D1736270

The State and Social Change in Germany, 1880–1980

The State and Social Change in Germany, 1880–1980

Edited by
W.R. Lee
and
Eve Rosenhaft

BERG
New York/Oxford/Munich

Distributed exclusively in the US and Canada by
St. Martin's Press, New York

First published in 1990 by
Berg Publishers Limited
Editorial offices:
165 Taber Avenue, Providence, R.I. 02906, USA
150 Cowley Road, Oxford OX4 1JJ, UK
Westermühlstraße 26, 8000 München 5, FRG

© Berg Publishers Limited 1990

Library of Congress Cataloging-in-Publication Data
The State and social change in Germany, 1880–1980 / edited by W.R. Lee
and Eve Rosenhaft.
    p.   cm.
ISBN 0-85496-234-4
1. Germany—Officials and employees—History. 2. Alien labor-
-Germany—History. 3. Finance, Public—Germany—History.
4. Germany—Social policy. 5. Finance, Public—Germany (West)-
-History. 6. Germany (West)—Social policy. I. Lee, W. Robert.
II. Rosenhaft, Eve, 1951–
JN3541.S73 1989
303.48'4'0943—dc20   89–36579
                                                              CIP

British Library Cataloguing in Publication Data
The state and social change in Germany, 1880–1980.
   1. Germany. Social change. Role of state, 1866–
   I. Lee, W.R. (William Robert), *1946–*
   II. Rosenhaft, Eve
   943.08
   ISBN 0-85496-234-4

Printed in Great Britain by Billing and Sons Ltd, Worcester

Contents

Contents

Tables

German Organisations

Allgemeiner deutscher Lehrerinnenverein	German General Association of Women Teachers
Arbeitsgemeinschaft für Volksgesundung	Working Group for Improving the Health of the Nation
Arbeitsgemeinschaft für Wohlfahrtspflege	Working Group for Welfare Work
Beratungsstelle für Auslandskredite	Foreign Credit Advisory Bureau
Bund der Festbesoldeten	Federation of Permanent Salaried Staffs
Bund der Kinderreichen	League of Large Families
Bund deutscher Frauenvereine	Federation of German Women's Associations
Bund für Volksaufartung	League for Regeneration
Bundesverband der deutschen Industrie	National Association of German Industry
Bundesvereinigung deutscher Arbeitgeberverbände	National Confederation of German Employers' Associations
Centralverband deutscher Industrieller	Central Association of German Industrialists
Deutsche Arbeiterzentrale	German Labour Agency
Deutsche Arbeitsfront	German Labour Front
Deutsche Gesellschaft für Gewerbehygiene	German Society for Occupational Hygiene
Deutscher Beamtenbund	German Federation of Civil Servants
Deutscher Lehrerverein	German Teacher's Association
Deutscher Medizinalbeamtenverein	German Association of Medical Officers
Deutscher Städtetag	Conference of German Cities
Deutscher Verein für öffentliche Gesundheitspflege	German Association for Public Health
Deutscher Verein für öffentliche und private Fürsorge	German Association for Public and Private Welfare
Deutscher Verein zur Fürsorge für jugendliche Psychopathen	German Association for the Care of Young Psychopaths

Gesellschaft für Heilpädagogik	Society for Educational Therapy
Gesellschaft für Rassenhygiene	Society for Race Hygiene
Gesellschaft für soziale Reform	Society for Social Reform
Gesellschaft zur Bekämpfung der Geschlechtskrankheiten	Society for Combating Venereal Diseases
Gewerkschaftsbund der Angestellten	Trade Union Federation of Salaried Employees
Institut für Arbeitsphysiologie	Institute for the Physiology of Work
Interessengemeinschaft Deutscher Beamtenverbände	Combination of Associations of Civil Servants
Interessengemeinschaft Deutscher Reichs- und Staatsbeamtenverbände	Combination of Associations of German Imperial and State Civil Servants
Preußische Feldarbeiterzentrale	Prussian Farm Labour Agency
Reichsausschuß für hygienische Volksbelehrung	National Committee for Health Education
Reichsbund der Kriegsbeschädigten, Kriegsteilnehmer und Kriegshinterbliebenen	National Federation of War-Wounded, Veterans and War-Widows
Reichslandbund	National Agrarian League
Reichsverband der deutschen Industrie	National Association of German Industry
Reichsverband der verheirateten Lehrerinnen	National Association of Married Women Teachers
Verband der Gemeinde- und Staatsarbeiter	Association of Municipal and State Workers
Verband der deutschen Reichspost- und Telegraphenbeamtinnen	Association of Female Postal and Telegraph Officers
Verband deutscher Tiefbauunternehmer	Association of German Civil Engineering Contractors
Verband mittlerer Reichspost- und Telegraphenbeamten	Association of Middle-level Postal and Telegraph Officers
Verband wirtschaftlicher Vereinigungen Kriegsbeschädigter	Association of Economic Organisations of Wounded Veterans
Verein für Socialpolitik	Association for Social Policy
Verein sozialistischer Ärzte	Association of Socialist Physicians
Werksärztliche Arbeitsgemeinschaft	Working Group of Works Physicians
Zentralverband der Angestellten	Central Association of Salaried Employees

Abbreviations

ADLV	Allgemeiner deutscher Lehrerinnenverein
BDA	Bundesvereinigung deutscher Arbeitgeberverbände
BdF	Bund deutscher Frauenvereine/ Bund der Festbesoldeten
BDI	Bundesverband der deutschen Industrie
BVP	Bayerische Volkspartei (Bavarian People's Party)
CDU	Christlich-Demokratische Union (Christian Democratic Union)
CSU	Christlich-Soziale Union (Christian Social Union)
DBB	Deutscher Beamtenbund
DLV	Deutscher Lehrerverein
DST	Deutscher Städtetag
DVP	Deutsche Volkspartei
FDP	Freie Demokratische Partei (Free Democratic Party)
IG	Interessengemeinschaft Deutscher Beamtenverbände
KPD	Kommunistische Partei Deutschlands (Communist Party)
LA	Local Authority
NSDAP	Nationalsozialistische Deutsche Arbeiterpartei
PAV	Personalabbauverordnung
RDI	Reichsverband der deutschen Industrie
RVL	Reichsverband der verheirateten Lehrerinnen
SPD	Sozialdemokratische Partei Deutschlands (Social Democratic Party)
USPD	Unabhängige Sozialdemokratische Partei Deutschlands (Independent Social Democratic Party)
VRT	Verband der Reichspost- und Telegraphenbeamtinnen

Preface

This volume brings together nine essays on one of the most central issues in German history, namely the role of the state in the complex process of social change in Germany in the period from the end of the nineteenth century to the 1980s. Germany inevitably presents an interesting context in which to examine the interplay between state and society. Even in the pre-industrial period, the state had a high profile in German social and political thought and the division of the German-speaking population of Europe into numerous small states before 1871 spurred speculation about the nature of states and the character of the eventual national state. On the other hand, the Prussian state had since the seventeenth century provided a model both for extensive state intervention in the daily life of the population, and for the creation of a professional administrative establishment and with it a social group (the bureaucracy) directly dependent on the state for its status and livelihood. With national unification in 1871 and increasing industrialisation, Germany added to the absolutist 'police state' the elements of the modern welfare state, pioneering the introduction of insurance schemes for sickness, disability and old age in the 1880s. Again in the 1920s Germany led in the development of social policy, including a national unemployment insurance scheme and municipal social programmes (particularly in public housing) which were renowned all over the world. Germany is also interesting in that it has been home to five different forms of state or types of political regime in the period covered by this volume, and a vigorous debate focusing on the specific nature of the state form within the context of a tradition of municipal and regional autonomy has prevailed in most of Germany during this period.

Inevitably in confronting the issue of the role of the state in social change historians are confronted by a variety of interdependent issues, including the actual definition of the state, in terms of its different structures and levels of operation. Given the nature of German political development since the last decades of the nineteenth century, any analysis of this issue must also confront the problem of discontinuity over time in Germany of the state form itself, the role and action of particular interest groups, and the general problem of legitimation. Equally important as part of the general agenda for research on the role of the state is the debate concerning the political and ideological reaction to state intrusion, particularly in the sphere of social policy.

The empirical studies contained in the present collection were all presented at a conference on 'The State and Social Change in Germany, 1880–1960', hosted by the Centre for Interdisciplinary German Studies at the University of Liverpool in January 1986. Gratitude is owing to the Economic and Social Research Council (ESRC) for providing initial support for the meeting, and, of course, to the participants at the conference for their individual contributions to what was a lively and open debate, and which emphasised the interdisciplinary nature of the theme. Taken as a whole, the conference represented a unique attempt to bring together economic, political and social historians, historians of medicine, sociologists and political scientists to discuss relevant approaches to the study of the state and state policy in the German context. The editors also owe a further debt of gratitude to all our contributors, and to Marion Berghahn of Berg publishers for the patience they have shown in seeing this volume through the press. We hope that they will be satisfied with the final product, and that their collective contributions to this volume will encourage further academic research on this important issue in German history. There was also common agreement at the conference that further work on the state and social change in Germany would need to be undertaken within a comparative framework, in order to view the potential peculiarities of Germany's development within the context of the experience of Central Europe as a whole, and within a broader international dimension.

W.R. Lee
Eve Rosenhaft   **University of Liverpool**

1
State and Society in Modern Germany: *Beamtenstaat, Klassenstaat, Wohlfahrtsstaat*

Eve Rosenhaft and W.R. Lee

Introduction

The essays in this volume examine the relationship between state and society in Germany during the last hundred years or so. Attention is given mainly to those periods when German society was characterised by parliamentary government, a federal structure and capitalist production relations, namely the pre-first World War Wilhelmine Reich, the Weimar Republic (1918–33) and the German Federal Republic (West Germany, since 1949). The particular concern of the authors is the ways in which state policy encouraged, directed or reflected changes in social organisation and popular attitudes – the specific contours of complex interplay between the realm of political decision-making and that of economic and social action. The very visible and controversial forms that the state has taken in Germany, both in the periods under discussion here and more notably in the period of National Socialist rule, make Germany a particularly attractive testing ground for ideas about state and society in modern Europe. The papers in this volume aim to contribute to the discussion of the nature of the state in capitalism, the origins of National Socialism and the peculiarities of German history, as these themes intersect in particular historical debates. On the other hand, we offer no contribution that focuses specifically on the experience of National Socialism, as there is already extensive literature on this subject. Nazism functions here as a premiss, one possible consequence of a crisis of 'normal' relations between state and society; several of the present contributions make extensive reference to National Socialist policies, and they all underline the extent to which the most radical of those policies were built on

1

plans already under discussion before 1933 and whose realisation was made possible by the new constellation of social power that National Socialism introduced. The focus of this volume is on the relationship between state and society in the finer, if sometimes more precariously balanced, systems that preceded the installation of the Nazi regime in Western Germany and which later succeeded it. The increasing role of state agencies in shaping economic and social life has been a characteristic of all developed countries in the last hundred years, and this is apparent even in systems in which the initiative and self-organisation of private individuals is regarded as the principal basis of social good, such as in liberal democracies. The state has emerged not simply as the active and acknowledged manager of the market or referee between private interests but also as an employer among other employers, as a direct dispenser of material benefits in the form of social welfare, and as the main guarantor of the physical and mental health of the population. This development was a consequence of changes in social and economic structure, the most obvious being the industrial revolution and the growth of the working class. It has in turn affected perceptions of the state and its functions and led to the growth of new kinds of popular organisations, ranging from public-service trade unions to welfare rights groups. Through its direct involvement in economic life the state may present itself as an adversary or negotiating partner to groups in the population; at the same time, the democratisation of political life may offer opportunities for participation in decision-making about vital issues that remain blocked in the private sector. The extension of state activity has thereby posed an equal challenge to the two accounts of the relationship between state and society that have been most influential in the European tradition. On the one hand, there is the vision of a self-regulating civil society best governed when governed least that is enshrined in liberal economic and political theory, and on the other hand the classical Marxism with its emphasis on the primacy and persistence of identities and conflicts generated at the point of production, and its insistence that the state exists to maintain the interests of a ruling class.

Since the first quarter of the twentieth century, that challenge has been answered by various adaptations of theory that focus on the increasing articulation between the activities of the state and private capital and identify it as a particular phase in the development of capitalism. One of the earliest attempts to come to grips with these issues resulted in the coining of the expression 'organised capitalism', a term which was originally coined in the 1920s to describe the German situation.[1] Before the First World War its author, the Social Democrat Rudolf Hilferding, had been developing an argument about the epochal significance of the increasing concentration of capital and the gradual merging of the interests and controlling structures of its different representative sectors (industrial, commercial and financial). If the checks on competition that this concentration involved implied 'the replacement of the capitalist principle of free competition with the socialist principle of planned production', then the increasing activity of the state in the economic sphere provided a formal element of socialisation. The change in the form of the state from the authoritarianism of the Wilhelmine Reich to the parliamentary democracy of the Weimar Republic appeared to confirm a (in Social Democratic terms) positive development, in which the state could be used by the organised working class as a 'political instrument for the construction of socialism'.[2]

After several decades of disuse, the term enjoyed a revival during the 1960s and 1970s, when it was used primarily by non-Marxist scholars to characterise societies with a combination of features. These included not only the growth of new relationships, structures and organisations outlined above but also changes in ideologies and attitudes in both the public and private spheres. Marxist-Leninist scholars, notably in East Germany, have developed analogous observations within the context of the theory of 'state monopoly capitalism'; although derived in the first instance from Lenin's theory of imperialism, the so-called 'Stamokap' theory has been applied with increasing subtlety in order to take account of aspects of state activity that are not compatible with a simple definition of the state as 'class rule'.[3]

1. For a discussion of 'organised capitalism', see H.-J. Puhle, 'Historische Konzepte des entwickelten Industriekapitalismus. "Organisierter Kapitalismus" und "Korporatismus"', *Geschichte und Gesellschaft*, vol. 10 (1984), pp. 165–84; H.A. Winkler (ed.), *Organisierter Kapitalismus. Voraussetzungen und Anfänge*, Göttingen, 1974.
2. See B. Brauckmüller and R. Hartmann, 'Organisierter Kapitalismus und Krise', in W. Luthardt (ed.), *Sozialdemokratische Arbeiterbewegung und Weimarer Republik*, Frankfurt am Main, 1978, vol. 1, pp. 354–421.
3. Puhle, 'Historische Konzepte', p. 171; D. Baudis and H. Nussbaum, *Wirtschaft*

Eve Rosenhaft and W.R. Lee

The Nazi State

At the root of the 'Stamokap' theory lies the particularity of German developments at the turn of the century, interpreted as characteristic of a general trend of western societies towards modernity. The rise of Nazism, which disappointed Hilferding's hopes for a peaceful development towards socialism, appeared in other respects to offer confirmation of the thesis of an epochal change in the role of the state. Although the Nazi system itself proved to be no more than an episode in the history of the relationship between state, capital and society in Germany, it has continued to present itself as the extreme case against which to test theories of politics and the state.

The peculiarities of Nazism begin with the character of the popular movement itself. The Nazi Party established itself in power on the basis of an appeal which to some extent cut across class lines. As an ideology, National Socialism explicitly denied the reality of class; it replaced conflict between economic interests with conflict between 'racial' groups, social divisions with gender divisions, control over production with control over reproduction as the aims and essence of policy.

Once in power, National Socialism was characterised by a peculiarly ambivalent relationship between the machinery of state and party, and also between the demands of the state and the interests of private capital. As long as the new regime concentrated its attack on the organisations of the labour movement, it was possible for more orthodox Marxists to maintain that its policies constituted a simple form of class-domination, its corporatist ideology a mere blind. But from the mid-1930s, National Socialism developed features that complicated the picture. In its economic preparations for war, the Nazi system depended on the combination of a thriving corporate capitalism with extensive elements of a command economy in which limits were set to capitalists' freedom of action. The prosecution of war evinced a high degree of sensitivity to the demands of the private economy, both in terms of the large-scale plundering of occupied territories and the systematic involvement of private firms in the exploitation of captured resources, plant and labour. At the same time it was motivated,

---

und Staat in Deutschland vom Ende des 19. Jahrhunderts bis 1918/19, Berlin, 1978, pp. 21ff.

4

perhaps primarily, by a racist ideology whose murderous demands in some respect ran counter to strategic and economic rationality. If, as both classical Marxist and liberal theory propose, the state's primary function is to guarantee the reproduction of social relations, then the Nazi war economy represents a genuine paradox. The logic of preparation for war led inexorably through the absolute exploitation and actual immiseration of the working class, into a war in which the Nazi regime was destroyed and Germany itself was threatened with annihilation. Similarly, the political theory of National Socialism made the principle of power so absolute as to drain politics of its meaning. The Nazi state asserted (and its legal theorists enshrined in jurisprudence) a power to discipline, coerce and physically destroy its own citizens which was justified by the needs of the Volk as defined by its deputy, the Führer, and subject to no independent assessment or appeal. In effect, the very concept of state lost its meaning against the transcendental (but inactive) Volk and the all-powerful Führer, while in practice policy was very largely made as a process of reaction of the various sections of party and state apparatus to issues and problems as they presented themselves.[4]

The Nazi system has thus provoked a series of theoretical reassessments of the relationship between the state and particular social interests, which share an emphasis on the relative independence of the state apparatus. It appeared to critical Marxists of the Frankfurt School as part of a general development towards the 'authoritarian state'. Already apparent in the Soviet Union – like Nazi Germany a dictatorship whose power rested on a dual apparatus of party and state administration – this kind of state (and not, after all, democratic socialism) was therefore the characteristic socio-political formation of an age distinguished, not only by the growth of the interventionist state and the concentration of economic power, but also by the culture and politics of the mass.[5] A similar, if less sophisticated approach appears in the totalitarianism theory of the 1950s. The revival of the Marxist theory in the 1960s brought with it

---

4. See I. Staff, *Justiz im Dritten Reich. Eine Dokumentation*, Frankfurt am Main, 1978.

5. A. Arato and E. Gebhardt (eds.), *The Essential Frankfurt School Reader*, New York, 1978, pp. 3ff, 71–117; M. Jay, *The Dialectical Imagination. A History of the Franfurt School and the Institute of Social Research 1923–1950*, 2nd edn, London, 1976, pp. 143–72.

5

debates around the thesis of the 'primacy of politics' in National Socialist policies (a primacy which however might yet be found to rest on demands arising out of social structures and conflicts). At the same time, there was renewed interest in the concept of 'Bonapartism', produced by Marx himself in his first attempt to come to terms with a form of political domination (plebiscitary dictatorship) that presented itself as a deformation of class politics. And in Marxist writings since the 1970s, fascism has been cited as an extreme example of the 'relative autonomy' of the state, within the general framework of its function of guaranteeing the reproduction of social relations and therewith of existing structures of power.[6] The most recent interpretative impulses have come from a different theoretical corner, namely that influenced by the work of Michel Foucault. For this school of thought, the (self-) conception of the Nazi state as the embodiment of absolute power, placing collective biology at the centre of political argument and the individual body as the focus of social discipline and political control, is a culmination of the central tendency in the development of Western society.[7]

If National Socialism in power provides a kind of ultimate test of general theories of the state, discussions of its origins have never been without reference to its location within the context of the specifically German variant of state development in western industrial societies. Indeed, in its historically unique character, Nazism has provided the basis for debate by two generations about the 'peculiar' development of German politics and society since the nineteenth century. Against an interpretation that described the rise of National Socialism to be the result of a flawed process of modernisation, in which cultural and political institutions lagged behind economic development, it has recently been argued that the crisis that brought Hitler to power bore all the structural features of a crisis of modernity.[8] This argument is compelling in its proposal that that crisis is explicable in terms of the logic of developed

6. A good summary of these discussions and a guide to the literature is provided by Ian Kershaw, *The Nazi Dictatorship*, London, 1985.
7. This approach is more than implicit in the work of Detlev J.K. Peukert, *Volksgenossen und Gemeinschaftsfremde. Anpassung, Ausmerze und Aufbegehren unter dem Nationalsozialismus*, Cologne, 1982, esp. pp. 295ff. (English edn: *Inside Nazi Germany*, London, 1987.)
8. D. Blackbourn and G. Eley, *The Peculiarities of German History*, London, 1985; D. Peukert, *Die Weimarer Republik*, Frankfurt am Main, 1987.

6

capitalism, without recourse to historical peculiarities apart from the particular ways in which class interests were institutionalised in the 'organised capitalism' of the Weimar Republic.[9] At the same time, the form that the resolution of the crisis took, and in particular the broad consensus among German elites and in the bourgeois public on the acceptability of an authoritarian solution, cannot be explained adequately except by reference to the ideological and social consequences of a particular state tradition.

Concepts of the State

The task of examining the nature of the interaction between state power and social formation is complicated in the German case by a philosophical tradition that conceptualised 'the state' as an entity standing outside and above society. Emerging in the state-building process of the early-modern period, it informed state policy through the direct influence of philosophy on individual 'enlightened monarchs' and through its institutionalisation in the ethos of the Prussian bureaucracy. It continued to inform attitudes to the state, particularly among the intelligentsia, even after the emergence of popular politics and self-conscious class organisation that accompanied industrialisation and the extension of the franchise in the late nineteenth century.

German political theorists recognised the state as a distinct apparatus of power, to which they ascribed a particular 'individuality'.[10] The political and philosophical antecedents of what has been described as a uniquely German pattern of ideas on the state[11] were clearly diverse. The growth of the absolutist state in the eighteenth

---

9. D. Abraham, *The Collapse of the Weimar Republic . Political Economy and Crisis*, 2nd edn, New York, 1987; G. Eley, 'What Produces Fascism: Pre-industrial Traditions or a Crisis of the Capitalist State?', in idem, *From Unification to Nazism. Reinterpreting the German Past*, London, 1986, pp. 254–82.

10. K. Dyson, *The State Tradition in Western Europe*, Oxford, 1980, p. 165.

11. J.A. von Rantzau, 'The Glorification of the State in German Historical Writing', in H. Krohn (ed.), *German History. Some New German Views*, London, 1954, p. 165. It could be argued that German political theory is 'unique' primarily by contrast with the British tradition; there are parallels in other North European national traditions: cf. Dyson, *State Tradition*; F.X. Kaufmann, 'The Blurring of the Distinction "State versus Society" in the Idea and Practice of the Welfare State', in F.X. Kaufmann *et al*, *Guidance, Control and Evaluation in the Public Sector*, Berlin/New York, 1986, p. 131.

century, with its three distinct elements – bureaucracy, militarism and mercantilism – provided an image of the state as an organisational replica of society as a whole. Legal concepts of *mutua obligatio* and *prudentia*, together with the rise of neostoicism, reinforced the idea of authority vested in the state apparatus.[12] Nineteenth-century theories of the state, as propounded by Hegel, Ranke and Treitschke, uniformly assigned it substantial organisational power, as a force for offence and defence.[13] Significantly the view of the state as an 'organic being' was one that was held by many German liberals, and various strands of Social-Democratic theorising also accepted the need for an activist state.[14]

In the eighteenth and early nineteenth centuries, the distinction between the state and society, as drawn by political theorists, went along with a perception of the state as a structure of both moral and legal order superimposed on society. This view found its classical formulation in Hegel's description of the state as a condition for rational freedom.[15] More than this, however, the state was expected to be active in enforcing order. Moreover, it was perceived to be acting on the whole of society. The cameralist concept of *Polizey*[16] proposed that in order to maintain general prosperity the state, as a civil organisation, was empowered to regulate, discipline and control the community. J.P. Frank's concept of 'medical police' (1779),[17] perhaps the best expression of the radical claims of the developed concept of the *Polizey-Staat*, was essentially only one facet of the general acceptance that the state had a duty to discipline all sections of society for the common good. It was significant for the subsequent course of German development that successive rulers in Prussia took these theories to heart in the simultaneous pursuit of military strength, moral regeneration and general *Glückseligkeit*. The absolutist system of state regulation which achieved its fullest development (and its programmatic justification)

---

12. G. Oestreich, *Neostoicism and the Early Modern State*, Cambridge, 1982, p. 162.
13. J.A. Aho, *German Realpolitik and American Sociology*, New Jersey, 1975, pp. 29, 38.
14. H. Heller, *Staatslehre*, 3rd edn, Leiden, 1963.
15. N. Johnson, *State and Government in the Federal Republic of Germany. The Executive at Work*, 2nd edn, London, 1983, p. 17.
16. Oestreich, *Neostoicism*, p. 155.
17. J.P. Frank, *System einer vollständigen medizinischen Polizey*, 9 vols., Mannheim, 1779–89.

under Frederick the Great has sometimes been characterised as a welfare state.[18] But in eighteenth-century Prussia prescription out-ran provision, and that was a function of the particular aims of policy; at this stage, welfare was an aspect of the administrative function of social discipline and prophylaxis (*Gefahrenabwehr*).[19]

The direct political consequences of such a concept were considerable. Not only did it enable the state to make authoritative decisions for society in isolation from contemporary political forces,[20] but it implied that the executive authority of the state could function independently of political constraints. Although the Prussian Law Code of 1794 did contain one germ of spiritual freedom (namely freedom of religion and conscience), and also made reference to the idea of social contract, it was generally a compilation of unequal rights based on estates.[21] Moreover, the absence of any great distinction between public and private law in Germany provided the means by which state regulation could be articulated and implemented. As a result, the development of an extensive state administrative apparatus preceded the formation of representative bodies. Older representative forms, such as the Landschaften, may well have continued to play an important role at the local level (as under the Bavarian Landesverordnung),[22] but the increasing obsolescence of representative constitutionalism in the face of the expansion of the absolute state was not accompanied by any new concessions to participatory political principles.

In contrast, in the Prussian tradition, the function of mediating between society and state was vested in the bureaucracy (*Beamtenschaft*, *Beamtentum*). Its members (*Beamte*) were so selected and trained as to be 'representative' in ideal terms, that is perfectly equipped to recognise the needs of society and translate them into policy; at any rate this was the essence of their self-image, and it was in this sense that Hegel identified the Prussian bureaucracy as the

18. R.N. Dorwart, *The Prussian Welfare State before 1740*, Cambridge, Mass., 1971.

19. T. Fischer, *Städtische Armut und Armenfürsorge im 15. und 16. Jahrhundert*, Göttingen, 1979.

20. Johnson, *State and Government*, p. 18.

21. J.H. Shennan, *The Origins of the Modern European State 1450–1725*, Cambridge, 1974, p. 124.

22. Oestreich, *Neostoicism*, p. 191; P. Baumgart (ed.), *Ständetum und Staatsbildung in Brandenburg-Preußen*, Düsseldorf, 1983.

9

historical embodiment of the rational principle.[23] The predominance of two social groups – the nobility and the middle class – in the bureaucracy, the rigorous insistence on state qualifying examinations which reinforced the academic character of the bureaucracy, and a high degree of self recruitment were important factors which helped to create the presumption that state officials could initiate policy in default of effective political leadership.[24] At the same time, top Prussian civil servants were committed in the eighteenth century to those social and political values that supported paternalistic and absolutist state authority, an attitude that was derived from Prussian pietism as well as secular and jurisprudential sources.[25] By the nineteenth century the state bureaucracy had become one of the strongest props of the political order, bureaucratic elite theories had penetrated much of German political thought, increased professionalisation had been accompanied by greater social exclusiveness and political authoritarianism, and the bureaucracy had become the 'means of all means'.[26]

Through the expansion of the administrative apparatus and the deliberate construction of an educational establishment to train its personnel, the absolutist state played a major part in the shaping of a new bourgeoisie. In the social and philosophical ferment of the late eighteenth century, this new class found itself on both sides of the (in Germany still metaphorical) barricades: on the one hand, as bearer of the absolutist *Beamtenstaat*, and on the other as representative of the values of reason and humanity that challenged absolutism. The statist tradition in Germany thus generated a particularly ambivalent social opposition, with the result that political crises were repeatedly resolved by 'revolutions from above'. In the wake of the French Revolution, for example, it was not a mass movement of the people but a series of reforming ministers who introduced

23. G.W.F. Hegel, *Grundlinien der Philosophie des Rechts oder Naturrecht und Staatswissenschaft im Grundrisse*, Berlin, 1821, pp. 287–301; W. Struve, *Elites against Democracy. Leadership Ideals in Bourgeois Political Thought in Germany 1890–1933*, Princeton, 1973, p. 33.
24. Johnson, *State and Government*, p. 171.
25. E. Hellmuth, *Naturrechtsphilosophie und bürokratischer Werthorizont*, Göttingen, 1985.
26. Struve, *Elites*, p. 31; J.R. Gillis, *The Prussian Bureaucracy in Crisis, 1840–1860*, Stanford, 1971, p. 212; W. Fischer and P. Lundgreen, 'The Recruitment and Training of Administrative and Technical Personnel', in C. Tilly (ed.), *The Formation of National States in Western Europe*, Princeton, 1975, p. 509.

into Prussia the 'modern' institutions of a popular army, free entry into trades and the end to servitude on the land. Similarly, the German constitution of 1871, with its progressive features of manhood suffrage and an elected national parliament (Reichstag), was not an agreement between free parties.[27] In their particular historical and ideological context, however, these measures, like Bismarck's later social insurance legislation, tended to reinforce the image of the powerful state as the most secure haven of individual freedom.[28]

This was as true for the politically organised and articulate middle classes in the nineteenth century as for political theorists. In particular, the state continued to be accorded a major role in regulating social relations and in initiating social policy. Karl Welcker (1790–1869) argued that the state must promote general welfare by intervening in social problems,[29] and many of the leading entrepreneurs of the early nineteenth century, such as Harkort and Mevissen, advocated government action not only to correct the abuses of industrialisation, but also to ensure the progress of reason and morality. Here it is possible to identify a shift in emphasis in ideas regarding the functions of the state, within the framework of the general appeal to the state as regulator of social relations. As Dietrich Milles suggests (Chapter 6), the emergence of a proletariat and a 'social question' in the first phase of industrialisation led to a redefinition of the proper object of state-sponsored regulation and discipline, from the whole of society to the lower or working classes. The articulate bourgeoisie, now defining itself against the 'mob' rather than (as in a previous generation) being against the aristocracy and absolutists, thus attempted to claim the powers of the state for its own protection. In this sense, the birth of capitalist class relations brought with it native impulses towards the creation of a *Klassenstaat*, specifically a state exercising power (or abstaining from the exercise of power) in the interests of the bourgeoisie.

At the same time, the German bourgeoisie failed to establish the central political institution that in England and France represented

27. E.M. Hucko (ed.), *The Democratic Tradition. Four German Constitutions*, Leamington Spa, 1987, p. 27.

28. Cf. J.J. Sheehan, *German Liberalism in the Nineteenth Century*, Chicago/London, 1978.

29. D.G. Rohr, *The Origins of Social Liberalism in Germany*, Chicago, 1963, p. 114.

the characteristic form of bourgeois control over state policy, namely representative government. Even prominent liberals, such as Eduard Lasker, who argued for the primacy of the Reich as an expression of the general interest over local state laws, were singularly closed to the idea of a popular assembly as the means of establishing the actual forms of general interest; they feared an opening of 'the floodgates of desire'. As a result there was no direct attempt to secure ministerial responsibility to parliament in Prussia after 1866,[30] and until 1919 the national executive was neither elected nor accountable to the Reichstag. Instead, in the nineteenth century liberal reformers were primarily concerned with securing the rule of law in the form of the *Rechtsstaat*,[31] or, like Gustav Schmoller, who was lavish in his praise of the unifying and rationalising effects of bureaucratisation, invested their hopes for social progress in the perfection of the *Beamtenstaat*.[32]

The Nature of State Power

The question of responsible government in the late nineteenth century touches an important theme in the history of the state in Germany. At the beginning of the period with which the present volume is concerned, the institution of a German state was new. The Bismarckian constitution that came into effect following unification in 1871 was superimposed on a collection of previously independent states. That constitution acknowledged the continued existence of historical regions in the form of federal states (Länder), granting them their own constitutions, state parliaments (Landtage) and extensive powers, particularly in the fields of education, culture and social policy. This pattern was repeated in the constitutions of the Weimar Republic and the Federal Republic; only under National Socialism and in the German Democratic Republic since 1958 have the Länder surrendered their historical autonomy to a unitary, fully centralised state. Historically German towns, too, have enjoyed a high degree of political independence from central government, being largely self-governing through representative institutions of some

30. J.F. Harris, *A Study in the Theory and Practice of Liberalism. Eduard Lasker, 1819–1884*, Lanham/London, 1984, p. 77.
31. Johnson, *State and Government*, p. 9.
32. Aho, *German Realpolitik*, p. 86.

kind; the Prussian cities were among the last to gain the right of municipal self-government, as a result of the reform movement of the early nineteenth century.[33] At the same time, the political units comprehended within the broad category of self-governing towns have always exhibited a startling variety. In size and economic importance, they range from towns with less than 2,000 inhabitants governed by mediaeval *Stadtrecht* to metropolises like Berlin and Frankfurt, incorporating a multitude of historical municipalities, employing large numbers of people and implicated through large-scale capital projects in the national and international economies. In constitutional terms, too, there is variety, the most notable aspect of the German scene being the persistence into the present day of the institution of the city-state in the form of municipalities that have the status of Länder in their own right (Hamburg and Bremen since the nineteenth century, and West Berlin since 1949).

The fragmentation of state power both locally and regionally has had important implications for the precise role of the state. Increasingly it is clear that pressures at the local level circumscribed the freedom of political leaders on the national scene,[34] and that from a comparatively early date local economic interests were actively articulated by dominant elites.[35] Pressure-group politics, even in the early stages of industrialisation, as during the discussions on free trade or protectionism at the Frankfurt National Assembly (1848/9), already reflected significant regional differences in Germany's economic and social structures at a local level.[36] Within the Reich, variations in regional constitutional forms and administrative attitudes meant that the character and accessibility of 'the state' as experienced by the population in daily life varied. While two-thirds of the Germans before 1918 were subject to a Prussian constitution

33. J. Reulecke, *Geschichte der Urbanisierung in Deutschland*, Frankfurt am Main, 1985.
34. G.R. Eley, *Reshaping the German Right*, New Haven, 1980; R.J. Evans, 'Introduction: Wilhelm II's Germany and the Historians', in idem (ed.), *Society and Politics in Wilhelmine Germany*, London, 1978, pp. 11–39; L. O'Boyle, 'Some Recent Studies of Nineteenth-century European Bureaucracy: Problems of Analysis', *Central European History*, vol. 109, 1986, pp. 386–408.
35. G. Zang (ed.), *Provinzialisierung einer Region*, Frankfurt am Main, 1978.
36. H. Best, 'Die regionale Differenzierung interessen-politischer Orientierungen im frühindustriellen Deutschland – ihre Ursachen und ihre Auswirkungen auf politische Entscheidungsprozesse', in R. Fremdling and R.H. Tilly (eds.), *Industrialisierung und Raum. Studien zur regionalen Differenzierung im Deutschland des 19. Jahrhunderts*, Stuttgart, 1979, pp. 251–76.

that was more restrictive in its franchise provisions than that of the Reich, inhabitants of the south German states and many municipalities enjoyed more liberal local regimes. The contributions in the present volume also make it clear that the character of administrative policy in such areas as public-sector employment varied significantly between the Länder, and this continues to be the case in the Federal Republic.

Many apparent contradictions of state development in Germany are explicable in terms of a history of fragmentation of state power. A relative lack of initiative on the part of central government, for example in broad areas of social policy in the nineteenth century (see Chapters 4 and 6), becomes comprehensible against the background of increasing activity at the regional and local levels. Indeed, both Marxist and non-Marxist analyses attribute a particular political function to the autonomous activities of the 'local state', whether in underpinning the stability of state systems by mediating between national government and the people, obscuring the state's essential function of maintaining class rule, or (with the optimism of Hilferding) in offering opportunities for socialists to gain some measure of state power and use it to consolidate their popular constituency and demonstrate the advantages of socialist policies (municipal socialism). An example of the collapse of that functional relationship between the national and local state is provided by Harold James and Jeremy Leaman in their studies of municipal finance in the Weimar Republic (Chapters 8 and 9). The new republic provided a particularly promising context for the development of the local state, with its combination of extended participatory democracy and expanded social provision under the aegis of an apparently triumphant labour movement. Under the impact of the depression, however, an apparent crisis of municipal finance fuelled a confrontation between national and local government, which became part of the general crisis of the parliamentary system.

The independent policy initiatives of the municipalities in the nineteenth and twentieth centuries rested on ideologies of local patriotism and self-government (*Selbstverwaltung*) variously rooted in mediaeval practice or cherished as a more recent achievement of reforming or revolutionary movements.[37] The crisis of relations

---

37. M. Walker, *German Home Towns*, Ithaca, 1971; V. Wünderich, *Arbeiterbewegung und Selbstverwaltung*, Wuppertal, 1980.

between central state and local government during the depression, however, was not articulated as such; the Communist Party, for example, attempted to mobilise opposition to the central government policy not in the name of local autonomy but as a form of resistance to the capitalist state.[38] To a striking degree, it has been the state in the form of central government that has provided the reference point for articulate politics, and the object of political sentiment for the left as well as for the right in Germany. It is probably a reflection of Prussia's hegemonic role within the new federation, institutionalised in the personal union between the Prussian and Imperial executives, that administrative and popular attitudes associated with the strong state in Prussia were to a considerable extent transferred to the Reich after 1871. This may at any rate provide some justification of our use of the term 'state' in the following pages to refer primarily to the institutions of central government.

The Role of the Civil Service

It has been suggested above that the German state of the mid-nineteenth century resists simple characterisation as a capitalist or bourgeois state, in terms either of the mechanisms of policy-making or of the intentions or functions of policy. During the period covered by this volume, the structures of public life changed significantly. Before 1914, the 'second industrial revolution', with the growth of employment in industry and the tertiary sector and explosive urbanisation, was accompanied by the development of a popular politics to which the authoritarian state of Prussian tradition was increasingly vulnerable. The labour movement grew steadily in organisational and electoral strength, on the basis of an expanding network of cultural and press activities, and established itself as the most vociferous advocate of political democratisation. During the 1890s the emergence of extra-parliamentary movements and pressure groups on the right challenged the compromise between bourgeois and traditional elites on which the stability of the authoritarian state rested. At the same time, the character of the

38. Wünderich, *Arbeiterbewegung*; cf. E. Rosenhaft, 'Communisms and Communities: Britain and Germany between the Wars', *Historical Journal*, vol. 26, 1983, pp. 221–36.

Eve Rosenhaft and W.R. Lee

state apparatus itself began to change with the massive expansion of public employment;[39] if the fact that Germany had proportionally the largest public workforce in Europe at the end of the nineteenth century itself reflects the particular character of the state tradition there, then the expansion of the class of *Beamte* to include (however half-heartedly) such groups as female telephone operators threatened a dilution of the bureaucratic ethos. Genuine democratisation of the political system, in the form of universal franchise (for women as well as men) and responsible government, was enshrined in the constitution of the Weimar Republic and perfected in that of the Federal Republic. Against this background of significant transformations in structures and expectations, the German scene remains characterised by certain continuities.

The bureaucracy continued to enjoy substantial scope for intervention in the definition of policy objectives, to the extent that Treitschke could describe the *Beamtentum* as a ruling class of Germany.[40] The assimilation of civil service attitudes in such spheres as business organisation and management also indicates the hegemonic force of the particular bureaucratic ethos within German society as a whole.[41] The role of the civil service in influencing legislation and formulating social policy objectives was strengthened by the fact that before 1914 Imperial and Prussian governments consisted largely of career bureaucrats. The establishment of specialised *Verwaltungsakademien* in the early twentieth century reflected the increasing diversity of responsibilities and tasks confronting the bureaucracy, even at the local level, and at the same time heightened internal awareness of the special role of the bureaucracy as a unique agency capable of realising the common good. Although the obligation to political loyalty was never legally defined, state administrators by and large showed themselves to be willing instruments of executive authority, providing the Nazis, for example, with a veneer of formal legality.[42] Even within the Federal Republic the formulation of legislation tends to be more the product of ministerial rather than legislative design, which not only

39. P. Cullity, 'The Growth of Governmental Employment in Germany 1882–1950', *Zeitschrift für die gesamte Staatswissenschaft*, vol. 123, 1967, pp. 201–17.
40. Struve, *Elites*, p. 37.
41. J. Kocka, 'Capitalism and Bureaucracy in German Industrialization before 1914', *Economic History Review*, vol. 33, 1981, pp. 453–68.
42. H.J. Rejewski, *Die Pflicht zur politischen Treue im preußischen Beamtenrecht*, Berlin, 1973; H. Mommsen, *Beamtentum im Dritten Reich*, Stuttgart, 1966.

provides the bureaucracy with a continuing and important sphere of influence, but lends credence to the claim that top civil servants still see themselves as belonging to an authoritarian, yet open, élite.[43]

The ethos of service to the state thus continues to provide a background or ideological point of reference against which the actual functions of the bureaucracy, and the concrete relations between its members and the state, have become increasingly diversified. Few outside observers have argued that the bureaucracy historically has ever acted from a neutral standpoint. In the nineteenth century, it played the role of mediator among the various segments of the upper class, omitting the proletariat from consideration,[44] and since the 1920s its expanded function as a conciliator between conflicting interest groups, although now taking organised labour within its purview, is essentially a conservative one. In its administration of policy, it tended to reproduce the ideology embedded in the tasks set for it by the power elites. As a result, although its authority and self-image were of a different source and substance from those of the economically dominant classes, it did not act as a brake on the institutionalisation of policies that operated in their interests. But the civil service cannot be regarded in its official functions as a simple instrument of class. Higher civil servants of the Empire were less conservative and less socially homogeneous than those of Prussia, and the fact that provincial training academies for civil servants failed to break the traditional monopoly of lawyers in higher administrative posts indicates an increasing conflict between more established concepts of the bureaucratic function and adherents of a more technocratic approach to local and central administration.[45] The work of Andreas Kunz and Helen Boak (Chapters 2 and 3) demonstrates the extent to which public servants were drawn into the social ferment generated by social and economic change, in ways which challenged the traditional corporate ethos and led to long-term transformations in the relationship between organised civil servants and the state. These changes seldom occurred without conflict and antagonism.

43. U. von Beyme *et al* (eds.), *German Political Systems. Theory and Practice in the Two Germanies*, Beverly Hills, 1976, p. 5; Struve, *Elites*, p. 63.

44. Gillis, *Prussian Bureaucracy*, p. 217; H.U. Wehler, *Das deutsche Kaiserreich 1871–1918*, Göttingen, 1973 (English edn: *The German Empire 1871–1918*, Leamington Spa, 1985); O'Boyle, 'Some Recent Studies'.

45. Struve, *Elites*, p. 37.

Eve Rosenhaft and W.R. Lee

Recent research on the shocks to their economic security and status suffered by *Beamte* in the Weimar Republic and National Socialism, has challenged the image of an unproblematic continuity of corporate acquiescence to state authority.[46] If the bureaucracy tended at times to operate as a separate interest group, then, it did not – indeed could not – pursue its own advantage as a coherent class interest. The widening of recruitment to public service since the nineteenth century tended to reinforce the importance of social function, rather than social origins, as a common point of reference, and this represents a more relevant criterion for understanding the role of state bureaucrats.[47]

The State and the Articulation of Political Interests

The sense of social function nevertheless had concrete implications for the class character of legislation even in the twentieth century, for it formed the link between a class-specific ideology and the civil servants' power to initiate policy. This power was in turn a function of the limitations on access to state power and the executive apparatus, which we need to consider before going on to look at the character of policy.

Even if Wilhelmine Germany, particularly after the mass politicisation of the 1890s, was far from being unpolitical,[48] or a simple plebiscitary system legitimising an irremovable government, access to the state apparatus remained severely restricted. The explicit acceptance of an independent executive and the deliberate limitation of democratic rights in the pre-1914 period nullified the Reichstag, which functioned, according to one assessment, largely as a sounding-board for imperial policy-makers.[49] In consideration of this tradition, the drafters of the Weimar Constitution introduced

46. A. Kunz, *Civil Servants and the Politics of Inflation in Germany 1914–1924*, Berlin, 1986; J. Caplan, 'Recreating the Civil Service: Issues and Ideas in the Nazi Regime', in J. Noakes (ed.), *Government, Party and People in Nazi Germany*, Exeter, 1980, pp. 34–56; cf. idem, '"The imaginary universality of particular interests": The "Tradition" of the Civil Service in German History', *Social History*, vol. 4, 1979, pp. 299–317.

47. S. Corrigan and P. Leonard, *Social Work Practice under Capitalism, A Marxist Approach*, Cambridge, 1978, p. 104.

48. S. Suval, *Electoral Politics in Wilhelmine Germany*, Chapel Hill, 1985.

49. Struve, *Elites*, p. 55.

the figure of the *Reichspräsident*, a popularly elected *Ersatzkaiser*, equipped with extensive emergency powers (Article 48). The use of these powers in the economic and political crisis of the early 1930s eased the slide into dictatorship, while the *Rechtsstaat* tradition made supporters of the republic hesitate to resist what were, even in Hitler's hands, formally legal measures. Indeed the legacy of this approach to political development is manifest even in the Federal Republic, with a perceptible separation between the legislature and the executive, and a view of Parliament (the Bundestag) as primarily a legislative machine.

Even in periods of democratic constitutionalism, policy has been made to a considerable extent through a process of lobbying and interest-group politics. But this has never operated on a pluralist basis, in the sense of an absence of systematic policy bias or equal participation in the political process by all pressure groups.[50] The articulation of political interests always took place within a fairly confined social grouping, and while the circle has been gradually extended, it has yet to be completely opened.

Certainly the development of Prussian society from the eighteenth century onwards reveals a process whereby various social groups effectively obtained preferential treatment in gaining access to positions of power and privilege within the state.[51] Attention has frequently been focused on the privileged access to state power open to the Junkers, the nobility and members of the officer corps. The admission of the representatives of business and industrial interests to the circle of *Hoffähige*, the social concomitant of the alliance of 'rye and iron' on which the Bismarckian constitution rested after 1879, reflected a history of contacts between industry and the state. From an early date the state's legislative, administrative and entrepreneurial functions had generated a constant process of interaction with the economy. Even during periods of increasing liberalisation in the nineteenth century, state administrators and entrepreneurs, particularly at the lower and middle levels, remained closely interrelated.[52] In specific sectors, such as the railways, the

---

50. See P. Taylor-Goodby and J. Dale, *Social Theory and Social Welfare*, London, 1981, p. 179.
51. Struve, *Elites*, p. 56.
52. H.-W. Niemann, 'Die Anfänge der staatlichen Elektrizitätsversorgung im Königreich Sachsen', *Zeitschrift für Unternehmensforschung*, vol. 23, 1978, pp. 98–117.

mixed system of dual ownership strengthened the informal relationship between business and government.[53] Industrialists quickly appreciated the benefits which would accrue from state social welfare legislation,[54] and Dietrich Milles highlights the role of lobbyist Trade Associations in actually structuring the social insurance system.

The emergence of political pressure groups such as the Pan-German League and the German Navy League in the Wilhelmine era represents the assimilation of new forms of popular mobilisation to the lobbyist system that already existed among those groups committed to the support of the state. As Martin Forberg indicates (Chapter 4), trade unions also increasingly sought such a role, advocating state intervention in the development of a public labour-market policy, but their influence remained limited, as did their aims – in this case the defence of the interests of native labour against those of foreign workers. This appears to be characteristic of the way in which the Wilhelmine state responded to lobbying and other external attempts to initiate policy. In the Bismarckian mode, legislation was used when and as necessary to maintain a balance of political forces favourable to the monarchical constitution and to the government in power, rather than to effect or direct social development. Economic policy thus reflected the attempt to balance the interests of those groups identified as supportive of the state, while social policy was deployed to pacify the working class, whose disaffection was axiomatic, and was complemented by the legal suppression of working-class parties and organisations. Although Bismarck's successors in government after 1890 began to develop a broader social vision (in accordance with the increasing complexity of the social and political crisis of the Reich), this policy orientation persisted. In areas of policy not obviously relevant to the central questions of power, the state responded in a relatively unsystematic way to individual issues (or lobbies) as they arose, and abstained from making policy in broad areas of public concern. Dietrich Milles demonstrates that even the centrepiece of Bismarckian social

53. D.F. Vagts, 'Railroads, Private Enterprise and Public Policy – Germany and the United States 1870–1920', in N. Horn and J. Kocka (eds.), *Recht und Entwicklung der Großunternehmen im 19. und frühen 20. Jahrhundert*, Göttingen, 1979, pp. 604–18.
54. M. Boeger, *Die Haltung der industriellen Unternehmer zur staatlichen Sozialpolitik in den Jahren 1878–1891*, Frankfurt am Main, 1982.

legislation reveals a state content to make policy and leave its execution to private interests; although welcomed in some quarters as an answer to the social question, the establishment of a national system of social insurance was tantamount to a withdrawal of government from responsibility. In the case of foreign workers, the state's abstinence from policy-making seems to reflect a lack of interest in forging a coherence between the two aspects of policy; while the Prussian government actively encouraged anti-Polish feeling for political reasons, it failed to legislate against immigration and thereby endorsed by default the employers' interest in importing labour. It was only relatively late in its history that the Wilhelmine state began to develop what Andreas Kunz calls public policy, in the sense of an integrated approach to identifying and solving social problems.

This process received a decisive impulse in the First World War, when the state saw itself obliged to take extensive measures to reorganise social and economic life on the home front in order to maintain the war effort. In its wake, the Weimar Republic undertook what appears in retrospect as a concerted effort to manage social and class relations through constitutional provision, legislation and executive measures, which failed in many respects, however, to go beyond the emergency measures of wartime and their extension in the demobilisation decrees (as Richard Bessel makes clear in Chapter 7). A feature of the social policy which Weimar inherited from the wartime regime was the acceptance of organised labour as a partner in the development and execution of policy. The new republic went further, however, and attempted to deal with social conflict by binding both labour and capital into a system of state-sponsored co-operation and conciliation. The Weimar constitution not only held out the promise (never fulfilled in practice) that the organised representatives of labour and capital would participate in official economic policy-making (Article 165), but also (Article 164) maintained the principle of selective and preferential policies designed to meet the needs of specific groups within society. The state was constrained to foster by legislation the interests of the agricultural, industrial and commercial *Mittelstand*.[55] The expansion of participation in policy-making thus took place in the form of

---

55. See H. Lebovics, *Social Conservatism and the Middle Classes in Germany 1914–1933*, Princeton, 1969, pp. 13ff.

an inchoate corporatism rather than a democratic free-for-all. Nazi experiments with the corporate reorganisation of labour, industry and agriculture did not essentially discredit corporate theories, which historically existed in a complex dialectic with specifically liberal values (particularly in German-speaking Central Europe). The Federal Republic, although committed at its birth to a more radical principle of market economy than any previous German state, nevertheless relies on a system of negotiation and conciliation between the interests of labour and business organised at the regional and national level to maintain social and economic stability. From the 1950s to the 1970s (at least), a continuing tendency within the West German system to criminalise groups that stood outside the consensus represented and enforced by these conciliatory mechanisms (the Communist Party, terrorists and their sympathisers, and a broadly interpreted category of enemies of the constitution), and to justify such measures with reference to the *rechtsstaatlich* principles of the democratic constitution, could be read as a legacy of the Bismarckian politics of negative integration.

The existence of legal provisions that protect or privilege their interests has never been seen by the business community as an adequate guarantee of influence on policy-making, however. In the 1920s, the existence of an 'industrial nobility' reinforced the active articulation of business interests, and a range of strategies were employed to influence policy in their direction. These included the channelling of funds to political parties, the sponsorship of political candidates, and active involvement of individual businessmen in politics. Through the presence in government of politicians expressly committed to the business interest, organised capital was able to exercise decisive influence at key moments in the stormy history of the Weimar Republic, although it was equally, and more fatally, prepared to prejuduce political decisions through the use of economic power in disregard or contempt of constitutional forms.[56] After a period of increasing heterogeneity in business strategies (especially in the channelling of political funds), the adoption of the Adolf Hitler-Spende after 1933 reflected a return to a more systematic basis of effecting political influence on the part of the business community.[57] After 1945 the further development of conveyer

56. H.A. Turner, *German Big Business and the Rise of Hitler*, New York, 1985; B. Weisbrod, *Schwerindustrie in der Weimarer Republik*, Wuppertal, 1978.
57. A.J. Heidenheimer and F.C. Langdon, *Business Associations and the Financing*

techniques and the high membership coverage of business associations helped to re-establish the 'primacy of the economy'.[58] The persistent and powerful manipulation of the political agenda by sections of the German business community in the twentieth century appears to confirm the structuralist analysis of the overriding importance of decisions in the market sphere, and the cognizance of business interests by government.

The fact that the stability of capitalist production relations appears to be more effectively enforced as the political order becomes more democratised – not necessarily through the direct influence of organised capital, but through a broad consensus that defines economic health in terms of the fortunes of the private economy (*die Wirtschaft*) – may be read in Marxist terms as a development towards the mature capitalist state. This development was an uneven one, however; during the Weimar Republic, for example, the extent to which industrialists saw themselves forced to act outside the law was a measure of the extent to which the new democracy was committed to an approach to a social policy that combined Christian social ideas of class conciliation with Social Democratic concepts of planning and wealth redistribution. The primacy of the economy had to be defended by extra-constitutional and dictatorial means against the demands of a working population which, as Richard Bessel shows, took the promises of the new state all too seriously.

The State and Social Policy

This brings us to the question of the character and functions of social welfare. Bessel demonstrates that the capacity of the Weimar 'welfare state' to deliver on its promises was limited from the very beginning, and that this had ambivalent political consequences.[59] Similarly, although Harold James and Jeremy Leaman argue from

---

of Political Parties, The Hague, 1968, p. 39.

58. Ibid., p. 45; R. Schulze, 'Representation of Interests and the Recruitment of Elites: The Role of the *Industrie- und Handelskammern* in German Politics after the End of the Second World War', *German History*, vol. 7, 1989, pp. 71–91.

59. See D. Geary, 'Welfare Legislation, Labour Law and Working-class Radicalism in the Weimar Republic', in D. Hay *et al*, *Law, Labour and Crime in Historical Perspective*, London, 1986.

Eve Rosenhaft and W.R. Lee

different theoretical standpoints in their studies of municipal finance in the Weimar Republic, they are agreed on the severe limitations that face municipal enterprise as a form of public sector economic initiative in capitalism, and their findings also underline the structural vulnerability of public welfare schemes.

In pursuing his study into the 1980s, Jeremy Leaman argues persuasively that even the development of more sophisticated and humane forms of crisis management has not changed the status of public-sector provision as a low-priority mechanism for social pacification. This represents one interpretation of state welfare provision understood as a means for guaranteeing the maintenance and reproduction of capitalist social relations, namely that even though such policies may embody at least some short-term interests of the working class, they constitute at best a form of appeasement whose partiality is bound to reveal itself at moments of crisis.[60] German social insurance legislation clearly fits into this mould, in terms of the intentions behind its introduction in the nineteenth century, and of the way in which the contributory principle ties its benefits to productivity (individual and general) rather than need.

In the German context, and particularly in the light of the experience of National Socialism, historians examining developments in such areas as poor-relief and family welfare in the nineteenth and early twentieth centuries have tended to adopt the more radical paradigms of social control or social discipline to characterise the integrative and mediatising functions of welfare. At the very least, it can be said that even institutions conceived of as a service imply expectations about the character of their clients, which they then serve to enforce. By the early nineteenth century, welfare had finally ceased to be a police concern, and had become a separate administrative function in most German states. This transition did not diminish the function of social welfare as an important element in enforcing conformity, however. Poor-relief was so designed as to instil into the new proletariat the qualities of conscientious workers and subjects, with the workhouse, its functions situated 'in the border territory between public order legislation and criminal law', as the disciplinary institution of last resort.[61] The Elberfeld system

---

60. N. Ginsburg, *Class, Capital and Social Policy*, 2nd edn, Cambridge, 1985, p. 2; Taylor-Goodby and Dale, *Social Theory*, p. 183.
61. C. Sachße and F. Tennstedt, *Geschichte der Armenfürsorge in Deutschland*, Stuttgart, 1980, p. 254 and *passim*.

24

(introduced in 1853 and adopted by numerous German cities in the following thirty years) may be seen as aspiring to exercise social discipline on the whole of the emerging class society. It systematised a new role for the bourgeoisie in an individualised form of voluntary poor-relief at the same time as – for the poor themselves – it linked relief with the duty to work, and aimed to channel their labour to private employers.[62] The medicalisation of poverty has been viewed as a form of social disciplining,[63] and Dietrich Milles emphasises the way in which medical insurance schemes embodied and enforced a social vision when they took as their object the human being as worker.

Medicine is an area of social provision in which, historically, Western states have worked at best indirectly, through the delegation of authority to professionals and private or voluntary administrations. It is a virtue of both 'social control' and 'social discipline' as analytical concepts that they draw attention specifically to this realm of semi-official institutions. In Marxist analyses, social control commonly refers to broadly cultural institutions and practices, through which the ideologies are generated that enforce acquiescence to the class structure; the Althusserian concept of 'ideological state apparatuses' expresses the conviction of a functional connection between such institutions and the machinery of class power.[64] The concept of social discipline that follows the approach of Michel Foucault is relatively uninterested in the operations of class or state power; but it also locates the construction of decisive social power precisely in the relatively autonomous realms of social exchange which generate knowledge (closely associated with the will to oversee and order society, and to exercise the constructive and controlling force of definition). Recent German work in the history of socialisation has also drawn attention to the affinity between Foucault's pessimistic vision of modernity and the work of Norbert Elias, who argues for a functional connection between the growth of the modern state, with its characteristic

62. Ibid., pp. 214ff.

63. U. Frevert, *Krankheit als politisches Problem 1970–1880*, Göttingen, 1984; G. Göckenjan, *Kurieren und Staat machen. Gesundheit und Medizin in der bürgerlichen Welt*, Frankfurt am Main, 1985, pp. 286ff.

64. L. Althusser, 'Ideology and Ideological State Apparatuses (Notes Towards an Investigation)', in idem, *Lenin and Philosophy and other Essays*, London, 1971, pp. 121–76.

25

Eve Rosenhaft and W.R. Lee

monopoly on the use of force, and the emergence of the social ideal
of a human adult systematically educated to self-discipline, modesty
and reflective action.[65]
This approach is attractive in the German case not simply because
National Socialism presents itself as a Foucauldian nightmare, but
because German traditions of *Polizey* historically privileged the role
of experts and professionals in policy-making. In the formulation of
social welfare policy, the German state repeatedly appears as responding less to the demands of gross class interest than to various
representations of the general interest, which in turn appealed to the
state's acknowledged function of enforcing social values (or ideology). But the interchange between experts and the state was a
complex process, and it did not take place independently of class-
and power-relations. The public sector evolved increasingly as a
complex area in which a multiplicity of relatively autonomous, but
nevertheless interdependent, actors interacted and sought to exercise political influence.[66] In the nineteenth century, when constitutional access to political decision-making was limited, professionals
and academics with plans for reform had the ear of the bureaucracy.
State administration itself was now characterised by an increasing
emphasis on *Leistung*, in the sense both of technical efficiency and
of the service (as distinct from police) functions of the state, and this
development was associated with a continued trend towards recruitment of civil servants from the upper- and lower-middle classes.[67]
As a consequence equally of their social origins and of their acknowledged function, members of the civil service shared with the
experts an ethos of academic qualification, commitment to public
service and rationality that typifies the *Bildungsbürgertum*. Moreover, they belonged to that broadly bourgeois public within and
through which reformers agitated for change, with meetings,
speeches, and pamphlets as well as through direct contacts with
representatives of the state; they formed its cutting edge.[68] This was

65. M. Foucault, *Histoire de la sexualité. La volonté de savoir*, Paris, 1976;
N. Elias, *Über den Prozeß der Zivilisation*, 2 vols., Frankfurt am Main, 1980. For a
discussion of these influences in recent German historiography, see D.J.K. Peukert,
*Grenzen der Sozialdisziplinierung. Aufstieg und Krise der deutschen Jugendfürsorge
1878 bis 1932*, Cologne, 1986, pp. 18ff.
66. Kaufmann et al, *Guidance*, esp. p. 790.
67. H. Henning, *Die deutsche Beamtenschaft im 19. Jahrhundert*, Stuttgart, 1984.
68. M.L. Plessen, *Die Wirksamkeit des Vereins für Socialpolitik von 1879–1890*,
Berlin, 1975.

the power which middle-class liberals acknowledged and aimed to employ in the perfection of the political order, and it is characteristic of the affinity between the *Beamtenschaft* and a wider bourgeois public that its members on the whole tended to support liberal parties.[69] The civil service thus provided a channel for the introduction of the concepts and aspirations of the educated middle classes into the policies of the monarchical state.

Before the First World War, the successes of these reformers had a manifest class and political bias. The academic crusaders for an enlightened social policy known as *Kathedersozialisten*, whose members formed the Verein für Socialpolitik in 1872, not only aimed to reconcile the industrial working class to the monarchical state,[70] but used political leverage to secure the implementation of ideological conformity within German universities. The passing of the Lex Arons in 1896 effectively barred Social Democrats from taking up university positions. Similarly, at the end of the century middle-class anxieties about the collapse of the family were expressed in policies that laid working-class families open to direct state interference. The fear of increasing juvenile delinquency as a function of rapid urbanisation prompted changes in criminal law, which allowed state governments unprecedented powers to remove youths and younger children from parental control.[71] The ban on political activity by young people, after the turn of the century, reflects the way in which anxieties about the social order tended to be linked to concerns about the political order.

Legislative provision for young people also provides an example of how state policy, by endorsing and institutionalising public discourses about social problems, served to consolidate the creation of new 'problem' or client groups. In a complementary process, the state collaborated in the professionalisation of key social groups, such as doctors, lawyers, teachers and social workers. The central role of government in administering higher education and technical training in Germany, as well as controlling employment in state-administered services, meant that the state was implicated in the general social process of professionalisation to a higher degree there than, for example, in the United States or Great Britain. The official

---

69. Kunz, *Civil Servants*, p. 26.
70. G. Iggers, *The Social History of Politics. Critical Perspectives in West German Historical Writing since 1945*, Leamington Spa, 1985, p. 7.
71. Peukert, *Grenzen*.

acknowledgement of the competence of experts to make policy within their own fields of expertise that professional status implied, in turn reinforced their claim to exercise influence on the formulation and implementation of state policy in the social sphere.[72]

The expansion of social welfare provision in the twentieth century was accompanied by the emergence of medically and technically trained officials, who came to constitute an important and powerful interest group. Far from acting as objective instruments of public policy, professional groups increasingly played an active role in the specification of policy objectives. Paul Weindling points out, for example (Chapter 5), that the bleak picture of deteriorating social conditions in the 1920s portrayed by welfare experts not only reinforced the necessity for their services, but also justified the allocation of state resources for psychopath welfare, eugenic data banks and criminal biology. Professional groups within this context represented a 'new and more subtle type of police authority'. Not only did their methods differ from those of official institutions of surveillance and discipline; the objects and the internal dynamics of their policing were also new, inasmuch as the logic of their scientific model of society strove towards realisation in a utopian effort to catalogue the whole population as the basis for guaranteeing the quality of future generations. Here again, we are drawn to the paradoxical conclusion that the more democratic state, by virtue of its aspirations to comprehensive welfare provision, was more susceptible to the extra-constitutional exercise of power by special interest groups than the authoritarian state that preceded it.

It has been argued against both social control and social discipline that (as ideal types, at least) they ignore the ambiguities of social and ideological structures and thus treat societies as closed systems. Social control offers the working class no way out of its subordination, while the seamless web of discourse that enforces social discipline leaves no way in for shifting structures of economic and political power. Social legislation creates its own constituency; it not only generates interests, but may also have an empowering effect among those on whom it works, as well as among those who

72. C. Huerkamp, *Der Aufstieg der Ärzte im 19. Jahrhundert*, Göttingen, 1985; W. Conze and J. Kocka (eds.), *Bildungsbürgertum im 19. Jahrhundert. Teil I: Bildungsbürgertum und Professionalisierung im internationalen Vergleich*, Stuttgart, 1985.

develop and administer policy.[73] The totalising claims of the new
public medicine in the 1920s remained a tendency; its proponents
operated on the basis of an existing class society, and their policies
in the first instance served to underline and reinforce class inequalities. This was true even of the more ambitious population policies
of the Third Reich.[74] At the same time, popular politics in the
Weimar Republic was driven in part by a conviction that state
welfare provision (if it could be properly funded and administered)
was a positive good.

The State, Gender and Class

The ambiguities of social policy are particularly apparent in the case
of women. In spite of the hegemonic growth since the eighteenth
century (even in politically conservative Germany) of liberal theories about the sanctity of the private sphere, relations between men,
women and children in the household remained subject to forms of
legal prescription and regulation, with a logic and a chronology
distinct from those that characterise the law governing other forms
of social relationship. In fact, it was one of the functions of family
law in the nineteenth century to underpin the sanctity of the private
sphere by guaranteeing 'social peace' within it. This was achieved
through the systematic denial to women of the civil, economic and
political rights granted their male counterparts, a denial which took
a more radical form in Germany than (for example) in Great
Britain.[75]

The legal subordination of women as a form of state support for
the family reflects the ambiguities of the functions of the state, as
well as of the social status of women. Here the state is fulfilling its
(perhaps) most characteristic function, in the legal enforcement of
ideology. The relationship of gender ideologies to material, and

73. Peukert, *Grenzen*, p. 23.
74. G. Bock, *Zwangssterilisation im Nationalsozialismus*, Opladen, 1986.
75. U. Gerhard, *Verhältnisse und Verhinderungen. Frauenarbeit, Familie und
Rechte der Frauen im 19. Jahrhundert*, Frankfurt am Main, 1976; idem, 'Die
Rechtsstellung der Frau in der bürgerlichen Gesellschaft des 19. Jahrhunderts.
Frankreich und Deutschland im Vergleich' and U. Vogel, 'Patriarchalische Herrschaft, bürgerliches Recht, bürgerliche Utopie. Eigentumsrechte der Frauen in
Deutschland und England', both in J. Kocka (ed.), *Bürgertum im 19. Jahrhundert*,
vol. 1, Munich, 1988.

especially class interests, is a problematic one. In the legal regulation of women's paid employment, which has received considerable attention in the historical literature on Germany, concepts of the family and the feminine character clearly play a role that is relatively independent of employer interests. It is easy to demonstrate that ideas of proper work for women endorsed by the state through legislation (or the absence of legislation) can be instrumentalised in the immediate service of capital, as for example in the state's toleration of low wages for women, or its resistance to applying the same social and protective legislation to home workers as to factory workers.[76] Studies of the way in which various kinds of work become gender-typed as they emerge with new technologies have also underlined the mutability of state-endorsed gender ideologies in the face of the economic imperatives of a segmented labour market.[77] In the long run, however, restrictions on women's hours and places of work limit the employer's freedom to exploit women's labour to the full, and the experience of the Nazi war-effort has been cited to suggest that even a strong state may find itself helpless to mobilise women workers if it has been too effective in propagating the ideology that motivates legislation.[78]

Of course, modern gender ideologies have a social background. German legislation in this field since the nineteenth century can be regarded as enforcing characteristic bourgeois values against the demands of capital accumulation – or specifically as privileging the values of the *Bildungsbürgertum* above the interests of the indus-

---

76. R. Dasey, 'Women's Work and the Family: Women Garment Workers in Berlin and Hamburg before the First World War', in R.J. Evans and W.R. Lee (eds.), *The German Family*, London, 1981, pp. 221–55.

77. See for example U.D. Nienhaus, 'Femininity and Skill: The Telegraph and Telephone Operating Case (1858–1889)', *Gender and History*, vol. 1, 1989; idem, 'Technological Change, the Welfare State, Gender and Real Women. Female Clerical Workers in the Postal Services in Germany, France and England 1860 to 1945', *Internationale wissenschaftliche Korrespondenz zur Geschichte der deutschen Arbeiterbewegung*, vol. 23, 1987, pp. 223–30.

78. S. Salter, 'Class Harmony or Class Conflict? The Industrial Working Class and the NS Regime 1933–1945', in Noakes (ed.), *Government, Party and People*, pp. 89–91; T. Mason, 'Women in Germany, 1925–40', *History Workshop Journal*, no. 2, 1976, pp. 5–32. The thesis of Nazi failure to mobilise women has been challenged: R.J. Overy, 'Mobilisation for Total War in Germany, 1939–1941', *English History Review*, vol. 103, 1988, pp. 613–39; cf. also C. Sachße, *Betriebliche Sozialpolitik als Familienpolitik in der Weimarer Republik und im Nationalsozialismus*, Hamburg, 1987, p. 436.

trial bourgeoisie.[79] On the one hand, of course, such a division of labour within the bourgeoisie may be viewed as functional to the maintenance of social order and social reproduction in the long term, not least because, alternatively, men of all classes found their interests served by the subordination of women.

The mesh of ideology and material interest in the very particular relationships between state, gender and class in the nineteenth century is nicely illustrated by the debate over female telegraphists in the 1870s. These jobs in the public service were reserved for the daughters of the middle class, a policy urged on the government by liberal parliamentarians and justified by the responsible authorities in terms of the state's obligation to public welfare.[80] The logic of the ostensible charitable function of such employment, as well as the contemporary attitude to women's proper role, determined that female telegraphists must be unmarried. For German women, the contradiction between work and family was enshrined in the Civil Code until 1976, in the form of the stipulation that a married woman had the right to work insofar as work was compatible with her (equally statutory) duty of care for her family and household. When the principle of inequality implicit in this stipulation was challenged by Article 128 of the Weimar Constitution ('All discriminatory regulations against female civil servants are lifted'), as Helen Boak's work suggests, the state itself was caught in a real contradiction. As an employer, it had not only to deal fairly with its own employees but also to set an example for other employers, the latter obligation being a function of its ideological role. As far as the employment of married women was concerned, though, the law represented two distinct views. Boak shows the policy-makers succumbing to conventional ideas about women's role in their treatment of married women employees, but it is also clear that the choice between discrimination and equality was prejudiced by the constant demands for cuts in the public payroll.

79. B. Duden and K. Hausen, 'Gesellschaftliche Arbeit – geschlechtsspezifische Arbeitsteilung', in A. Kuhn and G. Schneider (eds.), *Frauen in der Geschichte*, Düsseldorf, 1978, pp. 11–33. Elisabeth Meyer-Renschhausen argues for the historical identity of the bourgeois and feminine characters: 'Das radikal traditionelle Selbstbild. Zur Selbsteinschätzung des "gemäßigten" Flügels der Frauenbewegung um 1900 und seine politische Interpretation seitens der Nachgeborenen', *Geschichtsdidaktik*, vol. 10, 1985, pp. 128–48.

80. Nienhaus, 'Femininity and Skill'.

In reference to another area of state policy towards women, it has been argued that the subordinating effects of discriminatory legislation are counterbalanced by social policies directed at families. These have the effect of drawing women into direct negotiation with the state and state-sponsored professionals, in their role as consumers, responsible parents and household managers.[81] This exchange may prove a source of relative power within the family, for example when financial support is paid directly to the mother, or when the law gives women as mothers the means to defend themselves against their husbands or grown children. This remains a controversial thesis, and empirical research in German history has not yet produced the data against which it might be tested.[82] There is an example of social policy administration providing women with a forum in which to articulate their dissent from the ideal of family embodied in legislation. It is shown in the ways that women responded when insurance schemes premissed on a conventional division between housework and gainful employment, and between men's and women's work, were introduced in an area where a worker-peasant type of household economy still prevailed.[83] A different kind of alliance between women, professionals and the state is provided by women's involvement in social work since the nineteenth century. Before 1918, the expanding network of state and (still primarily) voluntary social agencies unquestionably provided a basis for autonomous activity for middle-class women, and at the regional level even meant that women could take up responsible positions in public administration. This may be seen as the collaboration of middle-class women in the disciplining of the working class.[84] It was manifestly not viewed this way by the social workers themselves, often members of the women's movement, who saw themselves as working in common cause with their female

81. See J. Donzelot, *La police de familles*, Paris, 1977.
82. For a relevant comment on the potential of social policy in contemporary Europe, see U. Gerhard, 'Den Sozialstaat neu denken?', *Vorgänge*, no. 87, 1987, pp. 14–32.
83. J.H. Quataert, 'Social Insurance and the Family Work of Oberlausitz Home Weavers in the Late Nineteenth Century', in J.C. Fout (ed.), *German Women in the Nineteenth Century*, New York/London, 1984, pp. 270–94; idem, 'Teamwork in Saxon Homeweaving Families in the Nineteenth Century', in R.B. Joeres and M.J. Maynes (eds.), *German Women in the Eighteenth and Nineteenth Centuries*, Bloomington, 1986, pp. 3–23.
84. U. Frevert, 'The Civilizing Tendency of Hygiene', in Fout (ed.), *German Women in the Nineteenth Century*, pp. 320–44.

clients. The welfare establishment of the Weimar Republic offered new career prospects for women, and was in turn permeated by the spirit of 'organised motherliness' of the older generation of feminists.[85] Some of the features of the Weimar scene persisted in the National Socialist welfare state, which allowed women a special role in the administration of family policy while bringing to fatal realisation the fantasies of the Weimar eugenicists. But this development has to be seen against the background of an initial dismantling by the Nazis of the network of social provision, which included the reduction or suspension of operations of state offices, as well as the closure or physical destruction of voluntary agencies and advice centres, in actions in which antifeminism as well as antisemitism and antisocialist resentment found expression.[86] It is the question of the ambivalences of state social policy, given new relevance by innovations in the study of gender relations and lent particular piquancy by the German historical experience, that may be expected to generate the most interesting new research in the near future.

85. I. Stoehr, '"Organisierte Mütterlichkeit" – Zur Politik der deutschen Frauenbewegung um 1900', in K. Hausen (ed.), *Frauen suchen ihre Geschichte*, Munich, 1983, pp. 221–49; C. Sachße, *Mütterlichkeit als Beruf. Sozialarbeit, soziale Reform und Frauenbewegung 1871–1929*, Frankfurt am Main, 1986.
86. On the National Socialist instrumentalisation of women's philanthropic and welfare work, see, most recently, C. Koonz, *Mothers in the Fatherland*, London, 1987. On the Nazis' handling of the social welfare system and of social workers in the early 1930s, see D. Kramer, 'Das Fürsorgesystem im Dritten Reich', in R. Landwehr and R. Baron (eds.), *Geschichte der Sozialarbeit*, Weinheim/Basel, 1983, pp. 173–217.

2

The State as Employer in Germany, 1880–1918: From Paternalism to Public Policy

Andreas Kunz

Introduction

The expansion of the public sector of the economy during the last three decades of the nineteenth century may be viewed as a general feature of the overall development of advanced industrial societies. While this growth process is itself well known, it is often overlooked that public sector expansion also led to decisive changes in employment patterns and thus in the labour markets of advanced industrial societies. With the quantitative growth in governmental employment, a new and sizeable internal labour market was created whose significance as a testing ground, if not as a pace-setter, for social policy legislation began to be increasingly apparent around the turn of the century.[1]

It is in connection with the latter development that the role of the state as an employer likewise underwent a remarkable change. While the absolutist state of the eighteenth century, and even the partially reformed constitutional monarchies of the early and mid-nineteenth century, had treated its comparatively small staff of civilian employees as 'servants to the crown', the modern industrial welfare state which had emerged by the turn of the century would prove to be unable to maintain this kind of authority over its

1. On the expansion of the service sector in general, see R.M. Hartwell, 'The Service Revolution: the Growth of Services in the Modern Economy 1700–1914', in C.M. Cipolla (ed.), *The Fontana Economic History of Modern Europe, Vol. 3: The Industrial Revolution*, London, 1973, pp. 358–96. On the growth of the public sector, see Peter Flora *et al.*, *State Economy and Society in Western Europe 1815–1975: A Data Handbook, Vol. 1: The Growth of Mass Democracies and Welfare States*, Frankfurt am Main/London/Chicago, 1983, Chapter 5.

employees.[2]

Aside from the purely quantitative developments already mentioned, several other reasons can be cited which set this process of transformation into motion. For one, the internal structure of the governmental workforce changed over time as the 'civil service elite' of the eighteenth century was replaced by an army of public employees, now including blue-collar workers. While the orientation and social status expectations of public employees may still have reflected a traditional civil service mentality, they also began to view themselves as economically dependent employees (or workers), as ready to take their demands to their (public) employers as their counterparts in the private sector of the economy. Rather than relying exclusively on measures of social welfare handed down to them by a benevolent, albeit paternalistic employer, public industrial workers and civil servants increasingly chose to defend their own interests through representative organisations.[3]

Secondly, one can observe that matters pertaining to the social welfare of public employment were slowly wrested from the exclusive jurisdiction of governments and placed squarely within the responsibilities of parliamentary legislation. Thus, the material (and legal) conditions of public employees began to be debated within the context of the social question and of social reform in general, that is, they became an integral part of public policy.

The timing of either acceptance or rejection of freedom of association, of forms and institutional patterns of negotiation, and of the public debate over these two issues varied greatly, and was dependent on the social and political structure, as well as on the political culture of the country in question. That is to say, the road from 'paternalism' to 'public policy' was travelled differently, at a different pace, and at slightly different times in France, Great Britain, and Germany.[4] By all accounts, Wilhelmine Germany was a late-

---

2. For the German case, see Bernd Wunder, *Geschichte der Bürokratie in Deutschland*, Frankfurt am Main, 1986, Chapter 1.

3. In a wider context, these organisational developments in the public sector must be viewed in connection with a more general trend toward interest organisation that began in the late nineteenth century in most Western European industrial nations. See Suzanne D. Berger (ed.), *Organizing Interests in Western Europe: Pluralism, Corporatism and the Transformation of Politics*, Cambridge, 1981.

4. A comprehensive international comparative study of these developments is still lacking. For an attempt at comparing only two countries, see Andreas Kunz, 'Arbeitsbeziehungen und Arbeitskonflikte im öffentlichen Sektor. Deutschland und

starter on what turned out to be a rocky road indeed. This may not be all too surprising, since it stands to reason that in Germany, the *Beamtenstaat* (civil-service state) par excellence, the unionisation of civil servants would be frowned upon, to say the least.[5] Yet of the three nations mentioned above, Imperial Germany had by far the largest public workforce. For this reason alone the process of transformation and social change resulting from the advancement of more modern forms of collective action in the public sector was bound to be as difficult as it would be significant historically.

The aim of this study, therefore, is to reconstruct and analyse the German state's reaction to socio-political changes in the public sector, by focusing on what may be considered the most important element in the transition from paternalism to public policy: the right of public employees – civil servants as well as industrial workers[6] – to associate freely in representative organisations and to negotiate their terms of employment and conditions of work. The concept of freedom of association emerged as the most controversially debated issue within a larger debate over the political rights of civil servants (and other state employees), which took place in Germany in the 1890s and in the first decade of the twentieth century.

The main contestants in this struggle were first, the Prussian State Ministry, which was allied with interested departments of the Reich government, especially the Reich Postal Administration, secondly, the newly-formed associations of civil servants and state workers in Prussia and other German states, and thirdly, parliaments, political parties and other supporters of public policy (e.g. the press). If in the context of this study the story will be told mainly from the vantage point of the state, this is not to deny the importance of the

---

Großbritannien im Vergleich', *Geschichte und Gesellschaft*, vol. 12, 1986, pp. 34–62.

5. Indeed, prior to 1890 this was not an issue at all in Germany, while in France, for example, the first battles had already been fought. On this, see Judith Wishnia, 'French Fonctionaires: The Development of Class Consciousness and Unionisation, 1884–1926', unpublished PhD thesis, Stony Brook, 1978.

6. It may be pointed out that there existed three forms of public employment in Germany, then as now: (1) civil servants (*Beamte*), including teachers, whose terms of employment were governed by public law (i.e. civil service law); (2) industrial workers (*Staatsarbeiter*) and (3) contractual public employees (*öffentliche Angestellte*), whose terms of employment were governed by private (contract) law. In the present study, the last two groups will be referred to summarily as 'state workers', since the *Angestellte* did not play a major role quantitatively at that time.

other two contestants. It is done in the conviction that the government's ambivalent, often shifting, attitude towards the freedom of association of its own employees provides a remarkable example of the German state's response to social change in the late nineteenth century.

The State as an Employer

In the three decades between 1880 and 1910 public employment in Germany increased dramatically. According to the occupational census of 1882, some 661,855 persons were employed in government service – national, state and local – in 1881; the 1907 census, by contrast, already lists 1,548,312 government employees.[7] The increase affected civil-service personnel as well as industrial workers in government service, although the latter were relative newcomers and the 'non-traditional' element in the German public workforce. According to one contemporary estimate, the number of blue-collar workers (*Arbeiter*) rose from some 100,000 in 1880 to more than 700,000 in 1913. Of these, about 80,000 were employed by the Reich Government, mainly in the Postal Administration (10,000), on the Alsace-Lorraine Railways – then under the administration of the Reich government – (12,000), in military workshops (30,000), and in the Imperial dockyards (26,000). Some 60,000 workers were under contract to municipal governments (the *Gemeindearbeiter*). The greatest number by far, however, was made up by the blue-collar workforce of the federated states (the *Bundesstaaten*). In Prussia alone some 500,000 industrial workers, the majority of whom worked on the Prussian-Hesse Railways (310,000) and in the state-owned mines (180,000), were on the payroll in 1913. As the contemporary source from which these figures have been drawn noted, the Prussian Ministry of Public Works had become by 1913 the 'largest employer in the world'.[8]

This is even more obviously the case if the Civil Service is taken into consideration as well. If one includes civil-service personnel (*Beamte*), some 560,000 persons were employed by the Prussian-

7. Figures are based on a recent recalculation of census data by Richard C. Eichenberg, 'Bureaucracy and Public Employment: Historical Data for the Western Democracies', HIWED Report No. 10, mimeo, Mannheim, 1979.

8. *Soziale Praxis* (*SP*), vol. 27, 1913, col. 1127.

Hesse Railway Administration in 1913. Altogether, there were about one million civil servants (including teachers) in Germany, working either at the national, state, or local level of government.[9] The total public workforce, then, amounted to some 1.7 million individuals in 1913, of which the vast majority, nearly two-thirds, were employed by the State of Prussia.

It stands to reason that the enormous size of the workforce under its direct jurisdiction created a new situation for the state in its role as an employer. To take care of the selection, training and remuneration of a handful of civil servants is one thing; to handle the complex affairs of a modern industrial labour force is quite another. Just how the German state met this challenge – if indeed it was able to do so at all prior to 1914 – will be one important subject of the present discussion. There are several ways to investigate the capacity of the German state to rise to this task. One approach would certainly be an in-depth examination of the social policy conducted by the various public employers. The results of such an investigation may well confirm the impression, already advanced by contemporary observers, that with regard to social-policy measures, large public employers such as the Prussian Railway Administration or the Reich Postal Service were indeed at the forefront when it came to matters regarding the welfare of their employees. As the world's pioneer of state-initiated social policy legislation, it only made sense that the Prussian government, as well as the Reich government, ensured that social insurance schemes, medical protection and the like were implemented in their own establishments.[10] Thus one may or may not doubt the sincerity in the words of the Prussian Minister of Public Works, Budde, for example, who in 1904 declared in the Prussian Chamber of Deputies that a large portion of his work was devoted to the general welfare of the workers. According to Budde, one of the most important duties of the Prussian Railway Administration was 'to solve the social question through means of social welfare (*Fürsorge*)'.[11] Budde, however, was the same man who only

9. On the numerical growth of civil service employment during this period, see Andreas Kunz, *Civil Servants and the Politics of Inflation in Germany, 1914–1924*, Berlin/New York, 1986, Chapter 1.
10. For a detailed contemporary analysis of governmental social policy measures in the Reich Postal Administration, see Kurt Kleemann, *Die Sozialpolitik der Reichs-Post- und Telegraphenverwaltung gegenüber ihren Beamten, Unterbeamten und Arbeitern*, Jena, 1914.
11. Haus der Abgeordneten (HdA), 37th session, 3 March 1904, clipping in

one year earlier had proclaimed in front of the same audience that any railway employee who did not obey his orders 'could pack his bags and go elsewhere to find work'.[12] Such pronouncements encapsulate rather well, I believe, the parameters of state employment in Germany and Prussia at the time: social welfare at the expense of succumbing to the unquestioned authority of the state as a public employer.

Despite the tendencies of repression, the relatively high level of social welfare, coupled with a level of employment security unmatched in the private sector, made government service highly attractive to prospective employees. For manual workers, the possibilities of advancing to the lower ranks of the civil service was an added incentive, since it would add status and prestige and provide for an even greater amount of employment security.[13] Recruitment was never a problem for public employers, therefore, and this increased their leverage in conflict situations with their employees.

In spite of welfare schemes and paternalistic social policies on the part of the state, the level and intensity of social unrest within the public workforce increased throughout the last two decades of the nineteenth century. There were several reasons for this development. For one, the growth of the public workforce played a role, since it increased the danger of hiring potential troublemakers, i.e. persons with leanings toward the (then outlawed) Social Democratic Party (SPD). The sources reveal that state agencies clearly became worried over this situation. In 1878, for example, the Prussian Minister of Public Works admonished the heads of the regional railway districts that 'in the interest of public welfare' the employment of civil servants and blue-collar workers who had ties to the Social Democratic Party 'should not be tolerated any further'.[14] Apparently alarmed by a report from Breslau, where allegations had been made that nearly all manual labourers and lower-

Geheimes Staatsarchiv Preussischer Kulturbesitz Berlin-Dahlem (GStA), Rep. 90, 2324, Bl. 48–50.

12. HdA, 28th session, clipping in GStA, Rep. 90, 2324, Bl. 43.

13. On this, see Klaus Saul, 'Konstitutioneller Staat und betriebliche Herrschaft. Zur Arbeiter- und Beamtenpolitik der preußischen Staatseisenbahnverwaltung 1890–1914', in Dirk Stegmann *et al.* (eds.), *Industrielle Gesellschaft und politisches System*, Bonn, 1978, pp. 315–36, in particular pp. 323ff.

14. Minister for Trade, Commerce and Public Works to chairmen of the regional railway offices, 3 July 1878, GStA, Rep. 90, 2323, Bl. 35ff. (excerpt).

grade civil servants in the railway district belonged to an SPD-oriented local organisation, the minister gave orders to eliminate 'such elements' from the railway service, either by immediate dismissal or, in the case of civil-service personnel, through disciplinary proceedings. Only if there was a chance for improvement in the future should the option of transfer to another location be used. The paternalistic attitude clearly emerges from the closing remark of the decree, where the minister raised hopes that some of those civil servants and workers 'who have been led astray' could be brought back to the right path by a benevolent but at the same time forceful method of disciplining them.

The initiative of the Minister of Public Works triggered off a longer debate within the Prussian State Ministry, about whether special legislation should be enacted to make possible the instant withdrawal of political rights from those civil servants or blue-collar workers in government service who were connected to the SPD in any way. Although favoured by some high-ranking members of the Prussian and Reich governments, among them Bismarck himself, the Cabinet followed the advice of the Minister of Justice and finally decided against special legislation, favouring the use of existing laws instead.[15] Apparently, the desire not to draw public attention to a highly sensitive issue, which therefore required discreet handling, played a role in the Cabinet's decision.

The Growth of Civil Service Associations

While in the early stages of the struggle with its employees the Prussian government had been chiefly concerned with the links between *individual* employees and political organisations – of which the SPD was only one, albeit the most significant one[16] – a

15. Letter from Bismarck to Vice-President of the State Ministry, 22 April 1879, copy in ibid., Bl. 42; Cabinet meeting 24 April 1879, ibid., Bl. 45ff.

16. Another case was the Polish Nationalist Party. As early as 1850 the Prussian Cabinet voted to outlaw the participation of civil servants in the Liga Polska. These and other documents have been taken from a compilation, put together by the Prussian State Ministry in 1909 and entitled 'Materialien zur Denkschrift betreffend der Beschränkung der Beamten in der Ausübung des Rechts auf freie Meinungsäußerung, des Petitions- sowie des Vereins- und Versammlungsrechts', a copy of which can be found in GStA, Rep. 90, Bl. 81–108. Henceforth this document will be cited as 'Materialien' with archival page numbers added. For a reference to the

few years later its attention was to turn to *associations* of civil servants and other state workers. While a possible connection between associations and the Social Democratic labour movement influenced this change in focus, the point of attack was undoubtedly broadened, since the very purposefulness of the formation of associations among public employees was now called into question. Once again the Minister of Public Works, the 'railway minister', spearheaded the attack. In November 1885 he alerted his cabinet colleagues to the fact that in his administration civil-service personnel had begun to band together in associations. While to the outside world these *Vereine* purported merely to promote the interests of their members at a very general level, the minister suspected that in reality their intention was to create a 'forum of opposition' and 'inappropriate pressure' vis-à-vis his administration. This, he added, would be 'in discord with the established political and administrative order of the realm'.[17] In the subsequent months, the minister apparently kept close surveillance over these associations, because one year later he proposed to the Cabinet that membership in them should be forbidden to public employees. After he had received the green light from his cabinet colleagues, he issued a decree stipulating that civil servants involved in the activities of these associations be removed from their posts and be made subject to disciplinary proceedings.[18] With this decree the Prussian government clearly had opted for a course of confrontation towards interest organisations of public employees.

While in the late 1880s only a few associations were affected – since only very few existed at the time – the implicit issue of freedom of association was to take on renewed significance, when in the 1890s an ever greater number of associations appeared on the scene. Two things are of importance in this context. First, the issue was now transferred from the (Prussian) Railway to the (Reich) Postal Administration (no doubt a result of the success of the 1886 decree which virtually prohibited the founding of associations among railway personnel), and secondly, it almost exclusively concerned *civil servants*, who had moved to the forefront of

---

Denkschrift itself, see below p. 51 and note 54.

17. 'Materialien', Bl. 94ff.

18. Cabinet meeting of 10 November 1886, and Decree of 14 December 1886, both excerpted in ibid., Bl. 95.

association-building in the public sector. Unions of blue-collar workers appeared only later, in the late 1890s, after the initial battles had already been waged.[19]

Given the peculiar social and legal status of the *Beamte* in German society, it is not surprising that in the second half of the nineteenth century civil servants had already begun to come together in separate organisations. Most of these were fraternal associations (*Standesvereine*), however, which did not attempt to represent the interests of their members. They remained concerned mainly with welfare and insurance matters, dealt with issues of professional education (*Fortbildung*) and offered general sociability.[20] In a sense, they explicitly avoided other functions, not least in an attempt to demonstrate to the state authorities their difference and distance from the labour movement. Most of these early associations were local associations; very few attempted to recruit on a regional level.

Two groups within the German civil service do not fit into this general picture: primary school teachers (*Volksschullehrer*) and postal officers (*Postbeamte*). Their organisational history reveals that from early on the idea of interest representation and the founding of larger, more centralised associations to support their claims, played a major role, at least among the leaders of these nascent movements.[21] Much has been written about German teachers in this context,[22] but this essay will highlight very briefly their contribution to association building in the period before 1890.[23]

The idea of association appeared as early as the late eighteenth

19. A national union organising municipal and state workers, the Socialist Verband der Gemeinde- und Staatsarbeiter, was founded in 1890, but initially it remained small and thus powerless. On the situation of organisations of railway workers, see Saul, 'Konstitutioneller Staat', pp. 319–22.

20. On these early associations, as well as on the formation of the civil service movement in general, see Kurt Ritter von Scherf, 'Die Entwicklung der Beamten und ihre Interessenvertretung', unpublished dissertation, University of Greifswald, 1919, pp. 76 and *passim*.

21. There is a striking parallel to France, where teachers and postal employees were the driving forces of organisational developments in the public sector. In Great Britain postal officers played a similar role as well.

22. Most recently by Rainer Bölling, *Volksschullehrer und Politik. Der Deutsche Lehrerverein 1918–1933*, Göttingen, 1978, which contains a good bibliography.

23. My main sources are Scherf, 'Entwicklung', pp. 76–83 and Bölling, *Volksschullehrer*, pp. 32–42.

century among German primary school teachers. Problems of status definition and pay might have played a role early on, since *Volks-schullehrer*, in contrast to university-trained teachers, were poorly paid and much less well respected than their counterparts in secondary schools. In 1848, during a period of revolutionary turmoil, a General Association of German Teachers was founded in Berlin. Not least as a result of an assumed 'revolutionary tinge', this organisation soon found itself under attack by the school authorities (i.e. the state). Only four years later, in 1852, fewer than 300 teachers dared to participate in a general teachers' conference. The low attendance reflected the unhappy fact that the state governments in Prussia, Bavaria and Saxony had proscribed membership in the General Association for teachers under their jurisdiction. In the course of the 1860s these proscriptions were lifted again, however, so that in 1871 (arguably a much more promising date than 1848 from the perspective of the state!) the founding of the Deutscher Lehrerverein (DLV) could take place. It initiated a new wave in association-building among teachers, and after some factional strife the DLV in 1908 emerged as the winner and the main interest organisation of German primary school teachers.[24] By 1918, it had become an umbrella for some forty-seven associations (in turn combining more than 2800 [!] branch associations) and mustered an overall membership of nearly 115,000.[25] Although the German teachers' movement had its own organisational life (and consequently its own history) apart from its role in the German civil-service movement until 1920,[26] it must be emphasised that teachers and their associations provided important organisational impulses for other civil-service groups.

A second impulse toward association-building and interest activity in the German civil service emerged from personnel employed in large state-run enterprises, particularly those in the postal service. Postal officers took the lead in forming larger, more centralised associations, which then began to make claims at representing

24. Figures cited by Scherf, 'Entwicklung', pp. 76–83.
25. Rival organisations continued to exist, however, mainly organised along religious lines. There was also a separate association for women teachers and, of course, separate associations for secondary school teachers, in spite of the fact that in principle the DLV tried to organise *all* teachers.
26. In 1920 the DLV joined the Deutscher Beamtenbund (DBB), which had been founded in 1918. See Bölling, *Volksschullehrer*, p. 52.

the interests of their members vis-à-vis the government. In 1890 the Verband mittlerer Reichs- Post- und Telegraphenbeamten was founded in Berlin, a middle-level civil servants' organisation which in the literature is often regarded as the first genuine interest association within the German civil service. Indeed, its statutes proclaimed, 'The association has as its purpose [. . .] the representation of the postal officers' interests.'[27] However, this somewhat daring move on the part of the organisation's founders was not honoured by those whose interests were to be represented, nor by the state whose authority was called into question. Only 600 of some 25,000 postal officers joined the new organisation, and repressive measures taken by the Reich Postal Administration against the association and its leadership soon forced its leaders to erase the interest clause from its statutes. Subsequently, but only for a brief period, it receded into the more common role of a fraternal *Verein*.[28]

If the fate of the postal officers' association may be interpreted as an exemplary case of government repression of civil-service unionism, this victory was to be short-lived. In the mid-1890s attempts at interest articulation intensified amongst German civil servants, primarily as a result of the officials' worsening economic situation in the wake of renewed series of price increases that plagued the German economy in the last decade before the war.[29] The suspicions of the Postal Administration were roused once again, when in 1897 attempts were made at putting together an association of the (much more numerous) lower-grade civil servants in the postal service. The Reich Postal Office in Berlin quickly issued instructions to its regional district office in Hamburg, where the call for the founding of the organisation had appeared in an SPD-oriented newspaper. The district's chief was ordered to 'carefully investigate the affair' and to collect all materials that could link the association to the Social Democratic Party. Such materials, he was told, would be of use in a possible confrontation over the issue with the SPD in

27. Fritz Winters, *Geschichte des Verbandes mittlerer Reichspost- und Telegraphenbeamten*, Berlin, 1915, p. 44.
28. Ibid., pp. 157–68.
29. This point is made by Emil Lederer, 'Die Bewegung der öffentlichen Beamten', *Archiv für Sozialwissenschaft und Sozialpolitik* (*ASS*), vol. 31, 1910, pp. 660–709, in particular p. 660. Henceforth Lederer's reports on the civil servants' movement, all published in *ASS*, will be cited with the author's name, the year of the journal and the page number given.

the Reichstag. Furthermore, the senior official in Hamburg was advised to establish contact with the regional railway district in Altona in order to learn about the ways in which the Railway Administration had confronted similar agitation among its personnel.[30] In addition, the Reich Postal Office warned the other district chiefs about the incident and ordered them to report immediately if similar occurrences took place in their respective districts.[31]

The worries of the Reich Postal Administration were compounded by the fact that in the previous months similar developments had taken place among the ever restive railway personnel, and that the postal officials in Hamburg had established contact with an organisation of lower-grade railway civil servants. Organisations of this kind had been founded in Hamburg, as well as in Magdeburg and Leipzig, in the autumn of 1897.[32] Although the Railway Administration had tried to block these attempts by forcing the railway-men to sign a declaration agreeing not to join the association (as in Hamburg), or by simply dissolving it (as in Leipzig), these measures had apparently failed to stem the tide completely.[33] Perhaps as a result of general changes in the political climate, the state authorities were unable simply to suppress the organisations, since the latter found public support not only with the Social Democratic Reichstag delegation, but also among left-liberal social reformers.[34] Indeed, it may be said that by that time the freedom of association of public employees – civil servants as well as industrial workers – had become an important public issue. This, in turn, tended to force the government into a defensive posture with regard to possible repressive measures.

One example may suffice to illustrate the point just made. In the spring of 1898, lower-grade postal and railway officials in Hamburg did indeed convene a *joint* meeting and demanded publicly both groups be permitted to form trade unions (*Gewerkschaften*). The

30. Letter from State Secretary of the Reich Postal Office to Oberpostdirektor Vorbeck in Hamburg, 15 June 1897, GStA, Rep. 90, 2323, Bl. 143.

31. Directive to all regional offices (*Oberpostdirektionen*), except for Hamburg, 3 June 1897, ibid., Bl. 142.

32. *SP*, vol. 6, 1896/97, col. 61ff. Reasons given were the worsening conditions of work, especially long work hours and low pay.

33. Ibid., col. 557.

34. Their mouthpiece was the *Soziale Praxis*, which lent great support to these organisational attempts among public employees.

Postal Administration reacted swiftly and with great zeal. As a result of denunciations made to the authorities, those civil servants suspected of having taken part in the meeting were interrogated by a higher official. The aim was clearly to intimidate the lower ranks and to get at the 'agitators' in an attempt at disciplining them.[35]

It was perhaps a sign of the essentially defensive nature of the government's struggle against the unionisation of public employees that the State Secretary of the Reich Postal Office was forced to defend these measures in front of the Reichstag. His categoric statement that 'any direct or indirect participation of a civil servant of the Reich Postal Administration in the activities of the Social Democratic Party is incongruent with his oath of office' may have earned him the applause of the right, but also 'laughter' from the left.[36] In the end, the Postal Administration used the incident to issue a decree prohibiting the appearance of 'professional agitators' at meetings of postal officers, since the latters' sole aim, according to the Administration, was the disturbance of the 'harmonious co-operation' that allegedly existed between the various ranks in the postal service.[37]

The Response of the State

While the measures described thus far have been confined to the two large state-run enterprises, the railways and the postal services, there were similar developments happening at the same time which prompted the Prussian Cabinet to take up the associational question at a more general level. The initiative came from the Prussian Minister of Finance, Johannes von Miquel, who in 1897 complained to his cabinet colleagues about the activities of civil service associations during the parliamentary debates on the fixing of civil service pay scales. He proposed to the Cabinet that membership in an association should be allowed only if the association in question agreed to limit its activities to the social welfare of its members. Civil servants should be warned not to take up membership in those associations that exerted pressures on government agencies or par-

35. *SP*, vol. 7, 1896/97, col. 599.
36. Reichstag session, 3 March 1898, clipping in GStA, Rep. 90, 2323, Bl. 147ff.
37. The decree was published in the official gazette of the Reich Postal Office, the *Amtsblatt*. Cited from a clipping in GStA, Rep. 90, 2323, Bl. 151.

liamentary bodies while trying to attain their goals. If civil servants persisted in their support of such organisations, their active participation in associations of this kind should be prohibited.[38]

A decision could not be reached at cabinet level, however, mainly because the Minister of Justice was opposed to an outright prohibition.[39] To iron out these differences, an inter-ministerial committee was formed. With some delay, the committee reported back to the Cabinet in February 1899, suggesting (1) the proscription of membership in a number of associations, and (2) the issuing of a warning to civil servants on membership in 'harmful associations', in conjunction with a reminder of possible disciplinary actions in cases of outright disobedience.[40] In a meeting of the Prussian Cabinet in March 1899, where the content of the report was discussed, Miquel pushed for the immediate implementation of these measures, since they would come at precisely the right moment to prevent renewed activity by the associations during the current budget discussions in the Prussian Chamber of Deputies. While the Cabinet agreed to publish the warning,[41] it decided against taking the more general prohibitive measures Miquel had suggested. The latter was left to the discretion of the heads of individual departments and ministries.[42]

It is not quite clear why the Prussian Cabinet failed to establish general guidelines on the basis of the Miquel Report. During the deliberations in the Cabinet the Minister of Justice upheld, implicitly at least, the principle of a *Rechtsstaat*, governed by the rule of law under the constitution rather than by the arbitrary use of force, and his objections may have carried enough weight to prevent the issuing of a formal decree. As a consequence, implementation of the report's findings was entrusted to individual departments, and this led to the unhappy fact that the attitude – or degree of repression – towards associations of public employees also continued to vary from department to department. The most repressive policies were undoubtedly pursued by the Prussian Railway Administration, which

38. In a meeting of the Prussian Cabinet on 10 July 1897, quoted in 'Materialien', Bl. 95ff.

39. Ibid., Bl. 96ff.

40. Ibid., Bl. 98. Twenty-seven associations in five administrative branches are listed for proscription in the source.

41. It appeared in the *Reichs- und Staatsanzeiger*, 17 April 1899.

42. 'Materialien', Bl. 99.

used the mandate given to it by the Cabinet on several occasions in an effort to curtail the power and influence of associations of civil servants and blue-collar workers under its jurisdiction. In 1905, for example, a decree was issued prohibiting civil servants from joining associations with an avowed interest-group character. According to the decree, these were organisations which strove for 'the attainment of political power by exerting influence on governments and parliaments'.[43] Obviously, the Railway Administration was responding to the appearance of supra-regional associations which had been formed in spite of all previous measures enacted to prevent such a development.[44]

Two years later, the Railways Ministry again issued stiff guidelines regarding the founding and operation of professional associations among its personnel. According to a ministerial decree issued in February 1907, the statutes of associations had to be confirmed by the district administration in which the Verein had its seat. All association activities had to be placed under constant surveillance. Moreover, associations were obliged to refrain from political or church-related activities – the latter a warning-shot fired at unions close to the Catholic trade-union movement. Finally, membership in associations was restricted to those civil servants (or blue-collar workers) still on active duty or to those officially retired. Two-thirds of an association's executive committee, including its chairman, had to be actively employed.[45] The last two measures obviously aimed at maintaining direct control over the activities of the associations, since disciplinary proceedings could be taken against employees still on the payroll (or even against retired staff), while the establishment of an independent and thus uncontrollable associational bureaucracy was rendered difficult, if not impossible.

Later on in the same year, the association issue was once again placed on the agenda of a Cabinet meeting. The Prussian Finance

---

43. Directive of the Ministry of Public Works, 24 and 31 December 1905, GStA, Rep. 84a, 3144, Bl. 5ff.

44. One of the measures had been the founding of 'company unions' at the instigation and under the supervision of the Administration, the so-called 'Buddevereine', named after the Minister of Public Works, von Budde, who promoted this scheme. On this, see Carl Schwarz, 'Zur Koalitionsbewegung der Eisenbahnarbeiter in Deutschland', unpublished PhD thesis, University of Kiel, 1923, pp. 98ff.

45. Directive of the Ministry of Public Works, 21 February 1907, excerpted in 'Materialien', Bl. 102ff.

Minister had been forewarned of a general meeting of an association of middle-level customs and tax officials, who apparently had sent out invitations to parliamentary delegates as well as to heads of departments. The minister suspected that if the meeting were to be held as planned, it could be interpreted as a signal to other associations that the Administration had become all too lenient in the matter. This, he claimed, would endanger the internal discipline of the Civil Service as a whole. As a remedy, the Finance Minister proposed that the Cabinet reissue a warning to civil servants on the basis of the Decree of 1899. He cautioned, however, that the timing for such a step was problematic, since the National Assembly could pick up the issue once the draft bill of a new Associations Law, then pending in the Reichstag, had reached the floor. If an appropriate rider were attached to the bill, the right of association of civil servants might then become part of the new law.[46] The Finance Minister's cabinet colleagues shared these misgivings about possible 'unpleasant debates' in the Reichstag and therefore agreed that 'drastic measures' against civil service associations were inopportune at the moment. Things should be handled on a case-by-case basis instead, for example by supervising leave-of-absence regulations or by invoking the penalties of the disciplinary code against 'zealots' (*Exzedenten*) amongst the associations' leaders.

Once again the issue had been shelved, rather than resolved, although the references to the Reichstag may be taken as an indication that the Prussian Cabinet's room for manoeuvre had become considerably reduced. One reason for this is that the associations in question had by then taken on a public dimension, as is demonstrated by the parliamentary deliberations and passage of the Associations Law of 1908. The civil servants' struggle for associational freedom during these years must be viewed in connection with the preparation and passage of this bill, which, as they hoped, would improve their affairs as much as those of any other citizen. As it turned out, however, the Administration would reserve to itself the right of interpreting the applicability of the Associations Law to the civil service in each concrete case, particularly when matters of pay became intertwined with interest representation.

---

46. Meeting of the Prussian Cabinet, 19 November 1907, GStA, Rep. 90, 2324, Bl. 62ff.

Andreas Kunz

National Association and State Repression

Such a scenario was to develop only two years later, when once again the formation of a new, now nationwide civil-service federation produced a sharp reaction from the government side. In April 1909, a 'national meeting of civil servants' (*Deutscher Beamtentag*) had been summoned to convene in Berlin.[47] Although the plan of founding a national organisation of civil servants was not achieved, the momentum of creating some kind of national umbrella association did not evaporate entirely. In conjunction with parliamentary struggles over a major reform of the civil service pay scale in 1909, a Bund der Festbesoldeten (BdF) was founded by a number of persons who had been active in the general meeting of 1909.[48] As an organisation, the BdF tried to cut across occupational and hierarchical divisions within the civil service by appealing to *all* civil servants rather than to a specific 'category', 'class' or 'group'. It may thus be viewed as a first attempt at achieving organisational unity within the deeply divided German civil servant movement. Emil Lederer, one of the most astute observers of social movements in Imperial Germany, even considered the BdF the nucleus of a new, modern civil service movement, whose contribution to the development of German society was, in his opinion, of central importance.[49]

If in the long run the BdF did not live up to such high expectations – a fact which was ruefully admitted by Lederer himself in later reports on the development of the German civil servant movement[50] – this was primarily due to the fact that it tried to organise public officials (*Beamte*) and so-called 'private officials' (i.e. salaried employees, or *Angestellte*) in private industry at the same time. By subsuming two different social groups, *Beamte* and *Angestellte*, under the artificial rubric of the *Festbesoldete* (permanent salaried staffs), the BdF lacked a clear social basis.[51] Thus it

47. Mentioned in 'Materialien', Bl. 106ff.
48. Some documentation on the politics of the BdF can be found in Zentrales Staatsarchiv Potsdam (ZStAP), RMdI, 2742. On the history of this organisation, see Scherf, 'Beamtenbewegung', pp. 99ff, and Lederer, *ASS* 1910–1915. For a recent appraisal, see Kunz, *Civil Servants*, pp. 94–101.
49. Lederer, *ASS* 1910, p. 662.
50. Lederer, *ASS* 1913, pp. 659ff.
51. This fact is stressed in some of the 'official histories' of the civil service movement, written by association leaders. See, for example, Albert Falkenberg, *Die deutsche Beamtenbewegung nach der Revolution*, 2nd edn, Berlin, 1920, pp. 18ff. See also Kunz, *Civil Servants*, pp. 95ff.

never could attract a large membership and remained at the fringes, rather than moving into the centre of a new civil service movement. When in 1913 the BdF joined the small-business oriented Hansa League for Trade, Commerce and Industry as a corporate member, the attachment to an umbrella organisation of producer interests represented the final act in the demise of the first, but ultimately unsuccessful, central civil servant association.[52]

Ironically, though, it was precisely the BdF's unsuccessful attempt at integrating civil servants and contractual employees which worried the state authorities the most. The government's rationale was obvious: not only would an 'employee mentality' (*Arbeitnehmergedanke*) spread into the civil service, but mass organisations of this kind also had a better potential of becoming more formidable adversaries in conflicts with the state. In April 1909, therefore, the Prussian Cabinet decided that this time a more thorough examination of the entire issue was called for. A committee was installed whose task it was to draw up a report regarding past experiences and future dealings with civil service associations, and, implicitly, with organisations representing other public employees as well.[53] The committee's report, subsequently issued in the form of a government memorandum, was completed only three months later, in July 1909, which may be taken as an indication of the high importance attached to the matter at this juncture. Its comprehensiveness makes this report a document of considerable significance for the argument of the present study. Its content shows once again, I believe, that repressive measures taken against civil service associations were not only random acts by senior officials in different ministries, but part of a comprehensive government policy designed to stabilise the existing social and political order of Imperial Germany.[54]

The memorandum begins with the reiteration of the 'fundamental principle' that a civil servant should submit totally to the interest and the welfare of the state. Any deviation from this 'iron principle' would entail a violation of the Civil Service Code and, if exposed,

---

52. Lederer, *ASS* 1913, p. 660.

53. The Cabinet meeting is mentioned in a letter of the Minister of Public Works to the Minister of Justice, 27 April 1909, GStA, Rep. 84a, 3144, Bl. 4. The activities of the Cabinet obviously were related to the *Beamtentag* mentioned above.

54. 'Denkschrift betreffend der Beschränkung der Beamten in der Ausübung des Rechtes auf freie Meinungsäußerung, des Petitions – sowie des Vereins- und Versammlungsrechts', copy in GStA, Rep. 90, 2324, Bl. 71–80.

should therefore be subject to established disciplinary measures. The inner commitment to unwavering loyalty to the state, the memorandum stresses, separated civil servants from the rest of the citizenry and curtailed their rights as citizens (*Staatsbürger*). Any existing infringement of basic political rights could only affect, in the first instance, the relationship between civil servants and those political parties which aimed at 'the destruction of the very foundation of the state', i.e. the Social Democratic Party and, to a lesser degree, the Polish Nationalist Party.

With regard to the issue of freedom of speech and freedom of association, similar, if more subtle, prohibitions and infringements appeared. For one thing, it was declared, the Prussian government could not tolerate any longer the practice of bringing pressure to bear on government agencies and parliamentary bodies through 'agitation' in the associational press. Thus, the civil service press, which had been subject to censorship in the past, would become so again in the future; additional pressure could be applied, if necessary, by monitoring subscriptions with the help of the Postal Administration.

The civil servant's right of petitioning, the memorandum stated, should be strictly regulated as well. While individual petitions could be tolerated, if filed in a proper way and through the correct channels, *collective* petitions, including those formulated and sent by civil service associations, were either not permitted or, at least, 'not desired'. Furthermore, all petitions, including those sent to parliamentary bodies, required the approval of the civil servant's immediate superior. Petitions which in any way advocated changes in existing government policies, or in legislative bills pending in the Prussian Diet, should be strictly forbidden.

With regard to the civil servants' right of association, the memorandum pointed out that the government commission, installed in 1897 at the behest of Minister of Finance Miquel, had stopped short of recommending the proscription of civil service associations altogether, but had warned that mass-organisation with the aim of coercing government agencies into concessions regarding social demands would not be tolerated by the state. While legally civil servants enjoyed the freedom to combine, their associations were in practice strictly regulated by governmental authorities. These regulations, the memorandum stressed, should again be 'sharply accentuated', even if it was necessary to avoid too much open regimentation 'in order not to stir up the sensitivity of the parliament with regard to alleged infringements of so-called [sic!] basic rights'. The Prussian government's insistence on curtailing, if necessary, the organisational activities of its civil servants, and the inherent dilemma it faced in enforcing these measures, is well captured in the closing phrase of the document. While civil servants, like other citizens, were free to join associations for the benefit of their common interests, the government had the right to prevent its civil servants from actively participating in these associations if the latters' aims were directed against the interests of the state.

The content of this memorandum, especially its last clause, shows that at this point governmental policies designed to repress *totally* the emergence and activities of civil servant associations had become partially eroded. The renewed sharp accentuation of repressive policies advocated in 1909 may also be taken as an admission that previous policies had failed to completely stem the tide of the creation of more centralised, general civil-service associations at the national level.

Given this state of affairs, it is surprising indeed that the findings of the committee were *not* used as a blueprint for further measures taken by the Prussian State Government. To be sure, the debate in Cabinet, where the matter was discussed on 15 December 1909, was perhaps the most heated one on the matter so far.[55] The Minister of Public Works in particular forced the issue by insisting that appeals to the civil servants' loyalty would not suffice any longer, but that clear-cut preventive measures had to be taken if the government was to maintain authority over its personnel. While he was supported in this opinion by his colleague, the State Secretary of the Postal Administration, a majority in the Cabinet argued that any harassment of the associations, especially of the BdF, would produce a harsh reaction at the parliamentary level and thus, would do more damage than good. Even a 'paternal warning' (*väterliche Mahnung*) of the kind issued in 1899 was considered too dangerous under the existing state of affairs, since it would only serve to enhance the importance of the associations in the eyes of the members of the civil service. Public policy had, in a way, finally replaced 'paternalism', when the Cabinet decided *against* the issuing of a renewed

55. Meeting of the Prussian Cabinet, 15 December 1909, GStA, Rep. 84a, 3144, Bl. 104–8.

decree, opting instead to await an interpellation in the Reichstag in order to present its position in response to a parliamentary motion. When further investigations into the activities of the BdF, conducted by Minister of State von Delbrück, later revealed that the publisher of the associations' gazette had connections to former Reich Chancellor Bülow, and that the former Chancellor had publicly supported the efforts of the association, the matter became a sensitive political issue and was dropped entirely.[56]

Several years later, in July 1917, the issue would reappear briefly in official correspondence, this time in response to yet another organisational attempt made by persons connected with the by then moribund BdF. But at this juncture what was at issue was not whether or not the new organisation – a national umbrella organisation for civil servant associations called the Interessengemeinschaft Deutscher Reichs-und Staatsbeamtenverbände (rapidly renamed the Interessengemeinschaft Deutscher Beamtenverbände, or IG) – should be suppressed or not, but whether it should be granted its wish to participate in the political decision-making process.[57] This clearly shows that the actual *existence* of civil service associations was not at issue any longer. The war and the *Burgfrieden* (party truce) of 1914 had solved this problem in a swift, if informal way. What remained controversial, however, was the *legal* protection of the associations and their *recognition* as negotiating partners and legitimate representatives of the interest of their members.

The First World War and State Concessions

The outbreak of war and the *Burgfrieden* mentality created within German society produced an immediate impact on the two principal rights withheld from civil servants, namely the full right of association and the right to engage actively in partisan politics.[58] While

---

56. Correspondence on this matter in ibid., Bl. 113, 209–20.

57. State Secretary of the Interior to Reich Chancellor, 4 July 1917, ZStAP, RMdI 2742, Bl. 97. The State Secretary explicitly refers to the 'BdF affair' in the beginning of this letter. The IG had demanded that it be consulted in the preparation of new custom and tax laws.

58. For a recent discussion of the civil servants' political rights from a jurist's point of view, see Hermannjosef Schmahl, *Disziplinarrecht und politische Betätigung der Beamten in der Weimarer Republik*, Berlin, 1977.

these two issues were certainly intertwined, we shall concentrate in the subsequent analysis on the problem of freedom of association as the more pertinent issue. It will be placed in the context of organisational behaviour and the emergence of civil service interest politics during the First World War.

Just as the Prussian government was forced to make concessions with regard to the appointment of SPD members to elected civil service positions at the municipal level,[59] it felt obliged rather early in the war to suspend the practice of enforcing a declaration of non-membership in the SPD, or in SPD-oriented trade unions, from prospective employees, whether they were civil servants, contractual employees (*Angestellte*) or blue-collar workers.[60] By the same token, membership in civil service associations ceased to be a major source of conflict between the associations and the government in Prussia as well as in the other German states. In a speech delivered to the Bavarian Diet in the autumn of 1914, for example, the Bavarian Minister of Finance grudgingly accepted the activities of civil service interest organisations as a 'phenomenon of modern life, if not a very pleasant one.' He expected, however, that in return the organisations would use their influence to ensure continued discipline within the civil service. Widely reported in the civil service press, the incident was interpreted as a first step towards a less repressive attitude, not only on the part of the Bavarian state government, but of 'government' as such.[61] Membership in 'striking unions' continued to be illegal for Bavarian civil servants, however, as well as for blue-collar workers in government service, which prompted one observer to comment that in reality the position of the Bavarian state government had not changed all that much.[62]

Indeed, if one probes into the internal operations of the government bureaucracy on this issue, it appears that senior officials in the relevant ministries remained sceptical, if not hostile, towards the emerging associations of government employees. This latent

59. The practice of not confirming these appointments was discontinued during the war. There is some documentation on this in ZStAP, RMdI, 2172.

60. Decided in a Cabinet meeting on 31 December 1914, GStA, Rep. 90, 2324, Bl. 132–41.

61. Reported by *Deutsche Beamtenrundschau (DBR)*, 1 October 1914.

62. Lederer, *ASS* 1915, p. 915. In early 1916 the Minister of Public Works had still insisted on placing a clause in the personnel regulations adopted in 1915, explicitly prohibiting membership in 'striking unions'. See *SP*, 9 March 1916, col. 534.

animosity increased even further, once the associations began putting pressure on parliamentary bodies to obtain material support in the face of mounting inflation. Activities of this kind were still regarded as 'highly objectionable' by high-ranking government officials.[63] Their misgivings increased even further, when in mid-1916 civil service associations began pressing for *formal* recognition as bargaining agents of civil service interests. The reform of the Associations Law of 1908, undertaken by the Imperial government in 1916 as one of the concessions made to the Social Democrats and to the Socialist Free Trade Unions, whose stigmatisation as 'political asociations' was to be thereby changed,[64] was seized upon by civil service organisations to enhance their standing vis-à-vis the government.

In April 1916, the leaders of fifteen large civil service associations met to devise a strategy to ensure that civil servants would benefit from the proposed reform of the Associations Law then pending in the Reichstag. There had been rumours that civil service associations would specifically be *excluded* from any improvements brought about by the new law. The assembled associational leaders decided to send a joint petition to the Reichstag and to the Bundesrat, in which the civil servants' demands concerning the new law were to be formulated. Obviously, this was a clear departure from the pre-war practice of not interfering with governmental legislative bills, and, as such, a sign of a new sense of power. As Anton Hoefle, an associational leader and a prominent member of the Centre Party told his colleagues, 'the opportunity for such a move is splendid, because the war has demonstrated that organisations are indispensable to our modern national economy'.[65]

Whether or not the petition created an impact during the parliamentary deliberations of the bill is difficult to ascertain. Several left-wing parties, however, did introduce a resolution calling for the recognition of civil service associations in such a way that the provisions of disciplinary law could not be used any longer by the government to overrule the stipulations of the new Associations Law. Government representatives refused to make any concessions,

63. Reich Office of the Interior to Reich Chancellery, 10 January 1916, ZStAP, RMdI, 2738, Bl. 53.
64. See Gerald D. Feldman, *Army, Industry and Labor in Germany, 1914–1918*, Princeton, 1966, pp. 121–3.
65. Based on a report of this meeting in *DBR*, 16 May 1916.

however, arguing that civil servants and contractual employees in the public service could not be regarded as regular employees (*Arbeitnehmer*), and that therefore the anticipated legal changes in the status of employee organisations could not be applied to civil service associations. While in the case of public wage-earners (*Staats-arbeiter*) the government was forced to make concessions in response to trade-union and SPD pressures,[66] it won out in the civil service question. Despite the fact that during the plenary debate in the Reichstag the civil servants' cause was taken up forcefully by the Progressive Party, no amendment regulating the legal status of civil service associations was written into the new law.[67] In a way, therefore, the initiative of the organisations had failed, and there was some resignation in the words of Ernst Remmers, the founder and first chairman of the IG, when in October 1917 he demanded that the government should place more confidence in the political and organisational skills of civil servants by recognising their associations, and by co-operating with them in all questions relating to civil service policy.[68]

Despite its ultimate failure, however, the offensive undertaken by the associations regarding the reform of the Associations Law may be interpreted as the first example of a modern type of interest politics conducted by civil service organisations in Germany. Characteristically, the very position of the associations within society, particularly vis-à-vis the government in its role as employer, was at stake. Civil servants had tried to benefit from changes in the relationship between the state authorities and interest organisations which had appeared in the first two years of the war. In the long run, however, active participation in social policy matters was to be wrested from public employers not by legal reforms, but by the mere existence of a potentially powerful mass organisation, which, although not recognised officially, could not be ignored any longer by the state.

In the course of the last two years of the war, a process of adaptation to changing social realities took place between the government and its principal adversary, the IG. At its first general

66. Feldman, *Army*, p. 122.
67. *Stenographische Berichte der Verhandlungen des Deutschen Reichstags*, vol. 307, pp. 1011–21.
68. Reported by *Die Gemeinschaft* (*DG*), 1 July 1917. *DG* was the official paper of the IG.

meeting in 1917, and at later occasions as well, the IG openly demanded recognition as the legitimate professional representative (*Standesvertretung*) of the civil service in a first step towards full integration into the socio-political system of the Empire. As a second step, the IG proposed the quasi-institutionalisation of governmental recognition by requesting a seat in the upper house of the Prussian legislature, the *Herrenhaus*, whose reform was being discussed in late 1917. At the middle and lower administrative levels, the process of institutionalisation of influence was to be accomplished by establishing civil service committees (*Beamtenausschüsse*) and civil service chambers (*Beamtenkammern*).[69] The government responded to these demands, some of which were modelled on similar gains scored by blue-collar workers in the Auxiliary Service Law of 1916,[70] with great hesitation. The establishment of civil service chambers and committees was among the many 'unfulfilled wishes' of the *Beamtenschaft* mentioned by Remmers in an address to the Gesellschaft für soziale Reform in the spring of 1918.[71] With regard to the IG's demand for representation in semi-parliamentary bodies like the *Herrenhaus* in Prussia, the State Secretary of the Interior advised the Reich Chancellor in mid-1917 that these were 'far-reaching demands indeed'. He questioned the usefulness of consulting with civil service representatives in matters not directly related to civil service policy, and he advised the Chancellor not to respond to the IG's proposal.[72]

Less than a year later, however, the integration of the IG into the political decision-making process had made further progress, and the umbrella association's political significance and leverage had increased accordingly. At the IG's second congress, which was convened in June 1918 in Berlin, a large group of parliamentary representatives attended, spanning the political spectrum from the left-liberal Progressive Party to the moderate-conservative Deutsche Reichspartei – an indication of the increased importance with which

69. 'Wünsche der Beamten zur Reform des preußischen Herrenhauses', *DG*, 16 December 1917.

70. For a splendid analysis of the impact of the Auxiliary Service Law on industrial relations in a regional setting, see Gunther Mai, *Kriegswirtschaft und Arbeiterbewegung in Württemberg 1914–1918*, Stuttgart, 1983.

71. 'Für Sozialpolitik nach dem Kriege', *Schriften der Gesellschaft für soziale Reform*, vol. 8, Jena, 1918, pp. 38ff.

72. Draft letter, State Secretary of the Interior to Reich Chancellor, 4 July 1917, ZStAP, RMdI, 2742, Bl. 97.

the IG was now being viewed in the bourgeois political camp. Delegates from the Social Democratic Party and the Socialist Trade Unions – not to speak of the radical-left Independent Socialists – were conspicuously absent, however, and this shows that the IG had either remained a bourgeois-oriented association, or that links to the labour movement which may have existed already at this juncture were at least not publicly disclosed.[73]

If the attendance of party delegates can be interpreted as a sign of the increasing importance of the IG and of its closer links with the parliamentary sphere, it is of equal, if not greater significance that government representatives attended the association's 1918 meeting as well. Moreover, they had come not as official watchdogs, as had been the case before 1914, but as invited guests of the association and its leaders. According to the inter-ministerial correspondence on the matter, the government had found it 'useful' at this point to send a delegation to the meeting, although none of the ministers or state secretaries themselves had been 'inclined to attend'.[74] Still, the fact that the government had sent an official delegation to a meeting of a civil service association was noted by Chairman Remmers in his opening remarks to the congress 'with great pleasure and satisfaction'.[75] Speaking for the government delegation, Privy Councillor von Jacobi of the Reich Office of the Interior promised to take the civil servants' wishes to their respective ministers and see to it that, if possible, they would be granted.[76] This, indeed, was a new tone, and the incident shows that a kind of working relationship had finally been established between government and interest group.

73. IG meeting 1918, report in *DG*, 1 July 1918. That these links did indeed exist would become clear only a few months later in the course of the November Revolution. On this, see Kunz, *Civil Servants*, pp. 132–58.

74. State Secretary of the Interior to IG, 20 June 1918, ZStAP, RMdI, 2738, Bl. 179ff, informing the organisation that Privy Councillor von Jacobi would attend the meeting as the official government representative. A note attached to the letter explains the position of the other ministries. Of all departments, only the Reich Office of Justice had refused to send a delegate to the meeting.

75. *DG*, 1 July 1918.

76. Ibid.

Conclusion

The reform of the political structure of the Empire in the wake of the so-called October Reforms of 1918, the last German 'revolution from above', did not drastically change the civil service organisations' leverage on the conduct of civil service policy, although the reforms did confirm the civil servants' full political rights as citizens.[77] In any case, such reforms as were undertaken were soon eclipsed by the 'revolution from below' of November 1918, which, as one might expect, was to lead to further changes in the relationship between civil servant organisations and the government as employer. In two early pronouncements issued by the revolutionary governments of Prussia and the Reich, the right of civil servants and state workers to associate freely was finally explicitly confirmed.[78] This fact has often led to the false conclusion that it was the November Revolution that introduced associational freedom in the German public service. This is a myopic interpretation at best. For what at first sight might appear as a gift of the revolution of 1918–19 was merely the endpoint of a much longer struggle between public employees and the government as an employer, a struggle which even prior to the revolution had propelled social policy in the German public sector from the paternalism of the 1880s and 1890s to the public policy of the first decade of the twentieth century.

---

77. The relevant documents on this in GStA, Rep. 90, 2324, Bl. 279ff.
78. Pronouncements published in *Reichsgesetzblatt* 1918, p. 1303 ('Das Vereins- und Versammlungsrecht unterliegt keiner Beschränkung, auch nicht für Beamte und Staatsarbeiter') and, for the Prussian government, in *Preußische Gesetzessammlung* 1918, No. 38, 7 December 1918, ('Durchführung der uneingeschränkten Koalitions- freiheit für alle Staatsarbeiter und Beamten').

3

The State as an Employer of Women in the Weimar Republic

Helen Boak

Introduction

'Through the German constitution the German woman has become the freest in the world,' proclaimed Gertrud Bäumer in August 1919.[1] The Weimar Constitution of 11 August 1919 granted women equality before the law, to add to the political equality the early days of the Republic had given them. In keeping with the spirit of the Constitution professions previously closed to women were opened in the early years of the Republic, and the foundations were laid for women to obtain equality with men. The census statistics of 1925 and 1933 furnish valuable information on employment patterns, making it possible to monitor the role of women in the economy and their progress towards economic independence of men, which, for some, is a prerequisite of female emancipation.[2] Within a fairly stable female work force women were leaving their traditional areas of employment (agriculture and domestic service) for industrial, white-collar and professional work, the number of women in white-collar employment increasing, while female manual workers tended to continue the wartime trend of leaving their traditional industries for newer, previously male-dominated ones.[3]

I should like to thank Ian Kershaw, Richard Bessel, Cornelie Usborne and the editors for their comments on an earlier draft of this article, and the University of Manchester and the German Historical Institute for financial support of the research on which this article is based.

1. Gertrud Bäumer, 'Die neuen Grundrechte der deutschen Frau', *Karlsruher Zeitung*, 15 August 1919.

2. Clara Zetkin, 'Die Arbeiterinnen- und Frauenfrage der Gegenwart', in Gisela Brinker-Gabler (ed.), *Frauenarbeit und Beruf*, Frankfurt am Main, 1979, pp. 134–46.

3. In 1925 there were 11,478,012, in 1933 11,479,041 women classed as working: *Statistik des deutschen Reiches* (subsequently *SdR*), vol. 402, pp. 452ff., vol. 458,

It was not until 1933 that separate classifications for white-collar workers and civil servants were introduced, but in 1925 women made up 27.1 per cent of white-collar workers and civil servants, in 1933 30.7 per cent. However, in the two branches of the public sector where figures are available, the railways and the Reich Postal Service on the one hand, and the administration and the health service on the other, the women's share not only lay below the national average in this classification, but actually fell between 1925 and 1933, completely against the secular trend.[4] It is the purpose of this essay to investigate the reasons behind this fall, and to examine government attitudes towards its female employees. Public sector workers range from postmen to state secretaries, from cleaning ladies to judges, and while it is the task of one important group among them to administer government policy, the government itself can use its own policy towards its employees to set an example to other employers.

Among public sector employees civil servants (*Beamte*) enjoyed a special status; their terms of service were governed by a body of public law which ensured life tenure and a guaranteed level of pay and of work. The state also employed contractual employees (*Angestellte*) and manual workers (*Arbeiter*). Few of the latter were female; in 1933 there were 19,018 women among 488,549 manual workers in the Reich Postal Service and on the railways.[5] In this essay, therefore, attention will be centred on female civil servants at Reich level, for only at Reich level can one talk of a uniformity of treatment and conditions of public sector employees. Many, of course, were employed by the Länder or local administrations. Indeed, in 1933, half the female civil servants in Germany, some 64,157, were employed as teachers by the Länder and their condi-

---

p. 75. Of these 11,319,088 in 1925 and 10,336,455 in 1933 were 'economically active', i.e. actually working, the decrease reflecting the effects of the depression on employment: *Statistisches Jahrbuch für das deutsche Reich* (subsequently *StJbdR*), 1935, p. 19. For men these figures are: 1925 – 20,531,288, of whom 20,053,335 were 'economically active'; 1933 – 20,817,033, of whom 16,104,601 were 'economically active'.

4. Number of white-collar workers and civil servants in the Reich Postal Service and railways: in 1925 = 657,734, of whom 66,758 (10.2%) were women; in 1933 = 557,919, of whom 54,760 (9.8%) were women. Number of white-collar workers and civil servants in the administration and health service: in 1925 = 1,378,601, of whom 374,269 (27.1%) were women; in 1933 = 1,235,541, of whom 235,204 (19.0%) were women (*SdR*, vol. 402, p. 428; vol. 453, pp. 37, 41).

5. Ibid., vol. 458, p. 43.

tions of service varied significantly, although on the whole the regional authorities were quick to follow the Reich's lead in their treatment of female employees.[6]

To date, little research had been carried out on women civil servants in the Weimar Republic, which may well reflect not only the smallness of their numbers, but also the lack of information available. I know of no study carried out during the Weimar Republic on the subject of women in the civil service, to complement the many on manual and white-collar workers.[7] Following a brief look at women's role as civil servants before and during the war, this chapter will concentrate on the government's treatment of its female civil servants during the Weimar Republic, as illustrated in its legislation, and will highlight areas of discrimination and prejudice.

The Growth in Women's Employment by the State

Before the war women were only to be found in any number in civil service jobs in education and in the communications and transport sectors. Women were first employed in the telegraph offices on Baden's railways in 1864, although it was to be the turn of the century before they appeared in the ticket offices and in the administration of other railway networks.[8] One source puts the number of women working in any capacity on the railways at 6,332 in 1907.[9]

6. Some 33,843 out of a total of 128,670 female civil servants were to be found in the Reich Postal Service. 3,564 women civil servants worked for the railways: ibid., p. 37.

7. I know of only one recent article on women civil servants: Claudia Hahn, 'Der öffentliche Dienst und die Frauen – Beamtinnen in der Weimarer Republik', in Frauengruppe Faschismusforschung, *Mutterkreuz und Arbeitsbuch*, Frankfurt am Main, 1981, pp. 49–77. Contemporary studies on women workers include: Deutscher Metallarbeiterverband, *Die Frauenarbeit in der Metallindustrie*, Stuttgart, 1930; Deutscher Textilarbeiterverband, *Erwerbsarbeit, Schwangerschaft, Frauenleid*, Berlin, 1925; Susanne Suhr, *Die weiblichen Angestellten*, Berlin, 1930.

8. Josephine Levy-Rathenau and Lisbeth Wilbrandt, *Die deutsche Frau im Beruf*, Berlin, 1906, pp. 105–11. Women were first found in ticket offices on the Prussian railways in 1901, and in Württemberg in 1902.

9. H. Oppenheimer and H. Radomski, *Die Probleme der Frauenarbeit in der Übergangswirtschaft*, Mannheim/Berlin/Leipzig, 1918, p. 127. Bajohr has a similar figure: Stefan Bajohr, *Die Hälfte der Fabrik: Geschichte der Frauenarbeit in Deutschland 1914–1945*, Marburg, 1979, p. 121. Oekinghaus, however, puts the figure at a mere 3,633: Emma Oekinghaus, *Die gesellschaftliche und rechtliche Stellung der deutschen Frau*, Jena, 1925, p. 97.

While the wives of railway workers were favoured for jobs cleaning trains and stations, office employees had to be single women or childless widows, and celibacy was a prerequisite for all civil service jobs for women before 1919. Far more women were to be found in the Reich Postal Service, an amalgamation in 1877 of the postal and telegraph administrations, the latter having taken over ninety-nine women telegraphists from Baden in 1871 and begun to appoint women in very small numbers from other areas of the Reich. Bavaria and Württemberg, however, continued to maintain their own postal and telegraph services. In 1877 it was decided to phase out the employment of women in the Reich Postal Service and it was only the introduction of the telephone which caused this decision to be reversed, women being taken on once again from 1889 onwards, with their numbers rising from 137 civil servants out of 50,968 in 1876 (0.26 per cent) to 2,408 out of 114,055 (2.11 per cent) twenty years later. In 1898 the Secretary of State for the Postal Service, General Podbielski, designated three areas of the service as suitable for women: the telephone and telegraph sections and certain clerical and administrative tasks within the postal service. In 1911 women were allowed behind the counter in small, rural post offices, although such women were not eligible for civil service posts. The total number of women in the Reich Postal Service, therefore, rose quickly, reaching 30,987 in 1913, of whom 22,252 were civil servants.[10] Not only did the applicants have to have a solid educational background, tested by an entrance examination, be healthy with good sight and hearing and no disfiguring afflictions, but they also had to be free of debt and have proved themselves worthy and respectable.[11] After nine years' employment they were entitled to be made civil servants, but they had to leave on marriage. Life tenure was only granted to women civil servants with fifteen years service on 1 January 1918, although those women first

10. 1886 = 193 women civil servants out of 69,471; 1906 = 13,102 women civil servants out of 185,192; 1910 = 19,441 women civil servants out of 209,589. Figures from Zentrales Staatsarchiv Potsdam (subsequently ZStA), Reichstag 3328, 167. 1913 figure from Oekinghaus, *Stellung*; W. Chemnitz, *Frauenarbeit im Kriege*, Berlin, 1926, p. 127, and Oppenheimer and Radomski, *Probleme*, p. 128. For the history of women in the Reich Postal Service see 'Die Frau als Post- und Telegraphenbeamtin', *Unter dem Reichsadler*, vol. 4, no. 4, 22 February 1912, pp. 75–7; Josephine Doerner, 'Neun Jahrzehnte Frauenbeschäftigung bei der Postverwaltung', *Jahrbuch der deutschen Bundespost*, vol. 7, 1956–7, pp. 377–402.
11. Rathenau and Wilbrandt, *Frau im Beruf*, p. 101.

appointed in Baden and those working for the postal services in Bavaria and Württemberg were given life tenure. There was no possibility of promotion to middle-ranking and senior civil service positions, probably because they did not possess the necessary educational qualifications. A grammar school education was the prerequisite for a middle-ranking civil servant's post and education at a girls' senior school was not considered to be the equivalent.[12] As a university education was generally the prerequisite for senior civil service posts and German universities did not begin to admit women until 1900, it is easy to see why very few women, save those who had attained university degrees abroad, were eligible for such posts. In addition, the lack of clear career guidelines may well have impaired women's advancement within the civil service as a whole. The position of factory inspector provides an illustration of this. Some states merely required practical experience, others also a knowledge of economics and the law, while one state, Baden, demanded a university education. In 1900 it appointed Dr Marie Baum, educated at Zürich university, on equal conditions with a male factory inspector.[13] As has already been pointed out, the employment conditions of many civil servants – those in education, Land and local administration, for example – varied from region to region. While male and female prison warders in Bavaria were paid the same, in Baden women averaged 75 per cent of their male colleagues' salary. In some states women had to leave on marriage with no rights to compensation, while in others they lost life tenure.[14] In spite of these restrictions jobs in the public sector were much sought after, even those of typist and clerk in local administration, which rarely led to a civil servant position.

The war was to bring just as significant changes to women's employment in the state sector as elsewhere, with women being drawn in to replace the men called to the front. Women now entered occupations previously closed to them and took on senior

12. M. Trenge, 'Die Frau im Staat', *Jahrbuch des Bundes deutscher Frauenvereine* (subsequently *JbBdF*), Berlin/Leipzig, 1912, pp. 111–19. For educational qualifications as demarcation lines for civil servants, see Jane Caplan, '"The imaginary universality of particular interests": the "Tradition" of the Civil Service in German History', *Social History*, vol. 4, 1979, pp. 299–317.

13. Her annual salary was 2,900 marks. In other states women served as assistants: Rathenau and Wilbrandt, *Frau im Beruf*, pp. 81ff.

14. Women first entered the prison service in 1840, becoming civil servants after ten years service: Elisabeth Süersen, *Die Frau im deutschen Reichs- und Landesstaatsdienst*, Mannheim/Berlin/ Leipzig, 1920, pp. 1, 2, 92, 117–19.

administrative tasks, even if they lacked the necessary legal training. With the setting up of a women's section in the War Ministry of Labour in December 1916, whose aim was the 'mobilisation of women by women' and the subsequent founding of branches of the Central Office for Women's Work throughout Germany, women were given high administrative posts for the first time.[15] Dr Marie-Elisabeth Lüders was appointed to head the section, assisted by Dr Agnes von Harnack. For the first time women were allowed to teach in boys' senior schools and married women were permitted, even encouraged, to teach or to work in the Reich Postal Service, on the understanding that once their husbands returned they would give up working.[16] On the railways women were employed as ticket inspectors and even stokers and drivers of local trains. Their numbers in the Prussian railway service rose ten-fold between 1914 and 1918, from about 10,000 to 100,000, though very few of these women were given civil service posts.[17] In the towns women ticket inspectors on the trams became a common sight, Mannheim, for example, employing 241 such women in 1915, while two years later women were to be seen driving its trams.[18] In the Reich Postal Service, where women were now used to deliver the post, their numbers increased to 36,304 in 1916, of whom 24,449 held civil service posts, with promotion for a further 3,000 female employees to the status of civil servants envisaged in the 1917 budget.[19] Lüders put the number of female civil servants in the Reich Postal Service at the beginning of 1918 at 31,000.[20] Such an increase may seem modest and this can be explained by the fact that the Reich Postal

15. In January 1917 the women's section was transferred to the War Office (Staff) and became known as the Central Office for Women's Work: Ursula von Gersdorff, *Frauenarbeit im Kriegsdienst 1914–1945*, Stuttgart, 1969, pp. 22–5, 118, 128; Marie-Elisabeth Lüders, 'Die Entwicklung der gewerblichen Frauenarbeit im Kriege', *Schmollers Jahrbuch*, vol. 44, 1920, pp. 241–67, 569–87.

16. Else Wex, *Staatsbürgerliche Arbeit deutscher Frauen 1865 bis 1928*, Berlin, 1929, p. 94; Else Fisch, 'Die Abfindung der wegen Heirat ausscheidenden Beamtin', *Die Frau* (subsequently *DF*), vol. 37, no. 4, January 1930, pp. 210–13.

17. Figures in Bajohr, *Hälfte*; Marie-Elisabeth Lüders, *Das unbekannte Heer*, Berlin, 1935, pp. 153–5; Charlotte von Hadeln, *Deutsche Frauen, deutsche Treue 1914–1933*, Berlin, 1935, pp. 162–6.

18. In 1916, 343 women inspectors were employed: Walter Friedrich, *Schicksal einer deutschen Stadt: Geschichte Mannheims 1907–1945*, Frankfurt am Main, 1950, p. 242.

19. Oppenheimer and Radomski, *Probleme*, p. 128; Chemnitz, *Frauenarbeit*.

20. Lüders, *Heer*, p. 153. Same figures in Gersdorff, *Frauenarbeit*, pp. 218ff.

Service, like the railways, took on many unskilled temporary workers, their numbers rising from 5,919 in 1913 to 101,000 in the summer of 1918.[21] Needless to say, these women were the first to be dismissed in the demobilisation later that year, although single women in civil servants' posts could not, of course, be dismissed.[22] However, the need to incorporate returning soldiers back into their civil service jobs and to provide such positions for long-serving soldiers (*Militäranwärter*) meant that opportunities for women to obtain a civil servant's post were restricted. Women waiting to be given civil servant status on the railways were told that there was no possibility of such promotion, while in Baden young women were warned against a career in teaching because of the large numbers of men returning from the Front looking for a teaching job.[23] The number of women civil servants in the Reich Postal Service, however, seems to have continued to increase steadily, as women serving in small, rural post offices were given the right to be transferred to civil service posts from 1 April 1920, and some 15,810 new non-regular (*außerplanmäßig*) civil servant posts were allocated to single women in March 1921.[24] Furthermore, jobs in the postal order offices, first set up in 1909, were deemed to be reserved for women, highlighting the beginning of an official reappraisal of women's role within the postal service. One woman, Frau Margarete Kinsberger, was appointed a consultant (*Referentin*) on all matters concerning female personnel in the Reich Postal Ministry in 1919, and women were given the right to sit on interviewing panels in 1920.[25]

21. Dora Lande, 'Die Frauenbewegung', *Sozialistische Monatshefte*, vol. 25, 1919, p. 744.

22. Demobilisation orders of 7 November 1918 and 28 March 1919. On the speedy dismissal of women war workers from the public sector, see Wex, *Staatsbürgerliche Arbeit*, pp. 93ff; *The International Woman Suffrage News*, vol. 13, no. 3, December 1918, p. 31; ZStA, Reichstag 127, minutes of the 84th sitting of the National Assembly on 20 August 1919. On the demobilisation of women in general, see Richard Bessel, 'Eine nicht allzu große Beunruhigung des Arbeitsmarktes', *Geschichte und Gesellschaft*, vol. 9, 1983, pp. 211–29.

23. *Freiburger Zeitung*, 11 May 1920; Marie Baum, *Rückblick auf mein Leben*, Heidelberg, 1950, p. 224.

24. *Unter dem Reichsadler*, vol. 12, no. 3, 12 February 1920, p. 29; vol. 13, no. 6, 24 March 1921, pp. 90ff; Doerner, 'Neun', p. 384. Kunz attributes the rise in women civil servants within the postal service to women's growing importance in general administrative and supervisory functions: Andreas Kunz, *Civil Servants and the Politics of Inflation in Germany 1914–1924*, Berlin, 1986, p. 52.

25. *Unter dem Reichsadler*, vol. 11, no. 17, 11 September 1919, p. 180; vol. 12, no. 16, 26 August 1920, p. 201; vol. 13, no. 13, 14 July 1921, p. 200. The Reich Postal

The demobilisation decrees at the war's end sought to return the labour market to its pre-war state. While the war might have brought some women into occupations and positions previously closed to them, it did not change attitudes to female employment, and indeed the mass slaughter of World War I emphasised, if anything, women's biological role and the need to increase the population. It is hardly surprising, then, that married women headed the list of those to be dismissed and indeed, many of them welcomed the chance to give up employment outside the home. But what of those married women, in particular those in civil servants' posts, who did not want to leave their jobs? They had been employed at a time when service regulations stated that women civil servants must remain single, a condition some women's organisations had campaigned to have revoked, albeit not very vociferously.[26]

Women's Equality and the Persistence of Discrimination

This situation, however, was to change with the Weimar Constitution of 11 August 1919, which not only proclaimed women's equality with men before the law, but also stated in Article 128: 'All citizens without distinction are to be admitted to public office in accordance with the laws and according to their ability and qualifications. All discriminatory regulations against female civil servants are lifted.'[27] Female civil servants could no longer be dismissed upon marriage, a development which brought little joy to the Reich Postal Minister, who complained bitterly of the bad experience his organisation had had with married women civil servants during the war, or even to the Verband der deutschen Reichspost- und Telegraphenbeamtinnen (VRT), which felt that the married woman civil servant should remain a rarity.[28] Although the VRT's programme

Minister also decreed that women in rural post offices should be trained to replace the male postmaster if necessary: ibid., vol. 13, no. 12, 23 June 1921, p. 184.

26. *JbBdF*, 1917, p. 82; Katherine Anthony, *Feminism in Germany and Scandinavia*, 1916, p. 189; Helene-Lange-Archiv Berlin (subsequently HLA), E/Eb1, 'Programm der liberalen Frauenpartei', 31 January 1907.

27. 'Die Verfassung des deutschen Reiches vom 11. August 1919', *Reichsgesetzblatt* (subsequently *RGBl*), 1919, pp. 1383–418.

28. The Reich Postal Minister felt that a married woman civil servant was worth only half the labour of a single one: ZStA, Reichstag 3328, 292. On the VRT:

had initially called for the repeal of the celibacy clause, which it regarded as an unwarranted intrusion into the rights of the individual, many of its branches did not support this call and it was cut from the VRT's programme at its second congress in 1913. Instead the VRT began to call for compensation for women civil servants leaving on marriage, which would not only benefit the women themselves, allowing the couple to set up home, but also the administration, the economy and the job market. The VRT believed that women should not become accustomed to combining marriage and a career, which it regarded as a double burden, nor should a household become used to relying on the incomes of both man and wife. A married woman civil servant meant one less civil service post for single women.[29]

While some, but not all, states were quick to bring their regulations into line with the Constitution, the Reich Postal Minister, Giesberts, of the Centre Party, was writing to the Reich Interior Minister seeking clarification.[30] He felt that the fact that a female civil servant was married made her unable simultaneously to do her work and to fulfil her duties to her husband and family as listed in the Civil Code of 1900. With 40,000 women civil servants on his staff, of whom an average 1,500 got married annually with half that number staying at work, he envisaged having to employ 7,000–8,000 married women civil servants within a few years.[31] He suggested offering women civil servants a gratuity to encourage them to leave on marriage, a proposal on which he had received a 56-page submission from the VRT on 9 July 1919, a time when women were still forced to leave on marriage and for whom the VRT sought some

---

Bundesarchiv Koblenz (subsequently BAK), Nachlaß Lüders 135, VRT letter to BdF of 18 November 1920.

29. 'Zur Gründung des Verbandes der Post- und Telegraphenbeamtinnen', *Unter dem Reichsadler*, vol. 4, no. 8, 25 April 1912, pp. 179–82; ibid., vol. 5, no. 11, 12 June 1913, pp. 256–8; 'Verbandseingabe betr. Abfindungssumme', ibid., vol. 12, no. 14, 22 July 1920, p. 165; 'Die Abfindungssumme', ibid., vol. 12, no. 21, 11 November 1920, pp. 271–3; 'Die Bestimmungen über die Weiterbeschäftigung verheirateter Beamtinnen', ibid., vol. 13, no. 3, 10 February 1921, pp. 34–36; 'Verbandseingabe über die Abfindungssumme', ibid., vol. 12, no. 3, 14 July 1921, pp. 194–6.

30. ZStA, Reichsministerium des Innern (subsequently RMdI) 2232, 2, letter of the Reich Postal Minister to the Reich Interior Minister of 9 October 1919. The budget committee of the Prussian Landtag accepted a bill revoking all discriminatory clauses against married women civil servants on 22 October 1919: Dora Lande, 'Die Frauenbewegung', *Sozialistische Monatshefte*, vol. 26, 1920, p. 198.

31. ZStA, Reichstag 3328; RMdI 2232.

form of compensation.[32]

Giesberts' suggestion led to a series of discussions in the Reich Ministry of the Interior between representatives of the government, the Länder and women's organisations about both the drawing up of guidelines on the legal position of the married woman civil servant and the granting of a gratuity to those willing to leave on marriage. The guidelines, issued by the Reich Interior Minister on 3 September 1920, instructed all Reich and Land departments to revoke all regulations demanding the dismissal of women civil servants on marriage, if they had not already done so, and detailed women's entitlement to service accommodation and maternity leave.[33] When states refused to comply with these guidelines, the Minister of the Interior had recourse to the Supreme Court. Such was the case with Bavaria. Paragraph 151 of its law concerning primary schoolteachers, which came into effect on 15 August 1919, made it compulsory for women to leave on marriage. In spite of repeated protestations from the Reich government in Berlin, the Bavarian Landtag refused to revoke the paragraph, maintaining that it had taken the decision not only for financial reasons, but also because of social and population policy. The sight of a pregnant primary schoolteacher was likely to invoke in her pupils 'thoughts and ideas which in the interests of education were much better avoided'. On 10 May 1921 the Supreme Court upheld the Reich Interior Minister's objection, maintaining that Paragraph 151 was incompatible with the Constitution and therefore invalid.[34]

The Bavarian law, however, had set a precedent: the granting of a gratuity as compensation to those women forced to resign on marriage.[35] There was, though, disagreement among the Reich and Land ministries about the granting of gratuities as enticements for women to resign their civil servant posts on marriage, and to

32. ZStA, Reichstag 3328; BAK, Nachlaß Lüders 233, *Unter dem Reichsadler*, vol. 12, no. 14, 22 July 1920, p. 165.
    33. ZStA, RMdI 2233, 189; BAK, R2/1291, 61–2; 'Richtlinien über die rechtliche Stellung der verheirateten Beamtinnen', *DF*, vol. 28, no. 1, October 1920, p. 25.
    34. BAK, Z.Sg.I.41/4, *Mitteilungen des deutschen Städtetages*, vol. 8, no. 8, 15 August 1921, pp. 321–5; Marie-Elisabeth Lüders, 'Grundsatz oder Vorteil', *DF*, vol. 36, no. 4, January 1929, pp. 198–201; 'Entscheidung des Reichsgerichts auf Grund des Artikels 13 Absatz 2 der Verfassung des deutschen Reiches. Vom 10. Mai 1921', *RGBl*, 1921, p. 735.
    35. Between 1 September 1919 and 31 August 1921, 523 female teachers in Bavarian primary schools received such a gratuity: BAK, R2/1291, letter of Bavarian Education Minister, not dated.

encourage them to trade their constitutional rights for a once-only payment. While the Reich Interior Minister, the Reich Postal Minister and the Reich Minister of Transport, who in 1921 had some 3,500 women civil servants on his staff of whom a mere 39 were married, were all in favour of such payments, the Reich Finance Minister expressed doubts, believing that such payments ran contrary to the principle that a civil servant, male or female, married or single, devoted his or her whole life to the state.[36] The competent authorities in Prussia, Saxony and Thuringia rejected the idea, believing it disadvantaged men leaving the civil service voluntarily, while those in Bavaria, Baden and Württemberg were only in favour of such payments if they possessed the right to dismiss women civil servants on marriage, although Baden later favoured the introduction of gratuities with no preconditions.[37] The women's organisations concerned, the VRT, the Association of Female Transport Civil Servants in Bavaria and Württemberg, and Catholic and Protestant women's groups all favoured the introduction of gratuity payments and called for a public campaign against combining marriage and a job in the civil service.[38] Although the large Allgemeiner Deutscher Lehrerinnenverein (ADLV) was reluctant to discriminate against married women, there can be no doubt that women civil servants in general shared the prevalent opinion that marriage was a career in itself.[39] Indeed, the VRT, whose motto was 'Work and Be Happy', was well placed to claim to speak on behalf of its members. Founded in Berlin on 25 February 1912 with thirty-two branches and some 6,519 members, who at the time constituted 23.7 per cent of the total number of women civil servants in the Reich Postal Service, it expanded rapidly to include 47,231 members in 1923 (74 per cent of the Reich Postal Service's total women civil servants) before its numbers fell, although in 1933

---

36. ZStA, RMdI 2233, 2, letter of Reich Postal Minister of 9 October 1919; 17, letter of Reich Finance Minister of 12 January 1920; 121, letter of Reich Interior Minister of 10 August 1920; 242, letter of Reich Transport Minister of 9 March 1921.

37. ZStA, RMdI 2233, 118, discussion of 12 May 1922; 185, discussion of 18 August 1922; Generallandesarchiv Karlsruhe, 231/3969, letter of Baden Finance Minister of 11 April 1922; 231/630, Baden Landtag minutes of 14 July 1922, 3699–703.

38. BAK, Nachlaß Lüders 135, letter of VRT to BdF of 18 November 1920.

39. ZStA, RMdI 2233, 420, ADLV's general meeting in Karlsruhe in May 1923, central committee decision not to recommend any restrictions on the rights of married women teachers.

it claimed to include 85 per cent of Reich Post women civil servants among its members.[40] This represented a high unionisation of women – women's highest share of the Free Trade Unions was 21.8 per cent in 1919, falling to 14 per cent in 1931, while women's share in both white-collar unions, the Gewerkschaftsbund der Angestellten and the Zentralverband der Angestellten only rose gradually throughout the Weimar Republic to reach 31.5 per cent of the former and 50.1 per cent of the latter by 1931. The relative success of the VRT might well be attributable to the fact that women civil servants were aware of the need for an organisation to represent their interests, either because they felt threatened or because they were educated enough to realise the benefits of union membership, although it may reflect the VRT's efficient organisation at a local level. The VRT leader from its inception to its dissolution on 28 May 1933 was Else Kolshorn, who in 1928 was appointed a member of the Administrative Council of the Reich Postal Service.[41]

The continuing discussions on the granting of a gratuity, and calls in the Reichstag and Landtage for a draft law granting all Reich women civil servants a severance payment if they left on marriage, did little to ease the Reich Postal Minister's immediate problems.[42] His staff had been increasing constantly to reach 475,167 in 1921, swelled perhaps by the number of soldiers entitled to civil service jobs and the need to find jobs for civil servants previously employed in 'lost' areas of the Reich (see Table 3.1). By August 1922 the number of women civil servants in his employ had risen to some 69,000, and this might explain why new regulations had been introduced a month earlier, on 1 July 1922, detailing branches of the service reserved primarily for women and providing women with a career structure and the opportunity of entering middle-ranking

40. Figures given in '20 Jahre Verband der deutschen Reichs- Post- und Telegraphen-Beamtinnen', *DF*, vol. 39, no. 6, March 1932, pp. 362–4; 'Zwei Jahrzehnte Verbandsarbeit', *Unter dem Reichsadler*, vol. 24, no. 4, 25 February 1932, pp. 49–53. The VRT had 32,666 members at the time of its dissolution: ibid., vol. 25, no. 11, 8 June 1933, p. 165.

41. For trade union membership, see relevant years of *StJdR*. For Kolshorn, see *Nachrichtenblatt des Bundes deutscher Frauenvereine* (subsequently *NBl*), vol. 8, no. 11, November 1928, p. 84.

42. ZStA, RMdI 2233, 94, Reichstag printed paper no. 4552, question no. 1701 from Mende, Matz, von Oheimb (DVP) of 22 June 1922; BAK, Nachlaß Dingeldey 19, *Korrespondenz der DNVP*, 27 April 1920.

Table 3.1 The personnel in the Reich Postal Service

Year	Total	Of whom civil servants	Of whom women	% women
1906	277,968			
1910	305,427			
1913	334,064			
1919	423,246			
1920	444,453			
1921	475,167			
1922	441,322			
1923	334,756	252,380	51,752	20.5
1924	325,213	247,136	48,879	19.8
1925	332,732	250,680	47,784	19.1
1926	360,339	252,524	45,827	18.1
1927	366,795	248,896	43,508	17.5
1928	375,393	244,030	41,072	16.8
1929	378,198	243,773	39,679	16.3
1930	377,322	241,238	38,716	16.0
1931	358,978	237,359	37,578	15.8
1932	350,814	233,343	36,217	15.5
1933	350,832	222,969	33,422	15.0
1934	362,850	221,259	32,287	14.6

Source: Statistisches Jahrbuch für das deutsche Reich, 1906–1934

and senior positions for the first time. However, examination bars as good as closed the more senior middle-ranking and senior posts until 1931, while an emergency measure of 15 January 1923 to combat the surplus of male civil servants allowed men to be employed in those areas primarily reserved for women. In addition, for most of the life of the Weimar Republic, no woman was taken on by the Reich Postal Service as a candidate for a civil service appointment (*Anwärterin*); rather women were employed as 'helpers', contractual employees of whom the same qualifications were required so they could at some future date possibly be transferred to the civil service, although they had no legal claim to such a transfer.[43] The railways had experienced a similar increase in staff

43. ZStA, RMdI 2233, 186, figures given by chairman during discussions on the granting of a gratuity to married women civil servants on 18 August 1922. Oekinghaus puts the number of female civil servants in the Reich Postal Service in December 1922 at 63,057: Oekinghaus, *Stellung*, p. 97. On the new regulations, see

and from 1922 there were ministerial discussions on how to reduce
the number of civil servants, possibly by lowering the retirement
age and prioritising the order of dismissal – single male civil servants, for example, were to be dismissed before married ones with
children.[44] The Reichstag saw one way of cutting the budget and
reducing civil service personnel in the granting of a gratuity to
married female civil servants willing to leave their jobs in the
transport and communications sector, and in a debate on an amendment to the 1922 budget on 16 December 1922 resolved to ask the
government to instigate steps to this end. On 13 January 1923 the
Reich Finance Minister notified his cabinet colleagues of his willingness to accept the Reichstag's resolution. Accordingly, he gave
details of the scheme to the Reich Postal and Transport Ministers on
3 February 1923. Any married woman civil servant with five years
service willing to leave before 31 March 1923 would receive a
severance payment, the amount depending on the length of service.
Those women who had acted rather precipitously on the Reichstag
resolution of 16 December 1922 and resigned before 3 February
1923 received nothing, although those women who accepted gratuities soon found them to be worthless because of inflation.[45] In
the face of protests from Prussia and Württemberg – later seen to be
justified – that such a scheme would open the floodgates for all
women civil servants to demand a gratuity for their voluntary
resignation on marriage, the Reich Finance Minister was quick to
stress the once-only nature of the scheme, and that it had been

Hahn, 'Der öffentliche Dienst', pp. 59ff; Hugh Wiley Puckett, *Germany's Women Go Forward*, New York, 1930, p. 271; *DF*, vol. 39, no. 6, March 1932, pp. 362–4; 'Notstandsmaßnahmen', *Unter dem Reichsadler*, vol. 15, no. 4, 22 February 1923, pp. 37ff.

44. The railways' workforce grew from 782,731 in 1913 to 1,132,185 in 1919, falling to 1,034,662 in 1922: *StJdR*, 1920, p. 86, 1922, p. 102, 1923, p. 79. On discussions to cut the number of civil servants see documents in BAK, R43I/2612 and also Kunz, *Civil Servants*, p. 371.

45. BAK, R36/93, 5–7, letter of the Reich Finance Minister of 13 January 1923; 18–21, decree of 3 February 1923 and Reich Postal Minister's circulars to his divisional administrations of 17 February and 14 March 1923, also in ZStA, RMdI 2234, 111. As those women who resigned because of their intention to marry before 30 September 1923 only received their gratuity on the day of the marriage, the VRT petitioned the Reichstag to make these gratuities paid in late summer equivalent in real terms to those paid in March. In some cases the tram journey to collect the gratuity cost more than the gratuity received: *Unter dem Reichsadler*, vol. 16, no. 12, 19 June 1924, p. 189; vol. 16, no. 9, 8 May 1924, p. 131.

introduced purely because of the government's need to cut spending.[46] As only an estimated 3,000 of the 69,000 Reich Postal Service's female civil servants were married at this time, a reduction in their number would have done little to cut the Reich Postal Service's budget.

The Reich Postal Minister was happy to report the success of the scheme: 20 per cent of his married female civil servants were not eligible to receive a gratuity, 13 per cent had not applied, but 67 per cent had taken up the offer, and 2,252 married female civil servants, with a further 1,177 intending to marry before 30 September 1923, had resigned. Only 1,701 married women civil servants remained in their jobs on 1 April 1923. Indeed, the scheme was so successful in certain sections such as the postal order department that there were staffing shortages and so some of the women who had resigned were re-employed on a temporary basis.[47] The Reich Postal Minister looked forward to the introduction of a permanent scheme along these lines in the future and the Berlin City Council followed the Reich's example and introduced a similar severance plan from September 1923.[48] No personal details are available about the women who took up the offer, but the popularity of the scheme among the women eligible validates the VRT stance on this issue.

However, the Reich Finance Minister believed that the introduction of his scheme on a permanent basis would contravene Article 128 of the Constitution, and the Reich cabinet reaffirmed its endorsement of the 1920 guidelines on the legal position of the married woman civil servant on 24 July and 2 August 1923, a time when discussions on measures to cut the civil service threatened women's rights. On 4 August 1923, for example, a draft law on the reduction of the civil service envisaged the suspension, with

46. BAK, R2/1291, 6–7, letters of the Prussian Finance Minister of 31 January 1923 and of the Württemberg Finance Minister of 31 March 1923; 23, request of German Protestant Women Teachers' Association to the Reich Finance Minister of 7 June 1923.

47. BAK, R2/1291, 37–8, 65–6, letters of the Reich Postal Minister to the Reich Finance Minister of 21 June and 20 September 1923, also found in ZStA, RMdI 2233, 423–6. The VRT later said that 3,463 out of a possible 5,163 married women civil servants took advantage of the scheme (67%): 'Die Kernfragen des weiblichen Beamtentums bei der Deutschen Reichspost', *Unter dem Reichsadler*, vol. 23, no. 18, 24 September 1931, pp. 273–4.

48. BAK, R36/93, 81, 'Vorlage – zur Beschlußfassung – betr. die Weitergewährung von Abfindungssummen an verheiratete Beamtinnen im Falle ihres freiwilligen Ausscheidens', 9 March 1925.

adequate compensation, of married women civil servants whose husbands had permanent employment.[49] The Reich's difficult economic and political situation led the Reichstag to pass an Enabling Act on 13 October 1923 allowing the new government to take any financial, economic and social measures it felt necessary, and two weeks later it introduced a decree reducing expenditure on all state employees, not just civil servants (the *Personalabbauverordnung*, PAV).[50] Married women civil servants, however, were singled out for special attention. While Article 3 of the PAV allowed the temporary suspension of civil servants, with those affected receiving a gratuity or a pension, Article 14 permitted the dismissal with one month's notice of all married women civil servants at Reich, Land and local levels whose future seemed economically secure with no compensation.[51] The Reich Finance and Transport Ministers argued that marriage granted women economic security and therefore all married women civil servants could be dismissed, unless they could prove they were not economically secure. In practice, all married women were dismissed, irrespective of any hardship caused. The government refused to set a lower limit on a man's income which would indicate economic insecurity for the wife. Initially, even the wife of a man drawing unemployment benefit was deemed economically secure.[52]

Article 14 evoked strong opposition from women's and professional organisations, spearheaded by the ADLV and the middle-class women's umbrella organisation, the Bund deutscher Frauenvereine (BdF), many of whose leaders were or had been teachers, which led in part to an amendment of 28 January 1924 granting a pension to those women in need, incapable of earning their own

49. BAK, R43I/2612, 37–41, meeting of 4 August 1923; R36/93, 49–52, Reich Interior Ministry circular of 13 August 1923.

50. On the development of plans to reduce civil servants, see Andreas Kunz, 'Stand versus Klasse. Beamtenschaft und Gewerkschaften im Konflikt um den Personalabbau 1923/24', *Geschichte und Gesellschaft*, vol. 8, 1982, pp. 55–86.

51. 'Verordnung zur Herabminderung der Personalausgaben des Reiches. (Personalabbauverordnung) Vom 27. Oktober 1923', *RGBl*, 1923, pp. 999–1011.

52. BAK, R43I/2612, 167, letter of Reich Finance Minister of 8 November 1923; 174–7, letter of Reich Transport Minister of 13 November 1923; *NBl*, vol. 6, no. 7, July 1926, p. 51; 'Der Abbau der verheirateten Beamtin', *Unter dem Reichsadler*, vol. 16, no. 9, 8 May 1924, pp. 130–2; 'Der Kampf gegen Artikel 14 der PAV', ibid., vol. 16, no. 17, 11 September 1924, pp. 278–81.

living.[53] A month later the VRT successfully called upon the Reich Postal Minister to draw up guidelines for the dismissal of married women civil servants, allowing those whose husbands were ill, blind or were still studying to stay on at work.[54] In early 1925, with renewed discussions on a new civil service law and plans to change the PAV underway, dropping Article 3, numerous petitions were laid before the Reichstag and its budget committee calling for an end to Article 14 as well. Although in its second reading a draft bill extending Article 14 was defeated by 180 to 179, with all women Reichstag members voting against it, in its third reading it was accepted, with women voting according to the dictates of their party. The new Article 14 was to continue until 31 March 1929, and it was an improvement on the old one. The period of notice was extended to three months and the women concerned could only be fired if their dismissal was deemed necessary by the relevant authority. A married woman could now also resign with three months notice, if her leaving did not run contrary to official needs. The dismissed women had six months in which to claim either a severance payment or a pension.[55] Such improvements, however, cannot conceal the fact that married women civil servants remained the only group which could be compulsorily dismissed. Their numbers were not so large as to justify claims of huge savings in public expenditure. And indeed, the Reich government, in a confidential memorandum to the Reichstag budget committee, no longer made any such claim. Rather, it stressed that Article 14 was a socio-economic necessity in the light of the current level of unemployment, an argument that was to resurface in the early 1930s. The

53. For BdF's protests, see BAK, R43I/2614, letter of 29 October 1924; for BdF's repeated petitions see *NBl*, vol. 5, 1925, pp. 2, 5, 7, 10–11; ZStA, RMdI 2234. 42, ADLV petitions of 13 and 22 May 1925. For the history of the BdF see Richard J. Evans, *The Feminist Movement in Germany 1894–1933*, London/New York/Beverly Hills, 1976.
54. 'Geschäftsbericht', *Unter dem Reichsadler*, vol. 16, no. 12, 19 June 1924, p. 178.
55. The Reich Finance Minister had originally proposed March 1930 as Article 14's expiry date: BAK, Nachlaß Lüders 135, Dr Richard Grau, 'War die Aufrechterhaltung der Abbaubestimmungen für verheiratete weibliche Beamte ohne Erfüllung der Voraussetzungen verfassungsändernder Gesetzgebung zulässig?', *Archiv des öffentlichen Rechts*, vol. 10, no. 1/2, pp. 237–46; Regine Deutsch, *Parlamentarische Frauenarbeit II. Aus den Reichstagen von 1924 bis 1928*, Berlin, 1928, pp. 91–3; *NBl*, vol. 5, 1925, pp. 2, 8; 'Gesetz über die Einstellung des Personalabbaus und Änderung der PAV. Vom 4. August 1925', *RGBl*, 1925, pp. 181–4.

employment of both man and wife should be stopped if possible; the duties of a wife and mother made it impossible for a woman to fulfil her duties as a civil servant. Article 14 was necessary to maintain an efficient and economical service, the memorandum concluded, for married women civil servants tended to be absent from their jobs twice as often as single women or men. Indeed, they were absent on average for more than one-sixth of the year.[56] The repeated arguments about bad experiences with married women civil servants which concentrated on their frequent absences from work would seem to point to shortcomings in the services' regulations and disciplinary procedures, and cloak the government's desire to return to the status quo before 1919, when women were forced to leave the civil service on marriage.

In October 1923 it was the government's intention to cut public sector employment by 25 per cent, a reduction achieved by 31 March 1924. Contractual employees and manual workers bore the brunt of the cuts with reductions of 49.7 per cent and 32.9 per cent respectively, while the number of civil servants fell by 16.3 per cent.[57] Figures on the reduction of female civil servants and contractual employees in Reich Ministries and public corporations during the first months of the PAV are given in Table 3.2. By far the largest number of female civil servants was to be found in the Reich Postal Service, and their numbers fell by 15 per cent between October 1923 and 1 April 1924, against an overall cut of 14.1 per cent in the Reich Post's civil servants. The number of female contractual employees was reduced by 75.4 per cent against an overall cut of 62.2 per cent. There can be no doubt that women were hit far harder than men, and among the women, the cuts in married women were the harshest – a 98.75 per cent cut in the Reich Post's civil servants and a 100 per cent cut in contractual employees whose dismissal was permitted under Article 15 of the PAV. Table 3.3 shows the continued reduction in female personnel, the fall in the number of married women civil servants in the Reich Postal Service from 2,718 in 1923 to 181 in 1928, a reduction of 93.3 per cent, illustrating the effectiveness of Article 14. The Reich Postal Service made severance

56. BAK, Nachlaß Lüders 153, sub-committee 5b, printed paper, 27, 'Regierungserklärung zu Artikel 14 der Personal-Abbau-Verordnung', Berlin, 7 April 1925.

57. Figures given in Kunz, 'Stand', p. 63. Also found in BAK, R43I/2613, 289, 'Denkschrift des Reichfinanzministers über den Personalabbau', 15 May 1924.

Table 3.2 The reduction in female civil servants and contractual employees in Reich employment, 1 October 1923 to 1 April 1924

(a) Female civil servants

	1 October 1923		1 April 1924	
	Total	Of whom married	Total	Of whom married
Reich Ministries	578	93	488	14
Reich Post	60,883	2,718	51,752	21
Reich Railways	2,992	144	2,314	19
Total	64,453	2,955	54,554	54

(b) Female contractual employees

	1 October 1923		1 April 1924	
	Total	Of whom married	Total	Of whom married
Reich Ministries	13,402	596	7,761	139
Reich Post	5,410	106	1,332	–
Reich Stationery	315	42	152	–
Reich Railways	65	1	39	–
Total	19,192	745	9,284	139

Source: BAK, R43I/2613, Anlage II zur Denkschrift des Reichsfinanzministers über den Personalabbau, 15 May 1924. There was one woman civil servant in the Reich Stationery Office.

payments to a total of 11,258 women civil servants during the five-and-a-half years that Article 14 was on the statute books.[58] It would appear that following the initial harsh implementation of Article 14 in the winter of 1923/4, the Reich Postal Ministry began to take account of the personal circumstances of the women concerned and may also have kept married women civil servants on because of staff shortages in the sections in which they worked. The fluctuations in the number of female contractual employees highlights the ease with which they could be hired and dismissed, making them more attractive as employees than as civil servants in the public sector. No overall figures on the reduction of women civil servants at Land and local level are available. Although many states, such as Saxony, Prussia, Baden, Hamburg and Lübeck, adopted Article 14 as part of their own personnel reduction laws,

58. BAK, R2/1291, 237, Reich Post survey of July 1929.

Table 3.3 The reduction in Reich female civil servants and contractual employees 1924–1928, excluding the Reich railways

(a) Female civil servants

	Total	Of whom married	Total in RPS*	Of whom married
1.10.1924	50,237	90	49,760	80
1. 4.1925	51,608	119	51,146	110
1.10.1925	48,476	69	48,027	63
1. 4.1926	47,079	144	46,627	133
1.10.1926	46,334	381	45,887	362
1. 4.1927	45,430	282	44,988	268
1.10.1927	43,890	319	43,450	303
1. 7.1928			42,943	181

(b) Female contractual employees

	Total	Of whom married
1.10.1924	9,101	122
1. 4.1925	8,247	101
1.10.1925	10,465	96
1. 4.1926	10,215	132
1.10.1926	8,193	150
1. 4.1927	9,555	150
1.10.1927	11,122	214

* = Reich Postal Service
Sources: BAK, Nachlaß Lüders 153, Reichstag printed paper no. 2895, Reich Minister of Finance, ref. 19146, 7 January 1927, 'Übersicht über den Personalstand nach dem Stande vom 1. Oktober 1926', 26–8; Reichstag printed paper no. 3860, Reich Finance Minister, ref. IB 18233, 23 December 1927, 'Übersicht über den Personalstand', 3; BAK, Z.Sg.I.90/25, 'SPD Parteikorrespondenz 1929', 20.

other states, such as Bavaria, Hesse and Württemberg, did not dismiss their married women civil servants if they had already been granted life tenure. However, single women with life tenure lost it on marriage.[59] Such differences in the adoption of Article 14 highlight the continuing divergence in the treatment women civil servants received at Reich, Land and local levels. The magazine of the Reichsverband der verheirateten Lehrerinnen (RVL) published lists

59. Käthe Gaebel, 'Zur Rechtslage der Beamtinnen', *DF*, vol. 31, no. 8, May 1924, pp. 242–6; 'Der Abbau der verheirateten Beamtin', *Unter dem Reichsadler*, vol. 16, no. 9, 8 May 1924, pp. 130–2.

of women dismissed by various authorities, especially in the early years of the PAV, and frequent questionnaires were sent to the association's members. Between 1 May and 1 October 1924, for example, twenty-seven married women teachers were dismissed from schools in six Berlin districts, four remaining at work. A RVL survey conducted in the winter of 1926/7 was answered by 162 women, of whom 120 had lost their jobs. Another, answered by 103 women in 1929, showed that 63.7 per cent of the women teachers dismissed had between ten and twenty years service. Of 430 women who answered a further survey in the winter of 1930/1, 57.7 per cent had a similar service record, 58.1 per cent had no children, 41.6 per cent were married to civil servants and 81.6 per cent had cleaning ladies, who were probably dismissed when their female employers lost their jobs.[60] Insufficient material is available to enable conclusions to be drawn about the total number of married women teachers dismissed, but the women's share of the teaching work force remained stable throughout the Weimar Republic: 29.7 per cent in the schools' census of 1921/2 and 29.8 per cent in the census ten years later. To some extent the position of women was shielded by the male to female student-teacher ratios laid down by the Länder, although there were instances where men, not single women, replaced married women teachers, as they had done at the end of the war.[61]

Economic Crisis and the *Doppelverdiener*

Article 14 of the PAV came to an end on 31 March 1929, because there was not the necessary two-thirds majority in the Reichstag required for the extension of laws contravening the Constitution, much to the disappointment of the Reich Postal and Finance Ministers, the Prussian Minister of Education, the Bavarian and Württemberg Association of Female Transport Civil Servants, the

60. In Bavaria 30 out of 37 women were dismissed and in Anhalt 11 out of 14: Archiv des Allgemeinen Deutschen Lehrerinnenvereins (subsequently AADLV), packet 16, *Die verheiratete Lehrerin*, vol. 3, no. 2, March 1927, p. 10; vol. 5, no. 4, October 1929; vol. 7, no. 3, June 1931, p. 34.

61. As early as 1908, for example, Prussia decreed that the staffing ratio in its senior girls' schools should be one man to one woman: *JbBdF*, 1912, p. 115. The ratio of student male to female teachers was 3 : 2 in Baden, 4 : 1 in Saxony, 3 : 1 in Thuringia and Hesse: *DF.*, vol. 38, no. 10, July 1931, p. 630.

Housewives' Association, among others.[62] A Social Democratic Party (SPD) bill to introduce a gratuity to women civil servants resigning voluntarily on marriage was likewise defeated, the argument being that such payments were unfair to men who received nothing when they voluntarily left the civil service. It was decided, however, to call upon the government to introduce a law governing the employment and legal position of married women civil servants, with the implication that the Constitution did not do this.[63] The guidelines of September 1920 had long since been a dead-letter.

The campaign for the granting of a gratuity to women resigning from the civil service on marriage was reborn, the VRT submitting another memorandum to the Reich Postal Ministry before the expiry of Article 14. The VRT, at an extraordinary meeting on 10 March 1929, had decided that it must support the BdF in its call for the ending of Article 14 on 31 March 1929, but it determined to fight for the immediate implementation of gratuity payments for those women civil servants who wanted to leave their job on marriage, a campaign the ADLV had never supported.[64] Although the government was unwilling to set a precedent by introducing such a scheme at Reich level – indeed, it wanted to reintroduce Article 14 – other authorities were quick to implement one; Berlin, for example, reintroduced its 1923 scheme with effect from 1 April 1929. The Reich railways also adopted a severance system in May 1929, although the Prussian authorities refused to take the initiative, preferring instead to wait for the Reich's example.[65]

The deteriorating economic situation and the rise in unemploy-

62. In 1925 it was not thought the extension of PAV Article 14 required a two-thirds majority because it was an improvement on the original: BAK, Nachlaß Lüders 135, Reichstag printed papers nos. 867 of 28 February 1929 and 179 of 20 March 1929, minutes of budget committee of 20 March 1929 and of Reichstag of 18 March 1929, 1516–18; R431/2614, 182–3 on how Article 14 proved itself indispensable to the Reich Postal Service.

63. BAK, Nachlaß Lüders 135, budget committee minutes of 20 March 1929 and Reichstag minutes of 19 March 1929, 1547; *NBl*, vol. 9, no. 4, April 1929, p. 24; Gertrud Bäumer, 'Die Wiederherstellung der Rechte der verheirateten Beamtin', *DF*, vol. 36, no. 7, April 1929, pp. 423–7.

64. The VRT felt it could not betray the principles of the women's movement. The Bavarian and Württemberg women postal civil servants' organisation, however, wanted Article 14 extended until a new civil service law came into effect: 'Für und Wider den Artikel 14', *Unter dem Reichsadler*, vol. 21, no. 5, 14 March 1929, pp. 84ff.

65. HLA, D/Dd1/aa; BAK, R2/1291, confidential meetings held in the Reich Interior Ministry on 23 July and 19 September 1929; R36/93, 147, notice in *Berliner Börsen-Courier*, 7 June 1929; Nachlaß Lüders 135, order of Reich Railway manage-

ment led to a resurgence of latent ill-feeling against married working women, the so-called 'double-earners' (*Doppelverdiener*). The inflation of 1923, which saw the number of those receiving unemployment benefit rise from 85,418 in January to 1,473,688 in December of that year, had led to numerous calls for the dismissal of employed married women, with the Reich Minister of Labour Dr Brauns (Centre Party) writing to the Union of German Employers' Federations asking it to devote special attention to the question of 'double-earners' 'especially married women'.[66] Indeed, there were reports of mass dismissals of married women manual workers.[67] Increasing unemployment in the 1930s, however, meant such calls were made even more vociferously. Not only men, but also single women were against married women's employment.[68] One reason, perhaps, can be found in the increasing number of married women working outside the home between 1925 and 1933, while the numbers of working single, widowed and divorced women fell. In 1907 25.8 per cent of all married women worked, 28.7 per cent in 1925 and 29.2 per cent in 1933, making up 29.3 per cent, 31.7 per cent and 36.4 per cent respectively of the female workforce.[69] The increase in the number of married women working between 1907

---

ment of 22 May 1929, no. 52.504 pol.o; 'Die Abfindungssumme für verheiratete weibliche Beamte', *Rundschau für Kommunalbeamte*, vol. 35, no. 31, 3 August 1929, pp. 552–3.

66. *StJbdR*, 1924/25, p. 299; BAK, R43I/612, 193, Reichsarbeitsministerium X7607/23, 18 November 1923. On *Doppelverdiener* see Jill Stephenson, *Women in Nazi Society*, London, 1975, pp. 81–83, 151ff; Helgard Kramer, 'Frankfurt's Working Women: Scapegoats or Winners of the Great Depression?', in Richard J. Evans and Dick Geary (eds.), *The German Unemployed*, London, 1987, pp. 108–41.

67. Isa Strasser, *Frauenarbeit und Rationalisierung*, Berlin, 1927, p. 5; Jürgen Kuczynski, *Studien zur Geschichte der Lage der Arbeiterinnen in Deutschland von 1700 bis zur Gegenwart*, Berlin, 1965, p. 218.

68. A survey among the working class showed 68% against the employment of married women: Erich Fromm, *The Working Class in Weimar Germany. A Psychological and Sociological Study*, Leamington Spa, 1984, pp. 162–70.

69. Calculated from figures in *SdR*, vol. 402, pp. 424, 439–42; vol. 458, pp. 62, 75ff. In 1925 the female work force was made up of 6,802,135 single, 3,645,326 married and 1,030,551 widowed and divorced women. In 1933 these figures were 6,415,089, 4,117,404 and 886,548 respectively. The number of employed married women continued to increase after 1933, with 33.6% of all married women working in 1939: Tim Mason, 'Women in Germany, 1925–1940: Family, Welfare and Work', *History Workshop*, no. 1, Spring 1976, pp. 74–113 and no. 2, Autumn 1976, pp. 5–32. There was, however, very little change in the percentage of employed married women within the total number of married women. In 1907 72.9% of all married women were only housewives, in 1925 69.9% and in 1933 69.2%.

and 1933 (65 per cent) exceeded that of married women within the
population (47.8 per cent), as more and more couples were getting
married in the 1920s and having fewer children, thanks to the wider
dissemination of birth control methods.[70] It appears that married
women went out to work primarily for economic reasons; 74 per
cent of women married to agricultural workers, 21 per cent of
manual workers' and 11 per cent of white-collar workers' wives
were working in 1925.[71] For some, marriage was only possible if
both partners worked, although many women, of course, had seen
their marriage prospects severely reduced by the slaughter of the
First World War and therefore had to earn their own living. To
them the married woman worker was not only a competitor in the
job market, but also combined employment outside the home with
a job many single women might perhaps have preferred – that of
housewife.[72]

Attention was centred on the married female civil servant, both
out of envy, because she was in a job which was held in high esteem
and which it would not be demeaning for a man to do, and out of
expediency, because such employees seemed the easiest to dismiss
by legislation. The Reich could set an example to other employers.
However, although the Brüning government, in its 1930 draft law
aimed at reducing public expenditure, envisaged the permanent
reintroduction of Article 14, the measure was dropped because the
necessary Reichstag majority was not assured.[73] From December
1930 a steady stream of petitions was laid before the Reichstag,
Landtage and local councils calling for the dismissal of married
women from the public sector. Some petitions also called for a
restriction on the further appointment of women to the public
sector and the dismissal of single women with wealthy parents.[74]

In January 1931 the government set up a commission under Dr
Brauns, Minister of Labour from 1920 to 1928, in order to investi-

70. In 1900 there were 8.5 marriages and 35.6 live births per 1,000 population, in
1910 7.7 and 29.8, in 1920 14.5 and 25.9, in 1930 8.8 and 17.5 and in 1933 9.7 and 14.7
respectively: *StJbdR*, 1934, p. 27.
71. *SdR*, vol. 402, p. 440. In 1907 22% of married women aged 18 to 30 were
employed, in 1925 27% and in 1933 29%.
72. There were 1,000 men to 1,067 women in 1925: ibid., vol. 401, pp. 580ff.
73. *DF*, vol. 37, no. 10, July 1930, p. 600; Meta Corssen, 'Die Frauenbewegung',
Sozialistische Monatshefte, vol. 37, 1930, p. 920.
74. BAK, Nachlaß Lüders 135, *Deutsche Allgemeine Zeitung*, 3 December 1930,
DVP petition to Berlin city council; Bajohr, *Hälfte*, p. 186.

gate the unemployment problem. In its deliberations on 'double-earners' the commission was unable to agree. The majority believed that the dismissal of married women civil servants would infringe their rights and that the current situation was not so severe as to justify violating rights enshrined in the Constitution. The number of economically secure married women civil servants was so small that their dismissal could in no way alleviate unemployment. None the less, the majority favoured the introduction of severance payments to tempt women to leave the civil service. The minority, on the other hand, favoured the compulsory dismissal, with compensation, of all economically secure married women civil servants.[75] As we have seen, ever since March 1929 successive governments, keen to implement such a measure, had been deterred by the evident lack of support in the Reichstag. It was left to the Centre Party, always a staunch opponent of married women's employment and encouraged perhaps by the Pope's encyclicals *Casti Connubii* of 30 December 1930 and *Quadragesimo Anno* of 15 May 1931 which declared that a married woman's place was in the home, to lay a draft bill before the Reichstag on 15 October 1931 and to initiate inter-party negotiations to ensure that the necessary two-thirds majority was on hand.[76] The SPD agreed to support the bill, provided the clause allowing its extension to include married women civil servants in the Länder and local authorities was dropped, and the bill was passed accordingly on 12 May 1932 by 460 votes to 73.[77] The law stated that any woman who wished to resign could be released at any time; a married woman whose future seemed permanently economically secure could be dismissed with three months notice. In both cases women were entitled to receive compensation, and it was incumbent upon the relevant authorities

75. BAK, R43I/2039, 387–9, 'Gutachten zur Arbeitslosenfrage betr. Doppelverdiener', 27 March 1931.
76. Rudolf Morsey, *Die Protokolle der Reichstagsfraktion und des Fraktionsvorstandes der deutschen Zentrumspartei 1926–1933*, Mainz, 1969, pp. 507ff., 517ff., 550ff.; 'Die christliche Ehe. Enzyklika des Papstes Pius XI vom 31. Dezember 1930', *Archiv für Bevölkerungspolitik, Sexualethik und Familienkunde*, vol. 1, no. 1, 1931, pp. 24–55; Pius XI, *Rundschreiben über die gesellschaftliche Ordnung*, Munich 1932; Stephenson, *Women*, p. 19; BAK, R36/93, 173–4, Reichstag printed paper no. 1207 of 15 October 1931.
77. 'Gesetz über die Rechtstellung der weiblichen Beamten. Vom 30. Mai 1932', *RGBl*, 1932, pp. 245ff. The Communist Party voted against the bill, the State Party abstained: 'Das Recht der verheirateten Beamtin', *DF*, vol. 39, no. 9, May 1932, pp. 574–8.

to prove that the women concerned were economically secure.

The new law was in no way as severe as Article 14, or the SPD would not have supported such a bill. The SPD's spokesman in the Reichstag, the only man to speak in the debate, emphasised that the reasons behind the SPD accepting the bill were the same as those which caused the VRT to welcome it: the failure for the past eighteen months of the Reich Postal Service to appoint any woman to a permanent civil servant's post, and the threatened transfer of married women civil servants away from their homes.[78] Following the 1930 draft law for reducing personnel, the VRT had begun to reappraise its position in June 1930. The number of women civil servants in the Reich Postal Service had fallen between 1925 and 1930 by 18.8 per cent, that of male civil servants had risen by 2.9 per cent.[79] There was a fear that women were being systematically removed from civil service positions (*Entbeamtung*). The VRT decided, after some soul-searching, to support a law which would give the authorities the right to dismiss married women civil servants in exchange for a gratuity payment and it approached the political parties for support in the winter of 1930/1. When it became clear that no such law would receive the necessary support in the Reichstag, the VRT approached the Reich Postal Minister on 20 March 1931 to ask for a repeat of the early 1923 voluntary severance scheme which he rejected 'with regret'.[80] The question of the employment of married women civil servants had by now become inextricably linked with the whole question of their future in the Reich Postal Service. On 15 December 1930 the VRT was told that until the question of married women civil servants was resolved, no more women would be granted permanent civil service posts.[81] At a meeting in the Reich Interior Ministry on 5 January 1931, the Reich Postal Minister's representative stated that if mar-

78. 'Die Rechtsstellung der verheirateten Beamtin', *Die Genossin*, vol. 9, no. 5/6, May/June 1932, pp. 125–8; 'Die verheiratete Beamtin', ibid., vol. 9, no. 2, February 1932, pp. 29–31.

79. The number of women civil servants had fallen from 48,879 to 39,679, that of men had risen from 198,257 to 204,094: 'Der Abbau des weiblichen Berufsbeamtentums bei der Deutschen Reichspost', *Unter dem Reichsadler*, vol. 23, no. 7, 9 April 1931, pp. 97ff.

80. 'Verbandseingabe zur Frage der Abfindungssumme für verheiratete Beamtinnen', ibid., vol. 23, no. 6, 26 March 1931, p. 84; 'Zur Abfindungsfrage', ibid., vol. 23, no. 7, 9 April 1931, pp. 98ff.

81. The Reich Postal Minister issued a decree to this end on 16 December 1930

ried women civil servants could not be compulsorily dismissed, then the end of permanent female civil servants in the Reich Postal Service was nigh.[82] Nine months later, in September 1931, the Reich Postal Minister, forced by a fall in trade and increased automation to make staff cuts, ordered the dismissal of economically secure married female civil servants who did not have life tenure and of female 'helpers', a measure that had already been taken by the Postal Administrative Division in Hamburg. Those married women civil servants who were frequently absent because of ill-health were to be examined by the Service's doctor and, if it was thought beneficial to their health, transferred to the country, thus forcing them to resign if they wanted to stay with their husbands.[83] It was unthinkable for economically secure married women civil servants to be employed while single employees or civil servants without life tenure, many of whom had others to support, were dismissed. If married women were dismissed, according to the Reich Postal Minister, they could devote themselves to raising a family.[84] Considerations of population policy can never be overlooked when talking of women's role in German society in the inter-war years, and married female civil servants were criticised in some circles for having fewer children than other women.[85] The policy of transferring married women civil servants away from their husbands, however, did little to promote family life. There were also reports that Article 14 had

---

with effect from 1 January 1931: 'Zur Frage der Vorenthaltung der Unkündbarkeit bei der planmäßigen Anstellung', ibid., vol. 23, no. 10, 21 May 1931, p. 147.

82. *NBl*, vol. 11, no. 10, October 1931, p. 83. A similar conclusion was reached by the German Towns' Congress: BAK, R36/2198, 'Vorbericht für die Vorstandssitzung des Deutschen Städtetages am 20. März 1931'.

83. BAK, R43I/2041, 253–5, Reich Postal Minister to fellow ministers and his postal divisions, 15 September 1931.

84. BAK, Nachlaß Lüders 135, letter of Reich Postal Minister to M-E. Lüders of 3 January 1931.

85. Married female civil servants were such a new phenomenon that no surveys had been done on them. A survey of male Reich civil servants in 1926 showed them to have fewer children than average, with low-ranking civil servants having more children than middle-ranking ones, who in turn had more children than senior civil servants. Social class was the prime determinant of the number of children a family had, and women civil servants tended to marry professional men: Friedrich Burgdörfer, *Der Geburtenrückgang und seine Bekämpfung*, Berlin, 1929, pp. 81–9; *DF*, vol. 38, no. 9, June 1931, p. 570. A survey into the fertility of female graduates in the 1930s found that it did not differ from that of other women in their social class: Agnes Martens-Edelmann, 'Frauenstudium, Ehe und Mutterschaft', ibid., vol. 44, no. 2, November 1936, pp. 84–94.

forced some women civil servants not to marry, others to divorce in order to keep their jobs, and Katharina von Kardorff, a DVP (Deutsche Volkspartei) member of the Reichstag from 1920 to 1924, believed that Article 14 forced women to 'live in sin'.[86]

It was concern about women's future in the Reich Postal Service, however, that caused the VRT to continue its campaign for the introduction of a law allowing the compulsory dismissal of married women civil servants with a severance payment. Correspondence received from its membership caused it to believe that the vast majority of married women civil servants in the Reich Postal Service wanted to leave their jobs, but could not afford to do so without a gratuity. The VRT welcomed the Centre Party's draft law of 15 October 1931 and thanked the party when it became law. It believed the law, which it regarded as a significant success for its efforts, would be greeted with great joy, not only by married women civil servants, but also by those wanting to marry, those who would step into their married colleagues' shoes, and by those who had been refused permanent civil service posts since 1 January 1931. On 8 June 1932 the Reich Postal Minister lifted the ban on permanent civil service posts for women.[87]

Considerations of population policy and the financial and socio-economic reasons used throughout the Weimar Republic to justify the dismissal of married women civil servants – the need to make cuts in staff and expenditure, frequent absences, the high level of unemployment – hide the fact that the authorities concerned simply did not wish to employ married women, especially in highly re-garded civil service positions. The dismissal of the estimated 1,000 married women in the Reich Postal Service in 1932 would do little to ease the unemployment situation, especially as they would not be replaced if their dismissal was indeed due to the Reich Postal Minister's reported need to make cuts.[88] The law of 30 May 1932

86. BAK, Nachlaß Lüders 135, article entitled 'Erneuter Abbau verheirateter Beamtinnen?', December 1930; minutes of the Reichstag of 19 March 1929, 1548; Nachlaß Katharina von Kardorff, 38, pp. 110–16, lecture of 20 October 1930.

87. 'Zur beamtenpolitischen Lage', *Unter dem Reichsadler*, vol. 23, no. 20, 29 October 1931, pp. 305ff. 'Verheiratete Beamte und Abfindungssumme', ibid., vol. 23, no. 24, 24 December 1931, pp. 375ff. 'Das Gesetz über die Rechtstellung der weiblichen Beamten im Reichstag angenommen!', ibid., vol. 24, no. 10, 26 May 1932, pp. 145–7; 'Die unkündbare Anstellung der weiblichen Beamten', ibid., vol. 24, no. 12, 23 June 1932.

88. Figures given by Dr Völter (SPD) in his Reichstag speech: *Die Genossin*, vol. 9, no. 5/6, May/June 1932, pp. 125–8. The Brauns commission had estimated that

can, of course, be interpreted in another light: the Reichstag could be seen to be heeding public opinion on the matter of the *Doppelverdiener* and setting an example, while actually doing very little to harm married women's employment, as the SPD had refused to allow the law to be applied by the Länder or local authorities. This view fails to take into account the fact that the Reich authorities were constantly trying to remove married women civil servants from their jobs from 1919 onwards, either by persuasion or coercion. In the early years of the Republic, however, successive governments were keen to uphold the Constitution and it was to require an Enabling Act before they did break Article 128. But as we have seen it would be wrong to assume the government was acting out of concert with the staff organisations concerned. The authorities, the VRT and the women transport civil servants' association felt that the combining of marriage and a civil servant's job somehow devalued the civil service. In addition, women civil servants and contractual employees in the Reich Postal Service and Reich, Land and local administration were generally older than the national average for such women; perhaps they had pursued a career at the expense of marriage and begrudged their younger colleagues the opportunity of combining both.[89] Some surveys showed that a considerable number of women civil servants married men in the civil service and before the war it was a regulation in most Länder that a civil servant's wife did not go out to work.[90] The Constitution

---

1,000 of the Reich Post's 39,000 women civil servants were married, along with 5,000–6,000 teachers: BAK, R43I/2039, 388. Reports in early 1933 put the number of women leaving the Reich Postal Service at 2,000: AADLV, packet 16, *Die verheiratete Lehrerin*, vol. 9, no. 1, January 1933.

89. In 1925 77.6% of all female commercial and administrative white-collar workers and civil servants were under thirty; in the Reich Postal Service and in the administration this figure was 56.2% and 59.3% respectively. 6.1% of all the women in this classification were married; in the Reich Postal Service this figure was 2.1%, in the administration 6.0%: *SdR*, vol. 408, p. 170. The difference between the marriage figures for the Reich Post and the Reich, Land and local administrations is attributable to the fact that in the former the majority were civil servants, in the latter contractual employees. In 1933 6.9% of women civil servants in the Reich Post and on the railways were under 30 with 39.5% over forty, while in the administration 14.6% were under 30 with 50.2% over forty: ibid., vol. 458, p. 64. The difference between the 1925 and 1933 figures highlights the fact that the majority of the young women who worked in the administration and in the Reich Post were contractual employees.

90. Gertrud Bäumer, 'Staat und Familie', *JbBdF*, 1917, pp. 75–85. Of the women civil servants in the Reich Post marrying between July 1926 and 1929 33.7% had

could not change attitudes overnight. In its granting of equality to married women civil servants it was far too progressive for many. In some countries, like Great Britain, women civil servants continued to be dismissed on marriage, while in others, such as the Netherlands, Canada, Sweden and some parts of the United States of America, legislation was passed allowing married women to be dismissed during the 1920s and 1930s.[91] While the Constitution, not the government, might be seen to be out of step with the public's sympathies, it was the government's duty to uphold, not undermine the Constitution.

Public ill-feeling against married women's employment could not prevent many women marrying and staying at work, and, indeed, it had always been accepted practice among certain sections of the working class that a married woman would have to go out to work. Shopkeepers and small farmers expected their wives to help in the family business, as indeed they were required to do by the Civil Code. Now, however, married women were remaining in jobs in the white-collar sector, which before the war they had tended to vacate on marriage. Contrary to government belief, marriage did not provide all women with economic security. The increase in the number of married women employed outside the home, which was due primarily to the increased incidence of marriage, might have been greater had they not met such ill-feeling in the labour market. And yet it must be stated that private employers did not follow the government's example in dismissing its married female civil servants or heed the Reich Labour Minister's calls, made in November 1923, September 1926 and December 1930, not to employ 'double-earners' if other suitable workers were available.[92] Women were, of course, attractive as cheap, unskilled labour during and following the rationalisation of German industry in the 1920s.

---

married civil servants, 37.7% Reich or Land contractual employees: BAK, R2/1291, 237, 'Übersicht über die Berufe der Ehemänner der weiblichen Beamten der deutschen Reichspost', July 1929.

91. Stephenson, *Women*, p. 4; Meta Corssen, 'Die Frauenbewegung', *Sozialistische Monatshefte*, vol. 31, 1925, p. 706; vol. 36, 1930, p. 921; vol. 37, 1931, p. 679; Henri Fuss, 'Unemployment and Employment among Women', *International Labour Review*, vol. 31, 1935, pp. 463–97. For the British civil service, see Meta Zimmeck, 'Strategies and Strategems for the employment of women in the British Civil Service, 1919–1931', *The Historical Journal*, vol. 27, 1984, pp. 901–24.

92. BAK, R36/2198, Deutscher Städtetag, 31 December 1930. See also footnote 66.

The Reality of Women's Employment

Census statistics reveal that women's share of the total industrial work force fell slightly from 22 per cent in 1925 to 21.1 per cent in 1933, but if only 'economically active' persons are considered, namely those in work, then women increased their share to 24.5 per cent by 1933. Married women made up 25.1 per cent of the total female industrial work force in 1925, 29.6 per cent in 1933.[93] During the 1920s women's labour force participation shifted away from traditional jobs in textiles, clothing and food, as rapid technical progress in the second half of the decade facilitated their further penetration of male-dominated industries which had first begun during the war. The German Metal Workers' Union noted an increase of 25 per cent in the female work force in the precision and optical instrument branch between 1925 and 1929, while the male work force remained stable.[94] Women industrial manual workers were concentrated in the larger factories, doing mainly unskilled or semi-skilled work. In the metal industry, for example, 68 out of every 100 unskilled and 35 out of every 100 semi-skilled workers were women.[95] Employers felt it was not worthwhile training women, as they would only be working for a short time before marrying and having a family. Women's lack of training was used as a justification for the low rates of pay they received. The war had brought about a relative increase in women's wages, as compared

93. Calculated from figures in *SdR*, vol. 402, pp. 442, 446; vol. 453, part 3, pp. 4ff. Of those women actually working in any capacity in industry in 1933 30.3% were married.

94. Deutscher Metallarbeiterverband, *Frauenarbeit*, p. 11. The shift was gradual rather than dramatic: women's share of the manual work force in textiles fell from 58.7% in 1925 to 56.3% in 1933, in clothing from 58.7% to 58.3% and in food from 28% to 25%: calculated from figures in *SdR*, vol. 458, p. 43 and *StJbdR*, 1932, p. 20. During the rationalisation process there was a varying demand for female labour and once it was over men returned again, though not in the same domination, to their former industries. In some cases women, too, lost their jobs to the machine: Judith Grünfeld, 'Rationalization and the Employment and Wages of Women in Germany', *International Labour Review*, vol. 24, no. 5, May 1934, pp. 605–32 and 'Frauenarbeit im Lichte der Rationalisierung', *Die Arbeit*, vol. 8, 1931, pp. 911–24. For an overall view of women's employment in the Weimar Republic, see Renate Bridenthal, 'Beyond *Kinder, Küche, Kirche*: Weimar Women at Work', *Central European History*, vol. 6, 1973, pp. 148–66.

95. Grünfeld, 'Rationalization', p. 617. In the printing trade 2 out of every 100 skilled and 63 out of every 100 unskilled workers were female: Dr M. Schiller, 'Frauenentlohnung und Tarifvertrag', *DF*, vol. 36, no. 5, February 1929, pp. 306–9.

with men's, as did the inflation of 1923, although the differential then remained stable until 1945.[96] In the chemical industry between 1924 and 1928, an unskilled woman received 67 per cent of an unskilled man's wage, while in the metal industry women averaged 70 per cent of men's wages. The General Federation of German Trades Unions had to admit in 1929 that unskilled men in industry, as a whole, earned more than skilled women.[97] Poorer wages for women were justified by the fact that they were in the main young and unskilled, single with no family to support, for whom employment was a temporary stage before marriage. Other reasons for women's poor wages can be found in the vast reservoir of women workers and the lack of organisation among those women who did work.

Old attitudes and double standards prevailed. Attempts by left-wing parties (SPD/USPD) to curtail the dismissal of unmarried female civil servants with a child failed when the VRT protested to the Reichsrat against an amendment to the Civil Service Law of 31 March 1873 which stated that the fact of unmarried motherhood in itself formed no grounds for the instigation of disciplinary proceedings. The Reichstag had passed the amendment on 1 July 1922. The VRT regarded the unmarried mother within the civil service as a disgrace; she had failed to uphold the duty of maintaining the high moral standards expected of civil servants, a view shared by the Bavarian and Württemberg Association of Female Transport Civil Servants, the Reich Postal Minister and the Reich Interior Minister, among many others.[98] Unmarried mothers joined married women civil servants as another group which could not rely upon its staff organisation to fight for its rights.

For married women and unmarried mothers Article 128 was a dead letter. These women lost their jobs, but other women civil

96. Gerhard Bry, *Wages in Germany 1871–1945*, Princeton, 1960, p. 96 *et passim*.

97. *Jahrbuch des Allgemeinen Deutschen Gewerkschaftsbundes*, 1929, p. 191.

98. The ADLV wanted each case to be judged on its merits but saw grounds for disciplinary proceedings in unmarried motherhood: BAK, Nachlaß Lüders 152, SPD petition 6540 of 27 February 1924, letter of VRT to Reichsrat of 5 July 1922, SPD or USPD petitions of 29 October 1920, 17 March 1921, 25 June 1921, VRT congress in Düsseldorf in May 1921; Nachlaß Lüders 233, SPD petition of 9 March 1922; *The International Woman Suffrage News*, vol. 27, no. 1, October 1922, p. 10; Helene Lange, 'Die uneheliche Mutterschaft als Disziplinverfahren', *DF*, vol. 28, no. 9, June 1921, pp. 270–2. Unmarried motherhood became insufficient reason for dismissal in January 1939: Stephenson, *Women*, pp. 63–6.

servants experienced discrimination in the areas of pay, appointment to the civil service and promotion. Although in principle men and women received equal pay, women were often placed in lower salary groups than men doing the same work and, in addition, received fewer and/or smaller allowances. The 1920 Salary Law gave married men an additional allowance for their wives. Married women civil servants were only entitled to receive half the local allowance and the children's allowance, if their husband did not earn enough to keep them.[99] Although the 1927 Salary Law was generous in its increases, these had in part to be paid for by not filling every third permanent civil service post which became vacant over the next five years. As women had, perforce, to leave on marriage, this measure affected women more harshly than men. In addition, wife's allowances were abolished, with single civil servants under forty-five receiving a smaller accommodation allowance than their married colleagues.[100] The salary cuts introduced by the Brüning government in 1930 and 1931 which averaged 23 per cent affected single civil servants more than married ones, women once again suffering disproportionately, while at a Land level it became common practice in the late 1920s and early 1930s for women teachers to have their number of hours cut by 10 per cent, and their salaries likewise.[101]

Mention has already been made of the Reich Postal Service's failure to appoint women to permanent civil service positions from 1931, in an attempt to bring about legislation allowing the compulsory dismissal of married female civil servants. Throughout the

---

99. 'Besoldungsgesetz. Vom 30. April 1920', *RGBl*, 1920, pp. 805–6; *The International Woman Suffrage News*, vol. 15, no. 9, June 1921, pp. 138ff.

100. 'Reichsbesoldungsgesetz. Vom 16. Dezember 1927', *RGBl*, 1927, p. 349; Jane Caplan, 'Civil Service Support for National Socialism: An Evaluation', in Gerhard Hirschfeld and Lothar Kettenacker (eds.), *The 'Führer State': Myth and Reality*, Stuttgart, 1981, pp. 167–93.

101. Figure of 23% given in Jane Caplan, 'The Politics of Administration: the Reich Interior Ministry and the German Civil Service, 1933–1943', *The Historical Journal*, vol. 20, 1977, pp. 707–36; Ludwig Preller, *Sozialpolitik in der Weimarer Republik*, Düsseldorf, 1978, pp. 396, 410. Mommsen puts the figure at between 18% and 23%: Hans Mommsen, 'Die Stellung der Beamtenschaft in Reich, Ländern und Gemeinden in der Ära Brüning', *Vierteljahrshefte für Zeitgeschichte*, vol. 21, 1973, pp. 151–65. Prussian law of 17 December 1927 in *Das gesamte deutsche und preußische Gesetzgebungsmaterial*, Berlin, 1927, pp. 826ff; Baden law of 9 October 1931 in *Badisches Gesetz- und Verordnungsblatt*, Karlsruhe, 1931, p. 380; *NBl*, vol. 12, no. 7, July 1932, 54 for Hesse and Thuringia.

Weimar Republic, however, there had been a marked reluctance on the part of the Reich authorities to appoint women in the administration to civil service positions. We have already seen that female contractual employees outnumbered female civil servants in the Reich ministries 16 : 1 in April 1924. By 1927 the women's association concerned was calling for all female clerical workers in Reich ministries with more than nine years' experience to be made civil servants.[102] Their case was taken up in the Reichstag by Marie-Elisabeth Lüders and although the supplementary budget for 1928 made provision for the promotion of some clerical workers to civil service posts, members of the budget committee felt such an action would discriminate against men, and so a decision was delayed until the Reich Finance Minister drew up a list of principles governing the transfer of clerical workers into the civil service. The Reich Finance Minister found that male and female clerical workers were treated equally, with the same access to a civil service career, and that an increase in the number of civil service posts for women could not be justified in the prevailing economic climate.[103] The BdF, however, believed that it was much more difficult for a woman clerical worker than a man to become a civil servant, and there were even fears that women were being excluded from a career in the administration.[104] A survey of 190 towns in 1928, for example, revealed that of every 100 women in local administration, 16 held permanent civil service positions, while 76 were in clerical grades.[105] The reluctance to appoint women to civil service posts was also felt by professional women such as doctors, lawyers and judges. Women were admitted to the legal profession by a law of 11 July 1922 and by 1933 36 of Germany's 10,359 judges and 251 of its 18,641 lawyers were women.[106] While women lawyers could set up

102. BAK, R2/1291, 131, letter of Union of Female Civil Servants and Clerical Workers in Reich Authorities to Reich Finance Minister of 14 February 1927; 145, of 890 female clerical workers in five ministries 228 had held their jobs for over ten years.
103. BAK, Nachlaß Lüders 135, 'Denkschrift über die Frage der Überführung weiblicher Angestellter in das Beamtenverhältnis', 14 January 1930.
104. *NBl*, vol. 6, no. 10, October 1926, p. 2; vol. 10, no. 10, October 1930, p. 1; BAK, R45II/64, 1151, *Frauenrundschau*, 17 March 1932.
105. Women thus made up 5.7% of civil servants and 84.2% of clerical workers: BAK, Nachlaß Lüders, 279, 'Minderbewertung der Frauenarbeit in Reichs-, Länder- und Kommunalverwaltungen', 20 June 1930. In 1933 there were 10,432 women among 436,307 civil servants in Reich, Land and local administration (2.4%): *SdR*, vol. 458, p. 37.
106. *SdR*, vol. 458, p. 49.

in practice on their own, women judges were appointed by the Länder, some of which believed women incapable of dealing with all types of cases or of coping with the heavy workload. Others, like Bavaria, simply excluded women from a career in the judiciary.[107] Women doctors likewise found themselves excluded from public service positions, such as district medical officers, in part because in some states they were debarred from taking the necessary examinations, and also because other state authorities felt the workload too demanding for women.[108] It was, therefore, difficult for women to obtain and then to keep a civil service post in the Weimar Republic. Examination bars and the lack of the necessary legal qualifications as good as closed senior civil service positions to women. Even where women possessed the necessary qualifications, they were rarely promoted. The Reich Interior Minister, commenting on the admittance of women to middle-ranking and senior civil service posts, felt that women should only be promoted in those subject areas where their presence seemed desirable. He noted that women were not and would not be promoted to be men's superiors in the Reich Transport Authority.[109] Some women, however, were given senior civil service posts in Reich and Land ministries, so-called 'political' civil service positions from which women, along with socialists, liberals and Catholics had been excluded before 1918.[110] Thus Dr Gertrud Bäumer, BdF chairman from 1910 to 1919 and a leading member of the German Democratic Party (Deutsche Demokratische Partei), was appointed an under-secretary in the Reich Ministry of the

107. BAK, Nachlaß Lüders, 239, article entitled 'Frauen als Richter', *Führer-Stimmen*, no. 10, 4 January 1930, pp. 1–3; 'Frauen im Justizdienst', *NBl*, vol. 10, no. 2, February 1930, p. 15; M-E. Lüders, 'Die Frau in der Verwaltung', *DF*, vol. 34, no. 1, October 1926, pp. 15–19, and no. 2, November 1926, pp. 83–87. Jill McIntyre, 'Women and the professions in Germany 1930–1940', in A. Nicholls and E. Matthias (eds.), *German Democracy and the Triumph of Hitler*, London, 1971, pp. 175–213.

108. Käthe Gaebel, 'Die Berufslage der Akademikerinnen', *DF*, vol. 34, no. 4, January 1927, pp. 218–24 and no. 5, February 1927, pp. 278–82. Hahn refers to one woman doctor who obtained a civil service appointment: Hahn, 'Der öffentliche Dienst', p. 64.

109. BAK, R2/1291, 97–8, letter to the Prussian Finance Minister of 22 January 1924; Bajohr, *Hälfte*, p. 182.

110. Hahn, 'Der öffentliche Dienst', p. 51; Eberhard Pikart, 'Preußische Beamtenpolitik 1918–1933', *Vierteljahrshefte für Zeitgeschichte*, vol. 6, 1958, pp. 119–37; John C.G. Röhl, 'Beamtenpolitik im Wilhelminischen Deutschland', in Michael Stürmer (ed.), *Das kaiserliche Deutschland*, Düsseldorf, 1977, pp. 287–311.

Interior in 1920, while Marie Baum became a senior government adviser on welfare to the Baden government.[111] Senior women civil servants were concentrated in education and welfare, areas thought to benefit from women's experience, but their numbers were few. A BdF survey in 1928 revealed only fifteen women in senior administrative posts in Reich ministries.[112] They were, of course, prey to any change in the political climate and the dismissal of five of the nine senior female civil servants in Prussian ministries in the autumn of 1932 heralded things to come.[113] On 27 February 1933 Gertrud Bäumer was granted indefinite leave of absence 'for political reasons', one of the many dismissals among the small number of women in senior administrative positions.[114]

Conclusion

The Weimar Republic can scarcely be regarded as the halcyon era of female employment in the civil service, with blatant discrimination and prejudice being practised against certain groups of women. In its dismissal of married female civil servants and unmarried mothers, and its appointment and promotion policies, the government and its authorities violated the Constitution. And yet the majority of German women did not perceive anything wrong in the government's actions.[115] Indeed, it was left to the major civil servants' union to protest on principle against the erosion of civil

111. Other senior civil servants included Helene Weber, an under-secretary in the Prussian Welfare Ministry, Else Ulich-Beil (Saxon Interior Ministry), Else Lüders (Reich Labour Ministry), Dr Käthe Gaebel (Central Office of Employment Exchanges), Charlotte Lorenz (Reich Statistics Office): Stephenson, *Women*, p. 24, 154; McIntyre, 'Women', p.177; Baum, *Rückblick*, p. 229; Gertrud Bäumer, *Lebensweg durch eine Zeitwende*, Tübingen, 1933, p. 391. Bäumer became a German Democratic Party, later State Party, member of the National Assembly and the Reichstag from 1919 to 1932.
112. HLA, D/Dd1/aa, 'Frauen an leitenden Stellen bei den Ministerien des Reichs und der Länder nach dem Stande vom 1. April 1928'. One source puts the total number of women in senior civil service posts in Reich and Land ministries at 38: Alice Rühle-Gerstel, *Die Frau und der Kapitalismus*, Leipzig, 1932, pp. 306ff.
113. Law of 29 October 1932: 'Zum Abbau der weiblichen Beamten in Preußen', *NBl*, vol. 12, No. 12, December 1932, pp. 111ff, vol. 13, no. 1, January 1933, p. 4.
114. Stephenson, *Women*, pp. 155–9; BAK, Kl.Erw.296–1, 16, letter of Gertrud Bäumer to Dorothee von Velsen of 7 March 1933. Helene Weber and Else Lüders were also dismissed.
115. M.-E. Lüders, *Fürchte dich nicht. Persönliches und Politisches aus mehr als 80 Jahren 1878–1962*, Cologne/Opladen, 1963, p. 106.

servants' rights, and, along with the BdF and the ADLV, to appeal for the upholding of Article 128 of the Constitution. They received little support from the women transport civil servants' association or the VRT, whose prime concern in the early 1930s was ensuring women's future within the permanent civil service, at the expense of the married woman civil servant.[116] The government was not acting out of step with public opinion or the beliefs of its female civil servants, who were described at the 1921 SPD women's conference as the 'most backward and conceited of all women'.[117] It was, however, out of step with the slowly changing overall pattern of women's employment, with more women marrying and staying at work.

Women had established themselves in education and, thanks to the belief that their presence was necessary for girls' education, their position was more secure than that of other women civil servants. It was, perhaps, this feeling of security that enabled women teachers to express opposition to discriminatory government legislation. During the Weimar Republic women's career structures within the civil service were laid down for the first time, giving women the opportunity of establishing themselves in this area of public service as well. However, a decreasing number of women was able to benefit from this opportunity; apart from the discriminatory measures taken against married women civil servants and unmarried mothers, the state increasingly preferred to appoint contractual employees rather than civil servants, whether male or female.[118] While the number of

116. BdF petitions found in numerous editions of *NBl*. The BdF, even while protesting about the measures taken against married women civil servants, insisted that a married woman's duty was her work in the family, and that this should be seen as a full-time occupation, although those women who also chose to pursue a career should be free to do so: 'Frauenarbeit in Familie und Beruf', ibid., vol. 11, no. 6, June 1931, pp. 41–3. The Deutscher Beamtenbund (DBB) protests against the compulsory dismissal of married women civil servants are found in *DF*, vol. 37, no. 10, July 1930, p. 600; vol. 39, no. 9, June 1932, pp. 574–8. For DBB protests against the erosion of civil servants' rights during the Weimar Republic, see Caplan, 'Politics', p. 711.

117. *Protokoll über die Verhandlungen des Reichsfrauentags der sozialdemokratischen Partei Deutschlands*, 1921, p. 38. The remark was made in connection with attitudes to unmarried mothers, but could be equally apposite for attitudes to married women's employment.

118. Between 1925 and 1933 the number of women civil servants in the Reich Postal Service fell by 30%, the number of civil servants and white-collar workers in the Reich Postal Service and the railways by 18%. See footnote 4 and Table 3.1. The DBB complained about the simultaneous reduction in the number of civil servants

civil service posts available for women was dwindling, the number of women who would have been able to seek such jobs as well as promotion within the civil service was growing. Girls' share of those taking the *Abitur*, the school leaving certificate necessary for university attendance, rose from 9.1 per cent of all pupils in 1926/7 to 23.5 per cent in 1931, while women's share of the student body rose from 9.2 per cent in the summer term of 1919 to 18.5 per cent in 1932.[119] Nor could women be accused of failing to carry out their civil service duties to a high enough standard. Those women who were given senior administrative posts acquitted themselves admirably. Gertrud Bäumer had to be replaced by two men, a fact which afforded her no small amount of satisfaction.[120] But the government did nothing to nurture the seeds of equality sown in the Constitution. It did nothing to promote the interests of women, both within the civil service and outside it, nor did it attempt to alter popular opinion on women's role in society. Indeed, its actions merely reinforced prejudice against married women, unmarried mothers and employed women in general.

---

and the increase in contractual employees, referring to a dismantling of the career civil service: 'Der Abbau des weiblichen Berufsbeamtentums bei der Deutschen Reichspost', *Unter dem Reichsadler*, vol. 23, no. 7, 9 April 1931, pp. 97ff.

119. *StJbdR*, 1929, pp. 406ff.; *StJbdR*, 1933, p. 521. Bäumer puts the figures at 10.9% in 1925/6 and 24.85% in 1931/2: Gertrud Bäumer, 'Krisis des Frauenstudiums', *DF*, vol. 39, no. 6, March 1932, pp. 322–7 and no. 10, July 1932, pp. 611–19. Student percentages calculated from *StJbdR*, 1933, pp. 522ff.; *StJbdR*, 1921/1922, p. 320.

120. Stephenson, *Women*, p. 155; Emmy Beckmann, *Des Lebens wie der Liebe Band. Briefe*, Tübingen, 1956, p. 50.

4
Foreign Labour, the State and Trade Unions in Imperial Germany, 1890–1918

Martin Forberg

Introduction

The employment of foreign labour in the German *Kaiserreich* is a subject closely connected with the questions of economic transition and social change. The recruitment of workers from abroad was at least partly a response by employers to a structural crisis in the agriculture of north-eastern Germany. At the same time it was a factor responsible for aggravating this crisis.[1] For particular industrial sectors – whose rise, accompanied by an increasing labour demand, intensified the agony of agriculture – the employment of foreign labour was a prerequisite for further development. Or, as

This article is based upon my unpublished M.A. thesis: 'Freie Gewerkschaften und ausländische Industriearbeiter, 1890 1918', Münster, 1985. I am grateful to Professor Klaus J. Bade, Teresa McKiernan, John Jeep, Arnd Schneider and Jerry Sheridan. More or less extensive use has also been made of two recently published works: U. Herbert, *Geschichte der Ausländerbeschäftigung in Deutschland 1880 bis 1980. Saisonarbeiter, Zwangsarbeiter, Gastarbeiter*, Berlin/Bonn, 1986; F. Zunkel, 'Die Stellung der Freien Gewerkschaften zur Beschäftigung ausländischer Arbeiter im Deutschen Reich vor und während des Ersten Weltkrieges', in H. Henning, D. Lindenlaub, E. Wandel (eds.), *Wirtschafts- und sozialgeschichtliche Forschungen und Probleme. Karl Erich Born zur Vollendung des 65. Lebensjahres zugeeignet von Kollegen, Freunden und Schülern*, Ostfildern, 1987, pp. 288–309.
    1. For the context of labour migration in Imperial Germany, see D. Langewiesche, 'Wanderungsbewegungen in der Hochindustrialisierungsperiode. Regionale, interstädtische und innerstädtische Mobilität in Deutschland 1880 – 1914', *Vierteljahresschrift für Sozial- und Wirtschaftsgeschichte*, vol. 64, 1978, pp. 1–40; D. Langewiesche and F. Lenger, 'Internal Migration', in K.J. Bade (ed.), *Population, Labour and Migration in 19th and 20th Century Germany*, Leamington Spa, 1987. For an overview in a north-western European context, including pre-industrial migration: J. Lucassen, *Migrant Labour in Europe 1600–1900: the Drift to the North Sea*, Beckenham, 1987.

Martin Forberg

the Austrian socialist Otto Bauer put it in 1907, labour immigration 'eases the rise of new and the expansion of already existing enterprises', thus in the long-run making possible the increased employment of indigenous labour.[2] In addition, the increased demand for foreign labour was related to the phenomenon of upward social mobility by elements of the indigenous working class – in the sense that the workers from abroad formed an inferior social stratum, thus allowing the 'rise' of some of their German colleagues. The strategy of foreign labour employment was also a reaction to the increased self-confidence expressed by German workers and their organisations. For various employers the immigration of labourers regarded as frugal was partly connected with the hope of creating 'a less demanding working class' in Germany.

As proletarian migration into Germany can be interpreted both as a result and a catalyst of socio-economic change, a specific examination of the role of the state in the context of its involvement in labour-market problems allows us to consider the more general features of state intervention in the economic sphere as a whole. In fact, in the pre-Weimar period, there were only very limited signs of coherent state intervention in that sphere, in terms of a strategy for systematically influencing the labour market. From this point of view the following contribution is limited to 'pre-historical' observations, which nevertheless may illustrate some of the origins of state labour-market policy. The general notion that the state in Imperial Germany was no uniform apparatus, but was shaped by substantial frictions between different levels of government and administration – partly due to the federal structure of the Reich – is entirely borne out by policy developments towards foreign labour, while the role of interest groups and the way they tried to influence state decisions emerge as a further crucial aspect of policy-making and its consequences. The problem of foreign labour also raises very urgently the question of a basic tension between nationalism (or a policy towards different nationalities as a reflection of the multi-ethnic structure of Imperial Germany) on the one hand, and a purely economic rationality on the other, which will be addressed later in this chapter. An essential aspect only incidentally touched on here is the relevance of the succession of different political

2. O. Bauer, 'Proletarische Wanderungen', *Die Neue Zeit. Revue des geistigen und öffentlich Lebens* (hereafter *NZ*), vol. 25, no. 2, 1906/7, pp. 476–94, here p. 486.

systems in Germany for the genesis of foreign labour employment policy during the years in question.

Immigration and Employment of Foreign Workers in Germany, 1890–1918: An Outline

Between 1871 and 1913 Germany experienced a substantial transition 'from an agrarian state with powerful industry to an industrial state with a strong agrarian basis'.[3] This process was accompanied by different forms of labour migration overlapping each other. Transatlantic migration, mostly originating in the agriculturally structured north-eastern regions of Germany and directed primarily towards the United States, reached its peak between 1880 and 1893; this 'third wave' of overseas emigration at the same time marked the beginning of its decline. Internal migration from East to West, which was primarily oriented towards the industry of the Ruhr region, in some respects resembled a genuine process of immigration in terms of the problems of acculturation and assimilation with which the migrants from the Prussian eastern provinces – the majority of whom were Polish – were confronted.[4] The third form

---

3. See K.J. Bade, 'Transnationale Migration und Arbeitsmarkt im Kaiserreich: Vom Agrarstaat mit starker Industrie zum Industriestaat mit starker agrarischer Basis', in T. Pierenkemper and R. Tilly (eds.), *Historische Arbeitsmarktforschung*, Göttingen, 1982, pp. 182–210.

4. K.J. Bade, 'Massenwanderung und Arbeitsmarkt im deutschen Nordosten von 1880 bis zum Ersten Weltkrieg: Überseeische Auswanderung, interne Abwanderung und kontinentale Zuwanderung', *Archiv für Sozialgeschichte*, vol. 20, 1980, pp. 270–5, 184ff., 227–80; idem, 'German Emigration to the United States and Continental Immigration to Germany in the Late Nineteenth and Early Twentieth Century', in D. Hoerder (ed.), *Labor Migration in the Atlantic Economies. The European and North American Working Class During the Period of Industrialization*, Westport, Conn., 1985, pp. 117–42 (first pub. *Central European History*, vol. 13, no. 4, 1980, pp. 338–77); idem, 'Transatlantic Emigration and Continental Immigration: The German Experience Past and Present', in Bade (ed.), *Population*, pp. 135–62; R.R. Doerries, 'German Transatlantic Migration from the Early 19th Century to the Outbreak of World War I', in Bade (ed.), *Population*, pp. 115–34; C. Kleßmann, *Polnische Bergarbeiter im Ruhrgebiet 1870–1945. Soziale Integration und nationale Subkultur einer Minderheit in der deutschen Industriegesellschaft*, Göttingen, 1978, pp. 337–45; idem, 'Long Distance Migration, Integration and Segregation of an Ethnic Minority in Industrial Germany', in Bade (ed.), *Population*, pp. 101–14; C. Kleßmann and K. Myrzynowska, 'The Polish Press in the Ruhr District and the Leading Role of Wiarus Polski, 1891–1923', in C. Harzig and D. Hoerder (eds.), *The Press of Labor Migrants in Europe and North America*, Bremen,

of labour migration, which is most important for our purposes, developed as 'continental immigration' of foreign workers and became a mass movement with the expansion of industry and agriculture in Germany from the 1890s on.[5] The state of contemporary statistics does not permit firm conclusions about the precise scale of foreign labour immigration, but in 1907 nearly 800,000 foreign workers were registered by the Occupational Census, the equivalent of 4.1 per cent of the total number of employed workers (see Tables 4.1, 4.2 and 4.3).[6]

From the beginning of the twentieth century more than 50 per cent of the foreign labour in Imperial Germany was absorbed by industry. A high proportion of foreign employees was registered in the building trade, the coal, iron and steel industries, in the stone industries and in the textile and metal industries. Foreign working women in the industrial sector were predominantly employed in the textile industry as well as in brickworks. Immigrant workers

---

1985, pp. 129–55. For critical comments on my paper concerning the relationship of migration, foreign labour employment and labour market policy I am grateful to Stephen Hickey.

5. Bade, 'Transnationale Migration', p. 185; Bade, 'Transatlantic Emigration'.

6. The figures on the development of the foreign population between 1871 and 1910, according to nationality (Table 4.1), can only give a 'vague clue about the real number of foreign migrant workers in Germany' (H. Schäfer, 'Italienische "Gastarbeiter" in deutschen Kaiserreich (1890–1914)', *Zeitschrift für Unternehmensgeschichte*, vol. 27, 1982, p. 96). They are based on the quinquennial census, probably the most questionable category of statistical material on the subject; K.J. Bade, 'Arbeiterstatistik zur Ausländerkontrolle: die "Nachweisungen" der preußischen Landräte über den "Zugang, Abgang und Bestand der ausländischen Arbeiter im preußischen Staate" 1906–1914', *Archiv für Sozialgeschichte*, vol. 24, 1984, pp. 166ff. The professional census of 1907 furnishes the most reliable data at the Imperial level (see Table 4.2). Nevertheless, these more accurate figures – which give a more realistic impression about the extent of foreigners' employment during the annual peak, but, according to Klaus J. Bade, are still 10% too low – are quite isolated, and thus cannot give any hints about the temporal development: Bade, 'Arbeiterstatistik', p. 167; K. Dohse, *Ausländische Arbeiter und bürgerlicher Staat: Genese und Funktion von staatlicher Ausländerpolitik und Ausländerrecht. Vom Kaiserreich bis zum BRD*, Königstein, 1981, p. 49; Schäfer, 'Italienische "Gastarbeiter"', pp. 210ff. According to this professional census, 11% (or 50,179) of foreign workers in industry were women, whereas this proportion was much higher in the agricultural sector, where 126,299 women (or 48.5%) were employed; F. Syrup, 'Die ausländischen Industriearbeiter vor dem Kriege', *Archiv für exakte Wirtschaftsforschung*, vol. 9, 1922, pp. 278–80. The statistical source which is most accurate unfortunately only refers to Prussia: the 'lists on the arrival, departure and stock of foreign workers in the Prussian state' ('Nachweisungen über den Zugang, Abgang und Bestand der ausländischen Arbeiter im preußischen Staate') include the period from 1905/6 to 1914. Some figures from these lists are given in Table 4.3 (for a critical edition of these lists see Bade, 'Arbeiterstatistik', pp. 163–284).

Table 4.1 Foreigners in Germany by nationality, 1871–1910

State of Origin	1871	1880	1885	1890	1895	1900	1905	1910
Austria-Hungary	75,702	117,997	156,762	201,542	222,964	390,964	525,821	667,159
Russia	14,535	15,097	26,402	17,107	26,559	46,967	106,639	137,697
Italy	4,019	7,115	9,430	15,570	22,693	69,738	98,165	104,204
Switzerland	24,518	28,241	34,904	40,027	44,875	55,494	62,932	68,257
France	4,671	17,273	24,241	19,659	19,619	20,478	20,584	19,140
Luxembourg	4,828	7,674	9,310	11,189	11,755	13,260	14,169	14,356
Belgium	5,097	4,561	6,638	7,312	8,947	12,122	12,421	13,455
Netherlands	22,042	17,598	27,191	37,055	50,743	88,085	100,997	144,175
Denmark	15,163	25,047	33,134	35,924	28,146	26,565	29,231	26,233
Sweden	12,345	8,483	10,943	10,924	8,937	9,622	8,932	9,675
Norway		1,416	1,727	2,012	2,154	2,715	2,921	3,334
Great Britain/Ireland	10,105	10,465	13,959	14,713	15,290	16,130	17,253	18,319
Rest of Europe	1,177	1,414	2,139	2,322	3,316	5,011	7,114	10,044
United States	10,698	9,046	12,685	14,074	15,788	17,419	17,184	17,572
Other countries	1,855	4,630	3,327	3,824	4,416	4,167	4,197	6,253
Total	206,755	276,057	372,792	433,254	486,202	778,737	1,028,560	1,259,873

Source: I. Britschgi-Schimmer, *Die wirtschaftliche und soziale Lage der italienischen Arbeiter in Deutschland*, Karlsruhe, 1916, p. 34.

Table 4.2 Foreign workers in Germany according to the occupational census of 12 June 1907

Occupational categories	Number of foreign workers	As % of all workers
Agriculture, Horticulture Fishing	279,940	3.8
Industry (total)	440,800	5.1
Skilled workers	187,670	3.8
Unskilled workers	251,466	7.1
Coal, iron and steel	76,906	8.5
Skilled workers	27,296	6.6
Unskilled workers	49,596	10.1
Stone and ceramic	69,055	10.7
Skilled workers	13,960	7.8
Unskilled workers	55,014	11.9
Textiles	46,393	5.4
Skilled workers	19,113	4.9
Unskilled workers	27,090	5.9
Construction	124,645	7.9
Skilled workers	40,915	4.4
Unskilled workers	83,687	13.3
Trade and commerce	45,205	2.3
Casual wage labour	9,120	1.9
Domestic service	24,798	2.0
Total	799,863	4.1

Source: W. Böhmert, 'Die ausländischen Arbeiter in Deutschland', *Der Arbeiterfreund*, vol. 51, 1913, p. 35.

worked primarily in industrial sectors which were 'to a high degree dependent on natural and physical strength',[7] and where the representation of foreigners amounted to 10 per cent; in the Ruhr mining sector, it ranged from 6 to 9 per cent between 1902 and 1911. Most of the foreign workers were occupied in the lower sphere of a

7. On the employment of foreign (and Prussian Polish) women in the textile industry and in brickworks: F. Jerchow, *1883–1983. Die Geschichte der Bremer Wollkämmerei zu Blumenthal. 1 Jahrhundert im Dienste der Textilwirtschaft*, Bremen, 1983; K.M. Barfuß, *"Gastarbeiter" in Nordwestdeutschland 1884–1918*, Bremen, 1986; Schäfer, 'Italienische "Gastarbeiter"; I. Britschgi-Schimmer, *Die*

Table 4.3 Numbers of foreign workers in Prussia at the end of the year, 1906–1914*

1906	218,725
1907	268,388
1908	271,985
1909	282,939
1910	291,412
1911	310,774
1912	332,488
1913	360,510
1914	516,938

* Based on figures for numbers arriving, leaving and remaining in the State of Prussia, in Klaus J. Bade, 'Arbeiterstatistik zur Ausländerkontrolle', *Archiv für Sozialgeschichte*, vol. 24, 1984, pp. 163–284.

split labour market: they had to do jobs that were of above-average risk and did not demand a high level of skill.[8]

From the 1890s, however, foreign labour was also being recruited increasingly into agriculture, particularly in the Prussian eastern provinces. This development has to be interpreted against the background of fundamental structural changes in the agricultural economy and labour markets of these regions.[9] Agricultural entrepreneurs from the 1880s on had tried to overcome the harmful effects of the crisis, which had become evident in this sector by the early 1870s. The main trend was towards the intensification of production, which mostly meant the introduction of root vegetables, and in particular sugar-beet. Given the notorious shortage of capital characteristic of many of the north-east German agrarian employers, the potential for and the pace of mechanisation were limited and thus a dramatic increase was required in the number of

---

wirtschaftliche und soziale Lage der italienischen Arbeiter in Deutschland. Ein Beitrag zur ausländischen Arbeiterfrage, Karlsruhe, 1916; G. Michels-Lindner, 'Die italienischen Arbeiter in Deutschland', *Der Arbeitsmarkt*, vol. 14, 1911, pp. 101–35; M.L. Danieli Camozzi, 'Die Auswanderung italienischer Frauen nach Deutschland und der Schweiz', *Soziale Praxis*, vol. 18, 1909, pp. 1284–9. For a comparative examination: H.-M. Habicht, 'Probleme der italienischen Fremdarbeiter im Kanton St. Gallen vor dem Ersten Weltkrieg', unpublished doctoral diss., Zürich, 1977, pp. 62–80. On industrial sectors with concentrated employment of foreign workers: Dohse, *Ausländische Arbeiter*, p. 48.

8. K.J. Bade, '"Preußengänger" und "Abwehrpolitik": Ausländerbeschäftigung, Ausländerpolitik und Ausländerkontrolle auf dem Arbeitsmarkt in Preußen vor dem Ersten Weltkrieg', *Archiv für Sozialgeschichte*, vol. 24, 1984, p. 106.

9. The following mainly refers to Herbert, *Geschichte*, pp. 19–22, 29ff.

employed workers. In fact, what the agrarian employers needed was an additional labour force influx at specific seasons of the year. The ratio between the highest and lowest labour requirement level during the course of the agricultural year was 4 : 1 for sugar-beet, compared with 1.6 : 1 for cereals. Thus in these peak times masses of seasonal workers appeared to augment the indigenous labour supplied by the stratum of semi-independent peasants and traditional agricultural labourers.

The latter also underwent substantial changes in status and mentality: the social type dominating the landscape of rural life in the German East now was no longer the peasant, but the wage-earner. Seasonal labour migrations in the north-eastern German agricultural regions were at first orientated towards the Prussian province of Saxony – a phenomenon which gave rise to the contemporary term *Sachsengänger* (migrants to Saxony). Settled rural strata became mobile and practised different forms of labour migration, thus aggravating the problem of *Leutenot* (shortage of hands) so frequently complained of by local landlords.

By the beginning of the 1890s it seemed quite clear that only a re-admission of labour from near-by Russian and Austrian regions (in both cases mostly inhabited by Poles) into the agrarian labour market of the Prussian eastern provinces could mitigate this shortage. But in reality this solution did not bring to an end the complex network of labour migration. On the contrary, increased immigration into the eastern German agrarian regions increased the disposition of resident workers to leave the local labour market. Thus, the massive employment of foreign labour, although originally intended as a means of avoiding any profound modernisation of agricultural production and substantial wage increases, tended to become itself a factor accelerating the – already quite advanced – dislocation of the traditional 'landlord order'.[10]

Foreign labour was cheaper both because of nominally lower pay, and because of its highly disposable character, since incapacity to work led to deportation. Nevertheless, it is not so easy to evaluate the average level of wages foreign workers earned in comparison with indigenous colleagues as a reproach often used against them – that they brought down wages – might suggest. Labour immigrants had their own specific expectations concerning wage levels and

10. Ibid., p. 29.

working conditions in Germany. By and large they primarily wanted to improve their living conditions.[11] There was a small heterogeneous group of skilled foreign workers that often earned relatively high wages,[12] but the observation of an Italian contemporary, Jacini, probably better reflects the general situation. He stated that Italian workers in the German construction sector should theoretically have received the standard wage. In reality, however, they earned 10 pfennigs less per hour because of their unorganised status.[13]

Jacini's observation draws our attention to a further complicating factor affecting the situation of foreign labour and contemporary attitudes towards it. Foreign labour could be used as manoeuvrable manpower in times of crisis and prosperity alike, which could lead to an aggravation of labour competition in the lower ranges of a split labour market. Such highly explosive constellations, for example, continuously fed the conflict over the preferential employment of indigenous labour on public construction projects (see below). This situation of 'worker's competition' (*Konkurrenz der Arbeiter*, a term frequently used in contemporary trade unionist papers) was one side of the story. Another was that foreign labourers could form part of an inferior social stratum, thus allowing the professional and socially upward mobility of domestic workers. The relevance of this fact was conceded even by contemporary observers who had their reservations about the employment of foreign labour.[14]

Public and Official Attitudes

There is evidence for the existence of an institutionalised mechanism

11. Bade, '"Preußengänger"'; Schäfer, 'Italienische "Gastarbeiter"', pp. 206, 121.
12. Britschgi-Schimmer, *Die wirtschaftliche und soziale Lage*, pp. 56–62, 72–6; Schäfer, 'Italienische "Gastarbeiter"', pp. 204ff.; Michels-Lindner, 'Die italienischen Arbeiter', pp. 110, 126; Bade, '"Preußengänger"', p. 106.
13. S. Jacini, 'Die italienische Abwanderung nach Deutschland', *Weltwirtschaftliches Archiv*, vol. 5, 1915, p. 131; Michels-Lindner, 'Die italienischen Arbeiter', pp. 123, 128; Britschgi-Schimmer, *Die wirtschaftliche und soziale Lage*, pp. 85–95, 100–5, 168.
14. Bade, '"Preußengänger"', pp. 107, 109 (labour competition); O. Becker, *Die Regelung des ausländischen Arbeiterwesens in Deutschland*, Berlin, 1918, p. 112; A. Winnig, 'Zur Einwandererfrage' (Part II), *Der Grundstein. Offizielles Organ des Zentralverbandes der Maurer Deutschlands* (hereafter *GST*), no. 36, 1916, pp. 189ff., especially p. 189 (upward mobility of domestic workers).

of discrimination against foreign workers designed to exclude them from occupational promotion. This discrimination was sustained by state agencies. In 1911, the Royal High Office of Mines in Breslau described a practice of reserving the worthwhile jobs for indigenous workers. The language decrees issued for the coal, iron and steel industries in the late 1890s had a similar effect: labourers who could not prove sufficient knowledge of the German language were excluded from qualified positions. It was their superiors' duty to determine this competence, a factor which evidently strengthened the immigrants' dependence on these persons.[15] The readiness to discriminate on nationalist grounds, particularly against Poles, was an important element of much of Prussian policy in the Imperial period. The Kaiserreich inherited, amongst other problems connected with the structure and history of the Prussian state, the precarious Prussian-Polish relationship. In the context of the official intention to bring about a 'national homogenisation' in Imperial Germany, this latent tension developed into a sharp conflict.[16] Against the background of a preoccupation with German cultural superiority and the image of a Polish unification movement threatening the security of the Prussian-German state, different battlegrounds for an anti-Polish policy of Germanisation inside Germany were defined.

Two prominent areas of conflict deserve mention: first, measures of discrimination against the language and culture of 'Prussian Poles', and secondly, an agrarian policy that tried to undermine the material security of Poles in the Prussian eastern provinces.[17] Prussian policy tried to restrict immigration by foreign workers of Polish nationality, either from Russian or from Austro-Hungarian parts of the former Polish state, by controlling their numbers,

15. Bade, '"Preußengänger"', p. 105 (Königliches Oberbergamt Breslau); Bade, 'Transnationale Migration', p. 204 (Sprachenverordnungen).
16. See H.-U. Wehler, *Das deutsche Kaiserreich 1871–1918*, Göttingen, 1983, pp. 110–18 (Eng. edn: *The German Empire, 1871–1918*, trans. Kim Traynor, Leamington Spa, Dover, NH, 1985); H.-U. Wehler, 'Polenpolitik im Deutschen Kaiserreich', in H.-U. Wehler, *Krisenherde des Kaiserreichs 1871–1918. Studien zur deutschen Sozial- und Verfassungsgeschichte*, 2nd, rev. and ext. edn, Göttingen, 1979, pp. 181–200; M. Broszat, *Zweihundert Jahre deutsche Polenpolitik*, Frankfurt, 1978, pp. 129–200; R. Blanke, *Prussian Poland in the German Empire (1871–1900)*, New York, 1981; W.W. Hagen, *Germans, Poles, and Jews. The Nationality Conflict in the Prussian East 1772–1914*, Chicago, 1980.
17. See Wehler, *Kaiserreich*, pp. 114ff.; Broszat, *Zweihundert Jahre*, pp. 164ff.; Kleßmann, *Polnische Bergarbeiter*, pp. 90ff.

periods of entry and geographical distribution. The various restrictive regulations against foreign Poles – which will be described in more detail below – were to a large extent responsible for the fact that Imperial Germany did not become a country of immigration in the proper sense, but a 'labour-importing country', in which migrant workers were prohibited from acquiring comprehensive civil rights and maintained as a disposable labour force.[18] The case of nearly 32,000 Poles of either uncertain or Russian and Austrian citizenship, who were expelled from the Prussian eastern provinces in 1885 and 1886 could be seen as a prelude to a period of a harsh anti-Polish policy, only softened during the short 'period of reconciliation' under Caprivi between 1890 and 1894. The mass deportations of the late Bismarck era[19] also throw light on another crucial aspect of foreign labour employment policy and German nationalism during the period under consideration. Nearly 9,000 out of the expelled were Jews, and the anti-Semitic connotations of the deportations were quite clear.[20] On the other hand, the deportations provoked sharp criticism, even from the ranks of conservative politicians, although this was partly motivated by the interests

18. See K.J. Bade, 'Politik und Ökonomie der Ausländerbeschäftigung im preußischen Osten 1885–1914: die Internationalisierung des Arbeitsmarktes im "Rahmen der preußischen Abwehrpolitik"', in H.J. Puhle and H.-U. Wehler (eds.), *Preußen im Rückblick*, Göttingen, 1980, pp. 273–99; Bade, 'Arbeiterstatistik'; idem, 'Kulturkampf auf dem Arbeitsmarkt: Bismarcks Polenpolitik 1885 – 1890', in O. Pflanze (ed.), *Innenpolitische Probleme des Bismarck-Reiches*, Munich, 1983, pp. 121–42.

19. For this context: H. Neubach, *Die Ausweisungen von Polen und Juden aus Preußen 1885/86*, Wiesbaden, 1967; Broszat, *Zweihundert Jahre*, pp. 142–52; H.-U. Wehler, 'Die Polen im Ruhrgebiet bis 1918', in Wehler, *Krisenherde*; Dohse, *Ausländische Arbeiter*, pp. 30ff.; Bade, 'Kulturkampf'; idem, 'Politik und Ökonomie', pp. 281ff.

20. For the whole subject, see (besides the literature just referred to): Hagen, *Germans, Poles and Jews*; S. Jersch-Wenzel, 'Die Lage von Minderheiten als Indiz für den Stand der Emanzipation einer Gesellschaft', in H.-U. Wehler (ed.), *Sozialgeschichte heute. Festschrift für H. Rosenberg*, Göttingen, 1974, pp. 365–87. On Social Democracy and anti-Semitism: R. Leuschen-Seppel, *Sozialdemokratie und Antisemitismus im Kaiserreich. Die Auseinandersetzungen der Partei mit den konservativen und völkischen Strömungen des Antisemitismus 1871–1914*, Bonn, 1978. A work focusing on anti-Semitism and East European Jews in Germany, although mainly referring to the time of the Weimar Republic: T. Maurer, *Ostjuden in Deutschland 1918–1933*, Hamburg, 1986, especially pp. 22ff. (comparative remarks Germany – Great Britain concerning the state attitude towards East European Jews); pp. 161–74 (relation of xenophobia, racism and anti-Semitism); pp. 219–29 (Social Democratic and communist press). By the same author: 'The East European Jew in the Weimar Press: Stereotype and Attempted Rebuttal', *Studies in Contemporary Jewry*, vol. 1, 1984, pp. 176–98.

of agrarian landowners who were afraid of losing a cheap and disposable work force. The employment of foreign labour in agriculture, however, had not yet reached a large scale. In the decades that followed the so-called *Leutenot* on the land became such a pressing problem that the Prussian administration had to make considerable concessions to the economic interests of the agrarian entrepreneurs concerned.[21] To summarise, it can be stated that the 'Polish question' was a key issue in the context of foreign labour employment policy, especially in the Prussian case.

But to examine the issue of labour migration in Imperial Germany and the attitudes towards foreigners expressed by the German state and society, there are still other factors to be taken into consideration. To clarify these points, three main questions, which are only touched on here, need to be discussed.

First, one has to distinguish the respective attitudes of different Länder, as well as the practical implementation of foreign labour policy at different levels of government (municipality, Land, Reich, etc.). In certain Länder a specific anti-Polish bias was nearly absent from decision-making concerning foreign labour (for example, in the southern states of Baden, Württemberg and Bavaria, and – in the north – in Bremen or in the Duchy of Oldenburg.).[22] To state this is not to maintain that Prussian influence had no relevance. Federal diversity, however, must be seen as a constituent element of state policy towards foreign labour in Imperial Germany. In this context the second question arises: what forms of nationalism and resentment did migrant workers of different ethnic or national origins have to face? Or to put the problem in a more general framework, were specific images for respective national groups at all relevant? That forms of xenophobia directed against all groups of seemingly strange or foreign workers and combining 'social discrimination with national prejudices' existed, cannot be doubted.[23] The *Rheinisch-Westfälische Zeitung*, for example, a paper close to Pan-German circles, demanded in 1907 that all Italian, Galician and Croatian workers should be kept out of Germany and should be 'eradicated' (*ausmerzen*) where they were already present.[24] Such

21. Herbert, *Geschichte*, pp. 18ff.
22. See Becker, *Die Regelung*; on Oldenburg, see Barfuß, *"Gastarbeiter"*, especially pp. 181–5.
23. Herbert, *Geschichte*, p. 80.
24. Quoted from ibid., p. 32.

rhetoric, however, already relatively close to later Nazi termin-
ology, was probably too radical for the average anti-Polish minded
Prussian civil servant. And although anti-Slavic resentment was
sometimes even to be found in trade union journals, the Prussian
'policy of prevention' was to such a high degree specifically anti-
Polish, that the Prussian bureaucracy tried to push the employment
of 'slavic' Ruthenian (i.e. Ukrainian) workers as a substitute for the
'slavic' Polish ones. Similarly there does not appear to have been
any political strategy in the various Länder of Imperial Germany to
prevent Italian workers as such from entering the German labour
market. Nevertheless, there was sharp popular resentment and
various forms of discrimination against Italians in different regions.
The image of the Italian strike-breaker was a notorious one.[25]
Angiolo Cabrini, a socialist deputy in the Italian parliament active
in migration matters, pointed out in 1904 that anti-foreign sentiment in Germany was mainly to be found in the indigenous working class and in the 'petty bourgeoisie'.[26] Although this notion still
needs closer examination, Cabrini's remarks throw light on a third
question concerning attitudes towards foreign workers in Imperial
Germany: which individuals, groups, and strata expressed different
kinds of sentiments? And how pervasive were these popular attitudes in different circumstances and for different classes of society,
for example, in influencing the response of indigenous workers to
issues affecting the work-place, industrial action, or housing?

At the beginning of the 1890s the pressure exercised by landowners in the north-eastern regions of Germany on the Prussian
government to re-admit foreign Polish workers had reached a level
which could no longer be ignored by the Caprivi government. Thus
a scheme for their re-admission was elaborated that had to satisfy
these economic interests without challenging the government's
anti-Polish nationalist policy.[27] A permanent settlement by Polish
migrant workers as well as their migration to the industrial western
regions of Germany, where they could have united with Prussian
Poles working there, had to be prevented. Thus the relevant decrees,
issued in November and December of 1890, only allowed the
presence of foreign Poles in the Prussian eastern provinces from

25. In this context, see Michels-Lindner, 'Die italienischen Arbeiter'.
26. *Correspondenzblatt der Generalkommission der Gewerkschaften Deutschlands* (hereafter *CB*), no. 32 1904, pp. 523–7, here p. 525.
27. The following mainly refers to Herbert, *Geschichte*, pp. 22–7, 34–9.

15 November to 1 April – a period that was extended in the years that followed. Migrants of Polish nationality were only allowed to immigrate as individuals, not with their families. Pregnancy was grounds for expulsion. From April 1891 onwards the employment of Polish migrants was also possible in the western Prussian provinces, but their exclusion from industrial occupations in these areas was a constant bone of contention for industrial employers, who frequently tried to obtain official exemptions.[28]

The intention of keeping Polish immigration on a 'rotating basis' was by and large realised. In 1906, nine out of ten Polish workers from outside Germany re-migrated in the late autumn, whereas 53 per cent of the non-Polish foreigners stayed during the whole year.[29] By 1910 statistics recorded a figure of 1,259,000 foreigners in Imperial Germany, or 1.9 per cent of the whole population, against only 260,000 people from abroad (0.5 per cent) in 1871.[30] Nearly 50 per cent of the foreigners in 1910 came from Austria-Hungary. In the same year, together with those people from Russia, Italy and the Netherlands they formed 83 per cent of the foreign population in Germany.

From the late 1890s up to 1907 a further important element in the Prussian-German system of controlling transnational in-migration emerged. A range of different interests was concerned to improve control of mass migration, especially Polish, into the German labour market. The state in Prussia, but also in other parts of Germany, intensified its interest in monitoring the various migrations, Polish or non-Polish, from beyond its borders, but the people moving in at that time were only superficially under the control of state agencies. This fact was partly due to the more or less private character of workforce recruitment. Intensified control of labour migration was also demanded by industrial and agricultural entrepreneurs to prohibit the large-scale arbitrary leaving of workplaces by migrant workers. Especially for foreign workers employed in the agriculture of the German north-east this escape was often the only means to evade miserable working and living conditions.[31] The Preußische Feldarbeiterzentrale (Farm Workers'

28. Bade, '"Preußengänger"', pp. 113–16; idem, 'Politik und Ökonomie', pp. 282ff.
29. Ibid., pp. 27ff.
30. Ibid., pp. 23ff.
31. Ibid., pp. 35–9, 44ff.

Agency), which was called the Deutsche Arbeiterzentrale from 1912 onwards, seemed to be an appropriate institution to guarantee a centralised control of labour immigrants. As a private organisation it was exempt from parliamentary control, yet it had been entrusted with administrative functions.

The institution was of minor importance in the recruitment of foreign labour, but it played a crucial role because of its monopoly power to 'legitimate' (i.e. to control) foreign workers. This activity was based on a decree of the Prussian Ministry of the Interior, issued in December 1907, which provided for the issuing of identity cards for foreign workers. Although at first primarily aimed at Poles, this compulsory legitimation was extended in 1909 to all labourers from abroad who intended to come to Prussia.[32] These identity cards and the corresponding bureaucracy that was created for their supervision, tended to abolish freedom of movement for the migrant workers affected, who in fact, were now confined to one place of work.

None of this should be confused with a consistent state policy towards foreign labour employment in Prussia. As late as 1904, the Prussian Ministry of the Interior had to admit that it was unable to compile a comprehensive list of the instructions on this subject currently in force in the various Prussian provinces. In practice, Prussian ministries represented various interest-groups seeking to exercise influence on this issue: while the Ministry of the Interior was a kind of 'clearing agency'[33], the Ministries of Culture and War called for a strictly restrictive anti-Polish course. The Ministries of Agriculture and Commerce reflected the economic interests of agricultural and industrial employers, and competed with each other for the promotion of 'their' respective sectors. Prussian policy also strongly influenced state behaviour towards foreigners in the whole empire. However, many Länder had only partially intro- duced the Prussian system of control before the First World War, despite the pressure the Prussian government tried to exercise. States as important for Italian immigration as Baden, Württemberg

32. Dohse, *Ausländische Arbeiter*, pp. 66ff., 69–71; K.J. Bade, 'Arbeitsmarkt, Ausländerbeschäftigung und Interessenkonflikt: der Kampf um die Kontrolle über Auslandsrekrutierung und Inlandsvermittlung ausländischer Arbeitskräfte in Preußen vor dem Ersten Weltkrieg', in L. Elsner (ed.), *Fremdarbeiterpolitik des Imperialismus*, no. 10, Rostock, 1981, pp. 29–33, 38–41; Bade, '"Preußengänger"', pp. 121–5.

33. Bade, 'Politik und Ökonomie', p. 297.

and Bavaria did not 'import' the obligatory legitimation cards.[34]

Indeed there was no labour market policy in a general or systematic sense in Germany before 1914. A relevant strategy with its corresponding institutional framework was only implemented for the first time during the Weimar Republic, with a policy towards foreigners as an integral element. Between these two periods, that is during the time of the war economy, different forms of coercive labour, accompanied by far-reaching state intervention, dominated the scene.[35] For the period prior to the First World War only few state initiatives in that direction can be identified. They were mainly intended to reduce the influence of the various professional employment agencies and to lessen the dangers of political instability, that might result from the problem of unemployment.[36] Only some Länder and municipalities tried to develop a more coherent strategy. Here we find the first instances of a rudimentary unemployment insurance and measures like special employment programmes in times of crisis. In connection with this there was also an intention to take labour exchanges into public hands. In particular, the southern German states of Bavaria, Baden, Württemberg and

34. Ibid., p. 290; Becker, *Die Regelung*, pp. 114–19, especially p. 114; K.J. Bade (ed.), *Auswanderer – Wanderarbeiter – Gastarbeiter. Bevölkerung, Arbeitsmarkt und Wanderung in Deutschland seit der Mitte des 19. Jahrhunderts*, Ostfildern, 1984, p. 129.

35. Dohse, *Ausländische Arbeiter*, pp. 77ff., 82; K.J. Bade, 'Arbeitsmarkt, Bevölkerung und Wanderung in der Weimarer Republik', in M. Stürmer (ed.), *Die Weimarer Republik: Belagerte Civitas*, Königstein, 1980, pp. 160–87; idem, 'Labour, Migration and the State: Germany from the late 19th Century to the Onset of the Great Depression', in Bade (ed.), *Population*, pp. 59–86; idem, *Vom Auswanderungsland zum Einwanderungsland? Deutschland 1880–1980*, Berlin, 1983; idem, 'Die ausländischen Arbeiter in der Landwirtschaft der östlichen und mittleren Gebiete des deutschen Reiches während des 1. Weltkrieges. Ein Beitrag zur Geschichte der preußisch-deutschen Politik', unpub. thesis, Rostock, 1981; idem, 'Die polnischen Arbeiter in der deutschen Landwirtschaft während des ersten Weltkrieges', MS, Rostock, 1975; idem, 'Liberale Ausländerpolitik oder Modifizierung der Zwangsarbeitpolitik? Zur Diskussion und zu den Erlassen über die Behandlung polnischer Landarbeiter in Deutschland 1916/17', *Jahrbuch für Geschichte der sozialistischen Länder Europas*, vol. 22, no. II, 1978, pp. 85–105; idem, 'Belgische Zwangsarbeiter in Deutschland während des ersten Weltkrieges', *Zeitschrift für Geschichtswissenschaft*, vol. 11, 1976; idem, 'Zur Haltung der rechten SPD- und Gewerkschaftsführer in der Einwanderungsfrage während des 1. Weltkrieges', *Wissenschaftliche Zeitschrift der Universität Rostock. Gesellschafts- und Sprachwissenschaftliche Reihe*, 1976, pp. 687–91; F. Zunkel, 'Die ausländischen Arbeiter in der Kriegswirtschaftspolitik des 1. Weltkriegs', in G.A. Ritter (ed.), *Entstehung und Wandlung der modernen Gesellschaft*, Berlin, 1970, pp. 280–311.

36. The following mainly refers to A. Faust, 'Arbeitsmarktpolitik in Deutschland im 19. und 20. Jahrhundert: die Arbeitsvermittlung im Wechsel arbeitsmarktpolitischer Strategien', in Bade (ed.), *Auswanderer*, pp. 216–53.

the *Reichslande* of Elsaß-Lothringen implemented a scheme, consisting of co-ordinated public labour exchanges at the district (*Re-
gierungsbezirk*) level in order to achieve a certain balance between
the supply and demand for labour. These agencies also became more
or less successful competitors with the professional private labour
exchanges. Thus in 1909 in Bavaria the public exchanges could claim
to have made twice as many job-placements as the private agencies,
whereas at the beginning of the century, the two kinds of labour
exchange had enjoyed a rough parity.

Nevertheless, taken as a whole, the public labour exchanges' role
in the labour market of Imperial Germany before 1914 remained
relatively marginal – although one of the few initiatives undertaken
on an Imperial level in this period, the Law Concerning Employment Agencies of 1910, had indeed managed to weaken the position
of the relevant private institutions.[37] According to an estimate by
Anselm Faust, the share of the various public labour exchanges in
labour market placements in the Reich in 1912 did not exceed 30 per
cent: for Westphalia the comparable figure for 1913 was 13 per
cent.[38] In contrast to the relatively elaborate system of foreign
workers' control which Prussia and other Länder had implemented
before 1914, the responsible Feldarbeiterzentrale – itself not a
public, but a private organisation only charged with functions
defined as public – had only a minor influence on the recruitment of
labour from abroad. Thus the freedom of employers to recruit
foreign labour was not effectively limited by this agency, as long as
the employers obeyed the primarily politically motivated regulations for controlling foreign workers. The more or less bizarre
state of things in Prussia can be neatly illustrated by the fact that it
was the duty of the local police, not of public labour exchanges, to
oversee the observance of these regulations. It was thus left to the
southern German states and to some municipalities rather than to
Prussia to meet half-way the trade unions' increasingly articulate
demands for a public labour-market policy. In 1909 the Bavarian
state ministry issued a decree on the introduction of municipal
institutions for unemployment insurance, which provided for the
public funding of appropriate trade union insurance schemes
(*Genter System*),[39] along similar lines to the system introduced by

37. Ibid., p. 226.
38. See ibid., p. 236.
39. M.T. Wermel and R. Urban, *Arbeitslosenfürsorge und Arbeitslosenversicherung*

the municipality of Strasbourg in 1907.

A similar co-operation between unions and the state in the south of Germany and in a number of municipalities could be found in related areas of social policy. Thus in 1901 the unionist *Correspondenzblatt* praised the new principles for the award of public works, adopted by the Bavarian parliament following a Social Democratic initiative, as an 'essential step forward' in social policy.[40] In addition to regulations on wage levels and working time, a special section provided for the preferential employment of indigenous workers. It anticipated principles of foreign labour employment policy which on the Reich level were first realised in the Weimar Republic: 'The employment of other [than indigenous/M.F.] workers is only allowed at identical wage and working conditions'.[41] Although this kind of state intervention can indeed be interpreted as an early example of labour market policy in the proper sense of the word, it only affected the public works sector. For the Prussian regulations the contrary was true: they had a relatively broad scope (i.e. the labour market in Prussia as a whole), but only scratched the surface of labour employment policy, without doing serious harm to 'capital's freedom of recruitment' (Dohse) of labour as such. Of course, if Polish workers were concerned, the Prussian regulations could, in fact, be quite annoying for employers.

Trade Unions and Foreign Labour: A Precarious Relationship

The terms internationalism and protectionism seem to be appropriate categories for a preliminary examination of the trade unions' attitude to foreign workers. These terms are seen here as antagonistic poles between which concrete trade-union policy was formed. Before 1914, elements of both tendencies were latent in different factions of the Social-Democrat-orientated labour movement in Germany.[42]

---

in *Deutschland*, 3 vols., Munich, 1949, vol. I, p. 85; A. Faust, 'Arbeitsmarktpolitik in Deutschland: Die Entstehung der öffentlichen Arbeitsvermittlung 1890–1927', in Pierenkemper and Tilly (eds.), *Historische Arbeitsmarktforschung*, pp. 253–73, here pp. 262ff., 267.

40. *CB*, no. 47, 1901, p. 759.

41. Ibid., p. 759.

42. For another view see, for example, L. Elsner, 'Zur Stellung der Arbeiterbewe-

In the 1890s discussions of transnational labour migration were nearly always combined with a plea for international freedom of movement. As the *Grundstein*, the journal of the construction workers' union, wrote in 1894, this freedom had to be seen as a guarantee of 'international political freedom' and of economic development, just as any 'progress in the direction towards socialism' seemed unimaginable without that freedom.[43] The ultimate solution for the problems that arose from international labour migration, and which also affected indigenous labour, would come only from a 'profound . . . transformation of the mode of production'. In the meantime international labour legislation and an increased influence of the unions on the regulation of working conditions were seen as appropriate means to weaken 'international competition' among workers.[44] Nominally the idea of international freedom of movement remained a positive point of reference up to 1914; but in the first decade of the twentieth century its implicit meaning underwent substantial modifications. This is evident from the reception of the respective declarations of the Second International by German trade unions. Various trade-union papers praised the internationalist spirit of the Stuttgart resolution on 'Immigration and emigration' adopted by the International Socialist Congress in 1907.[45] But at the

---

gung zur Ausländerbeschäftigung im wilhelminischen Kaiserreich und in der BRD', in idem (ed.), *Fremdarbeiter*, no. 4, 1978, pp. 10ff.; idem, 'Zur Haltung der Arbeiterbewegung zu Migrationen, zur Ausländerbeschäftigung und Ausländerpolitik imperialistischer Länder im 20. Jahrhundert', in idem (ed.), *Fremdarbeiter*, no. 15, 1983; idem, 'Deutsche Arbeiterbewegung und eingewanderte ausländische Arbeiter 1900 bis 1933', in idem (ed.), *Fremdarbeiter*, no. 16, 1985, pp. 15ff.; J. Nichtweiß, *Die ausländischen Saisonarbeiter in der Landwirtschaft der östlichen und mittleren Gebiete des Deutschen Reiches 1890–1914*, Berlin, 1959, pp. 156–68.

43. *GST*, no. 23, 1894, p. 2.

44. Ibid., p. 2; *GST*, no. 35, 1891, p. 6.

45. On the Internationalist Socialists' Congress, Amsterdam 1904: *GST*, no. 35, 1904, pp. 346ff.; Nichtweiß, *Die ausländischen Saisonarbeiter*, p. 157; *Internationaler Sozialistenkongreß zu Amsterdam 14. bis 20. August 1904*, Berlin, 1904, pp. 52ff. On Stuttgart 1907: *Internationaler Sozialisten-Kongreß zu Stuttgart 1907 vom 18. bis 24. August 1907*, Berlin, 1907, pp. 57–64, 119ff., especially pp. 58ff.; for the reception of the resolution in the literature, see for example: H. Anagnostidis, 'Gewerkschaften und Ausländerbeschäftigung', in E. Klee (ed.), *Gastarbeiter. Analysen und Berichte*, Frankfurt, 1972; P. Cinanni, *Emigration und Imperialismus*, Munich, 1976; M. Diamant, 'Bemerkungen zur sozialen und rechtlichen Lage der ausländischen Arbeitnehmer: Ausländergesetz '65 – Alternativentwurf '70', *studentische politik*, vol. 1, 1970; Dohse, *Ausländische Arbeiter*; Elsner, 'Zur Stellung'; idem, 'Zur Haltung der Arbeiterbewegung'; idem, 'Deutsche Arbeiterbewegung'; Nichtweiß, *Die ausländischen Saisonarbeiter*.

same time they insisted that the resolution subscribed to a credo of 'wise . . . restriction' of immigration. This was more a readjustment of the Stuttgart paper to their own position than a correct interpretation of the intentions of that declaration.[46]

In the last years before 1914 the attitude towards foreign workers on the part of German trade unions had been dominated by a resignation about the possibility of ever organising them.[47] There had been attempts to integrate migrant workers from abroad into the indigenous labour movement, relying on agitation by leaflets and journals and co-operation with labour organisations in different countries of origin, especially in Italy. But these attempts were not as successful as the German trade-union activists had hoped – to say the least. In 1912 August Winnig, an official of the construction workers' union, complained that only 6,000 to 7,000 of 130,000 Italian workers in Germany had joined the unions.[48] Various factors were responsible for this frustrating fact. The primary concern of foreign migrant workers was to improve their (or their relatives') living conditions by migratory work. Especially at the beginning of their career as migrants most of them did not want to threaten this objective by trade-union activities, which could always lead to expulsion. At the same time German trade unions had difficulty understanding the specific needs of their foreign colleagues. This became evident when the latter made their own way to class-consciousness and to industrial action. Immigrant or seasonal migrant workers, as well as Polish workers with German citizenship working mainly in the Ruhr (the so-called *Ruhrpolen*), displayed a capacity for taking part in industrial action and for organising themselves to defend their interests, as in the case of the Polish Professional Union (Zjednoczenie zawodowe Polskie, ZZP), founded at Bochum in 1902.[49] But whenever foreign workers attempted to

---

46. *GST*, no. 36, 1907, pp. 433ff.
47. *CB*, no. 22, 1912, pp. 249ff.; see Schäfer, 'Italienische "Gastarbeiter"', p. 209; *Protokoll der Verhandlungen des zehnten Kongresses der Gewerkschaften Deutschlands, abgehalten zu München vom 22. bis 27. Juni 1914*, Berlin, 1914, pp. 171ff.; *GST*, no. 27, 1914, p. 336.
48. *CB*, no. 17, 1912, p. 259.
49. *GST*, no. 11, 1903, p. 99; *GST*, no. 5, 1906, p. 53; *GST*, no. 9, 1902, p. 4; *GST*, no. 38, 1909, p. 448; *GST*, no. 5, 1901, p. 3; *GST*, no. 5, 1908, p. 49; *GST*, no. 25, 1909, p. 28; *GST*, no. 32, 1909, p. 378 ('danger of separatism'). Kleßmann, *Polnische Bergarbeiter*, pp. 110–25; Wehler, 'Die Polen', pp. 230–2; *CB*, no. 3, 1912, p. 41; no. 9, p. 132; *CB*, no. 9, 1914, p. 135.

form special branches within German trade unions or to found separate organisations for themselves, trade-union leaders were worried that this might foster the 'danger of separatism'.

As long as the foreign workers were perceived (for whatever reason) as competitors rather than potential trade union colleagues, protectionism appeared attractive, and it is clear that the statements of German trade unions tended to become more protectionist up to 1914. At the same time, their actual policies were characterised by continuing uncertainty which varied in particular with economic circumstances. There are indications of a positive correlation between protectionism and economic crisis during two periods at the beginning of the twentieth century. In 1900 – that is during the depression which lasted from 1900 to 1902 – a conference of the mine-workers' union held in Altenburg urged the Imperial government to prohibit a further 'import of alien labourers of foreign language into the mining districts' on the grounds that an inability to understand German might cause danger at the place of work. At that time the *Grundstein* used stronger words to characterise immigrant Italian workers (they were, for example, referred to as 'a public nuisance'), and this was formulated with explicit reference to 'economic crisis and employment'.[50] During the crisis of 1907–8, there is plenty of evidence for appeals addressed to employers to stop the 'import' of foreign workers, at least from representatives of the mine-workers' and the construction workers' unions.[51]

It was in these years, too, that the debate on a preferential employment of indigenous workers at public construction works (and the vehement agitation by the trade unions for this preference) reached its first peak. It is unclear, however, whether attitudes expressed at conferences or in trade-union papers were solely those

50. Wehler, *Kaiserreich*, p. 51 ('depression' 1900–1902); M. Schippel, 'Die Konkurrenz der fremden Arbeitskräfte. Zur Tagesordnung des Stuttgarter internationalen Kongresses', *Sozialistische Monatshefte, Internationale Revue des Sozialismus* (hereafter *SMH*), 1906, p. 739; Kleßmann, *Polnische Bergarbeiter*, pp. 18, 63ff.; Wehler, 'Die Polen', pp. 234–6; *Bergarbeiterzeitung. Organ zur Förderung der Interessen der Bergarbeiter und verwandten Berufe* (hereafter *BZ*), no. 26, 1901, p. 413; *CB*, no. 39, 1900, pp. 9–11; *Protokoll über die Verhandlungen des Parteitages der Sozialdemokratischen Partei Deutschlands. Abgehalten zu Mainz vom 17. bis 21. September 1900*, Berlin, 1900, pp. 188–200, especially p. 188. See also: G.A. Ritter, *Die Arbeiterbewegung im Wilhelminischen Reich. Die sozialdemokratische Partei und die Freien Gewerkschaften 1890–1900*, Berlin, 1963, pp. 192ff. (Altenburg conference 1900).

51. See *BZ*, no. 26, 1908, p. 1; no. 27, p. 4; no. 31, p. 5; no. 32, p. 1; no. 44, p. 6; no. 47, p. 3. *GST*, no. 11, 1908, p. 1; no. 41, p. 456; no. 44, p. 485.

of officials or if they represented the views shared by rank and file members as well. With some caution, it can be said that there were internationalist as well as protectionist currents among the rank and file of trade unions.[52]

In the years between 1914 and 1918 the trend towards protectionism strengthened. An indication of this was a debate on postwar immigration of foreign workers that took place in the trade-union press in 1916.[53] The debate was initiated by the *Grundstein*, which published about thirty articles and letters, but soon other trade-union and Social Democratic papers became involved. In the debate legal measures to guarantee priority to indigenous workers' interests were once again demanded, with statements coloured by nationalistic accusations against foreign labourers.[54]

---

52. In 1911 the *Grundstein* appealed to the unions' members not to vent their anger about Italian welfare in Tripoli on their 'Italian workmates'. Siegfried Nestriepke, a historian of the German trade unions' movement, stated in 1922 that strong discontent about the competition of foreign construction workers had been widespread among members of the organisation even before 1914, but that this had been suppressed by headquarters. On the other hand, especially local branches of the unions that had long-lasting experiences with migrant workers from abroad, insisted on an increased consideration for the specific situation of their foreign colleagues. They often rejected tendencies in trade-union policy which might have deepened the cleavage between domestic and foreign labourers. *GST*, no. 47, 1911, p. 573; S. Nestriepke, *Die Gewerkschaftsbewegung*, Stuttgart, 1922, vol. 2, p. 70; Deutscher Bauarbeiterverband (ed.), *Protokoll über die Verhandlungen des zweiten (außerordentlichen) Verbandstages*, Hamburg, 1914, pp. 61ff.; *GST*, no. 43, 1904, p. 417; *GST*, no. 7, 1906, pp. 86ff.; *GST*, no. 32, 1901, pp. 5ff.; *CB*, 1905, p. 210.

53. On the issue of the working-class movement and foreign labour in the First World War, see Bade, *Vom Auswanderungsland zum Einwanderungsland?*, pp. 46ff.; Dohse, *Ausländische Arbeiter*, pp. 77–83; Elsner, 'Die ausländischen Arbeiter'; idem, 'Die polnischen Arbeiter'; idem, 'Belgische Zwangsarbeiter'; idem, 'Zur Haltung der rechten SPD- und Gewerkschaftsführer'; idem, 'Liberale Ausländerpolitik'; Zunkel, 'Die ausländischen Arbeiter'; C.H. Riegler, 'Arbeitskräfterekrutierung für die deutsche Kriegswirtschaft in neutralen Ländern unter besonderer Berücksichtigung Schwedens, 1915 bis 1919', in L. Elsner (ed.), *Fremdarbeiter*, no. 10, 1981, pp. 63–81; G.P. Feldman, *Army, Industry, and Labor in Germany 1914–1918*, Princeton, 1966; R.B. Armeson, *Total Warfare and Compulsory Labor*, The Hague, 1964; U. Herbert, 'Zwangsarbeit als Lernprozeß. Zur Beschäftigung ausländischer Arbeiter in der westdeutschen Industrie im Ersten Weltkrieg', *Archiv für Sozialgeschichte*, vol. 24, 1984, pp. 285–304; H.-J. Bieber, *Gewerkschaften in Krieg und Revolution. Arbeiterbewegung, Industrie, Staat und Militär in Deutschland 1914–1970*, Hamburg, 1981; J.A. Moses, *Trade Unionism in Germany from Bismarck to Hitler 1869–1933*, London, 1982, vol. 1, pp. 177–212.

54. For the whole debate see Schäfer, 'Italienische "Gastarbeiter"', pp. 211–13; D. Kachulle (ed.), *Die Pöhlands im Krieg. Briefe einer sozialdemokratischen Bremer Arbeiterfamilie aus dem 1. Weltkrieg*, Cologne, 1982, pp. 23, 211; Elsner, 'Zur Haltung der Arbeiterbewegung'; idem, 'Zur Haltung der rechten SPD- und Gewerk-

It is quite evident that nationalist currents played a decisive role in the protectionist shift of the labour movement's attitude towards foreign labour during the war. An examination of other factors that may have influenced this shift is nevertheless illuminating. These might include the following:

(1) the quantitative development of immigration during the war,
(2) an increased demand for labour which might have enhanced the unions' self-confidence in confronting employers and the state,
(3) the fear by trade unions and other contemporary witnesses that an uncontrolled labour immigration after the war might aggravate the problem of unemployment.

One cannot deny that each of these factors had a specific importance. There was indeed increased immigration during the war, after a dramatic reduction of foreign labour during the first months of hostilities.

The increased number of foreign workers in the German war-economy from 1915 onwards was partly due to recruitment of labour in the occupied territories of Poland and Belgium. Their recruitment and working conditions once they arrived in Germany were by and large characterised by the use of force. That force had already played a crucial role in the pre-war policy towards foreign labour in Imperial Germany is something which may be recalled at this point. The existence of virtual forced labour in the war-economy as such cannot be denied, despite differing views among scholars on its spatial and temporal scale. The academic debate on this issue – which in the context of this essay can only be briefly mentioned – also raises the question of the continuities and discontinuities of foreign labour policy in Germany from the Imperial to the Nazi period.[55] According to official statistics, between 1915 and 1918 up

---

schaftsführer'. For the *Grundstein* statements referred to here, see e.g. *GST*, no. 29, 1916, p. 160; no. 49, p. 250; Forberg, 'Freie Gewerkschaften', pp. 113–22, especially p. 116 (complete lists of articles on that subject published in the *Grundstein*).

55. See Zunkel, 'Die ausländischen Arbeiter' on the one hand and Elsner, 'Liberale Ausländerpolitik'; Elsner, 'Belgische Zwangsarbeiter'; for a synthesis: Herbert, 'Zwangsarbeit'; idem, *Geschichte*, pp. 82ff. On the question of continuity see Bade, *Vom Auswanderungsland zum Einwanderungsland?*, pp. 52ff.; Herbert, *Geschichte*, pp. 173–8.

to 240,000 persons were recruited from Poland: the figure for Belgian workers amounts to 130,000. In the period of the war-economy even larger masses of highly disposable foreign labour were provided by prisoners of war. In 1916 1,105,000 out of a total number of 1,625,000 POWs in German custody (or 68 per cent) had to work inside Germany.[56] Agriculture absorbed 735,000 prisoners of war (or 45 per cent of the total number), whereas industry had to be content with the employment of 331,000 (or 20 per cent) and 39,000 (2 per cent) had to carry out so-called 'works of public utility' (*gemeinnützige Arbeiten*).[57] There was thus probably some reason for the trade unions to complain about the employment of such a large number of disposable competitors. And opinions of this kind are indeed to be found in the unions' press, where it was stated that the employment of prisoners of war in agriculture and the mining industry might lead to deteriorating labour conditions for indigenous workers. On the other hand, the number of labour migrants from Italy, who drew much attention in the debate of 1916, had actually fallen dramatically just at the beginning of the war. Whereas the legitimation figures counted about 65,000 Italian workers for the years 1913–14, only about 13,000 were reported for 1914–15.[58]

The debate of 1916 also reflected the fundamental change in the state's attitude towards trade unions during the war. The history of the Auxiliary Service Law of December 1916 in particular had shown that the state needed the unions for the maximum mobilis-ation of labour for the war-economy.[59] The unions in their turn could, and in fact did, expect the realisation of their long-standing demand for legal recognition. The 1916 debate was also influenced by the expectation that projected mass unemployment at the end of the war might be aggravated by a large scale immigration of foreign workers. This danger of mass unemployment connected with post-war demobilisation had already shaped the programme (*Leitsätze*)

56. Herbert, *Geschichte*, pp. 91, 96, 99ff.; L. Elsner, 'Ausländerbeschäftigung und Zwangsarbeitpolitik in Deutschland während des Ersten Weltkrieges', in Bade (ed.), *Auswanderer*, p. 539.
57. Herbert, *Geschichte*, p. 85.
58. Ibid., p. 87.
59. See Feldman, *Army*, pp. 197–249; for a summary of recent research on the subject, U. Ratz, 'Vom sozialen Protest zur kollektiven Interessensvertretung. Neuerscheinungen zur Geschichte der deutschen Arbeiterbewegung', *Neue Politische Literatur*, vol. 31, no. 1, 1986, pp. 5–20, especially pp. 10–18.

on labour market problems published by trade unions of all ideological tendencies and the Gesellschaft für soziale Reform in March 1915.[60]

As an alternative to protectionism trade unions could pursue a strategy of eliminating the legal discrimination that made foreign labour cheap and attractive to employers. Like the call for the protection of indigenous labour, this strategy brought the unions into direct dialogue with state institutions, in terms (the denial and assertion of civil rights) particularly familiar to both sides. The German Social Democratic labour movement as a whole condemned any measure taken by the state to push immigrant workers into an unequal position, whether in the political or juridical field. It was in this context that the government was strongly criticised for the shelter it gave to foreign (and domestic) strike-breakers.[61] The state's policy of arbitrary expulsions, which was not only directed against political activists, was bitterly attacked by the Social Democratic Party and the trade-union movement at every opportunity, both in parliamentary debates and at party rallies.[62] And it was with the same logic that the unions opposed any policy towards foreigners that gave them significantly fewer rights than natives. For in circumstances of legal discrimination, any attempts to organise foreign migrant workers in considerable numbers were bound to fail.

The right of foreigners in general and foreign workers in particular to take part in coalitions was an item of related importance, and the precarious situation of foreigners in respect to that right was frequently denounced.[63] In that context the Imperial Law on Associations (*Reichsvereinsgesetz*) provoked further opposition: leading figures in the trade unions reacted vehemently to the introduction

60. Zunkel, 'Die Stellung', pp. 298ff.
61. State and strike-breaking activities: K. Saul, 'Zwischen Repression und Integration. Staat, Gewerkschaften und Arbeitskampf im kaiserlichen Deutschland 1884 bis 1914', in K. Tenfelde and H. Volkmann (eds.), *Streik*, Munich, 1981, pp. 209–36, especially p. 225; Michels–Lindner, 'Die italienischen Arbeiter', p. 151 (Italian strike-breakers).
62. See Dohse, *Ausländische Arbeiter*, pp. 73–5.
63. Ibid. pp. 73–5; *CB*, 1895, p. 168; *BZ*, no. 17, 1906, pp. 1ff.; *BZ*, no. 6, 1907, p. 5; *BZ*, no. 52, 1909, p. 2; *BZ*, no. 49, 1909, p. 1; *GST*, no. 47, 1908, p. 520; *Protokoll über die Verhandlungen des Parteitages der Sozialdemokratischen Partei Deutschlands. Abgehalten zu Essen vom 15. bis 21. September 1907*, Berlin, 1907, pp. 276ff., 283ff., 287; see Nichtweiß, *Die ausländischen Saisonarbeiter*, pp. 161ff.; Elsner, 'Zur Stellung', pp. 13ff.

of the foreign workers' 'legitimation card' in 1907 – and did not confine themselves to strong words.[64]

The rudiments of an alternative policy towards foreigners were evolved by the trade unions and their press. In 1904 the *Correspondenzblatt* under the headline 'Foreign workers policy' tried to formulate a standpoint in accordance with the interests of the 'international working class'. It proposed treaties between different countries to guarantee their respective citizens all rights necessary for occupational activities in all signatory states. Equal rights for natives and foreigners alike was to be the guiding principle.[65] A 'social treaty' signed between France and Italy in 1904 was conceived as the model. Three years later the same journal advocated the legal guarantee of security of status for foreigners as well as a reduction in state administrative power: it also demanded that naturalisation be made easier. If these proposals were realised, the paper argued, a more effective control of immigration could be made possible. The article favoured bilateral treaties, with the additional argument that they might lead to 'social education amongst those nations which are inferior to us in culture and standard of living'.[66]

It was with the demand for the preferential employment of indigenous workers on public construction projects that the trade unions went most decidedly beyond the familiar (if not purely altruistic) defence of civil rights to urge a positive policy innovation and a direct intervention by the state in employment practices. The particular relevance of this problem was connected with the following factors: first, only where the state itself acted as sole employer could it decide on the composition of the labour force. Thus, different groups with quite contrary interests concerning the employment of foreign labour focused on this sector in order to influence state decisions. Secondly, the organisations of the indigenous working class had to defend their claim for a privileged treatment of German workers against strong interests. On the one hand, the bureaucracy was in favour of cheaper foreign labour in order to lower construction costs. On the other hand, agrarian employers

---

64. *CB*, no. 16, 1908, pp. 241–3; no. 15, pp. 228–30; no. 19, pp. 281–7; H. Block, 'Das Reichsvereinsgesetz', *NZ*, vol. 2, 1907, pp. 85–93; Nichtweiß, *Die ausländischen Saisonarbeiter*, pp. 165ff., 163ff., 166ff.; Dohse, *Ausländische Arbeiter*, p. 72.
65. *CB*, no. 31, 1904, pp. 507–10; no. 32, pp. 523–7.
66. *CB*, no. 30, 1907, pp. 465–7; no. 31, pp. 481–4; no. 32, pp. 497–500.

in particular tried to reduce the 'pull effect' on labour exercised by large canal construction works, and were therefore strongly interested in an increased employment of foreigners on such projects.[67] In the period before the First World War the trade unions were unable to achieve the realisation of their programme and the history of the issue itself was a chequered one. In the 1890s the employment of foreign workers on public works was discussed quite frequently in the press of the Social Democratic labour movement. On the occasion of the construction of the canal between the North Sea and the Baltic (Nord-Ostseekanal), the *Grundstein* criticised the fact that primarily 'Russians, Poles, Italians' had been employed there because these workers were 'cheaper and less demanding than Germans'.[68] During these years a positive discrimination in favour of indigenous labourers was sometimes demanded by Social Democratic and trade-union organisations at the local level. A Prussian decree of 1898, clearly issued to increase the number of foreign workers on public works at the expense of workers from the agricultural areas east of the river Elbe, caused strong protests by trade-union, Social Democratic and some 'bourgeois' papers as well. From that time on the demand for the preferential employment of indigenous workers on public works became an integral part of the Social Democratic labour movement's programme on labour market policy. Originally these aspirations could be seen as disorganised attempts by indigenous workers, more or less emotionally motivated, to block undesirable competition.[69] The leadership of both the Social Democratic Party and the trade unions gradually adapted themselves to that trend. The claim for a preferential employment of natives was initially to be limited to public works, and was only later to be extended to the whole construction industry. During times of economic crisis the supplementary demand for a systematic public organisation of the labour market in order to reduce unemployment was raised,[70] although this policy

67. Dohse, *Ausländische Arbeiter*, pp. 55–7.
68. *GST*, no. 28, 1908, p. 4 ('Nord-Ostseekanal'); *GST*, no. 1, 1892, p. 3 (Hanover); *GST*, no. 3, 1893, p. 4; no. 8, p. 6; no. 10, p. 6 Nuremberg; *GST*, no. 32 (1895), p. 5; no. 33, pp. 4ff.; no. 34, pp. 4ff.; no. 35, p. 3; no. 37, p. 4 (Flensburg) (local claims for positive discrimination in favour of indigenous workers).
69. Dohse, *Ausländische Arbeiter*, p. 56; Bade, 'Politik und Ökonomie', p. 286; *GST*, no. 19, 1898, p. 1; no. 24, p. 2; Nichtweiß, *Die ausländischen Saisonarbeiter*, p. 58 (Decree, 1898); Schippel, 'Die Konkurrenz', pp. 737ff.
70. See for example; *GST*, no. 45, 1901, pp. 1ff.; *CB*, 1902, p. 53.

did not go unchallenged within the labour movement. Critical voices warned against the danger of increasing divisions between indigenous and foreign workers by the programme of employment preference. Hermann Molkenbuhr, a prominent trade unionist and Social Democratic politician, in an article for the journal *Die Neue Zeit* stated that the 'natives first' slogan in fact meant a suspension of the principle of 'international solidarity' in times of crisis.[71]

The net effects of the labour movement's fight for preferential treatment for indigenous workers remained meagre in the period before 1914. In some Länder (particularly in Bavaria and Baden) and at the municipal level, public regulations were adopted which at least partly satisfied the aspirations of the Social Democratic Party and trade unions.[72] But they could not exert a substantial influence on public employment policy in Prussia. Especially in the years between 1907 and 1913 there were debates on the employment of foreigners for construction projects connected with the extension of the Nord-Ostseekanal, which involved different factions of the Prussian and Imperial bureaucracy, as well as deputies of political parties, representatives of both employers and employees, and the Labour Exchange Associations (*Arbeitsnachweisverbände*), especially in the north of Germany. At a session of the Prussian parliament on 27 April 1907 the Prussian Minister for Public Works, Breitenbach, mentioned the worry of agrarian employers that public works might entice hands away from their estates. Building entrepreneurs ought to be influenced to prefer foreign workers, the minister argued. Five days later the state secretary of the Imperial Ministry of the Interior, Posadowsky, advocated giving preference to 'German industry and German manpower' in the construction of the canal. At the same session this statement was avidly supported by a Social Democratic deputy. However, in 1908,

---

71. H. Molkenbuhr, 'Zur Frage der Arbeitslosenversicherung', *NZ*, vol. 2, 1901/2, pp. 723–30, especially p. 729.
72. *GST*, no. 45, 1901, p. 1 (Bavaria, Baden), *CB*, no. 47, 1901, p. 759; *CB*, no. 35, 1907, pp. 545–7; M. Schippel, 'Die fremden Arbeitskräfte und die Gesetzgebung der verschiedenen Länder, Materialien für den Stuttgarter Internationalen Kongreß', *NZ*, supplement to no. 41 (1906/7), p. 61 (Bavaria); *GST*, no. 49, 1908, p. 531–3; J. Ludwig, *Die wirtschaftliche und soziale Lage der Wanderarbeiter in Großherzogtum Baden*, Karlsruhe, 1915, p. 111 (Baden); R. Calwer in *Bremer Bürgerzeitung*, 18 January 1903; see also A.S. v. Waltershausen, 'Die italienischen Wanderarbeiter', in *Festschrift für A.S. Schultze*, Leipzig, 1903, pp. 91–3 (Saxony); Schippel, 'Die fremden Arbeitskräfte', pp. 60–3; Becker, *Die Regelung*, pp. 47–50, 53ff., 66; Dohse, *Ausländische Arbeiter*, p. 65.

Minister Breitenbach, in a letter addressed to the Verband deutscher Tiefbauunternehmer, promised that employers would be free to use foreign labour. This policy was commented upon in bitter terms by the *Correspondenzblatt*: '25,000 foreigners are employed on public works at a time when hundreds of thousands of German workers are without work; that indeed means dashing the bread out of the hands of the native workers . . .'.[73]

In 1909 the Imperial Canal Bureau issued a decree that prescribed the preferential use of German labourers, if two important conditions were met: 'appropriate' indigenous labour had to be available and in sufficient numbers. According to the decree employment exchanges should have an important function in the recruitment of indigenous workers. But given these conditions, it was not difficult for the employers to increase the employment of foreign labour: the indigenous labour supply could simply be classified as 'inappropriate'.[74] In fact the employment exchanges in various towns of North Germany had simply been ignored by the building employers. A survey from 1911 clearly showed that they would have been able to recruit 'appropriate' German labour if wages had been raised to the level of forty pfennigs per hour. The Canal Bureau's reaction to that criticism was quite ambiguous. On the one hand, it warned that to raise the wages would mean to disturb the employers' (and thus the state's) calculations. On the other hand, the entrepreneurs were urged to employ more indigenous labour, otherwise they might lose the permission to employ foreign labourers at all.

In the event the first condition prevailed: the calculation remained undisturbed and the proportion of foreign labour on the dry sector of the canal construction works went up to 36 per cent. A 'competition from foreign labour' was also felt in the wet sector which was taking on more qualified workers: in 1913, the union paper *Deutscher Maschinist und Heizer* (German Machinist and Fireman) reported that about two-thirds of the workers in the wet

73. See M. Grunwald, 'Die fremden Arbeitskräfte in Deutschland und die preußisch-deutsche Gesetzes- und Verwaltungspraxis', *NZ*, vol. 2, 1906/7, pp. 581–91, especially p. 584 (Breitenbach); *Stenographische Berichte des Reichstages*, vol. 228, 1907, p. 1314; see Dohse, *Ausländische Arbeiter*, p. 58; Grunwald, 'Die fremden Arbeitskräfte', p. 585; *GST*, no. 22, 1907, pp. 367ff. (Posadowsky); *CB*, no. 31, 1908, pp. 486ff., especially p. 486; no. 41, p. 456; see Bade, '"Preußengänger"', p. 103 (*Correspondenzblatt*).
74. *GST*, no. 32, 1911, pp. 392ff.

sector were foreigners, primarily Dutchmen. The coalition pressing for preferential employment of indigenous labour included not only labour movement organisations but also advocates of the Weberian theory of displacement, such as the agronomist Stieda.[75] But in spite of the breadth of support for the idea, it could not be realised until the complete reconstruction of state policy towards foreigners and employment in the Weimar Republic, when there was a marked shift away from a broadly (if not solely) politically motivated policy of prevention to a consistent employment policy. The years of the First World War and the war-economy had resulted in an accentuation of workers' protectionism. The success of that protectionism and its influence on state policy at the same time reflected the integration of important parts of the Social Democratic labour movement into the political system.

In the course of the war, and thereafter, a new state policy concerning the employment of foreign labour developed. This was accompanied by the creation of a public labour-market policy in the proper sense of the word.[76] The concept of the Social Democratic-oriented trade unions for the period of 'economic transition' was exemplified in a programme issued in July 1917, which made clear that they intended to solve the problems of foreign labour employment according to the principle of parity in decision-making, already practised in different realms of social and economic policy during the war.[77] The practical implementation of this concept passed its first test soon after the collapse of the old régime. The demobilisation decrees guaranteed the validity of collective agreements for individual labour contracts as an inalienable principle. For employers this implied a prohibition on undermining contract conditions by the recruitment of foreign workers. The latter now had to be employed with a contractual status equal to that of their domestic colleagues. Until March 1919 the majority of foreign workers then present in Germany were removed from the labour market, as well as from the country, in the course of demobilisation measures. This development could at the same time be interpreted as a further step to integrate trade unions as full partners into a

75. Dohse, *Ausländische Arbeiter*, pp. 63ff., 65; Bade, '"Preußengänger"', pp. 104ff.; Bade, 'Labour'.
76. See Zunkel, 'Die Stellung'; Faust, 'Arbeitsmarktpolitik', pp. 216–53.
77. See Zunkel, 'Die Stellung', pp. 305–9.

policy to regulate the labour market.

Now expulsions of foreign workers were not criticised but supported by the trade unions. Deportations now served to guarantee a 'Germans-first' policy on the domestic labour market. It would be interesting to compare the tendencies towards an exclusion of foreign workers from the domestic labour market with the attitude of trade unions concerning female labour – at least by the end of the First World War representatives of different unions were also calling for the 'deportation' of their female workmates out of the labour market.[78]

In the spring of 1919 German agricultural entrepreneurs again found themselves confronted with the familiar problem of a *Leutenot*. The recruitment of a sufficient labour force for agricultural work from the masses of unemployed German workers had proved impossible. Thus from the agrarian viewpoint the recruitment of foreign labour seemed once again to be in prospect. But it soon became evident that in the agricultural sphere, too, the legal and political position of trade unions had dramatically improved since pre-revolutionary times. The prospect of a further unlimited recruitment of foreign labour was blocked by the effective opposition of the agricultural labourers' trade unions. This opposition now paved the way for a definitive reform of the regulations for the recruitment of foreign labour. In March 1920 the national working group (*Reichsarbeitsgemeinschaft*) of the organisations of agricultural employers and employees elaborated a suitable scheme, which was intended to become a model for foreign labour employment on the whole German labour market. It included three main principles:

(1) preferential employment of indigenous workers,
(2) equal status for foreign workers in contractual matters,
(3) a proportional representation of trade unions in the agencies responsible for decisions on foreign labour recruitment.

Thus, ironically enough, trade unions had used their profoundly

---

78. See Bieber, *Gewerkschaften*, pp. 203–10; U. Daniel, 'Fiktionen, Friktionen und Fakten – Frauenlohnarbeit im Ersten Weltkrieg', in G. Mai (ed.), *Arbeiterschaft in Deutschland 1914–1918. Studien zu Arbeitskampf und Arbeitsmarkt im Ersten Weltkrieg*, Düsseldorf, 1985, pp. 277–323; Ratz, 'Vom sozialen Protest', pp. 13–15, especially pp. 14ff. For the whole discussion see also the contributions by Helen Boak and Richard Bessel in this volume.

increased ability to take part in decision-making on social and labour market policy in the environment of a changed political system to foster a relative 'freeze' of the German labour market. As a result, foreign labour employment in the Weimar Republic became a relatively marginal phenomenon, at least compared with the situation prevailing during the last three decades of the Imperial period.

It seems to be evident that this 'freeze' cannot be interpreted mainly in terms of nationalism. The limits to foreign labour employment in the Weimar Republic originated rather from an established political strategy designed to regulate the labour market. But nationalist currents had in no degree lost their importance for foreign labour policy in the Weimar Republic. Future developments in German society and the German state proved this in a catastrophic way. In this context the question of 'continuity' could, and should, be examined carefully. But this is a task far beyond the scope of this chapter.[79]

79. See Herbert, *Geschichte*, pp. 173–7.

5
Eugenics and the Welfare State During the Weimar Republic

Paul Weindling

Democracy and Professionalisation

The Weimar constitution marked the birth of the German welfare state, which assumed responsibility for the health and welfare of the family. This expansion of the role of the state ended the policy prevailing during Imperial Germany that welfare was a private philanthropic concern best left to voluntary organisations or to municipal initiatives. State welfare in the form of the poor law had been only for marginal groups of the utterly destitute and had been associated with moral and social stigma. The role of the Weimar state was redefined in terms of having a responsibility of maintaining the welfare of the total population. This meant that the concept of the welfare state was also expanded to incorporate diverse state authorities as well as municipal, insurance and voluntary agencies. Despite the ethos of scientific modernity attached to welfare, the welfare state had none of the clear and rational lines of a Bauhaus building: the welfare state was not a unitary construction but a ramshackle edifice that had insecure financial foundations and great gaps in its cover. The edifice of welfare was labyrinthine in its complexity and benefits were inadequate, unequal and selective. The break with past welfare schemes was thus less radical than it might have seemed. The co-ordinating and directing role of the state authorities had already been evident in the activities of officials and aristocrats as patrons of welfare organisations in Wilhelmine Germany and during the 1914–18 war. Municipal insurance and voluntary schemes continued and were indeed expanded. At the same time the composition of the state authorities was changing with the intrusion of medical and technically trained officials into central and local government.

This chapter seeks to challenge the view that the Weimar welfare state was a model product of democracy and altruistic social concern. The politicisation and public accountability of welfare policies can be seen to be limited, once policy formulation and its implementation are examined. Professionalisation, reinforced with scientific training, had authoritarian implications that were evident when expanding areas of Weimar welfare, such as the treatment of youth 'psychopaths', are scrutinised. Eugenics illustrates the authoritarian and nationalist side to welfare, as it blended modern scientific explanations of poverty and techniques of enforcing orderly behaviour with nationalist ideology of a fit and efficient body politic and of devotion to future generations. The democratic rights of the individual were subordinated to higher 'national' priorities. Eugenic measures permeated innovative areas of Weimar welfare policy as, for example, the health care of mothers, infants and school children, tuberculosis and venereal disease prevention, sexual counselling, and mental health. Innovative experiments in social medicine and social work focused on *Familienfürsorge* (family welfare). As welfare changed from a philanthropic to a scientific approach, convictions grew that simply providing benefits could not solve the problem of poverty, which essentially required radical solutions. On the positive side there were innovative schemes, for example, for new housing, but these were so expensive that they benefited only a fraction of the population. On the negative side there was the conviction that poverty could be prevented by discouraging the poor from having large families. There was a strong current of corporatism, that gave the organic totality precedence over the individual. Such corporatism was evident in the growing influence of social hygiene, social biology and eugenics. The authoritarianism implicit in these ideologies, which presupposed expert screening, registration and evaluation of the population, supports an interpretation of Weimar welfare as coercion. The concept of problem families emerged which were regarded as reservoirs of congenital disease and inherited deviancy. Eugenics culminated in plans for the screening of the total population as a preliminary for eradicating the so-called anti-social elements through custodial detention, and ultimately by sterilisation. By the end of the 1920s semi-autonomous initiatives in welfare were becoming grouped together as centralised structures under dictatorial professional control. These sought to co-ordinate diverse state agencies at the national, provincial and municipal level. The spread of eugenics, the proliferation of selected welfare schemes and the unification of official agencies, provides an important insight into how the coercive impulses of welfare authorities during the Weimar period ultimately undermined democratic rights.

The reputation of the Weimar welfare state is that it was a product of democratic socialism and that its lavish benefits brought Germany to the brink of economic disaster. This mythology was spread by conservative critics of the costs of welfare, and it has continued to pervade analyses of the slump. In fact local studies of the operations of the welfare state show that it was mean, penny-pinching and inadequate.[1] An analysis of specific policies and of the eugenic presuppositions of welfare work helps to explain how this situation came about. Professionalism in this context should be seen as a force countering radical socialist demands for lay-controlled welfare. The churches and other voluntary bodies also continued to play an important role. Despite its pretensions to rational efficiency and social planning, the welfare state was a chaos of competing authorities, under-funded agencies, and a mixture of voluntary and public bodies. Its diversity reflected its origins as a product of diverse political forces. Socialists, liberals inspired by the 'one nation' ideology of Friedrich Naumann, and the Catholic Centre Party combined to support its formation. The war and the subsequent economic upheavals, which led to a loss of wealth among many sectors of the bourgeoisie, meant that conservatives also initially acquiesced in the ideology of welfare for all. However, because welfare was supported by a coalition of parties as a national priority, this meant that it was regarded as an area best left to professional expertise. Democratisation of social policy was thus hindered.

Welfare meant not simply an extension of state powers, but a change in the social composition of administrators. Technically trained officials – *Fachbeamte* – had greater security than general administrators, particularly as senior ministerial appointments came to be regarded as political posts. In contrast to the political purging of senior administrators only 8 per cent of *Fachbeamte* were replaced

1. K. Borchardt, *Wachstum, Krisen, Handlungsspielräume der Wirtschaftspolitik*, Göttingen, 1982; R.J. Evans and D. Geary (eds.), *The German Unemployed*, London and Sydney, 1987.

between 1918 and 1932. Underlying the extension of state power was the growth of professionalism. The war accelerated the trend for welfare work to be a professional rather than voluntary activity. Many war-time voluntary welfare workers acquired professional qualifications, as in the fields of infant and child nursing, and social work. By 1925 there were 3,000 women social workers in Prussia,[2] and established professions like medicine developed new career opportunities by extending public health into the sphere of family welfare. The number of *Fachbeamte* with qualifications in economics, sociology and medicine increased disproportionately in relation to legally-trained *Verwaltungsbeamte*. The welfare state, therefore, emerged as a result of the acquisition of new professional skills by the bourgeoisie and the professionalisation of welfare had socio-political implications. In theory, socialisation of welfare found legitimation in Weimar's democratic constitution. In practice, the first beneficiaries of the welfare state were middle-class welfare workers. A problem, therefore, arises, as to whether professionalised welfare functioned primarily in the interest of its clients or whether 'higher' social interests like social control, surveillance and the overall health of the 'nation's body' (*Volkskörper*) transcended the democratic rights of the citizen. Professionalism, backed by official powers, meant that the Weimar concept of welfare helped to define new spheres for the exercising of coercive powers. This then raises the question of whether the instability of the Weimar republic was a result of something more than anti-democratic extremism on the part of the ultra-left and ultra-right. The 'technocracy' of professions and welfare administrators might be seen as erecting anti-democratic and coercive social structures by extending the welfare state.

Eugenics

During the war the state had overseen the formulation of a population policy designed to raise the birth rate. Welfare measures were regarded as a means of maintaining military fitness. The state also

---

2. C. Sachße, *Mütterlichkeit als Beruf*, Frankfurt am Main, 1986, pp. 286ff.; D.F. Crew, 'German Socialism, the State and Family Policy 1918–1933', *Continuity and Change*, vol. 1, 1986, pp. 235–63; W. Runge, *Politik und Beamte im Parteienstaat*, Stuttgart, 1968.

sought advice from innovators in social work and public health. State administrators were converted from quantitive to qualitative eugenic policies during the crisis of defeat and social disorder. Alarmed bureaucrats resorted to a biologically conceived nationalism. Officials condemned the Allies' hunger blockade as 'a war of extermination against the German race'. Spectacular accusations were made of 'child murder' and the Treaty of Versailles was hated as a calculated Allied attempt to destroy the German race. The condition of German youth was diagnosed as so bad that the *Volkskörper* was ruined. In this context the declining birth rate was taken as an indicator of a dying nation. Welfare policies can, therefore, be seen as having been inspired by nationalist and biologistic aims. Family-oriented welfare measures and social hygiene were regarded as a means to rebuild the biological fabric of the race and to restore national morale. Officials began to defend the family against 'epidemics', such as abortion, venereal disease and psychopathy. This official mentality is also evident in Theweleit's analysis of the Freikorps' idealisation of the family, of the sisterly nurse, and of racial purity. Experts in social hygiene aimed to root out and destroy degenerate characters and their campaign in defence of the German family invoked terrifying threats of impending extermination.[3]

Eugenic schemes for improving the quality of the population gained prestige in this atmosphere of crisis. Eugenic organisations had a membership composed primarily of doctors and other middle-class professionals. Before 1918 eugenics had permeated welfare organisations such as those combating 'racial poisons' like tuberculosis, venereal disease, alcoholism and mental defects. The state takeover of welfare meant that eugenics now became established in the state. Yet the eugenics movement had been split over attitudes to social welfare. Social Darwinists condemned therapeutic medicine and sentimental welfare, as curbing the invigorating effects of natural selection and allowing those with hereditary diseases to procreate. Other eugenicists argued that high mortality did not

3. O. Krohne, 'Die gesundheitliche Not des deutschen Volkes', 4 January 1923 in Zentrales Staatsarchiv Potsdam (ZStAP), 15.01, 9409, Bl. 101–5; Zentralstaatsarchiv Merseburg (ZStaM), Rep. 76, viii, B, 2049: Betr. volksgesundheitliche Fragen während des Krieges 1918–19; Bayerisches Hauptstaatsarchiv, Munich (BHStA), MF 68014: Medizinalwesen; K. Theweleit, *Männerphantasien*, Frankfurt am Main, 1977.

produce a healthier society. They emphasised the positive value of eugenics in improving the biological constitution of the nation and projected an image of eugenics as a scientifically modern and human method of preventive medicine and social welfare. Eugenics, often defined as 'being born well' (*Wohlgeborenwerden*), was to replace sentimentality as a component of welfare.[4]

Any interpretation of welfare as a system of social control and coercion must be weighed against some powerful limiting factors. Welfare was underfinanced, at a time when needs were greater than ever. Municipalities, voluntary organisations and sick funds were burdened by increasing obligations. The more enterprising promoted innovations in welfare, but were hampered by economic problems. There were flaws and inconsistencies in legislative provisions. The demarcation between state and municipal responsibilities was unclear and rivalries among authorities and professional groups arose. The professions suffered from internal disagreement, as between those doctors who preferred part-time posts to augment the responsibilities of family practitioners and those who wanted full-time posts in public health services. There was a clash of social interests between sickness insurances which supported municipal health centres (*Ambulatorien*), and the medical profession which organised strikes against these, as in 1923 and 1924. Political parties also disagreed over welfare. The Centre Party supported the role of voluntary welfare organisations, and the Social Democratic Party (SPD) advocated the socialisation of welfare services under state control. However, Communist (KPD) critics dismissed the whole edifice of the welfare state as merely shielding an ailing capitalist economy. The welfare state was divided, inconsistent, and chronically under-financed.

Regional and local circumstances were also subject to considerable variation. Few historians have been brave enough to attempt the long march through the Reich, Land, voluntary and municipal institutions in order to unravel the complexities of welfare provision, and relate policies to public responses and social conditions. Such an exercise, however, makes it possible to pinpoint when a

4. O. Peltzer, *Das Verhältnis der Sozialpolitik zur Rassenhygiene*, Munich, 1925; P. Weindling, 'Die Verbreitung rassenhygienischen/eugenischen Gedankengutes in bürgerlichen und sozialistischen Kreisen in der Weimarer Republik', *Medizinhistorisches Journal*, vol. 22, 1987, and idem, *Health, Race and German Politics between National Unification and Nazism*, Cambridge, 1989.

particular authority or policy succumbed to the eugenic ideas. It is important to emphasise the status of local case studies, as an analysis of pockets of deprivation frequently has advantages of greater authenticity over more optimistic national aggregates, and this was a point which influenced officials in the 1920s. The question of actual conditions should be separated from factors which motivated and structured policies, and how these policies themselves were derived from broader developments. Central state public health records permit an examination of official responses to social conditions, showing the social pressures underlying what was known as 'social hygiene'. Not only were social workers exposed to eugenics in their training, but one of the major forces in the rise of German eugenics was the medical profession. Doctors took a leading role in the development and dissemination of eugenic ideas, and eugenics can be seen as legitimating demands for greater professional powers. By looking at policies for 'out-door' welfare, such as clinics and measures to monitor the health of families, the extent to which eugenics had an impact on social policies can be gauged. Until now greater attention has been paid to custodial institutions, and the more lurid extremes such as sterilisation, rather than to the more ambitious positive aims of welfare. The role of welfare clinics, of monitoring organisations like school health services and efforts to instigate family health statistics offer the opportunity of examining what motivated the implementation of welfare. These issues also provide an insight into the Weimar state with regard to whether its comprehensive pretensions meant that it became a vast custodial institution or attempted to alleviate sickness and poverty.

The Structure of State Welfare

The power-seeking ambitions of professionals surfaced in 1919 with attempts to establish unitary administrative structures under professional control. Although medical plans for a centralised Reich authority for health and welfare failed, experts in social hygiene campaigned within the Social Democratic, Independent Social Democratic and Centre Parties for a Ministry of Health, Social Insurance and Population Policy. Such a ministry would have undermined the independence of Länder, municipalities and insurance funds, curbed democratic accountability of political appointments, and legitimised a coercive type of pro-natalism. The Reich Health Office objected that a centralised Ministry would not fit in with the new social order, as this was less a unitary state (*Einheitsstaat*) than a confederation (*Staatenbund*). It cautioned that if welfare was to be added to the responsibilities of a Ministry of Health, the powers of the Reich Labour Office would be infringed. Moreover, any authority with a doctor at its head would incur the opposition of the sickness insurance funds. Although Weimar social services were to develop on a decentralised basis, the aim of developing professionally controlled authorities continued to be pursued with the rationale of improving the efficiency, planning and co-ordination of politically fragmented administrative bodies.[5]

Although the Reich had legislative, monitoring and co-ordinating responsibilities, the Länder remained responsible for health and welfare policies. Prussia provides an outstanding example with the Ministry of Public Welfare (Ministerium für Volkswohlfahrt). That the SPD ceded control of this to the Centre Party (with Stegerwald and then Hirtsiefer as Ministers) showed how welfare was secondary to the priority of political stabilisation. It could be left to expert, professionally qualified administrators. The Department of Public Health (Abteilung für Volksgesundheit) was headed by a medical practitioner rather than a administrative civil servant. The new ministerial director, Gottstein, had pioneered infant and school health services in the municipality of Charlottenburg. In one sense his appointment represented the municipal 'outsider' becoming the central state 'insider'. But in another sense, Gottstein cemented the ties between public health officials and the medical profession.

Medical officials formed an independent-minded hierarchy within the state. Their career structure and professional outlook differed from that of other administrators. Medical officials were recruited from the ranks of district medical officers. Technically trained bureaucrats moved with greater ease into central positions, but maintained allegiances with their profession. At the level of the district (*Kreis*), the medical officer was on an equal footing with the provincial state official (*Landrat*). Professionalism, therefore, could

5. ZStAP, 15.01, 10948: Schaffung einer deutschen Reichsbehörde für das Gesundheitswesen; BHStA, MF 68014: Medizinalwesen; A. Labisch, 'Neue Quellen zum gesundheitspolitischen Programm der MSPD von 1920/22', *Internationale wissenschaftliche Korrespondenz zur Geschichte der deutschen Arbeiterbewegung*, vol. 16, 1980, pp. 321–47.

be a stronger bond between doctors in different sectors of public service than either administrative or political allegiances. Berlin's municipal medical officers (*Stadtärzte*) formed a radical left-wing grouping, keen to defend the decentralisation of state authority to a communal level. But they shared many authoritarian attitudes with state medical officers (*Kreisärzte*) or central state officials. There were links through professional welfare and eugenic organisations. For example, the Lichtenberg *Stadtarzt*, Georg Löwenstein, was Secretary of the Gesellschaft zur Bekämpfung der Geschlechtskrankheiten and active in the Red Cross and the state-directed Bund für Volksaufartung concerned with positive eugenics. Other municipal medical officers, like Drigalski of Halle and later of Berlin, or Tjaden of Bremen, had a classic training in bacteriology and either military or central government administrative experience.

Political accountability to elected state assemblies was offset by consultation with professional experts. A classical example of a pool of expertise was the Prussian Health Council (Landesgesundheitsrat), established in 1921. Its 120 members were responsible for advising on public health and social hygiene. This was a non-elected parliament of professionals including doctors and social workers and its committees included one for eugenics and population matters.[6] It urged that professional tribunals should be given extensive powers over such spheres as marriage and the family. The pattern was repeated in other states, as in Saxony, where there was a strong pro-sterilisation lobby.[7] Administrators also had links with professional and philanthropic organisations. The Prussian health administration ensured that most welfare organisations were directed by a prominent medical official,[8] which meant that the welfare organisations were subjected to direct control by the state. Smaller welfare organisations were dragooned into umbrella organisations like the Red Cross, the Evangelical Innere Mission, the Catholic Caritas and the Social Democratic *Arbeiterwohlfahrt*.[9] State control was exercised through financial subsidies, and

6. F.A. Weber, 'Die Unfruchtbarmachung geistig Minderwertiger, Schwachsinninger und Verbrecher', *Zeitschrift für ärztliche Fortbildung*, vol. 22, 1925, pp. 152–5.
7. K.-D. Thomann, 'Das Reichsgesundheitsamt und die Rassenhygiene', *Bundesgesundheitsblatt*, vol. 36, 1983, p. 206.
8. *25 Jahre Preußicher Medizinalverwaltung*, Berlin, 1927, p. 469.
9. ZStAP, 15.01, 26366: Unterstützung von Anstalten und Einrichtungen der Wohlfahrtspflege.

consultation over impending legislation and the implementation of official measures. The post-war inflation also made voluntary organisations dependent on state subsidies. Reforms like the Tuberculosis Law created new authorities which combined both state and voluntary interests. This fusion of state and voluntary interests often made any demarcation artificial and it is more appropriate to see both spheres as succumbing to the control of middle-class, professionally trained experts.

Eugenics provides a classic example of the fusion of professionalism and authoritarian administration. Otto Krohne, of the Prussian health department from 1926 to 1928, was chairman of the national Gesellschaft für Rassenhygiene and of its Berlin branch.[10] Financial subsidies directed eugenics efforts into acceptable areas like eugenics education and pro-natalism. Unacceptably radical eugenicists were removed. Eugenicists negotiated state subsidies for those welfare organisations supporting 'positive' eugenics and population policies in welfare bodies; the social hygiene expert, Grotjahn, intervened on behalf of the Bund der Kinderreichen.[11] The Bund für Volksaufartung boasted of the support of 50,000 registry officials (*Standesbeamte*), who were to give eugenic advice to those intending to marry. It is interesting to see how the Bund commanded the allegiance of medical officials, but not of the civic authorities. Thus Drigalski, medical officer of Berlin, was on its executive committee, although the municipality of Berlin declined any official support.[12] Similar situations occurred in Bremen and Hamburg, where medical officers wished to support eugenic organisations but their council refused.[13]

The Role of the Clinic

The basis of health and welfare lay in clinics (*Fürsorgestellen*). Prior to the war there had been competing strategies of local organis-

10. P. Weindling, 'Die Preußische Medizinalverwaltung und die "Rassenhygiene"', in A. Thom and H. Spaar (eds.), *Medizin und Faschismus*, Berlin, 1983, pp. 23–35, extended version in *Zeitschrift für Sozialreform*, vol. 30, 1984, pp. 675–87.

11. ZStAP, 15.01, 26234: Bund der Kinderreichen, Bl. 161.

12. Berlin Stadtarchiv, GB 877.

13. Staatsarchiv Bremen (StAB), V, 2, 1536; Staatsarchiv Hamburg, Medkoll II N50: Blutgruppenforschung; ZStaM, Rep. 76, viii, B, 2076.

ation. Socialists demanded municipal welfare centres, whereas state and military medical authorities urged that district health centres (*Kreisgesundheitsämter*) be established to co-ordinate welfare measures on a social hygiene basis. They were specifically envisaged for rural areas where it was not possible to rely on voluntary efforts. These rival concepts, however, became fused in the Weimar system of health, youth and welfare offices (*Gesundheits-, Jugend- und Wohlfahrtsämter*). But the system retained a certain duality. Towns tended to keep health, youth and welfare separate, whereas in the countryside the responsibilities were amalgamated. The state response to demands for the 'socialisation of medicine' was limited to the administrative reform of public health and welfare. Municipalities and insurance funds could be more radical. They drew on traditions of lay self-administration (*soziale Selbstverwaltung*) to establish health centres, based on the idea of doctors as official panel doctors. The KPD demanded health centres (*Gesundheitshäuser*) supported by a proletarian medical service. While these challenged the economic basis of medicine, the communist health centres were to be staffed by conventionally trained professionals.[14]

The traditions of administrative independence of municipalities were gradually eroded, as welfare legislation regulated the relations between central state and municipal services. Municipalities were empowered to take over central state functions in certain circumstances. However, the division of responsibility between state and municipal authorities became somewhat arbitrary, and was complicated by professional rivalries. The health offices were responsible for infants, children, tuberculosis, venereal disease, alcoholism, mental disorders, psychopathy, pregnancy and genetic counselling. Youth and welfare offices had overlapping responsibilities, for the blind, deaf and dumb, and 'feeble minded'. A local co-ordinating body, the Arbeitsgemeinschaft für Wohlfahrtspflege, linked voluntary and official measures. In Berlin the Central Health Office, Land Welfare Office and Youth Office were subject to the Central Administration for Welfare Work. Municipalities had the option of combining the posts of municipal and state medical officer, and agreed with the state on the transfer of certain services. Any

14. E. Hansen, M. Heisig, S. Leibfried and F. Tennstedt (eds.), *Seit über einem Jahrhundert . . .: Verschüttete Alternativen in der Sozialpolitik*, Cologne, 1981; P. Weindling, 'Shattered Alternatives in Medicine', *History Workshop Journal*, no. 16, 1983, pp. 152–7.

extension in existing services might require enabling legislation by the Reich, as for the marriage advice clinics (*Eheberatungsstellen*), which were meant to have eugenic functions in issuing health certificates for those intending to marry. The emphasis on co-ordination blurred traditional divisions between the state and municipalities, arguably preparing the way for an eventual unification under Nazism.

Clinics were a channel for introducing medical surveillance into daily life. One function of the clinics was to identify patients for referral to 'closed', 'total' institutions, like hospitals, sanatoria and asylums. The increase in the number of hospitals marked a change in standards and attitudes, as hospitals lost the traditional stigma of poor law institutions. Closed institutions like mental hospitals also served custodial policing and eugenic functions. The unproductive and hereditarily unfit could be detained and 'humanely' prevented from procreating. Yet such closed institutions were financially expensive. Moreover, they could only cope with a far smaller percentage of the population than was deemed to be unfit. Clinics and welfare centres provided alternatives to incarceration. A visit to the clinic would invariably result in a social worker inspecting the home. Clinics, however, had the advantage of being relatively cheap to run, and could be spread throughout the population. They could serve the fit and healthy by dispensing welfare supplements and hygiene advice, and focused on the need for everyone to have their own bed, bedding, cutlery and an adequate diet. Clinics provided health education, preventive medical measures, and mass screening for early diagnosis. They could be used to root out the degenerate, such as alcoholics, the venereally diseased, tuberculous and psychopaths. They were also to identify those who were apparently fit, but carriers of hereditary diseases, and those who suffered only mild forms of physical and mental disorders. The services were carried out by the social worker (whose gender and role were expressed in the term *Familienfürsorgerinnen*), and a medical officer had overall responsibility. The system was adaptable to both urban and rural conditions and the clinic was the best means of integrating diverse branches of welfare as a provision for the family and for extending overall surveillance of the population.[15]

15. Staatsarchiv Dresden (StAD), MdI, 15832: Ländliche Wohlfahrts- und Heimatpflege.

Table 5.1 Clinics in Prussia, 1928

	Official clinics	Voluntary clinics
Marriage advice	224	2
Ante-natal	898	7
Infants	2,656	342
Small children	1,517	150
Tuberculosis	1,322	89
Venereal disease	196 (=1929)	25
Alcoholism	277	55
Cripples	675	4
Psychopaths	339	11
War invalids	543	5

Source: Das Gesundheitswesen des Preußischen Staates im Jahre 1928, Berlin, 1929.

Indeed, officials were proud of a steady rise in the number of supervisory authorities and clinics. Most had been founded between 1919 and 1921. By 1928 there were 823 district and local authority welfare centres in Prussia, which exemplified the type of services provided and the resources that were allocated for such purposes. They were supported by 133 full-time district and communal doctors, and 294 part-time doctors. There were 2,244 social workers, with 675 attached to the public health offices. Official (i.e. state and municipal) measures had now overtaken voluntary initiatives (see Table 5.1).[16]

This apparent achievement was accompanied by extravagant claims as to the effect of clinics on health conditions. Welfare experts made the dubious assertion that they had reduced mortality rates from infant diseases and from tuberculosis. Yet there was rising mortality from diphtheria, scarlet fever, childbed fever and cancer. It was argued that a further extension of clinics and welfare services was vital. If mortality rates went down, here was proof of the efficacy of medical measures. If they went up, this showed that public health was under-resourced. Either way more resources were necessary. However, projected targets relating to the number of clinics and welfare workers were never attained.

Yet mortality was too narrow a front on which to be fighting for more public resources. Officials wished to show that health and

16. *Das Gesundheitswesen des Preußischen Staates im Jahre 1928*, Berlin, 1929.

social conditions were inextricably linked and this could greatly extend their sphere of operations. As a result, morbidity and psychological factors came to be regarded as more important than mortality. The Reich Health Office observed on the nation's health in 1923:

> It is not epidemics, not communicable diseases or acute illnesses, that cause anxiety, but rather a chronic process of morbidity of a particular kind, which leads us to fear the worst, manifesting itself in most people in a feeling of unsettled health, weakened physical and intellectual powers, immediate susceptibility to the appearance of communicable diseases, in nervousness, irritability, in anxious brooding and in world-weariness. Along with the physical strength to live, moral and ethical standards disappear.[17]

Eugenics and social hygiene were to remedy a social and psychological malaise.

The efficacy of clinics in terms of reaching the population for which they were intended, and in improving health, is difficult to assess. The intention of policy-makers was that such clinics should reach as large a percentage of the population as possible, and that data collection and the distribution of advice were grounds, in themselves, for demanding an expansion of clinics. Welfare experts were predisposed by eugenic theories of biological degeneration to believe that health conditions were worsening, and that any improvements were due to the efficacy of public health measures. Officials argued that mortality statistics did not give an accurate picture of health conditions. Mortality was lowest among some of the unhealthiest groups in society. The chronic ill-health of small children was recognised as 'statistically difficult to register'. Authorities used the reports of clinics to measure health conditions, and local reports indicated that disease and poor living conditions continued to be widespread. They analysed the health of children, by laboriously itemising the condition of those seen in clinics, including details of height, weight, nutrition, clothing, bedding and mental state.[18] Infant mortality was declining, but reports flooded in of how infants still suffered from malnutrition, rickets, skin conditions like eczema, due to a lack of nappies, diarrhoea and

17. ZStAP, 15.01, 9408, Bl. 450: Hygiene in der Nachkriegszeit, 1924.
18. ZStAP, 15.01, 9408, Bl. 432: Gesundheit in der Nachkriegszeit, 1924.

worms indicating poor nutrition, and tuberculosis. High percentages – between 25 and 75 per cent – of infants were reported as suffering from symptoms of malnutrition such as hunger oedema, chlorosis, rickets and scurvy; many did not have a bed, bed linen or adequate clothing, and were tired and nervous.[19]

The more clinics and welfare workers there were, the more evidence on disease and poverty were collected, although it was difficult to establish whether conditions were improving or worsening. To overcome such problems, the medical statistician, Roesle, of the Reich Health Office, suggested a new system of morbidity statistics designed to provide an index of total health. Instead of just registering those cases of disease which by chance were seen by clinics, hospitals or practitioners, he suggested small group investigations taking account of both the healthy and diseased. It would be necessary to undertake comprehensive screening programmes to establish the rates of not being ill. These 'biological health indices' would show the health of selected social groups, like the unemployed and their families. In 1931 the Reichswehr moved from a 'disease index' to a 'health index'. The aim of comprehensive family statistics to show 'biological character', therefore, coincided with the plans of eugenicists for comprehensive screening programmes.

Welfare legislation stressed the positive role of clinics in improving conditions. The venereal disease decree of 1918 had an element of compulsion, which became the basis of later legislation. The venereal disease measures were regarded as progressive, in that they allowed for compulsory treatment of men and women, and not just of prostitutes. The new laws represented a transfer of powers from police to medical authorities, with children and youth regarded as a priority. The Tuberculosis Law of 1925 was typical, with its stress on early diagnosis, especially in youth. The apparatus of youth welfare contained a strong medical element, and the demarcation of responsibilities between Youth Welfare Offices and other medical agencies was often arbitrary and problematic.[20] Prevention was linked to registration and compulsion, and the tuberculosis law provided for the registration of all outbreaks of disease. Medical

19. ZStAP, 15.01, 9409, Bl. 454f.
20. A. Gottstein, 'Der Entwurf eines preußischen Jugendgesetzes', *Deutsche Medizinische Wochenschrift*, vol. 44, 1918, p. 1029.

officers also gained discretionary powers to isolate patients.

The system of clinics was, therefore, susceptible to permeation by eugenic values. It was only a minority of administrators who welcomed the post-war conditions as fostering natural selection by exterminating cripples and weaklings.[21] More spoke in nationalist terms of a struggle for the nation to survive. It was emphasised how clinics must work to rebuild the strength of the nation. While clinics for genetic counselling and psychopathy represent the extreme of eugenic positions, it is worth noting how other clinics could be turned to eugenic ends. Officials wanted to make attendance at clinics compulsory and in 1925 the government caused an outcry when it tried to make maternity allowances conditional on visiting an infant health clinic. Compulsion fitted in with eugenic strategies. Children suffering from hereditary syphilis were inevitably a major concern. It was emphasised how this might be prevented by comprehensive ante-natal screening of mothers, by giving each a blood test. This gave rise to a discussion as to whether this should be 'voluntary' – that is, with a forceful recommendation by a doctor – or compulsory.

The proliferation of clinics made it necessary to train a new generation of staff. Eugenics, population policy and heredity formed part of the curriculum for training medical students, in the further education of doctors, and for medical officers at the new Social Hygiene Academies at Charlottenburg, Breslau and Düsseldorf.[22] Eugenics was also used in the training of midwives, nurses, child nurses and social workers, who were to screen for inherited diseases and mental disorders. Emphasis was placed on their primary duty of supervision.

School medical services were also to monitor health on a large scale. Several million school children were meant to benefit from regular examination of their physical and mental condition. Reports on post-war health emphasised that school children were among the worst hit of all social groups, although their sufferings were hardly reflected in terms of mortality statistics. Yet the ideology of concern with future generations inevitably made them a prime target for welfare. The alarmed reports on malnutrition were full of how the Allied blockade would have hereditary effects. Rickets, bone deform-

21. ZStAP, 15.01, 9406, Bl. 136; 9408, Bl. 430.
22. ZStaM, Rep. 76, viii, B, 335.

ities and tuberculosis were recorded as increasing. The proposed remedies of light, air and sun, education, sport, salt baths and ultra-violet light were conveniently cheap.[23] Medical care and nutritional supplements could be provided, and it was claimed that early diagnosis of rickets and tuberculosis could permit these to be cured. School medical services, in general, show a concern with diagnosis and cheap palliatives, rather than the provision of costly items such as school meals.

Moreover, there was much concern with the mental health of school children, who were seen as subject to increasing strain, resulting in delinquency. Teachers, school nurses and kindergarten assistants were to be made aware of the importance of 'constitution and heredity', and were given responsibilities for health education in 1926.[24] State authorities encouraged anthropometric surveys. The Reich Health Office attempted to standardise categories in 1921, accepting such categories as feeble-mindedness, psychopathic disposition and constitutional diseases. The racial hygienist, Max von Gruber, who represented the Bavarian Ministry of Education, demanded details of racial characteristics. Although this and other racial demands were rejected, hereditarian concerns permeated welfare services.[25]

A major limitation on school health services was that they fell far short of any ideal of comprehensiveness. In Prussia in 1921 only 5,712 out of 26,453 local councils provided school health services. Of 2,417 school doctors in 1922 only 177 – that is 7.4 per cent – were full-time. By 1928 several hundred thousand children were still not covered by medical services. Primary schools continued to attract more attention than secondary schools. In theory the school doctor was 'ever more in the front line in the fight against popular disease'; but the economic collapse meant that the ideal of comprehensive welfare could not be realised.[26] Clinics and school medical services were at the front line of the attack on ill-health and despite their fragmented and sporadic character, welfare agencies promoted social integration by bringing large numbers into contact with welfare. They also had a symbolic function of promoting ideologies of the health of the *Volkskörper*.

23. ZStaM, Rep. 76, viii, B, 2050.
24. ZStaM, Rep. 76, viii, B, 2833; StAD, MdI, 15224/1.
25. ZStaM, Rep. 76, viii, B, 2932: Hygiene in Schulen, Bl. 332.
26. ZStaM, Rep. 76, viii, B, 2833.

The Psychopath

It was feared that the post-war social turmoil had undermined the authority of the state, the church and the family by unleashing a wave of mental disorder. The new generation of professionals were convinced that these social upheavals had psychological and hereditary causes. This can be seen in a concentration of welfare resources on the problem of delinquent youth psychopaths. The Chairman of the Gesellschaft für Heilpädagogik, Egenberger, estimated that 25 per cent of all youths were psychopaths. He commented in 1923, 'The question of degeneration and loss of racial character [*Degeneration und Entartung*] is a vital question for the German people.' Educationalists and psychiatrists were concerned with the mild but widespread incidence of feeble-mindedness, neuropathy, and, the most disturbing of all, psychopathy. These definitions show how disorderly behaviour was to be classified (and thus to be controlled) by using medical rather than moral or social categories. The experts warned that psychopathic children would grow into a future generation of criminals, prostitutes and vagabonds.

Psychopathy was a problem requiring vast resources. After the war, the Bavarian and Prussian states organised a new branch of the welfare services known as 'psychopath welfare' (*Psychopathenfürsorge*) in response to demands by the Deutscher Verein zur Fürsorge für jugendliche Psychopathen.[27] A survey of treatment facilities for psychopaths was held by Prussia in September 1920, and the establishment of clinics was encouraged by a decree of November 1921. A symptom of psychopathy was diagnosed to be rootlessness, necessitating special measures for youth vagrants. The provincial reports emphasised the links between social and mental disorders, and some administrators saw clinics as a means of dealing with putschists and revolutionaries. Others were sceptical because, 'it is precisely these psychopaths, who imagine themselves to be smarter and more capable than everyone else, who will obstinately evade the influence of such clinics'. But those places with clinics emphasised how these were at the centre of networks of control. Clinics worked in association with the Youth Office, the school nurses and doctors, and the families of the mentally disordered.

27. ZStAP, 15.01, 9384: Psychopathen Fürsorge 1920–5.

Here was an ideal area for co-operation between doctors and educators. The aim was comprehensive care, and this focus was evident in many towns, with school children and youth as the main targets. Special departments for youth psychopaths were also established, as at the Landesheil- und Erziehungsanstalt Hadamar. Between 1920 and 1927 fifty-eight new homes and advisory centres were established for psychopathic youths.[28]

Professional demands clearly lay behind state measures. Egenberger, for example, was one of a Munich group of educators who were especially concerned with organic degeneration. They had links with psychiatrists like Max Isserlin, who established a neurological research centre for children and youths, and Ernst Rüdin, who headed the Genealogical Department of the German Psychiatric Research Institute. Rüdin considered psychopathy to be an intermediate condition between the diseased and the normal. Consequently most psychopaths were outside custodial institutions. The Verein zur Fürsorge für jugendliche Psychopathen, the Reichstag and various states consistently urged the need for a central collation of statistics.[29]

The Munich experts were distinct from a Berlin group consisting of Ruth von der Leyen (of the Verein), Walter Friedländer, and Friedrich Wilhelm Siegmund-Schultze (who developed the concept of a 'psychopathic constitution' and became the first director of the Berlin Youth Office). They constituted a liberal and progressive wing of youth welfare, and although they still had a biologistic approach, their efforts were directed to rehabilitation.[30] Harvey has analysed how Friedländer, a founder of the *Arbeiterwohlfahrt*, pioneered 'social pedagogy' and 'family welfare' in the Prenzlauer Berg Youth Office. He abandoned the concept of psychopath in favour of welfare education, preferring education to incarceration,[31] which also shows how biological concepts could have a progressive potential.

'Progressives' like Friedländer and von der Leyen, however, were

---

28. ZStaM, Rep. 76, viii, B, 1850: Einrichtung von Fürsorge und Beratungsstellen für psychopathische Kranke 1920–3.
29. ZStAP, 15.01, 9384, Bl. 341.
30. W. Jantzen, *Sozialgeschichte des Behindertenbetreuungswesens*, Munich, 1982.
31. E. Harvey, 'Sozialdemokratische Jugendhilfereform in der Praxis: Walter Friedländer und das Bezirksjugendamt Berlin Prenzlauer Berg in der Weimarer Republik', *Theorie und Praxis der sozialen Arbeit*, vol. 38, 1985, pp. 218–29.

condemned during the Third Reich. The hereditarian and authoritarian approach undoubtedly increased in influence during the 1920s. It was represented by individuals such as Rüdin, who was the major scientific adviser for the Nazi sterilisation law of 1933, and Werner Villinger, chief medical officer of the Hamburg Youth Office from 1926 to 1934 and the later adjudicator in the 'T4' medical killing programme. Concepts of social order, and biologistic and mystic ideas (for example, the concept of divine innocence or the vision of men as 'God's children') formed a bond between psychiatrists, youth social workers and the churches. Pastor Happich of the Hephata asylum illustrates how a concern with heredity and social order permeated the welfare institutions of the Innere Mission. In 1920 he revealed some of the motives for this fear: 'It is entirely characteristic that a twelve-year-old psychopath in our institution said recently: "I know what I'll be when I'm seventeen, I'll be a spartacist leader, I'm made for it." He sensed correctly where so many of his peers stand.' The pastor was to lead the campaign for the sterilisation of mental defectives.[32] Poore has also shown how attitudes towards cripples were similarly motivated by fears of anti-social and disruptive behaviour. The Prussian Cripples' Welfare Law of 1920 required that negative psychological traits be noted, as physical abnormalities were signs of potential social deviance.[33] Here too was a vast reservoir of potential danger, requiring the expertise of welfare.

Total Surveys

Demands by eugenically minded doctors for data-banks on heredity (*Erbkarteien*) inevitably extended medical powers in the sphere of social welfare. The aim was to correlate records of medical, school and criminal authorities. These data-banks formed the basis for research on the inheritance of diseases, mental disorders and crime, and of positive qualities like leadership, fitness and genius. Doctors argued that it was not enough to locate only the sick and their

32. F. Happich, 'Die Not unserer Psychopathen', *Die Innere Mission*, vol. 15, 1920, p. 81.
33. C. Poore, 'Der Krüppel in der Orthopädie der Weimarer Zeit. Medizinische Konzepte als Wegbereiter der Euthanasie', in B. von Braun *et al*, *Wie teuer ist uns Gesundheit?* (*Argument-Sonderband* 113), Berlin, 1984, pp. 67–78.

parents, because the healthy could be carriers of latent pathogenic genes. Medical experts, therefore, demanded the screening of the total population, and for this the support of local, provincial, state and Reich authorities would be necessary. Demands for health passports and hereditary data-banks began before 1914, and were linked to a long-term process of the medicalisation of social values, with psychiatrists and eugenicists taking a lead in instigating *Erbkarteien*. In May 1918 Kraepelin founded the German Psychiatric Research Institute, which was supported mainly by municipal and state funds. Its research was linked to immediate administrative needs, as in relation to the mental health of war invalids. The Institute claimed official status, and stressed its aim of protecting the public from the dangerous and burdensome mentally ill. Its Genealogical Department under Rüdin collected a massive data-bank with records of asylums, hospitals, parish councils, and prisons, and by interviewing families. Rüdin's aim was hereditary prognosis, in order to implement preventative medical schemes. By calculating the ratios and patterns of inheritance, it was hoped that effective genetic counselling and preventive measures could be provided. This was the scientific underpinning of the demand for marriage certificates and marriage counselling agencies.

Criminal biology was one of the first areas in which it was expected that social hygiene and hereditary biology could shed new light on social conditions. In 1919 Rüdin joined forces with Viernstein, a medical officer, for research using school records on the families of prisoners at Straubing in Bavaria. On 15 January 1920 the Ministry of the Interior gave its support.[34] In 1924 the Bavarian Ministry of Justice decided to have a central criminal biological data-bank based at Straubing. The Ministry of Culture ordered schools and parish councils to co-operate. In 1926 The Reich Ministry of the Interior gave the Genealogical Department official status and rights to consult state and criminal records. It was to supply information to prisons, police and law courts and the material was to be overseen by doctors, anthropologists and psychiatrists, and used for biological research, for example, for twin studies. In 1928 it was decided to transfer these records to the German Psychiatric Research Institute.[35] Here Rüdin was working

34. BHStA, Mk 11158: Psychiatrische Angelegenheiten.
35. BHStA, Mk 11779: Erbbiologische und kriminalbiologische Untersuchungen der Strafgefangenen; Bundesarchiv Koblenz (BAK), R86 2374, Bd. 1, Bl. 328f.

on a 'general demographic and biological register', as well as making surveys of districts, like Upper Bavaria, for inherited 'constitutional' diseases including cretinism, gall stones and goitre.

Criminal biological surveys were also organised in other states on the Bavarian pattern. In 1923 the eugenicist, Rainer Fetscher, began to use Saxon criminal records for research on sexual deviants. In 1925 he gained the support of the Saxon Ministry of Justice for a 'comprehensive card index' on the anti-social. Regular grants of between RM 5,000 and RM 8,000 annually were made until 1933 for work undertaken in conjunction with the police and welfare authorities. He commented: 'The records of the welfare offices, in particular, frequently contain important biological data.' These were to be of value for marriage counselling and career guidance for the juvenile courts, and in distinguishing those prisoners who could be re-educated from those who were hereditarily incurable. In 1925 he also emphasised the value of the data for sterilisation. The Labour Ministry and Welfare Ministry requested that they be allowed to consult the survey in order to pass on information to welfare and youth offices, and psychiatrists like Rüdin also exploited the data. By 1930 Fetscher had data on 800,000 individuals of 70,000 families. He recorded mental and psychological disorders, alcoholism, character, indebtedness, and, for women details of pregnancies, menstruation and menopause. The aim was to produce a 'psycho-biogramm' relating physical to mental qualities. Research on the organic basis of personality was combined with racial hygiene.[36] In Prussia there were also initiatives on a provincial level, as in East Prussia in 1928, and at particular asylums. Moreover, in 1930 a Prussian decree greatly expanded the scope of surveys.[37]

From 1921 Prussia supported the campaign for a national institute for hereditary and demographic research. The Reich Health Office advocated the statistical investigation of families in order to determine the inheritance of tuberculosis, cancer, nervous diseases, idiocy, feeble-mindedness and crime.[38] State and municipal funding of hereditary research indicated a general expectation of social benefits. For example, in 1929 Rüdin received funds from the Bavarian Minister President, the Reich Ministry of Labour, the

36. R. Fetscher, 'Zweck und Aufbau erbbiologischer Karteien', *Die Medizinische Welt*, vol. 7, 1933; StAD, Justizministerium, 1587: Erbbiologische Karteien.
37. ZStaM, 2074, Bl. 346; StAD, Kriminalbiologische Gesellschaft 1928–32.
38. ZStAP, 15.01, 9421: Menschliche Vererbungslehre und Bevölkerungskunde.

provincial insurance office of Berlin and from the city of Munich. Data were collected from medical institutions, homes for disabled, school and special schools (*Hilfsschulen*). Between 1925 and 1927 the Catholic eugenicist, Muckermann, raised one million marks from state, municipal and insurance sources for the Kaiser Wilhelm Institute for Anthropology, Human Heredity and Eugenics, which was to function as a national eugenics institute and data collecting centre.[39] The way in which institutions were founded shows that medical researchers established institutes both to centralise official data and to co-ordinate welfare measures.

Surveys show how pilot projects by medical researchers drew increasingly on state subsidies and resources so that they ultimately became part of the general administration. Local surveys were designed as stepping stones to total surveys of the population. The 1925 census offered opportunities for compiling statistics on such 'anomalies' as mental defects, and on the blind, deaf and dumb.[40] Other research projects followed a similar pattern of state and municipal funding, and research was carried out in co-operation with municipal, medical and welfare institutions. From the establishment of the Kaiser Wilhelm Institute for Anthropology in 1927, hospitals and schools were used for Verschuer's twin research on supposedly inherited diseases like tuberculosis. The Institute's Director, Eugen Fischer, planned a total survey of the population, which was launched in 1930. It included criminal biology, mental hygiene and anthropology, as well as the registration of blood groups. Medical officers, welfare administrators and school teachers were to be mobilised to carry out the survey. Even so, the survey was to be limited to only a very few districts.[41] By 1932 the Hamburg anthropologist, Walter Scheidt, who had been allocated 21 out of 63 districts for the survey, had collected material on 250,000 people on 464,400 cards.[42] These surveys marked the culmination of family surveillance, but despite their pretensions, they were never as comprehensively carried out as their advocates would

---

39. P. Weindling, 'Weimar Eugenics in Social Context', *Annals of Science*, vol. 42, 1985, pp. 303–18.

40. E. Rüdin, 'Klinische Psychiatrie und psychiatrische Erbbiologie', *Zeitschrift für die gesamte Neurologie und Psychiatrie*, vol. 40, 1925, pp. 535–63.

41. BAK, R 73/169: Rüdin to Notgemeinschaft der Deutschen Wissenschaft, 20 January 1930.

42. ZStAP, 15.01, 26242: Vererbungslehre und Rassenhygiene.

have liked. It was only after 1933 that clinics for 'hereditary and racial health' became the routine basis of public health.

'Biologising' Welfare

The eugenic data banks cemented links between welfare organisations and the state. Fetscher's data-bank was regarded as of practical value for genetic screening. In Saxony the law of 20 March 1926 for Marriage Advice Clinics gave this responsibility to the district charity organisation societies (*Bezirksfürsorgeverbände*), and money was allocated in 1927. The law provided for 'the co-operation of voluntary agencies, in particular women's organisations, as well as those responsible for social insurance schemes'. Welfare and youth offices were to co-operate with the churches and the schools in providing sex education[43] and there were numerous similar examples of connections between eugenics and welfare schemes.

Health education was clearly a priority, because this was a means for making up for a deficiency in resources and compulsory powers. Eugenicists spearheaded a campaign to inculcate the value of health among a broad public. The 1926 exhibition, GESOLEI ('Gesundheit, soziale Fürsorge und Leibesübungen' – Health, Welfare and Exercise), had a number of eugenic features. Fetscher issued a eugenic 'health passport' for regular inspection by the family doctor[44] and his work was popularised by the Dresden Hygiene Museum. Pamphlets, posters, postcards, lectures, exhibitions, films, radio talks, mothers' days and health weeks were also means of spreading the eugenic gospel. Much of this was subsidised by the state, through such organisations as the Reichsausschuß für hygienische Volksbelehrung. New techniques were developed for an eye-catching public presentation of health and demographic statistics. Popularisation of genetics claimed that science provided the solution to social problems, like vagrancy, crime and inherited diseases. Certain themes recurred in the propaganda, including the need to replace humanitarianism by a new scientific ethic and the claim that the idiot, the short-sighted, or the deaf and dumb could

---

43. R. Fetscher, 'Eheberatung in Sachsen', Eugenische Rundschau, in *Archiv für Soziale Hygiene und Demographie*, vol. 3, 1928, p. 473.
44. R. Fetscher, *Der Gesundheitspaß*, Dresden, 1927.

not survive in nature, but required institutionalisation in order to prevent procreation. Above all, it was necessary for people to act with self-control and responsibility in the interests of future generations. The perils of alcohol and sexual excess were to be avoided in favour of sobriety, industriousness and a large number of children. The message was repeated by popular health guides and other propaganda methods. Eugenics, christian morality and nationalism were, therefore, combined by such as Muckermann in a vapid organicist ideology, which masked many contradictions and inadequacies in the welfare state. It served to disseminate eugenic values in the hope that there could be voluntary consent to eugenic norms of behaviour.

Muckermann (of the Kaiser Wilhelm Institute for Anthropology) and Luxenburger (an expert on youth psychiatry who was Rüdin's assistant) gave innumerable lectures to Catholic welfare organisations, social workers and educationalists. Joseph Mayer (a theologian, an assistant at the Institut für Caritaswissenschaft and editor of the journal *Caritas*), fearing that the fit were being swamped by degenerates, organised a Caritas conference in 1929 on 'Eugenics und Welfare'. He justified sterilisation for the sake of the higher good of the body politic. Harmsen, who had researched under Grotjahn on population problems injected the spirit of eugenics into the Innere Mission. He directed the Arbeitsgemeinschaft für Volksgesundung, which was an amalgam of numerous organisations and engaged in a social purity campaign, that lent itself readily to eugenic ideas. One aspect of this was active propaganda for a 'German Mother's Day'. The Mother's Day idea was combined with the ideals of national health and racial hygiene and its supporters came from a variety of branches of eugenically oriented welfare organisations.[45]

In addition, welfare officers demanded autocratic powers. Administrators of psychiatric institutions, of homes for vagrants, and of welfare clinics demanded a law for custodial detention to detain anti-social parasites like vagbonds and psychopaths. In 1928 this was supported by the Deutscher Verein für öffentliche und private Fürsorge. A culmination of the fusion of eugenics and welfare was

45. K. Hausen, 'Mütter zwischen Geschäftsinteressen und kultischer Verehrung', in G. Huck (ed.) *Sozialgeschichte der Freizeit*, Wuppertal, 1980, pp. 249–80; Behr Pinnow, 'Vererbungswissenschaft und Eugenik', *Arbeitsgemeinschaft für Volksgesundung. Mitteilungen*, No. 17, 14 June 1929; ZStAP, 15.01, 26233–26235.

the congress organised by the Innere Mission in 1931. Harmsen spoke on the feeble-minded, the Christian eugenicist, Verschuer, spoke on the laws of heredity, and Pastor Happich spoke on the anti-social.[46] The conference sought to refute accusations that Christian charity resulted in a proliferation of the unfit, by accepting sterilisation and incarceration as recognised eugenic measures.[47]

The economic crisis of 1929, however, dealt a crippling blow to positive social welfare. Clinics were closed and benefits were cut, as the apparatus of positive welfare was dismantled. But the crisis also provided an opportunity for more selective welfare programmes with a eugenic rationale. New ideas were advanced of the need for selectivity in the choice of patients and welfare recipients. The conviction grew that a healthier society would result from letting natural selection freely take its course, and negative eugenics and sterilisation increased in importance as 'welfare measures'. The 1932 conference of the Prussian Health Council on sterilisation was called 'Eugenics in the Service of Welfare' and welfare organisations were strongly represented. Eugenics was seen as a means of attack on degenerate social dead weights, and the economics of welfare were much discussed.[48]

The Welfare State

It is tempting to see the authoritarianism of Weimar welfare as providing precedents for the Third Reich. Continuities have been traced between the Weimar concern with chronic illness and Nazi 'euthanasia' or the medical killing of unproductive, inefficient individuals. A case-study of Hamburg as a model district (*Mustergau*) has argued that here was a situation where racial ideology was a legal priority, but where efficiency and cost-effectiveness were priorities in the 'management' of the mentally ill and infirm.[49] Roth

46. H. Harmsen, 'Gegenwartsfragen der Eugenik', *Die Innere Mission*, vol. 26, 1931, pp. 336–9.
47. E. Klee, *Dokumente zur Euthanasie*, Frankfurt am Main, 1985, pp. 29–31; ZStAP, 15.01, 26243: Vererbungslehre und Rassenhygiene 1931–3.
48. J. Noakes, 'Nazism and Eugenics', in Roger Bullen and Hartmut Pogge (eds.), *Ideas into Politics*, London, 1984.
49. A. Ebbinghaus, H. Kaupen-Haas and K.H. Roth (eds.), *Heilen und Vernichten im Mustergau Hamburg*, Hamburg, 1984. For social work under National Socialism, see H.-U. Ott and H. Sünker, *Soziale Arbeit und Faschismus*, Bielefeld, 1986.

has accused the social hygiene movement of the 1920s of laying the basis for racial policies. He stresses the emphasis in public health on degeneration, reconditioning, protective custody, compulsory confinement in an asylum, culling, population measures like parenthood insurance (*Elternschaftsversicherung*) and propaganda to inculcate the 'will to procreate'. From such perspectives the economic crisis of 1929 was important in shifting the emphasis to negative eugenics.[50]

Against such arguments for continuity, a number of objections can be raised. Kater has contrasted the humanity of Weimar welfare (*Fürsorge*) with Nazi preventive measures (*Vorsorge*). However, he overlooks the extent to which social biology underpinned Weimar public health.[51] Roth's advocacy of continuity, on the other hand, is marred by empirical defects leading to interpretative errors. Through misdating and misattributing eugenic measures, he finds that the 1929 economic depression is the single, crucial turning-point, in comparison to which 1918 and 1932–3 are insignificant. But schemes like the eugenic data-banks and psychopath clinics derived from the post-war disorders and factors like professionalism had a greater role to play than purely economic variables.[52] It should also be pointed out that the Weimar eugenicists made a point of disengaging eugenics from anti-semitism and racist nationalism, and had to tread carefully so as not to antagonise radical lobbies such as those for abortion on demand and for nature therapy.

Key areas where continuity might be expected to occur in fact show major rifts. As Lilienthal has pointed out, 1933 marked a break in the continuity of eugenics.[53] One can substantiate this with many instances of eugenicists who were dismissed by the Nazis, like Fetscher, Muckermann and Jewish eugenicists and welfare experts. Others like the anthropologist Scheidt refused to co-operate with the regime while retaining their posts. In 1933 the organisation of eugenics fundamentally changed, as did the relations of eugenicists

50. K.H. Roth (ed.), *Erfassung zur Vernichtung. Von der Sozialhygiene zum 'Gesetz über Sterbehilfe'*, Berlin, 1984.

51. M.H. Kater, 'Die "Gesundheitsführung des Deutschen Volkes"', *Medizinhistorisches Journal*, vol. 18, 1983, pp. 349–75.

52. P. Weindling, 'Soziale Hygiene: Eugenik und medizinische Praxis – Der Fall Alfred Grotjahn', in *Jahrbuch für kritische Medizin 10: Krankheit und Ursachen* (*Argument-Sonderband* 119), Berlin, 1984, pp. 6–20.

53. G. Lilienthal, 'Rassenhygiene im Dritten Reich: Krise und Wende', *Medizinhistorisches Journal*, vol. 14, 1979, pp. 114–34.

to policy-making in public health. The biological values of the 1920s and 1930s reveal many contrasts; in particular anti-semitism and anti-socialism were alien to the 1920s ideology of rebuilding the *Volkskörper*. Perhaps most important were structural discontinuities in health and welfare administration. Labisch and Tennstedt have showed how the Law for the Unification of Health Services of 1934 was not the product of long-term efforts to reform public health in the Weimar Republic. It resulted from a fundamentally new programme by the Nazi medical officer, Gütt, and the Reich Ministry of the Interior. Public health was structured so as to be a means of implementing racial plans for a biological stock-taking and for sterilisation. Whereas the Reich Ministry of the Interior had a low profile in health matters during the 1920s, and indeed checked rather than supported eugenic demands for sterilisation, it was now to be the new authority with overall control of health offices.[54]

The extent to which there was a 'biologisation' of Weimar social policy does not depend on whether or not there was continuity after 1933. The Weimar welfare state ought to be judged on its own terms. Eugenics can be seen as occupying an important place in a system in which professional and scientific demands for the rationalisation of authority were at a premium. A search for those negative eugenic measures like sterilisation and aspects of population policy most closely related to Nazi measures, inevitably conceals many features of biologically-oriented, 'positive' health policies during the Weimar era. These features are analogous to the situation prevailing in Great Britain, France and Scandinavia, where eugenics was fused with innovative schemes of social welfare, and where a multiplicity of welfare agencies prevailed. The emergence of professionals demanding rights of intervention in the home and family was an international phenomenon. What gave Germany a distinctive authoritarian atmosphere was the acuteness of the crisis produced by military defeat and the opportunities provided for state social policy in the 1920s.

Moreover, there was an ambiguity in the aims and practices of welfare, which prevents any easy evaluation. While degeneration and the hereditary transmission of diseases were feared, the prime motives in the treatment of the sick, cripples and mentally abnormal

---

54. A. Labisch and F. Tennstedt, *Der Weg zum Gesetz zur Vereinheitlichung des Gesundheitswesens*, Düsseldorf, 1985.

still revolved around cure and rehabilitation. 'Open' systems of care based on the family were intended to be more humane than treatment in institutions. Case studies are clearly necessary to examine the extent and quality of care in specific branches of welfare. Welfare experts like Löwenstein might be eugenicists, but they still warned that eugenics could all too easily be a class weapon stigmatising poverty as degeneracy. Ferocious critics of social hygiene should also be given their due. The SPD retreated from eugenics over the refusal of people like Grotjahn to support abortion law reform and the doctor and dramatist, Friedrich Wolf, attacked the power of the medical profession as repressive, arguing in favour of lay nature therapy.

Welfare experts projected an image of deteriorating social conditions, thereby establishing the necessity for their services. Norms of behaviour were to be inculcated into the population. Deviance from hygienic precepts would result in disease, and intervention by sanitary authorities. Education was to bring about a docile population, conforming to a stereotype of the ideally healthy family. If necessary, coercive powers could be employed. A remarkable feature of the welfare lobby was its resilience and opportunism. During the post-war crisis experts argued for control of deviants and an extension of positive benefits. During the mid-1920s continuing high rates of morbidity and evidence of poverty showed the need for a more extensive network of clinics. After 1929 negative eugenics came to the rescue of welfare, scientifically proving the necessity for a far more comprehensive and radical programme of survey and sterilisation. In this context, therefore, elite groups trimmed their ideas and policies in accordance with economic and political fluctuations.

The extension of welfare indicates how the experts acquired powers to intervene in the home, family relations and sexual matters. Professionals constituted a new and more subtle type of police authority. The broad-ranging responsibilities of the state, the penetration of a new breed of professionals into administrative posts and committees, and the ideology of co-operating municipal, insurance, scientific and medical, voluntary and state authorities all served to blur the distinction between state and society. Integration was reinforced by the organicist ideology of the *Volkskörper*. The ideology and institution of welfare clearly had anti-democratic implications, although there was some opposition from socially

159

radical groups of professionals and left-wing politicians. There was also administrative inertia. Within the state there was considerable fragmentation: welfare schemes were continually sabotaged by Finance Ministries, and legal officials emphasised the limits of state and professional powers. Political divisions were also a deterrent to resorting to democratic processes for new legislation. Frustration with political and legal barriers to the implementation of comprehensive measures, therefore, prompted some welfare experts to see Nazism as an opportunity for imposing grandiose measures on a compulsory basis.

The divisions within the state, and the problematic co-ordination of a multiplicity of welfare authorities, suggest that welfare and health functioned best as autonomous and professionalised hierarchies. Local co-ordination of administrative offices, clinics and hospitals proved the viability of a welfare state that broke down the traditions of lay self-administration in favour of professional powers. Individual rights were transcended by 'higher' social needs like the health of the *Volkskörper* and of future generations. Scientifically-minded professionals were thwarted in their attempt at creating centrally administered welfare agencies under professional control. Although the feeling grew that a more authoritarian political climate would remove irritating obstacles, such as personal rights and political radicalism, that impeded the scientific solution of social ills advocated by professional experts, welfare workers accepted the constraints of the democratic structures for the time being, and were to some extent able to manipulate these to their own advantage. As welfare fell far short of the ideals of comprehensiveness, public health officials, psychiatrists and social workers maintained their power, not on the basis of real achievement, but because of monitoring and controlling functions. Alarmist predictions over the declining birth rate, the degeneration of the family, inherited mental and physical disabilities, and youth delinquency served to sustain and expand the new technocracy. Within this context, welfare and social medicine were innovative methods for the defence of national values. Officials had a sense of mission that they were to save the nation from racial extermination and restore it to fitness. Reports on the horrifying extent of disease, poverty and malnutrition were, therefore, very much in the interest of professional experts.

6
Industrial Hygiene:
A State Obligation?
Industrial Pathology as a Problem
in German Social Policy

Dietrich Milles

Origins and Handicaps

In the 1980s the various branches of the German social insurance system celebrated their hundredth anniversary (1883 health insurance, 1884 accident insurance, 1889 disability insurance). Hardly any social institution in Germany can look back on such an unbroken tradition and such a powerful influence.[1] From the point of view of the current preoccupation with continuities in German history, the social insurance system demands special attention. For not only were the central standards and values of bourgeois society

This chapter is based on research within the project 'Social conditions of preventive interventions in "industrial pathology" exemplified by the Occupational Medical Service', which was carried out at the University of Bremen under the direction of Professor Dr Rainer Müller in the research centre for 'Risks of reproduction, social movements and social policy' and subsidised by the Deutsche Forschungsgemeinschaft in their research programme 'Social conditions of socio-political interventions: state, intermediary authorities and self-help'.
1. See H. Rothfels, *Theodor Lohmann und die Kampfjahre der staatlichen Sozialpolitik 1871–1905*, Berlin, 1927; F. Kleeis, *Die Geschichte der Sozialversicherung in Deutschland*, Berlin, 1927; V. Hentschel, *Geschichte der deutschen Sozialpolitik (1880–1980). Soziale Sicherung und kollektives Arbeitsrecht*, Frankfurt am Main, 1983; P.A. Köhler and H.F. Zacher (eds.), *Ein Jahrhundert Sozialversicherung in der Bundesrepublik Deutschland, Frankreich, Großbritannien, Österreich und der Schweiz*, Berlin, 1981; W.J. Mommsen and W. Mock (eds.), *Die Entstehung des Wohlfahrtsstaates in Großbritannien und Deutschland 1850–1950*, Stuttgart, 1982; G.A. Ritter, *Sozialversicherung in Deutschland und England. Entstehung und Grundzüge im Vergleich*, Munich, 1983; F. Tennstedt, *Vom Proleten zum Industriearbeiter. Arbeiterbewegung und Sozialpolitik in Deutschland 1800–1914*, Cologne, 1983; E. Wickenhagen, *Geschichte der gewerblichen Unfallversicherung*, 2 vols., Munich, 1980.

(health and security) fixed in this system; it also established an interrelationship between scientific and official competences, between experts and authorities, and between the definition and treatment of problems, which was functional to the maintenance of the social order. In addition, its establishment meant that the state withdrew from many direct social responsibilities, because many problems could now be handed over to the self-governing social insurance system. Thus, from its very beginning, the system took over several socio-political tasks which before had been the province of poor-law policies,[2] as well as central tasks of *Arbeiterschutz* (workers' protection – a term which was later, especially under National Socialism, transformed into the meaningless term *Arbeitsschutz* [work protection]). In this respect, the triumph of the social insurance system – which had not been predictable at its inception – meant the withdrawal of responsibility from the state and the state's systematic renunciation of competence to make preventive interventions in the conditions governing risks to life and health in industrial society.

Not health insurance, which was introduced first, but accident insurance was the central problem when the Prussian-German social constitution was launched after the foundation of the German Empire in 1870–1. It would have been enough for a comprehensive system of health insurance to extend existing institutions, private insurance schemes and poverty policies.[3] But accidents touched on a sore point in society; they were symbols for everyday hazards and pauperisation. They were also a problem for civil law, which treated questions of liability in cases of injuries as questions of guilt in order to force the party responsible for the injury to act according to the law. On the other hand, accidents were an inevitable consequence of industrial development, and the legal accountability for existing injuries should not restrict entrepreneurial initiative. The solution, a replacement of entrepreneurial liability by socialising the hazards, was only insufficiently completed by the Liability Law of 1871. In

2. See S. Leibfried and F. Tennstedt, 'Armenpolitik und Arbeiterpolitik. Zur Entwicklung und Krise der traditionellen Sozialpolitik der Verteilungsformen', in S. Leibfried and F. Tennstedt (eds.), *Politik der Armut und Spaltung des Sozialstaats*, Frankfurt am Main, 1985, pp. 64–93.
3. C. Sachße and F. Tennstedt, *Geschichte der Armenfürsorge in Deutschland. Vom Spätmittelalter bis zum 1. Weltkrieg*, Stuttgart, Berlin, Cologne and Mainz, 1980.

keeping with its general approach, the Prussian-German government thought first about a system of general accident insurance. In this context, in 1876, Bismarck emphasised the idea of insurance instead of an extension of public control.[4] Leading industrialists intervened and achieved the deferral of plans for an Accident Insurance Law. Instead, a Health Insurance Law was elaborated relatively quickly and passed in 1883. Health insurance provided several advantages in the context of the threat of class division, conflict and rebellion which was then under discussion as 'the social question'; it could be invoked for a period of at least thirteen weeks, to cover any illness, regardless of the cause. Close interconnections between chronic diseases and conditions of work, accidents and industrial hierarchy, endemic disease and living conditions, etc., became indistinct. Social inequality in illness and death lost its scandalous direct expression. There was a long time between the cause of the injury and the clarification of the question of guilt. Even absolute poverty was counterbalanced to a certain, limited extent, though the insurance did not cover all necessities.

Nevertheless, health insurance raised problems because it tended to become the only form of insurance against hazards to life and health, and this implied the creation of a central, state-controlled institution. Employers and liberal politicians condemned such a tendency, labelling it 'state socialism'. It became ever more apparent as the prospect of a unification of the insurance and health systems was raised (e.g. in the preliminary stages of the Reich Insurance Statute in 1911). But the authority of the employer was retained in the special area of production. For example, the Accident Insurance Law of 1884, in combination with the Health Insurance Law, made it possible to transfer extremely serious individual cases of damage to health to accident insurance after thirteen weeks, if it could be proved that there was a strict causal relationship, that is, that the damage was the result of a sudden and 'external' event at the workplace.[5]

4. See R. Simons, *Staatliche Gewerbeaufsicht und gewerbliche Berufsgenossenschaften. Entstehung und Entwicklung des dualen Aufsichtssystems im Arbeitsschutz in Deutschland von den Anfängen bis zum Ende der Weimarer Republik*, Frankfurt am Main, 1984, pp. 35ff.; A. Pensky, *Schutz der Arbeiter vor Gefahren für Leben und Gesundheit. Ein Beitrag zur Geschichte des Gesundheitsschutzes für Arbeiter in Deutschland*, Bremerhaven, 1987.
5. For the implications of the concept 'accident', see H. Barta, *Kausalität im Sozialrecht. Entstehung und Funktion der sogenannten Theorie der wesentlichen*

The special role of accident insurance implied setting a course for workers' health protection. The view that prevailed was a restrictive one, which regarded technical development and technical measures as providing optimal protection. The concern with the protection of residents living near industrial plants and of consumers, which had been emphasised at the beginning, was also lost.

The first worker protection laws, such as the Prussian 'Regulation on the occupation of young workers in factories' of March 1839, were developed in a constellation of social interests which combined several different aspects. They combined an interest in a qualified workforce (i.e. the demand for compulsory school attendance for all children and the prohibition of child labour) with an interest in maintaining a population physically fit for military service and for work, an interest in regulating the conditions of competition so that the smaller companies could not compensate for relative technical backwardness by exploiting manpower ruthlessly, and an interest in maintaining social control through a redistribution of social power. From then on, workers' health protection ('protection of workers against dangers to life and health', as it was known in official parlance) was never an end in itself; there was no recognised basis for socio-political intervention and no direct pressure arose from the existence of industrial hazards. The progress of protection depended on its proponents arguing in terms of aspects relevant to large industrial nations: labour market considerations, fitness for military service, productivity, and order. But the dilemma of state-controlled workers' protection was thus fixed from the beginning: it soon came up against the narrow limits represented by the capitalist interest in exploitation and nationalistic definitions of suitability – paradoxically, the very terms which had first inspired it.

The Trade Regulations issued for the first time in Prussia on 17 January 1845 constituted the actual framework of workers' protection. They did not contain any direct regulation for health protection, yet they introduced the free employer-employee relationship, and thus the wage relationship, as the basis for all social regulation in companies. Paragraph 13b demanded only that employers take proper 'consideration for the health and morality' of journeymen, assistants, and apprentices. These two 'central terms of

---

Bedingung. Analyse der grundlegenden Judikatur des Reichsversicherungsamtes in Unfallversicherungssachen (1884–1914), 2 vols, Berlin and Munich, 1983.

work protection in the nineteenth century'[6] were directed against the 'excesses, tumults, and riots' which accompanied the extension of industrial society in the *Vormärz*.[7] Even the system of factory inspectors, which was established by the trade regulations in 1849 and 1853, was a response to the menacing rootlessness and social rebellion of the workers. From now on, factory inspectors, and later local police authorities with powers of oversight were instituted. But in contrast to the British example, until 1878 the factory inspectors in Prussia were only an optional institution with limited autonomy. The Trade Regulations of 21 June 1869 did not change a thing. They contained a provision on the licensing of dangerous plants (in §16) and ordered every employer 'to produce and install at his own expense all facilities which are necessary to protect the worker against hazards to life and health as far as is possible in keeping with the special character of the commercial enterprise or factory' (§107, later §120). To this day this has been a contradictory basis for health protection, because the terms 'in keeping with', 'as far as possible' and 'necessary' invite the exercise of an official discretion, which – in case of doubt – has commonly found against the interests of the employees.

Bismarck first thought of following the British example of factory inspectors. But after a series of strikes and the first crisis of rapid industrial expansion in Germany in the 1870s, he thought it wrong to solve 'the problems implied in the employer-employee relationship by creating a new class of civil servants, which contains all the elements for the multiplication of bureaucratic mistakes'.[8] While Bismarck thus adopted the views of the Centralverband Deutscher Industrieller founded in 1876, reform-minded experts of the ministerial bureaucracy, especially Theodor Lohmann, had proposed another way, taking other European states as examples. Lohmann saw the necessity of a political solution which fixed the degree of protective measures for the employer 'according to the state of the industrial development of a people'. While he thought the German

6. Tennstedt, *Vom Proleten*, p. 93.
7. A. Lüdtke, *"Gemeinwohl", Polizei und "Festungspraxis"*. *Staatliche Gewaltsamkeit und innere Verwaltung in Preußen 1815–1850*, Göttingen, 1982; R. Reith, *Der Aprilaufstand von 1848 in Konstanz. Zur biographischen Dimension von "Hochverrat und Aufruhr". Versuch einer historischen Protestanalyse*, Sigmaringen, 1982.
8. Letter to Achenbach, 10 August 1877, quoted by Simons, *Staatliche Gewerbeaufsicht*, p. 37.

Empire was progressive in its regulations (as far as child labour, night-work and Sunday work were concerned, and to a lesser extent women's work), he maintained that the institutions for carrying out and controlling the regulations were 'extremely backward', especially when compared to Great Britain and France. He demanded the extension of the factory inspector system.[9]

In the amendment to the Trading Regulations of 17 July 1878, factory inspection became, in fact, obligatory. Factory safety and health control was assigned to special officials who were appointed by the state governments. But their authorisation did not allow them to attack the causes of health hazards; their task was rather to mediate between employers and employees and to support the employers by giving advice.[10] The decision against an effective factory health and safety control system was at the same time a decision in favour of a social security system. From the 1880s, a 'dualism' of state institutions (factory health and safety control) and corporatist institutions (trade associations as representatives of the agency for accident insurance) developed in the sphere of workers' health protection. The lack of effective control on the part of the state became a central topic in the early 1890s, when anti-socialist legislation introduced in 1878 and the hard line of repression had failed and a positive cooperation between state and society was sought. The social reformers made the defects of workers' protection responsible for social hardship and therefore for the insufficient integration of the workers into bourgeois society.[11] Again an efficient extension of factory safety and health control was demanded. Instead of acting as night-watchman, the state should intervene 'with a great number of officials trained in technical questions, hygiene and social policy'.[12] During this period the number of officials in factory health and safety control increased rapidly, but it

9. T. Lohmann, *Die Fabrik-Gesetzgebung der Staaten des europäischen Kontinents*, Berlin, 1878, pp. 33ff.; cf. L. Machtan, 'Risikoversicherung anstatt Gesundheitsschutz für Arbeiter. Zum historisch-politischen Entstehungszusammenhang der Unfallversicherungsgesetzgebung im Bismarckreich', *Leviathan*, vol. 13, 1985, pp. 420–41.

10. T. Sommerfeld, 'Die Gewerbehygiene', in S.N. Kreiss (ed.), *Fortschritte der Hygiene 1888–1913*, Berlin, 1913, pp. 134–208.

11. U. Ratz, *Sozialreform und Arbeiterschaft. Die "Gesellschaft für Soziale Reform" und die sozialdemokratische Arbeiterbewegung von der Jahrhundertwende bis zum Ausbruch des Ersten Weltkrieges*, Berlin, 1980.

12. H. Herkner, 'Zur Kritik und Reform der deutschen Arbeiterschutzgesetzgebung', *Archiv für soziale Gesetzgebung und Statistik*, vol. 3, 1890, pp. 209–61.

was increasingly demanded that physicians should also participate in the control system. This demand was supported by physicians committed to public health, and by social reformers, less by representatives of the medical profession, and certainly not by the technically oriented factory inspectors.[13] Even though the Occupational Medical Service was established in this period, nothing was achieved in dealing with the fundamental problems of workers' health protection. These problems, however, have remained an insuperable handicap from the very beginning and have prevented effective work by state occupational physicians up to the present.

Approaches to Industrial Pathogenicity – A Problem Frequently Suppressed in Industrial Societies

The industrial production of goods and the social conditions caused by it imply numerous health hazards. Environmental groups have made this a topic for discussion in recent years. The sources of this industrial pathogenicity, however, attract little public and only limited political attention. The sphere of production has remained an arena resistant to politicisation. On the one hand, industrial development in itself seemed to guarantee social welfare; on the other hand, industrial law and work protection regulations seemed to suffice. But this is the case only as long as the relations that generate industrial pathology are dethematised, that is, as long, as their articulation and politicisation are inhibited.[14] The dethematisation of industrial pathogenicity safeguards the private sphere of production, relieves state or official responsibility and individualises the factual consequences. In the following pages I want to demonstrate paradigmatically how social policy measures against industrial pathogenicity have had an effect precisely because of their ineffectiveness.

Social policy has stood in the area of conflict between 'state' and 'society' from its very beginning.[15] The nineteenth-century term

---

13. For this discussion, cf. T. Sommerfeld, *Der Gewerbearzt*, Jena, 1905.
14. See D. Milles and R. Müller, 'Zur Dethematisierung sozialpolitischer Aufgaben am Beispiel des Gesundheitsschutzes für Arbeiter im historischen Rückblick', in F.X. Kaufmann (ed.), *Staat, intermediäre Instanzen und Selbsthilfe*, Munich, 1987, pp. 68ff.
15. Kaufmann (ed.), *Staat*, pp. 9f.

Social-Politik covered various areas in which state responsibility had been handed over to charitable institutions, trade unions, social insurance schemes, or employers' associations.[16] This process, which began in the middle of the nineteenth century, had two seemingly contradictory features; on the one hand socialisation (especially of risks connected with industrial production), on the other hand individualisation (especially of the ensuing damages). These aspects were successfully connected by constructing social policy as a system of social insurance, working according to the 'model of social correction'.[17] This model is based upon the principle of a positively desirable 'character of the factory', which promotes social welfare and makes protective and caring measures necessary only in special cases which lie outside the normal pattern of production. In these cases, state measures correct inequalities between the parties to a contract (e.g. in industrial law), limit the 'normal' pattern of production, guarantee consistent conditions of production, prevent advantages in competition that might be gained as a result of extreme hazards, provide support against pauperisation, and always contain aspects of social control. They aim at 'inclusion'[18] and support the 'obligation to social integration',[19] namely the imperative that individual and collective reproduction is carried out through gainful employment. Social policy not only sustains such an assumed 'normality', it also intervenes in order to bring about this normality. The recent diagnosis of a 'crisis of work-centred society'[20] emphasises the fact that this 'normalisation' has a paradoxical character; it takes place in spite of the fact that assumptions of 'normality' are no longer or only slightly relevant, and possibly just because of this fact. Thus, the tie between social security and gainful work becomes stronger even if mass unemploy-

16. Cf. E. Pankoke, 'Geschichtliche Grundlagen und gesellschaftliche Enwicklung moderner Sozialpolitik', in B. Schäfers (ed.), *Sozialpolitik in der Bundesrepublik* (*Gegenwartskunde*, Sonderheft 4), Opladen, 1983, pp. 23–40.

17. W. Däubler, *Arbeitsrecht*, 2 vols, Reinbek, 1986; D. Milles, 'Schwierigkeiten einer produktionsbezogenen Gesundheitspolitik', in R. Bauer and S. Leibfried (eds.), *Sozialpolitische Bilanz. II. Tagung der Sektion Sozialpolitik der DGS*, Bremen, 1986, pp. 251–67.

18. N. Luhmann, *Politische Theorie im Wohlfahrtsstaat*, Munich, 1981, pp. 30ff.

19. *Sozialpolitik und Sozialstaat* (Working papers of the Research Centre on 'Risks of reproduction, social movements and social policy', no. 51), Bremen, 1985, p. 399.

20. J. Matthes (ed.), *Krise der Arbeitsgesellschaft? Verhandlungen des 21. Soziologentages in Bamberg 1982*, Frankfurt am Main, 1983.

ment becomes a chronic and structural problem and 'normal' male full-time employment is increasingly the exception. The connection between social security and gainful employment stabilises the employer–employee relationship and binds the workers in a special way to the risks of their work. This has an effect especially on trade unions, which are oriented to gainful employment. Work-centred society rests on the obligation to pursue gainful employment and therefore legitimises values like productivity, economy, rationalisation and growth. It unites the people who profit and those who suffer from it.

According to Max Weber the supposition of normality in a work-centred society can be described as a secular form of the Protestant ethic. In dealing with hazards to life and health in connection with gainful employment, it is decisive that the individuals have internalised the obligation to pursue gainful employment as a work ethic and have transformed it into a 'finalisation' of the body.[21] The persons affected fulfil themselves the obligation which the social conditions impose. In accordance with the employers and other 'usufructuaries', they regard sickness as inability and health as ability to work. Thus, they accept the basic pattern of the social security system.[22]

In the nineteenth century social policy was elaborated in the area of conflict between the Bonapartist authoritarian state and bourgeois society; this process has been characterised by the terms 'legalisation, bureaucratisation, economisation, and professionalisation'.[23] The extension of social policy took place mainly in the area of positive help to individuals, whereas the areas of workers' and environmental protection seemed to be adequately regulated through the compensatory payments provided by social insurance.

21. M. Foucault, *Die Geburt der Klinik*, Munich, 1975; J. Attali, *Die kannibalische Ordnung. Von der Magie zur Computermedizin*, Frankfurt am Main, 1981; D. Milles and R. Müller, 'Workers' bodies in occupational medicine. A historical survey', Paper presented at the conference 'Historische, anthropologische und soziologische Aspekte von Gesundheit und Krankheit in Deutschland', Centre for Interdisciplinary Research, Bielefeld, 1987.

22. *Sozialpolitik und Sozialstaat*, p. 23.

23. See Kaufmann, *Staat*, p. 13; H. Achinger, *Sozialpolitik als Gesellschaftspolitik*, Reinbek, 1958; C. v. Ferber, *Sozialpolitik in der Wohlstandsgesellschaft*, Hamburg, 1967; F. Tennstedt, 'Sozialgeschichte der Sozialversicherung', in M. Blohmke *et al* (eds.), *Handbuch der Sozialmedizin*, 3 vols, Stuttgart, 1976, pp. 385–492; B. Badura and P. Gross, *Sozialpolitische Perspektiven. Eine Einführung in Grundlagen und Probleme sozialer Dienstleistungen*, Munich, 1976.

The effort to develop a preventive and creative social policy has been manifest only in a few historical epochs. The creation of an Occupational Medical Service by the state can be regarded as an important product of one of these epochs. Its subsequent history, however, reflects the problems that social policy (in this case health policy) faces when confronted with the demands of production.

Industrial pathogenicity covers first of all the special stresses operating on individual workers in certain jobs and trades. In addition, it covers the problems which the industrial pattern of production brings about in the environment and in the living conditions of residents, consumers, etc. Finally, industrial pathogenicity also refers to the constraints which prevent a social debate on or a preventative reform of the causes. As industrialisation progressed, an imbalance developed between the problems that were shifted onto each worker and citizen, and the individual's ability to influence and solve them which produced a call for social policy measures and for a redistribution of responsibilities.

Social policy measures against industrial pathogenicity were developed first in the framework of workers' protection following the example of industrially developed Great Britain. These measures, however, were subordinated to industrial development from the very beginning.[24] Employers, workers, the authorities and the Social Democrats all hoped, each in terms of its own ideology, that technical progress would eliminate problematic working and living conditions; they all hoped technical progress would bring about individual as well as social welfare. Therefore, the measures were mainly limited to the deployment of technical devices.

The foundation of the Empire in 1871 and the following crises made it obvious that Germany's technical, economic and social development demanded new strategies. Thus, in the 1880s the social insurance system was developed, which made a problem-orientated workers' protection superfluous and placed compensation in the centre of the social management of industrial pathogenicity. Official measures within the social insurance system followed the principles of a 'permanent extension of externalising solutions for the existential hazards of the workers'.[25] These externalising solutions were ineffective because they distracted attention from causal interrela-

24. Tennstedt, *Vom Proleten.*
25. Leibfried and Tennstedt, 'Armenpolitik', p. 74.

tions and amounted to little more than 'individualising legal positions'.[26]

The social security system promoted a selective, restrictive and compensating approach to the problems. The overlapping of workers' protection (its definition reduced to accidents and their prevention) with accident insurance meant that health protection for workers tended to become a protection against the consequences of the inability to work. The close linking of certain compensatory payments, like the pension paid to a victim of poisoning, to the proof of a causal relationship between the source of the disease and the disease itself, serves even today as a narrow filter, structured according to financial and legal criteria. Only individual claims can pass, and then with considerable difficulties. Doctors who were socially committed, such as Ludwig Teleky, Louis Levin, Theodor Sommerfeld, or Wilhelm Hanauer, wanted to expand this filter, using scientific arguments to demand the inclusion of occupational diseases in accident insurance. Together with social reformers in Germany and abroad, they expected that compulsory registration of these diseases would lead to an increase of knowledge in industrial hygiene and that compensation would mean a significant improvement for the persons affected. These endeavours, however, were directed against the effects of the insurance system, in which the social role of the doctor and clinico-scientific medicine are embedded in a way which stabilises society. Today these endeavours have reached a cul-de-sac, in which occupational diseases are marginalised.

Not even the differentiation of the subject hygiene under the influence of industrialisation[27] was able to bring about an effective connection between medical knowledge and social policy. This connection was on the agenda and even attempted in the 1880s with the concept of threshold values, i.e. the general fixing of maximum tolerable concentrations of poisonous substances or pollutants.[28] But at the very time when the social insurance system began to take

26. Ibid., p. 24.
27. M. Hubenstorf, 'Sozialhygiene und industrielle Pathologie im späten Kaiserreich', in R. Müller (ed.), *Industrielle Pathologie in historischer Sicht*, Bremen, 1985, pp. 82–107.
28. See D. Milles and R. Müller, 'Die relative Schädlichkeit industrieller Produktion. Zur Geschichte des Grenzwertkonzeptes in der Gewerbehygiene', in G. Winter (ed.), *Grenzwerte*, Düsseldorf, 1985, pp. 227–62.

root the medical approach was blocked by the 'triumph' of bacteriology, which supported a technical and mechanistic concept of the tasks of health protection for workers.

Health protection for workers was thematised in the context of the social reform movement only to a limited extent, although with increasing frequency.[29] In this context, however, not industrial pathogenicity but the 'social question' was central. Social reformers wanted to protect the health of the working masses in order to enable them to participate in society's material and cultural goods. State intervention in the sphere of material interests was an appropriate means to bring this about, so long as it was accompanied by a liberalisation of the existing political and legal system. They did not so much celebrate the existing capitalist-industrial social order as tolerate it, both because it appeared to be practically inevitable, and because any radical attempt to fight it appeared to retard rather than to advance the rise of the working class to full participation in contemporary culture.

The fact that a growing stratum could drop out of the existing social order because the consequences of capitalist-industrial development could not be effectively managed was viewed as a threat to society under the rubric 'social question' – especially after the failure of the anti-socialist laws. In this sense, social reform worked as a 'regulator of the system'.[30] It also worked as a stabilising force in the system insofar as health protection and participation in the 'light of culture' were not regarded as systemic, but rather as ancillary problems. Social reformers failed to perceive the artificial demarcation and individualisation of problems connected with the dominance of technical and compensatory strategies within the social insurance system. The causal interrelationship between industrial pathogenicity and the aims of industrial-capitalist social policy was no longer in focus. Two principles limited the scope for social change: the economy (ability to work, productivity, optimisation) and protection of the social hierarchy (factory organisation, self-legitimation of bureaucratic procedures). Social-reform

29. D. Milles, 'Zur Dethematisierung der industriellen Pathologie. Entwicklungslinien in der Geschichte der Gewerbehygiene vor 1933', in R. Müller *et al* (eds.), *Arbeitsmedizin in sozialer Verantwortung. Studien zur Epidemiologie und Bewältigung der industriellen Pathologie*, Bremen, 1985, pp. 9–37.
30. M.-L. Plessen, *Die Wirksamkeit des Vereins für Socialpolitik von 1872–1890. Studien zum Kathedar- und Staatssozialismus*, Berlin, 1975, p. 126.

positions were acceptable because they did not question capitalist development.[31] They were successful to a certain extent because they realised and paid attention to the importance of public opinion, of professionalisation, and, above all, of the political autonomy of institutions and practices.

The Occupational Medical Service, which was established in Munich in 1909 with the employment of the first state occupational physician (*Landesgewerbearzt*), bears all the features of a social reform policy. A certain practical helplessness resulted from a list of duties which was from the very beginning rather broadly defined and unspecific. The state occupational physician was challenged by the need to impose high standards, but had no equipment to achieve them.[32]

Looking back on his personal and institutional career, the first state occupational physician, Franz Koelsch, who regarded himself as the 'founder and representative of modern occupational medicine', wrote that the traditional 'so-called "hygiene problems" have today become a field for special technicians.' State occupational physicians should deal with physiological, clinical and medical-insurance questions instead and also develop a considered response to modern technology and social policy. Koelsch succeeded in giving a special justification for preventive measures by indicating the duty 'to use one's physical and mental forces as well as possible in the interests of the public'. Consequently 'manpower was under the state's special protection'. Occupational medicine had the task of 'maintaining and improving as far as possible the health and performance capacity [*Leistungsfähigkeit*] of the worker, preventing premature exhaustion, and preventing and counterbalancing injuries caused by work.' On these points Koelsch based his hopes

---

31. H.-J. v. Berlepsch, 'Überlegungen zur Reform der Arbeiterschutzbestimmungen in der Gewerbeordnungsnovelle von 1891', in Müller (ed.), *Industrielle Pathologie*, pp. 128–47.

32. See D. Milles, '75 Jahre Landesgewerbeärzte in Deutschland. Franz Koelsch und die Probleme einer Institution zwischen Gewerbeaufsicht und öffentlicher Gesundheitspflege', in R. Müller and D. Milles (eds.), *Beiträge zur Geschichte der Arbeiterkrankheiten und der Arbeitsmedizin in Deutschland*, Bremerhaven, 1984, pp. 580–602; D. Milles, 'Anfänge, Entwicklungen und Probleme des gewerbeärztlichen Dienstes in Deutschland', in R. Müller *et al* (eds.), *Industrielle Pathologie in historischer Sicht. Arbeitstagung*, Bremen, 1985, pp. 159–81; D. Milles and R. Müller, 'Der Beitrag der Landesgewerbeärzte zur Entwicklung der Arbeitsmedizin', in *Arbeitsmedizin, Sozialmedizin, Präventivmedizin*, vol. 21, 1986, pp. 116–20.

for support for the Occupational Medical Service.[33] Professionalisation of occupational medicine should be supported by the state because in this way the mutual obligation of citizen and society could be fulfilled. The conservation and improvement of workers' capacity to work seemed to be the focus where individual and social demands met.

The Physician in German Factory Inspection

There is a basic pattern in the history of the Occupational Medical Service. In a speech delivered before the Upper Bavarian medical council Friedrich Bauer linked the arguments which in the end led to the employment of Franz Koelsch as the first state occupational physician in Bavaria to a 'number of injuries which very frequently have as a consequence the illness and incapacity of the individual' and which have their causes in society. 'Public hygiene must, therefore, take its position beside individual hygiene if the individual is to have effective protection.' Economic and cultural progress were based on this. That is why

> the state, from the point of view of state egotism, has the greatest interest in protecting its citizens' health; but this is also its duty, since the individual loses the chance to protect himself on his own effectively against injuries arising from the social environment by integrating into the great society and subordinating himself to its living conditions and laws.

This task was, according to Bauer, particularly relevant for members of the working class, 'for whom in a great number of occupations the hazards to life and health are far greater than the rest and who, therefore, require more protection.'[34] The relationship between individual and society, between worker and employer, and between factory and state – conflict-ridden as it was in everyday life – seemed to be adjustable via the terms 'capacity to work' and 'productivity'.

Against this background, medical professionalisation of factory

33. F. Koelsch, 'Rückblick und Ausblick – der Weg der deutschen Arbeitsmedizin und ihre Forderungen in der Gegenwart', *Arbeitsmedizin*, vol. 1, 1962, p. 17.
34. F. Bauer, *Ärzte als Gewerbeinspektoren*, Munich, 1905, p. 4.

inspection started. It must, however, be emphasised that this professionalisation was rationalised in terms of the duties of the state.
The Deutscher Verein für öffentliche Gesundheitspflege postulated
in 1906: 'A beneficial development of industrial hygiene is unthinkable without the physicians' participation.'[35] This statement called
for the employment of state occupational physicians. From the
point of view of their duties, it particularly emphasised the changing
forms of pollution and dangers which could not be sufficiently
registered, analysed, and combated by existing technical factory
inspection. The medical professionalisation of factory inspection
was intended to create a system of experts which would supply the
necessary knowledge for the authorities in question, and, at the
same time, promote research and training. Such a professionalisation was also expected to provide higher labour productivity for the
employer: 'The intelligent employer is more and more convinced of
the fact that the more he ensures light and air, cleanliness and
tidiness in his factory, the more the workers' productivity rises, the
resistance against occupational hazards and accidents increases, and
premature exhaustion is prevented.' Therefore, every improvement
in the field of occupational hygiene meant at the same time an
economic improvement. The employers had recognised this, e.g. in
leaflets distributed in large companies, but in view of continuing
levels of morbidity and mortality this insight had to be further
propagated.[36]

This summary of the effects of professionalisation on companies
was a calculated one, since from the point of view of the employer it
was by no means clear why a medical professionalisation of factory
inspection was necessary for internal company training and instruction. Its author, Emanuel Roth, manoeuvred around the cliffs of the
employer–worker relationship by demanding, first 'a stricter control of measures taken in the interests of workers' protection',
secondly, 'corresponding instruction and education of workers by
factory physicians, occupational physicians, or state employed
physicians', and, finally, from the physician in all his activities an
awareness 'that he cannot demand what is technically impracticable

35. Quoted by E. Roth, 'Die gewerbehygienischen Aufgaben des Fabrikarztes,
des Gewerbearztes und des beamteten Arztes', in P. Fraenckel, E. Roth and J. Kaup,
Über Gewerbekrankheiten und Gewerbehygiene. Drei Vorträge, Berlin, 1915, p. 39.
36. Ibid., pp. 29f.

or what exceeds the capacities of the factory in question'.[37] Thus, occupational hygiene became a sort of bonus depending on increased productivity and corresponding profitability.

Accordingly, Roth had considerable trouble differentiating between the factory doctor and the state occupational physician. Factory doctors had, in fact, more knowledge than general practitioners.

> But they could never replace the occupational physician as an independent state officer. For the factory doctors are first of all *Vertrauensärzte*, i.e. doctors whom the factory management trusts, whereas the state has the obligation to control the measures enacted for the protection of the workers by authorities designed for this purpose. This is also relevant for the examination of workers before starting a job as well as at fixed intervals during the period of the employment, which have been stipulated for a great number of factories, and for the oversight of the sickness register in these factories by state employed doctors.

Factory managements should, wherever possible, be interested in having a reliable permanent staff of older workers at their disposal, but this was not a concern of the state.[38]

Even today a clear regulation of competences of medical practitioners, factory doctors, state occupational physicians, and doctors in the public health departments would be advisable, but Roth's proposed regulation was not that clear: if the social obligation to maintain and protect health and productivity is taken over by the employers and if only the *Vertrauensarzt* is capable of 'controlling permanently' the specific conditions which have to be taken into account, then the tasks fixed by the state can be carried out sufficiently and effectively by the factory doctors. The control by 'state-employed doctors', cannot suffice and must remain ineffective. Therefore, it was necessary to define which forms of oversight inside the factories had to be exercised by state-employed doctors and how state occupational physicians might qualify for this task (in terms of education, research and the demands of factory doctors).

Such a formulation of the question is relevant in historical perspective, because there were other models and procedures in other

37. Ibid., p. 31.
38. Ibid., p. 32.

European countries in those years, and because at that time people were particularly interested in knowing what was happening beyond their own frontiers, especially across the Channel.

Physicians in Factory Inspection in Europe

Before 1889, the year of the Berlin Workers' Protection Conference, only seven European states had established authorities to enforce laws for workers' protection: Great Britain, Denmark, France, Switzerland, the German Empire, Russia, Austria; in the same year Belgium, the Netherlands, Finland and Sweden joined them. The first comparative report of the International Labour Office in 1910 could name twenty-two European states which had established factory inspection. The international congresses for workers' protection in Zürich in August 1897 and in Paris in July 1900 also pursued the issue. The International Association for Legal Workers' Protection emerged from the Paris congress, which demanded in the words of its president, Professor von Philippovich, 'the employment of female medical inspectors and of inspectors coming from among the workers' and suggested that 'there should be an exchange of ideas between factory inspectors from different countries'.[39]

The subsequent activities of the International Association concentrated on individual regulations, especially on the specific protection of working women, on particular forms of poisoning, etc. In 1906, the congregation of delegates in Geneva decided that the sections in the member states should give reports to the Association's office about state measures 'to make sure that workers' protection was put into effect'. Kähler and Lösser wrote the report about Germany. In addition to the international report, which was compiled by Stephan Bauer, the papers on medical inspection by Theodor Sommerfeld and L. Carozzi also excited attention.

There was great international variety in the involvement of medical competence in factory inspection. There was a perceptible tension between the tasks which arose principally from technical conditions in the factories and in which physicians and technicians had to co-operate, and the tasks which arose from the state's

39. Quoted ibid., p. v.

obligation to maintain and improve hygiene, in which the physicians had the function more of advisers. In Great Britain, a stronger emphasis was put on the second task, which resulted particularly in reports and statistical investigations.[40] The British mortality statistics for the male population, classified according to occupations, were for many years the only reliable source of their kind and have provided a model to this day. But whereas in Germany the newly established institution of social insurance breathed new life into the scientific debates about social and industrial pathology, in Great Britain a clinging to out-dated forms of organising social security led to stagnation. It would be wrong to attribute to the German authorities a greater 'knowledge about the prevention of causes of occupational diseases',[41] yet the rapid medical professionalisation due to social insurance supported the endeavours for social medicine or social hygiene to a much greater degree than in Great Britain. The different traditions in terms of poor-law poverty policy, however, were even more important. Whereas social insurance in Germany addressed the qualified, skilled worker in a new way and, thus, assumed normal employment on the basis of the Protestant work ethic, the British insurance system was mainly aimed at those actually in need, i.e. those who could not maintain an existence on the basis of their own labour. The integrating and controlling regulation of behaviour through social insurance was much more effective in Germany and was responsible for the international attractiveness of this model.

The Occupational Medical Service – the Focal Point in the Approach to Industrial Pathology

The particular influence of social reformers, together with the fact that public hygiene lost its importance with the triumph of bacteriology, and the dominance of compensation had the effect that medical professionalisation of workers' health protection did not take place within a public health service. The inclusion of physicians

40. E.g. E. Chadwick, *Report on the Sanitary Condition of the Labouring Population of Great Britain*, London, 1842; S. Smith, *The Common Nature of Epidemics, and their Relation to Climate and Civilization*, London, 1866; W. Farr, *Vital Statistics*, London, 1885.
41. Ritter, *Sozialversicherung*, p. 67.

in the factory inspectorate which was made possible by §120 of the Trade Regulations of 1891, forced the physicians into an ambivalent position from the outset. They were pushed to and fro between the public health service, workers' protection, and the social insurance system, as well as between medical administration, the Ministry of the Interior, and the Ministry of Labour. This administrative conflict, however, demonstrates only the underlying discrepancy between fundamental problems and their social management.

In 1905, a physician of the medical college (Scheurlen) was assigned as permanent consultant to the factory inspection. In Baden a physician (Holtzmann) was given his own inspection district as factory inspector, and his duties also included the advising of technicians. On 1 January 1909 in Munich, Franz Koelsch began his long years of activity. Though he should have known better, he continually referred to himself as the Nestor of German occupational medicine. As State Occupational Physician for Bavaria he was under the supervision of the Central Inspector for Factories and Trade, but he had an independent range of duties which covered the whole kingdom. His employment led to the recruitment of more occupational physicians by the states only after the First World War (Thiele in Saxony in 1919, Teleky in Düsseldorf in 1921, as well as Beintker in Arnsberg and Münster, Betke in Wiesbaden, Gerbis in Erfurt, Neumann in Breslau, Nuck in Hanover in 1928, Rosenthal-Deussen in Madgeburg, Holstein in Frankfurt an der Oder).

In Prussia occupational medical officers (*Gewerbemedizinalräte*) were appointed, whose instructions listed the following fields of activity: (a) the counselling and support of officials in general factory inspection and mining inspection in questions of industrial hygiene; (b) an extension of knowledge about pathological changes in the bodies of workers caused by industrial work as well as their prevention and eradication; and (c) an extension of the scope of industrial hygiene.[42] Ludwig Teleky in particular interpreted these general instructions as including the development of reliable statistics about occupational diseases and mortality (on the basis of data from the local health insurance bureaux), the scientific examination of individual branches of industry and trade, the education and

42. See F. Syrup, *Handbuch des Arbeiterschutzes und der Betriebssicherheit*, vol. 1, Berlin, 1927, pp. 21–8.

further instruction of medical general practitioners, as well as the counselling of trade unions.[43]

The attractiveness of setting up a practice as medical practitioner, as well as of a career in a clinic, was one of the reasons why physicians with some social commitment were interested in these duties. It was this commitment that made the Occupational Medical Service the pivot in the approach to occupational pathogenicity; the facts that duties carried out in the public service could not be the objects of litigation and that no other institution had developed a comparable competence contributed to this position. The fact that the state occupational physicians were not engaged in bureaucratic procedures made them an institution which could deal with all aspects of the social problem. They dealt with:

(1) the trade union movement (the reports of the occupational physicians were evaluated in the working-class press; workers' representatives made applications for investigations and review; several occupational physicians established consultation hours for workers, etc.);

(2) the interests of employers (when inspecting factories; in cases of accidents and complaints about industrial hygiene; in reports and public statements; in clubs and associations, societies and boards);

(3) the institutions for practical workers' protection (the technical factory inspectors, the mining inspectors, the district physicians, the police authorities, the trade associations, the factory physicians, and the mining associations' physicians);

(4) the institutions enforcing the Reich Insurance Statute (together with the *Vertrauensärzte* and other appropriate physicians; from 1925 onwards as a centre and first point of reference for cases of occupational disease; in co-operation with insurance schemes or study-groups; as senior experts in disputes; as members of the Senate for Occupational Diseases in the Reich Insurance Office);

(5) the authorities of the Reich (under the jurisdiction of the Ministry of Labour, as members of the Imperial Health Department, as members of the preliminary Imperial Econ-

43. L. Teleky, 'Die Aufgaben des Arztes in der Durchführung der Gewerbe-hygiene', in A. Gottstein, A. Schloßmann and L. Teleky (eds), *Handbuch der sozialen Hygiene und Gesundheitsfürsorge*, vol. 2, Berlin, 1926, pp. 46–58.

omic Council, and as medical officers);

(6) the authorities of the *Länder* (as experts in the appropriate ministries, departments, and law courts in all questions of occupational medicine; as medical officers);

(7) societies and associations (Hartmannbund, the Deutsche Gesellschaft für Gewerbehygiene, the Deutscher Medizinalbeamtenverein, the Verein für Socialpolitik, the Gesellschaft für soziale Reform, and the Verein sozialistischer Ärzte);

(8) international institutions (the International Labour Office, the International Conference of Occupational Physicians, the international congresses for hygiene and demography, industrial hygiene, and social insurance); and

(9) medical science and its institutions (medical specialists and their congresses, the Institut für Arbeitsphysiologie, E.W. Baader's clinical section, B. Chajes's industrial hygiene clinic, the Academies for Social Hygiene in Düsseldorf and Munich, museums of occupational medicine, and accident hospitals).

The lack of integration in the relevant bureaucratic procedures, however, led to a systematic uncertainty concerning the activities of occupational physicians. The state occupational physicians demanded a reorganisation of procedures dealing with occupational diseases, and attempted in this way to get legally fixed medical duties.

The Reich Insurance Statute in 1911 had in §547 provided opportunities to extend compensatory payments at the same rates as accident insurance to work-related diseases not arising from accidents. Because of international pressure and despite particular resistance from the factory physicians in the large chemical firms, the First Statute on the Extension of Accident Insurance to Occupational Diseases was passed in 1925. It included a list of eleven diseases, of which, however, only diseases caused by lead and its alloys were of some relevance for industrial hygiene. Social reformers and socially committed physicians had demanded above all the extension of accident insurance in order to introduce compulsory registration and to increase compensation for afflicted workers. They expected an enormous increase of knowledge in the field of industrial hygiene and a legal fixing of the duties of occupational physicians. In the event the state occupational physicians were made responsible for collecting the notifications of occupational diseases from the physicians in attendance, and for inspecting the factories together with technical factory inspectors. Moreover, the statute established the state occupational physicians as responsible experts, especially in cases of dispute. By binding them to the Occupational Diseases Statute, however, it produced a tension between the possibility of intervening within the framework of factory inspection, and their activities as experts within the framework of an extended accident insurance.

The tradition of medical or sanitary police could hardly be claimed by the state occupational physicians. Even though industrial hygiene implied prevention, and there was no other way to legitimise the professionalisation of occupational physicians, only two fields of prevention remained for the public health service after the triumph of bacteriology: inoculation and health education. The factories remained closed to the public health service; but the licensing of new plants on the basis of the trade regulations, in which aspects of industrial hygiene were supposed to be of importance, resulted in the effective sanctioning of certain hazards which could be detected in retrospect. Whereas in the 1870s people had still attempted to make industrial hygiene a part of a public health service, the illusion that technical progress would simultaneously bring about individual and social welfare, suggested an association with workers' protection as propagated by the social reformers. Although it was close to the crucial causes of ill-health (the working conditions 'on the spot'), this very proximity made it subordinate to technical competence, for prevention in this context had to mean intervention in working conditions with the aim of structuring them in a human way. This could not be the genuine role of a physician. The professionalisation of occupational physicians in the context of factory inspection contributed to the development of a strategy based on standardising and controlling human occupations. Most state occupational physicians shrank back from this consequence and even those who, like Ludwig Teleky, tried to develop an 'appropriate workers' protection which strikes the right balance between all sides',[44] offered no comprehensive health policy strategies.

Thus, in the light of their own interests in professionalisation,

44. L. Teleky, 'Wandlungen der Gewerbeaufsicht in dem Arbeiterschutzgesetze', *Soziale Praxis*, vol. 36, 1927, pp. 470–4.

approaches prevailed which emphasised maintaining the health of the 'working man' as a special branch of medical administration – as the Deutscher Medizinalbeamtenverein had already stated in 1920. Franz Koelsch (who later called the years from 1933 to 1936 the best of his career, because he had been assigned to medical administration) declared: 'The Occupational Medical Service, then, is restricted to medical problems applied to the individual worker and his environment. The main stress lies on medico-scientific researching, expertise, and counselling activities – *not* on policing, on continual surveillance of factories and workshops. The latter is the duty of technical factory inspectors and the police, or the local health authorities.'[45] Of course, the Occupational Medical Service had to go into the factories, but only in order to examine and advise. Because it had a medical task, however, the Occupational Medical Service ought to become a special department of the general health service.

Yet this position is essentially an escape from the socio-political implications of industrial hygiene, especially from a debate about class antagonisms. The ideas of social reform, which had brought about the establishment of the Occupational Medical Service, did not offer any orientation in questions of health policy which might serve as a justification for its integration into the public health service on the basis of industrial pathology e.g. from an approach which today could be termed 'ecological'). On the contrary, there were ambivalent influences within social hygiene that sought an answer to socio-political problems in 'race-hygiene', or eugenics.

The Occupational Physician and the 'Welfare of the Whole People'

As early as 1929 W. Abelsdorff attempted to justify the extension of medical professionalisation in the field of industrial hygiene by reference to more general prophylactic duties. One proposal in this vein[46] was refused by the editorial staff of the journal to which it

---

45. F. Koelsch, 'Organisation des gewerbeärztlichen Dienstes in Deutschland', *Klinische Wochenschrift*, vol. 8, 1929, pp. 2013–6.
46. W. Abelsdorff, 'Einige Bausteine zur geplanten Verreichlichung der Arbeits-

was submitted, who argued from the perspective of the technical factory inspectors.

> Why? Are they hoping to keep the occupational physician under-occupied so that he'll be able to relieve his engineering colleagues? It is absolutely intolerable that this introductory remark [of the editorial staff for the essay mentioned above, D.M.] is motivated by professional egotism, at a time when we must assemble all our forces in order to make the coming generation forget the negative effects of the war on health and, above all, spare our sorely afflicted Fatherland inferior and useless offspring.[47]

Such a point of view corresponded with National Socialist propaganda, which focused on a 'highly competitive German people with a sound body and soul'.[48] Medical professionalisation received an enormous boost under this maxim. Industrial hygiene in the sense of medicine aimed at improving competitive performance, or *Leistungsmedizin*, also took part in this development. Starting in 1936 and especially from 1941 onwards, the system of factory physicians was rapidly extended. Occupational physicians employed by the state, however, tried only to keep their previous duties, although they were situated at a focal point of National Socialist health policy.

Reviewing the first twenty-five years of his work and envisioning the new political conditions, Franz Koelsch asked in 1933:

> What is the current conception of the occupational physician? He is a physician employed by the state, a physician in a public position with public duties; his occupation is medically defined from the very start; he has to work in special fields of public health care – like a forensic physician. These facts and their consequences are so clear and so unambiguous that differing opinions on this subject simply cannot arise. The range of duties covers medical advice for interested authorities, clinical, hygienic, experimental and medical-statistical analyses, medical surveillance and welfare for the working member of the nation [*Volksgenosse*],

---

aufsicht', *Mitteilungen des Vereins deutscher Gewerbeaufsichtsbeamten*, vol. 4, 1928, p. 10.

47. W. Abelsdorff, 'Die Mitarbeit von Ärzten in der deutschen Gewerbeaufsicht', *Ärztliches Vereinsblatt für Deutschland*, no. 10, 1 April 1929.

48. *Handbücherei für den öffentlichen Gesundheitsdienst*, vol. 3, Berlin, 1938, p. 1.

medical assessment for insurance purposes, hygienic information and instruction – no doubt medically oriented duties which, first of all, presuppose a close co-operation with all the branches of the state health authorities. These duties must not be regarded in isolation; they must be fitted into the framework of general health protection in close connection with the toughening up [*Ertüchtigung*] of the whole people which is being carried out with determination by the National Socialist state.[49]

Koelsch neither comprehended the full intentions of National Socialist health policy, nor did he understand that there was no logical necessity to professionalise occupational physicians, since neither the aim of differentiating their broadly defined duties, nor the effectiveness of the concrete duties carried out in association with the state authorities demanded it. Indeed, in the following years, the deep-rooted fear that the Occupational Medical Service could lose its importance because of the division of duties between the factory management and the state health policy was consolidated. In an account prepared for the official handbook for the public health service, Michael Bauer, Department Head in the Reich Ministry of Labour, did not make the new health policy developed by National Socialism the central issue, but emphasised instead the extension of factory inspection, which had prospered over the years, most recently with the support of a Führer decree of 2 May 1935 and an instruction from the Reich Minister of Labour of 20 June 1935. The duties Bauer listed tried to emphasise a frictionless co-operation on all sides, while a genuine formulation of duties which would distinguish the Occupational Medical Service from other institutions (such as the factory inspectorate, the institutions of the Nazi Party, the physicians' associations, the insurance companies, and the trade associations) could hardly be detected.[50]

Only the formal procedure governing occupational diseases provided support for Koelsch's position, and consequently it was developed further in this direction. The Third Occupational Diseases Statute of 16 December 1936[51] established a decisive role for the state occupational physicians, under the new title *staatlicher*

---

49. F. Koelsch, *25 Jahre Bayerischer Landesgewerbearzt. Rückblicke und Ausblicke*, Munich, 1933, p. 60.

50. M. Bauer *et al.*, *Dritte Verordnung über Ausdehnung der Unfallversicherung auf Berufskrankheiten vom 16. Dezember 1936*, Leipzig, 1937, pp. 284ff.

51. Ibid., *passim*.

Gewerbearzt, in proceedings concerned with the confirmation of reported occupational diseases; they were made 'masters of proceedings', as was emphasised in the preliminary discussions. According to §6 of the Statute the trade association (as chief insurer) had to send the original copy of a notification of an occupational disease to an appropriate state occupational physician within two days. He had to examine the notification; he could examine the sufferer himself or have him/her examined at the expense of the trade association. Then, he had to write a report or confirm an existing one. He could also carry out an investigation on the spot or delegate this task; investigations carried out by the association had to be reported to him. The new statute was thus especially important because it produced not only a new title for the state occupational physician, but also a consolidation of the institution itself. This was made possible, however, by an overemphasis on the statute as a key source of legitimation. In 1936, the structure of the Occupational Medical Service was equipped with facilities that are still in use.

The state occupational physicians welcomed the new regulations, which – as the trade associations also saw – promised a tightening and better legitimation of the restrictive procedures by emphasising medical competence. In retrospect, the physicians saw problems in the fact that – as a consequence of the statute – the Occupational Medical Service had been taken over into the responsibility of the Ministry of Labour. On the one hand, it united the fields of 'work protection' and social insurance, but on the other hand it separated the occupational physicians from the medical administration.

On the basis of the anti-semitic and anti-socialist Law on the Restoration of the Civil Service of 7 April 1933, Ludwig Teleky and Erika Rosenthal-Deussen were driven out of the Occupational Medical Service. According to a survey on the offices of state occupational physicians made in 1936 there were sixteen physicians in Prussia (Berlin, Breslau, Düsseldorf, Frankfurt an der Oder, Hanover, Magdeburg, Münster, Wiesbaden), three in Bavaria (Munich), five in Saxony (Dresden, Chemnitz, Leipzig, Zwickau), and one each in Württemberg (Stuttgart), Baden (Karlsruhe), Thuringia (Jena), Hessen (Darmstadt), Greater Hamburg (Hamburg), Mecklenburg (Schwerin), Oldenburg (Oldenburg), Brunswick (Brunswick), Bremen (Bremen), Lippe (Detmold), Saarland (Saarbrücken). The office of the state occupational physician in Austria was situated in Vienna in the building of the District Trade Inspectorate.[52] More occupational physicians were employed when the Occupational Medical Service was reformed on the basis of the statute (in Thuringia, Mecklenburg, and Brunswick). In Württemberg, a part-time occupational physician was promoted to full-time work; several part-time occupational physicians were employed (Hamburg, Hessen, Oldenburg, Bremen, Lippe-Detmold), in Saarland a full-time occupational physician was employed on 1 April 1937.[53]

Under the direction of Michael Bauer, who was responsible for medical questions of work protection and for medical factory safety and health control in the Ministry of Labour, the state occupational physicians actively pursued the National Socialist health programme, as it constantly emphasised the significance of the working person. They wanted to defend their own position because their institution was in the firing line of National Socialist 'purges' due to the social commitment of some of its members. 'A special significance' for 'the building of the National Socialist state' was assigned 'to the activities of officers of the factory safety and health control'; it was seen as 'absolutely relevant to the political sphere, too, because the shaping of social conditions in the factories is particularly important for the political attitudes of the workforce'. This shaping should be carried out in such a manner 'that threatening discord among the workforce and resulting disruptions' could be prevented. *Leistungsbereitschaft* (readiness to perform) should be increased particularly through education.[54]

Even the experience of National Socialist policy was not able to overturn the deeply-rooted belief that individual and social welfare depends upon increased productivity and technical progress. On the contrary, this belief constitutes one of the most important social bases for many continuities in the field of occupational medicine. This was personified in Franz Koelsch as in no other person. He was state occupational physician during the Empire, the Munich Soviet Republic, the Weimar Republic, National Socialism, the post-war occupation of the allied forces, and in the Federal Republic.

52. Ibid., p. 288.

53. *Der gewerbeärztliche Dienst in den Jahren 1935 und 1936*, Leipzig, 1938, p. 14.

54. Prussian Minister President to the Prussian Minister of Economy and Labour, 2 October 1933, Zentrales Staatsarchiv (ZSTA) Merseburg, Rep. 120/BB/VII/4/1, vol. 12, Bl. 302, 309.

He was still writing in 1944 in a popular publication:

> The working man stands at the centre of a purposeful economy. A people's wealth lies in the manpower and the willingness to work of the *Volksgenossen*. Therefore, it is our duty of far-reaching economic and social importance to maintain human capacity to work and to keep it from harm. . . . Only a disproportion between capacity to perform [*Leistungsfähigkeit*] and the demands of performance [*Leistungsbeanspruchung*], a utilisation of the whole organism or individual parts of the body which exceeds their physiological limits, a continual influence of harmful substances or conditions, and the like lead to disease. . . . The fundamental significance of the individual *constitution* for the capacity to perform and the achievement of work can be deduced from these explanations. By this, we understand the complete genetic inheritance [*Gesamtmasse des Erbgutes*] as well as the reaction of the body to environmental influences. We call a 'normal' constitution one which includes the regular composition of the body and its organs, with the regular functioning of these organs in the framework of the whole organism, with the capacity to adapt to and resist the hazards of daily life and particularly of work. But besides the *physical* aptitude for occupational work we expect the 'healthy' person to show a corresponding *mental* attitude to the experience of work: training ability, training endurance, work morale, capacity to adapt to a community of workers, etc. In the end, the frequency of accidents depends to the larger degree upon the *constitution*; this 'individual accident factor' is furthered by physical or mental deficiencies. From all this, the considerable relevance of medical selection for work and psychotechnical career guidance is clear.[55]

The obligation of the worker who hires out his labour to work for the economy in the service of all relieved occupational physicians of social responsibility and made it possible to adjust their activities smoothly to the existing social system. The duties of industrial hygiene listed by Koelsch even justify the activities of the factory physicians who were detested by the workers as *notorische Gesundschreiber* (notorious confirmers of health).[56]

In his post-war review of the first fifty years of the Occupational

---

55. F. Koelsch, *Was weißt Du von Berufskrankheiten und Gewerbehygiene?*, Berlin, 1944, pp. 3ff.
56. S. Graessner, 'Gesundheitspolitik unterm Hakenkreuz', in G. Baader and U. Schultz (eds.), *Medizin und Nationalsozialismus. Tabuisierte Vergangenheit – ungebrochene Tradition?*, Berlin, 1980, pp. 145–51.

Medical Service, Bauer, who was by this time a professor and worked for the Ministry of Labour in Bonn, omitted the period of National Socialist rule and gave the impression that industrial hygiene had been on a straight uphill path, which the state occupational physicians in particular had trodden, carrying out their duties 'in a healthy and socially responsible spirit for the welfare of the working people'.[57] While such a view is characteristic of the way the German medical profession in general came to terms with the National Socialist 'episode',[58] it is true that the state occupational physicians must be counted among those physicians who were least compromised by association with the Third Reich.

The orientation towards *Leistungsmedizin*, which fascist 'health policy' adopted after 1936 by way of the factory physicians,[59] was facilitated particularly by the Deutsche Gesellschaft für Gewerbehygiene. Its managing director Eger even exerted influence on articles in journals with the help of Ministry of Labour, when, for example, he called the publication of an article by Teleky, which Franz Koelsch supported, an 'impertinence'.[60] The state occupational physicians concentrated their activities almost entirely on the procedures concerned with occupational diseases. The social reform tradition, with which the Occupational Medical Service had started, was completely lost in this development.

Continuity of Dethematisation – Ways of Repressing Industrial Pathology and the Occupational Medical Service in West Germany after 1945

After the defeat of the National Socialist regime, some of the exiled physicians returned to Germany. Among them was Hugo Freund,

57. M. Bauer, 'Der gewerbeärztliche Dienst. Ein Blick über 50 Jahre', *Bundesarbeitsblatt*, Sondernummer '100 Jahre Gewerbeaufsicht', 1954, p. 32.

58. A. Mitscherlich and F. Mielke (eds.), *Medizin ohne Menschlichkeit. Dokumente des Nürnberger Ärzteprozesses*, 2nd edn, Frankfurt am Main, 1978; W. Wuttke-Groneberg, *Medizin im Nationalsozialismus. Ein Arbeitsbuch*, Tübingen, 1980; F. Kudlien, *Ärzte im Nationalsozialismus*, Cologne, 1985.

59. K.H. Karbe, 'Das Betriebsarztsystem und zum Schicksal der Arbeitsmedizin im faschistischen Deutschland', in A. Thom and H. Spaar (eds.), *Medizin im Faschismus. Symposium*, Berlin, 1983, pp. 107–19; Milles; 'Anfänge'; idem, 'Zur Kontinuität betriebsärztlicher Aufgaben und Sichtweisen', in H. Gerstenberger and D. Schmidt (eds.), *Normalität oder Normalisierung?*, Münster, 1987.

60. ZSTA Merseburg, Rep. 120/BB/VII/1, Nr. 130, Bl. 374, 376.

health policy expert of the Social Democratic Party executive before 1933, who returned via Haifa, New York, and London to Hanover in March 1948. Here, the party executive had employed new, young experts and had little interest in health policy.

Hugo Freund established a Social-Medical Bureau which he used for building up an Institute for Health Policy concerned with interdisciplinary approaches (medical, psychological, and socio-political). His attitude towards the problem of social rationalisation is particularly significant, because it was based on the assumption that the developed American economic system would spread in Germany, too.

> If rationalising measures are applied to a biologically prostrate work-force, whose occupational categories have been disrupted, there is a certain danger not only that manpower will suffer severely, but also that the most important goal of rationalisation, the increase in productivity, cannot be achieved. Even sophisticated methods of occupational science cannot be simply transferred and applied to the German situation today.[61]

Freund also referred to the methods developed in the USA which facilitated an increase in productivity without generating health hazards. These methods were directed towards 'group productivity' which could increase productivity by about 18 per cent 'simply by methods of democratising the factories (i.e. without any objective technical changes and without psychotechnical intervention)'.[62] In spite of the problematic fixation on productivity, Freund drew a conclusion which is remarkable even for the contemporary discussion about a humane reform of working conditions: 'The best safeguard against damages due to rationalisation could be attained if rationalisation could be carried out at the level of *real planning*. Then, health policy with *all* its methods (applied in a balanced manner) could take its appropriate position in the process of planning and in the framework of planning groups.'[63]

Although it was a far-sighted view of the problems and a pioneering attempt at solving them, the aspects that could actually be put

---

61. Information Nr. 3, Nachlaß Hugo Freund, Social Policy Archives University of Bremen.
62. Ibid.
63. Ibid.

into effect tended to restrain health policy and particularly industrial hygiene, because they were seen under the single criterion of economic efficiency (performance, productivity, cost-saving). The illusion that measures of industrial hygiene would also be economical and, therefore, in the interests of both employers and employees, runs like a red thread through the history of occupational medicine.[64] From a superficial point of view, it is astonishing that there was no discussion in the field of health policy after 1945 which could have destroyed this illusion.

Significantly, the social policy of the Social Democratic labour movement contributed to the fact that – alongside the continuity of individual and economic orientation – the system of factory physicians survived the overthrow of National Socialism relatively unaffected.

Emigré doctors in the United States committed to the question of health policy (Felix Boenheim, Käte Frankental, Kurt Glaser) published a petition demanding 'the construction of a democratic health system in Germany' as early as May 1945. They demanded the employment of factory physicians in all larger companies.[65] Even the state occupational physicians at their first congress after 1945 regarded the employment of factory physicians as necessary for the 'safeguarding of health and ability to work'.[66] The regional Medical Councils even had plans for legal regulations ready, but the Ministry of Labour under the first Adenauer government recommended a compromise between the parties concerned. The Werksärztliche Arbeitsgemeinschaft, an association of works physicians (as the factory physicians were called after the war), which continued to exist under the strong influence of the chemical industry, made an agreement with the German Trades Union Congress and the Employers' Federation on 3 June 1950. In it the Factory Medical Service is 'recognised as an important means to strengthen and improve the work- and health-protection of the working population'.[67] The trade unions regarded medical activities in the practical context of occupational work and disease as positive in principle.

64. Milles, 'Zur Dethematisierung', pp. 35f.

65. See S. Leibfried and F. Tennstedt, *Council for a Democratic Germany*, Bremen, 1981, p. 15.

66. Quoted by H.U. Deppe, *Industriearbeit und Medizin*, Frankfurt am Main, 1973, pp. 21ff.

67. See ibid., p. 171, for the complete document.

For them it was only necessary to develop a system of workers' participation and, thus, an opportunity for control by the person afflicted in order to prevent the doctors from acting on misconceptions about the nature of occupations.

The fact that Social Democratic workers' organisations saw no structural problems in dealing with industrial pathogenicity has to do with the fact that they favoured the prevention of injury by state regulation, and still saw the development of the productive forces as the main instrument for removing all structural defects. Fritz Tarnow explained in 1950, against all short- and long-term experiences, that the knowledge had been accepted that 'social expenses and improvements are by no means only cost factors for the economy ... Even from a purely capitalistic and business point of view, caring for the labour force could be an economic enterprise. During the last decades [!], knowledge about the interrelation of social security and the well-being of the economy has been extended significantly.'[68] Basically the old concepts of *Wirtschaftsdemokratie* (economic democracy) blocked the development of a critical and radical health policy strategy. Significantly, the elaboration of the Social Democratic social plan, which started in 1951 under the control of Ludwig Preller, was no longer concerned with new terrain in the field of health policy, but only envisaged compensation as the basic form of social security.[69] Preventive duties were discussed within the institutional context of the social insurance system.

In this situation, the state occupational physicians lacked the social basis on which they might have appealed for a thorough restructuring and updating of their duties. Instead the state occupational physicians retreated into their civil servants' shell. This resulted in a further fixation on their activities as experts in the framework of procedures dealing with occupational diseases.

The state occupational physicians had already complained after the Occupational Diseases Statute of February 1929 that they were

68. F. Tarnow, 'Soziale Sicherheit als Voraussetzung für eine gesunde Wirtschaft', *Gewerkschaftliche Monatshefte*, vol. 1, 1950, pp. 17–21.
69. L. Preller, 'Reform der sozialen Sicherung', *Gewerkschaftliche Monatshefte*, vol. 3, 1952, pp. 20–7; H.G. Hockerts, *Sozialpolitische Entscheidungen im Nachkriegsdeutschland. Alliierte und deutsche Sozialversicherungspolitik 1945–1957*, Stuttgart, 1980; K. Naujeck, *Die Anfänge des sozialen Netzes 1945–1952*, Cologne, 1984.

put under too much strain by the procedural reports and evaluations they were obliged to present. After the Third Statute had been passed in 1936, the reports occupied more and more of their time. This activity not only undermined the social-reformist claims for workers' protection, but reduced their ability to recognise medical problems and led, in the end, to a loss in medical competence. The factory physicians developed medical competence 'on the spot';[70] medical competence in questions of detail was taken over by medical specialists and hospitals. The state occupational physicians, however, fell between all stools because of the failure to reorganise the social constitution after 1945.

This is illustrated by a report by the American physician Irving R. Tabershaw, which was circulated in 1950 after an extended study of German conditions.[71] The report on the situation of industrial hygiene in the western zones of occupied Germany had been commissioned because American experts had noticed great shortcomings in workers' health protection. They regarded the practice of industrial hygiene in Germany as deficient, rudimentary, and tending towards ineffectivenes. This devastating appraisal of a political domain in which Germany had once proclaimed itself to be the world leader referred particularly to the prevention of diseases and injury resulting from accidents, as well as to the maintenance and improvement of the state of health of the workers.

The state occupational physicians were at the centre of the report; they played a decisive part in the whole problem, in both historical and legal terms. The report criticised the overwhelming dominance of compensatory regulations. A more general concept of health protection had been pre-empted, since the social security laws had reduced the physicians' competence to controlling access to insurance benefits and to handing them out. The activities of the state occupational physicians were, as far as the broad field of industrial hygiene was concerned, limited to medico-scientific, legal, and social-policy problems; the multiplicity of factors relevant for health hazards was not considered at all. The report noticed the discrepancy between the duties assigned to the state occupational physicians

70. A.M. Thiess, *Arbeitsmedizin und Gesundheitsschutz. Werksärztliche Erfahrungen der BASF 1866–1980*, Cologne, 1980.

71. I.R. Tabershaw, *Report on Industrial Hygiene in the Western Zones of Occupied Germany*, n.p., 1950.

in co-operation with the factory inspectorate in the fields of counselling, survey, and maintenance of health protection, and the preoccupation with procedures connected with the identification of occupational diseases. In the report the preoccupation with occupational diseases, particularly with writing appropriate assessments, on the part of state occupational physicians was regarded as the decisive factor in the practical inadequacies of occupational hygiene. Besides, the measures of health protection in the factories did not enjoy a high reputation and were oriented towards the institutions of the social security system (e.g. by seeing the prevention of accidents as the classical focus of prevention, just as the trade associations did).

The report evaluated the function and image the state occupational physicians had of themselves in the following résumé: 'None of the *Landesgewerbeärzte* have any concept that their functions embrace an interest in non-occupational disease, in the total health of the worker, or in furthering general public health!' The physicians who had played a decisive part in the development of occupational medicine and had as physicians wanted to be integrated into the public health system, did not develop any strategy in the field of applied occupational medicine and left it largely to the factory physicians. They had regarded the Occupational Disease Statute as a secure, promising path for the professionalisation of occupational medicine and not as a dead-end street.

Tabershaw emphasised the reduction in the whole range of activities of occupational medicine; systematic factory inspections, statistical analyses on the focal points of health hazards, and particularly preventive measures had dropped out of view. Contrasting the German situation with that in the USA, he stressed that the state occupational physicians, because they played a decisive part as experts in procedures governing occupational diseases, were held back from the research, surveillance and counselling which could serve to prevent work-related diseases. Hence, knowledge and practice of the occupational physicians remained in narrow, predetermined paths. The main argument he presented to the state occupational physicians assembled in Bochum on 28 October 1950, was, however, not so new: in contrast to the USA, the Occupational Medical Service in Germany did not operate as an institution of public health care.

The way society dealt with industrial pathogenicity did not lead to clearly defined responsibilities. The importance of the basic problems demanded regulation by the state. The differentiation of official and institutional treatment of these problems into the fields of public health, work protection, and the social security system inevitably led to overlapping areas of responsibility. A shifting of competence from one field to another can be reasonably justified only if it means a more effective awareness and treatment of problems. Such a development was, and still is, conceivable in the fields of public health service and workers' protection, and also in the context of a unified social security system. The decisive factor remains whether the orientation towards industrial pathogenicity as a structural problem is successful. Although the Occupational Medical Service today has lost the significance it had in the 1920s, there is still no other relevant institution that is in a better position to develop such an orientation.

The State Occupational Physician as an Institution of Preventive Medicine?

According to the official guidelines of 1966, the state occupational physician should be consulted together with the Land Medical Council when full-time works physicians were employed or the service of works physicians called on, as well as when such physicians were dismissed.[72] In subsequent years the Employment Security Law in particular further restricted the role of state employed physicians in comparison to private physicians in the field of occupational medical practice.

Whereas in the first years after the Second World War it was still maintained that the business of factory inspection was the protection of labour and not the control of trade and industry, this aspect was increasingly lost sight of during the economic boom. In official plans for new regulations, a sharp line was drawn between medical and technical factory inspection, the separate competence of technicians and physicians was emphasised and a vertical co-operation between technical and medical factory inspection attempted.[73] In

72. Guidelines of the Federal Ministry for Labour and Social Order on the medical care of employees at work and the services of works physicians, 10 June 1966.
73. K. Groggert, 'Der gewerbeärztliche Dienst und die technische Gewerbeauf-

this context, the role of industrial hygiene partly lost its contours: 'The state occupational physician must use the Trading Regulations, decrees issued in this context, and the other compulsory guidelines as a legal basis, in order to perform his advisory duties in all questions of industrial hygiene and in order to be able to intervene preventively if necessary.'[74]

The question was, however, whether §120 of the Trading Regulations could serve as a legal basis for an institutionalised preventive medicine. An extensive control of the conditions in the factory in accordance with the compulsory regulations would have been an immense advance, after all, if compared to the practice of the Occupational Medical Service. This consisted and still consists for the greater part in activities laid down by the Occupational Diseases Statute.

The fact that controlling activities were reduced in favour of expert advisory activities can be seen from an interesting revision of the official identity cards for state occupational physicians. While the card issued in 1958 underlines that the state occupational physician 'has all official authority of the police authorities, particularly the right to inspect industrial plants at any time', the card issued in 1977 takes only 'the tasks legally assigned to state factory inspectorate' into account and mentions that the inspectorate can inspect a factory at any time and apply administrative compulsion. Since the legal basis according to §139 of the Trading Regulations and §114 of the Criminal Code has remained unchanged, the text of the identity card has simply been expressed more vaguely.

At the same time as the controlling tasks were blurred, the chance was missed to use the discussion about an 'institution of preventive medicine' to extend the duties to predictable problem areas. According to §44, section 2, of the Decree for the Unification of the Health Service, the state occupational physician is responsible for local hygiene and air quality if the public health department is not in a position to judge the existing problems with certainty (e.g. in cases of concessions). Since the extension of industry in the 1960s this has become more and more relevant. But the state occupational phys-

---

sicht', *Berliner Zentralblatt für Arbeitsmedizin und Arbeitsschutz*, vol. 15, 1965, pp. 25ff.

74. K. Maerz, 'Staatlicher Gewerbearzt als Institution der Präventivmedizin', *Gesundheitsfürsorge*, vol. 18, 1968, p. 162.

icians have not made any efforts to include this aspect in their duties. It was only pointed out that they must be informed by the public health department and have the possibility of inspecting plants together with them.[75]

Instead, the defensive attitude of the state occupational physicians together with the importance of the Occupational Diseases Statute had the effect that the duties of the Occupational Medical Service were reduced by the trade associations. The self-governing trade associations referred to their historic role and practical successes and demanded 'real' responsibility. They saw themselves on the same level as the state factory inspectorate with an equal relationship to the central authorities.[76] This endeavour echoed a tendency of the legislators to simplify the legal regulations for labour protection and to transfer it to the level of negotiations between unions and management or other bodies.[77] The obvious tension between surveillance by the state and by the trade associations should, as F.J. Dreyhaupt has argued, be solved in such a manner that a confirmation of the autonomy of the employers goes parallel with an oversight of protective measures by the factory inspectorate.[78]

Instead of this perspective, the Employment Security Law considerably strengthened the trade associations in relation to the factory inspectorate. This was less obvious in the field of technical factory inspection than in terms of the relationship between the state occupational physicians and the employers within the accident insurance scheme, where the state occupational physicians were simply to provide 'limited assistance' to the trade associations. Only 'special expert knowledge in a specific aspect of the occupational diseases procedure relevant to the final decision' justified a sort of 'general co-operation' on the part of the state occupational physician.[79]

The propounder of this view, a representative of the Trade Association for Wood Products writing in 1985, had no particular

---

75. Ibid., p. 166.

76. See with a critical evaluation, F.J. Dreyhaupt, 'Verhältnis der staatlichen Gewerbeaufsicht zu den Berufsgenossenschaften', appendix to Jahresbericht 1974 der Gewerbeaufsicht des Landes Nordrhein-Westfalen, Geldern, 1975, p. NW3.

77. See §708 and 712 of Section 1 of the RVO.

78. Dreyhaupt, 'Verhältnis', p. NW9.

79. V. Kaiser, 'Rechtsfragen zur Zusammenarbeit der Staatlichen Gewerbeärzte und Unfallversicherungsträger bei der Entschädigung von Berufskrankheiten', *Die Berufsgenossenschaft*, vol. 12, 1985, pp. 107ff.

occasion to press his argument. Yet the situation seemed to be favourable for putting down markers, so to speak, and for confirming the independence of the employers within the accident insurance system. The apparently desperate situation of the Occupational Medical Service makes it quite understandable why he argued against, or at least from a point of view at variance with, the interests of the state occupational physicians. The position of the trade associations makes the dilemma of the Occupational Medical Service clear: when they base themselves on the occupational diseases procedure, the state occupational physicians not only have difficulty drawing a clear line between their own functions and those of the technical factory inspection, but they are also bound to concentrate their activity on individual compensation in particular cases and thereby confirm the role of the trade associations.

These difficulties have caused some physicians in the factory inspectorate to look for unused possibilities offered by the occupational diseases procedure which provide an opening for a preventive concept of the Occupational Medical Service. Such possibilities are seen in §3 of the Occupational Diseases Statute, which stipulates the obligation of an insurance system to counteract 'with all possible means' the danger that any occupational disease will arise, recur, or get worse. 'This obligation to intervene in individual cases corresponds to the task of the accident insurance system, namely to prevent occupational accidents and, thereby, occupational diseases.'[80] Although part of the Occupational Diseases Statute since 1968, this obligation on the insurer has remained a dead letter up to the present, but there have been efforts recently to make the public aware of its existence and to persuade employers to combine a recognition of the obligation with the growing trend towards regular preventive health checks. Such prophylactic examinations are included among the legal obligations on employers fixed in the Employment Security Law.

The enormous growth in the practice of prophylactic examinations at the workplace raises the question of whether and to what extent these examinations can be used to support a development of preventive activities on the part of the Occupational Medical Ser-

---

80. R.W. Gensch, '"Arbeitsmedizinische Vorsorge" in der Praxis – Gesundheitsschutz oder Arbeitsplatzverlust?', in G. Elsner (ed.), *Vorbeugen statt Krankschreiben. Betriebsärzte in der Praxis*, Hamburg, 1986, p. 81.

vice. If the registration and processing of the results of these examinations were not left to the companies alone, it would be more difficult for employees with damaged health to be marginalised and dismissed. It would also be possible to detect and remove the main sources of stress. The intention which informed the drafting of the Occupational Diseases Statute, namely that knowledge about health hazards and prevention of diseases should be improved, could eventually be fulfilled.

It seems strongly advisable to combine both systems: the preventive intention of §3 can only become reality if it is supplemented by an efficient system for detecting those circumstances that are the preconditions for the payment of insurance compensation. But the system of medical prophylactic examinations at work – if it expands any further – will reach its limits. From this point on, it loses its legitimacy because of its social consequences. It must be supplemented by regulations to safeguard the economic interests of those who pay the price for minimising work-related hazards, regulations such as can be found in section 2 of §3 of the Occupational Diseases Statute.[81]

History, however, demonstrates that the terms on which society is organised are not favourable to a 'combination of the detective component of occupational medical prevention with the safeguarding component of §3'. They tend rather to prevent, or at any rate to limit the effectiveness of such a combination, which will be problematic as long as the 'safeguarding component' is given such central importance, while the neglect of the 'detective component' actually relieves the strain on the safeguarding groups. The simplest solution, de-emphasising the 'safeguards', presupposes emphasising the detective component, but there is no evidence either of support for this within significant social groups or of a political power bloc which could put it into effect. Obviously, the Occupational Medical Service is still compelled or content to await its call to social effectiveness.

81. Ibid., p. 92.

7

State and Society in Germany in the Aftermath of the First World War

Richard Bessel

1918 – A Crisis of State Authority

Preparing their annual report to the Prussian Minister for Welfare in October 1919 about conditions in homes for youth in care, the regional authorities in Pomerania reviewed developments during the previous year, beginning with the effects of the revolution in 1918:

A large number of the older youths became rebellious, insolent and disobedient, and only reluctantly performed their work. Many were of the opinion that with the change in government all laws had been repealed at a stroke and that corrective education had ceased. Some fathers came into the homes, referring to the workers' and soldiers' councils, and demanded the immediate release of their children. In order to avoid further trouble, in some instances the heads of the homes gave in to the demands of these people and the youths were released.[1]

No doubt such experiences were traumatic for those whose task it

This is a much-revised version of a paper presented to the Conference on 'State and Social Change in Germany, 1880–1960', organised by the Centre for Interdisciplinary German Studies at the University of Liverpool on 8–10 January 1986. I would like to thank the participants at the Conference, especially John Breuilly and Dick Geary, as well as Dave Blackbourn, Detlev Peukert and Eve Rosenhaft for their comments on earlier drafts. I would also like to thank the Alexander von Humboldt Foundation and the Wolfson Foundation for the generous financial support which made possible the research for this paper.

1. Archiwum Panstwowe w Szczecinie (=APS), Oberpräsidium von Pommern, Nr. 2915: The Landeshauptmann to the Oberpräsident, 'Bericht über die Ausführung der Fürsorgeerziehung Minderjähriger im Rechnungsjahre 1918', Stettin, 5 October 1919.

had been to run youth-care institutions during the dark days of 1918 and 1919. For many, it seemed that the rug had been pulled from underneath their feet. To be sure, the war years had seen a deterioration in conditions in these institutions and in the behaviour of the youths committed to them, as fathers were called away to the military and discipline was eroded as a result of war-related pressures.[2] Indeed, youth running wild had been a theme constantly recurring in wartime discussions of social problems within Germany.[3] However, the upheavals of 1918–19 added a new dimension to the nightmare facing those who saw their task as stamping a sense of discipline and order upon Germany's wayward youth. During the War they had seen problems of delinquency increase, but the legal framework and structures of authority had remained in place – even if social pressures created by the War had reduced their effectiveness. Now the framework itself was shaken, and for a short period it seemed that the old structures of authority had disintegrated.

The reactions of the youths in care (and of their fathers) to the collapse of state authority are revealing. For them the change in government meant that now they could do what they wanted. The state no longer had the power to intervene in – and in this case determine the shape of – their everyday lives. For the adolescents in question and their fathers the revolutionary events of 1918–19 and the demobilisation did not signal the realisation of a coherent political programme or the possibility of constructing new sets of economic relationships – an observation which may be made of large sections of German society at that time.[4] Rather, it meant in the first instance casting off unwelcome state interference. This is not to assert that such actions and sentiments were devoid of political significance; this behaviour had profound political ramifications. But it was essentially a reaction to the interference of an

2. APS, Oberpräsidium von Pommern, Nr. 2915: The Landeshauptmann der Provinz Pommern to the Oberpräsident, 'Bericht über die Ausführung der Fürsorgeerziehung Minderjähriger im Rechnungsjahre 1917', Stettin, 3 October 1918.

3. Eve Rosenhaft, 'A World Upside-Down. Delinquency, Family and Work in the Lives of German Working-Class Youth 1914–1918' (paper delivered to the SSRC conference on 'The European Family and the Great War: Stability and Instability 1900–1930', Pembroke College, Cambridge, September 1983).

4. See Wolfgang J. Mommsen, 'The German Revolution 1918–1920: Political Revolution and Social Protest Movement', in Richard Bessel and E.J. Feuchtwanger (eds.), *Social Change and Political Development in Weimar Germany*, London, 1981.

authoritarian state: once the authority of the German state had been drastically, if temporarily, reduced, people seized the opportunity to get it off their backs.

It may well be argued that this, in essence, is what revolution is about. Certainly there was a strong element of such a sentiment in the left-wing militancy which characterised the revolutionary period in Germany after the First World War. Wolfgang Mommsen, in his stimulating discussion of the German revolution of 1918–20, has observed that, 'in the earlier phases of the revolutionary processes at least, the workers' and soldiers' councils deployed primarily defensive rather than offensive energies'.[5] And there can be little doubt that the leftward drift of workers from the Majority Social Democrats and towards the Independents had much to do with hostility towards a state with which the MSPD leadership had identified itself. The movement among miners for the nationalisation of the pits also was motivated by desire to remove authority. While the state may have been expected to provide the framework within which the hoped-for changes were to be instituted, the goal was not to introduce state control at the workplace. Thus, according to Mommsen:

> In no way whatever did the miners associate with a 'nationalisation' of the mining industry – albeit in a decentralised form – 'a fundamental restructuring of the social system as such', as had been part and parcel of the programme of all the socialist parties, but with different degrees of emphasis. Not the state and its agencies but the workers on the shop floor and their representatives should run the mines, while the administrative apparatus of the mines should go on operating more or less as before.[6]

Working-class militancy was not aimed so much at a takeover or control of state power as it was directed against established authority, whether in the form of employers or government – something which continued to shape the conflicts of the post-1918 period.

This should hardly come as a surprise. The revolution was, almost by definition, a reaction against state authority – in this case against a particularly visible state which had attempted, unsuccessfully, to extend its authority into almost all facets of Germans'

5. Ibid., p. 29.
6. Ibid., p. 33.

everyday lives. The obvious injustices and mounting chaos created by attempts to regulate food distribution during the War (what Robert Moeller has described as the 'poorly controlled controlled economy') provides perhaps the best example of the failure of such state intervention, of which more below.[7] State control became identified with chaos, and decontrol, by contrast, with the prospect of a return to order. The German state had utterly discredited itself through its conduct of the War and management of the economy and society between 1914 and 1918, and revolution was its reward.

There are, of course, many ways to conceptualise the state. Here it is used in two senses – what it was, and what it was perceived to be. On the one hand, we can define the state as a system of institutions and processes through which the political will of a society is developed and applied, and which claims a monopoly of legitimate force within a particular geographical area; on the other hand, we need to focus on the way in which the state is widely perceived – as a collection of bureaucrats, paid for out of taxes, who tell people what to do. This latter, essentially negative perception framed popular attitudes towards the state in Germany and was given an especially sharp edge during and after the First World War. The state was drawn into economic and social conflicts as never before and, as a result, in Weimar Germany it tended to be seen less in terms of its positive functions (for example, as the provider of schools or the ultimate guarantor of social justice) than in terms of functions which, perhaps inevitably, aroused antipathy.

No group reacted more directly, and with such far-reaching consequences, against state authority than Germany's soldiers, who during the latter stages of the War increasingly demonstrated their hostility towards those who had sent them into combat and allowed such severe hardships to be inflicted on their families back home.

---

7. See Gerald D. Feldman, *Army Industry and Labor in Germany 1914–1918*, Princeton, 1966, esp. pp. 97–116, 283–91; Jürgen Kocka, *Klassengesellschaft im Krieg. Deutsche Sozialgeschichte 1914–1918*, Göttingen, 1973, pp. 96–105 (Eng. edn: *Facing Total War: German Society 1914–1918*, trans. Barbara Weinberger, Leamington Spa, 1984); Jens Flemming, *Landwirtschaftliche Interessen und Demokratie. Ländliche Gesellschaft, Agrarverbände und Staat 1890–1925*, Bonn, 1978, esp. pp. 95–105; Robert G. Moeller, *German Peasants and Agrarian Politics, 1914–1924. The Rhineland and Westphalia*, Chapel Hill and London, 1986, pp. 43–67; Robert G. Moeller, 'Economic Dimensions of Peasant Protest in the Transition from Kaiserreich to Weimar', in idem (ed.), *Peasants and Lords in Modern Germany. Recent Studies in Agricultural History*, Boston, 1986, pp. 149–54.

The political revolution of November 1918 was, of course, initiated by servicemen. It was the collapse of the German armed forces which led the old political elites to abdicate, and revolts of soldiers stationed within Germany almost invariably preceded the mass strikes of local industrial work forces.[8] This was but the culmination of a longer-term deterioration of morale among the soldiers. Already during late 1917 up to 10 per cent of the troops being transported from the Eastern Front to the Western Front used the trip as an opportunity to desert,[9] and the numbers of deserters increased considerably after the spring offensives of 1918. More and more soldiers simply disembarked from the trains carrying them to replace troops at the Front, and the numbers of the so-called *Drückeberger* (shirkers) and men taking unauthorised leave rose greatly; one estimate put the number of the *Drückeberger* during the final months of the War at between 750,000 and one million.[10] By November 1918, with the approach of the Armistice, this disintegration accelerated to such an extent that the German army no longer existed as a disciplined fighting force: units, especially those behind the lines, disbanded themselves; soldiers failed to return from leave in the hope of sitting out the end of the War in safety within Germany; troops mutinied, as those stationed in the rear refused to go to the Front.[11] The authority of the state, in its most naked and important form – its disposal of armed force – had dissolved.

The hostility towards state authority continued into the demob-

8. See Ulrich Kluge, *Soldatenräte und Revolution. Studien zur Militärpolitik in Deutschland 1918/19*, Göttingen, 1975, p. 105.

9. Wilhelm Deist, 'Der militärische Zusammenbruch des Kaiserreichs. Zur Realität der "Dolchstoßlegende"', in Ursula Büttner (ed.), *Das Unrechtsregime. Internationale Forschung über den Nationalsozialismus. Band I. Ideologie – Herrschaftssystem – Wirkung in Europa*, Hamburg, 1986, p. 109.

10. Erich Otto Volkmann, *Der Marxismus und das deutsche Heer im Weltkriege*, Berlin, 1925, p. 193. See also Deist, 'Der militärische Zusammenbruch', pp. 115–17. For problems of morale, refusals to follow orders and mutinies on the Eastern Front during 1918, see Ulrich Kluge, *Soldatenräte und Revolution*, pp. 94–5.

11. See Erich Ludendorff, *Meine Kriegserinnerungen 1914–1918*, Berlin, 1919, p. 564; Heinz Hürten and Georg Meyer (eds.), *Adjutant im preußischen Kriegsministerium Juni 1918 bis Oktober 1919. Aufzeichnungen des Hauptmanns Gustav Böhm*, Stuttgart, 1977, p. 52; Deutsche Akademie der Wissenschaften, Zentralinstitut für Geschichte, *Deutschland im Ersten Weltkrieg. Band 3. November 1917 bis November 1918*, 2nd edn, Berlin, 1970, pp. 520–1; Hans-Joachim Bieber, *Gewerkschaften in Krieg und Revolution. Arbeiterbewegung, Industrie, Staat und Militär in Deutschland 1914–1920*, Hamburg, 1981, p. 568.

ilisation period. The soldiers knew that no one could compel them to obey orders, and they acted accordingly. Although many men marched from the Front back to Germany in reasonably good order, once they arrived in the Reich or crossed the Rhine large numbers took off on their own.[12] As the Reich War Ministry later admitted, in an account of the return of the German soldiers from the Eastern Front published in 1936, 'a mood developed among the troops which allowed only one single thought: to return home at any price!'[13] The overwhelming desire was to get out of uniform, to return to private life. Alarmed civilian authorities reported that among soldiers stationed within Germany 'a complete lack of discipline' prevailed, that soldiers had allowed their weapons to land in 'unauthorised hands', stole food and equipment from their units to sell to the civilian population, refused to follow orders and behaved in a 'threatening manner'.[14] And once they had shed their military uniforms the veterans displayed little desire to go where the government directed them. Despite the desperate need for farm labour, returning veterans turned a deaf ear to the repeated attempts of the Reich Demobilisation Office to induce them to accept employment on the land; similarly, the make-work projects set up by local authorities and subsidised by the Reich government to prevent mass unemployment during the post-war transition often were shunned.[15] Two things appear to have been at work here: first, unemployment among the returning veterans turned out to be a much less serious problem than those planning the economic

12. Staatsarchiv Hamburg (StAH), Demobilmachung 7, f. 11: Oberst Reinhardt, 'Rücktransport und Demobilmachung des Heeres (Sitzung mit dem Demobilmachungskommissar am 18.12.18)'; Ludendorff, *Meine Kriegserinnerungen*, p. 619.

13. Reichskriegsministerium, Forschungsamt für Kriegs– und Heeresgeschichte (ed.), *Die Rückführung des Ostheeres*, Berlin, 1936, p. 22.

14. This is well documented for Upper Silesia during November and December 1918. See Archiwum Panstwowe w Wroclawiu (APW), Rejencja Opolska Pr.B., Nr. 259, f. 1019: The Landrat des Kreises Tost-Gleiwitz to the Regierungspräsident, Gleiwitz, 26 November 1918; ibid., ff. 1027–8: The Landrat to the Regierungspräsident, Leobschütz, 25 November 1918; ibid., f. 1037: The Landrat to the Regierungspräsident, Oppeln, 10 December 1918.

15. See, for example, StAH, Demobilmachungskommissar, Nr. 50, f. 41: Stellv. Genko. IX. A.K., Abt. Ia/V, to the Demobilmachungskommissar bei der Stadt Hamburg, Dr Buehl, Altona, 19 December 1918; Richard Bessel, 'Unemployment and Demobilisation in Germany after the First World War', in Richard J. Evans and Dick Geary (eds.), *The German Unemployed. Experiences and Consequences of Mass Unemployment from the Weimar Republic to the Third Reich*, London, 1987, pp. 23–43.

demobilisation had assumed it would become. Secondly, the men who had just got out of uniform were not inclined to do what the authorities told them they ought to do – certainly not if that involved taking up undesirable outdoor work on farms or public-works projects. The German state was in no position to compel its citizens to work where they did not want to work.

The demobilised soldiers were not alone in expressing such feelings. Women too resisted state direction, in particular attempts by labour exchanges to place them in domestic service or in agricultural work after their wartime employment came to an end.[16] Thus in Silesia women displayed 'great resistance' to placement in domestic service or on the farm, and teenage girls responded to attempts to place them on the land with the argument that 'the farmers should do their dirty work themselves'.[17] The main desire, it seems, was to retreat to the private sphere once the employment opportunities which had opened up to women during the War were closed off again.[18] This helps explain, on the one hand, the relative ease with which women were removed from many types of employment during late 1918 and early 1919 and, on the other, their resistance to attempts to place them in unattractive jobs. It is in this context that the tremendous – and predictable – waves of births and marriages which followed the Armistice may be taken into account. The annual number of marriages in 1919 and 1920 was roughly three times what it had been during the War years and about two-thirds higher than immediately before the War; and the numbers of births showed a corresponding rise during the early 1920s.[19] Where the state was pushing women to return to the private sphere it was pushing against an open door; where it attempted to direct labour (without the commensurate authority to compel people to go where directed), there it met with resistance. During the demob-

16. See Geheimes Staatsarchiv preußischer Kulturbesitz Berlin–Dahlem (GStA), Rep. 180, Nr. 15913: 'Bericht über den Arbeitsmarkt in Danzig während des Krieges', Danzig, 17 February 1919.

17. Zentrales Staatsarchiv Potsdam (ZStAP), Reichsministerium für wirtschaftliche Demobilmachung (RMwD), Nr. 18/1, ff. 297–301: Kriegsamtstelle to the Reichsamt für wirtschaftliche Demobilmachung, Breslau, 8 February 1919; ZStAP, RMwD, Nr. 2, ff. 371–2: Arbeitsnachweis der Landwirtschaftskammer für die Provinz Schlesien to the Kriegswirtschaftsamt, Breslau, 4 January 1919.

18. See Richard Bessel, '"Eine nicht allzu große Beunruhigung des Arbeitsmarktes". Frauenarbeit und Demobilmachung in Deutschland nach dem Ersten Weltkrieg', *Geschichte und Gesellschaft*, vol. 9, 1983, esp. pp. 221–4.

19. See *Statistisches Jahrbuch für das Deutsche Reich 1926*, Berlin, 1926, p. 24.

ilisation period the German government was successful where it aimed to lift state controls; where it attempted to continue or extend them it inevitably ran up against difficulties.

These observations may help to explain one of the paradoxes of the post-war events in Germany, namely the apparent contradiction between the strength of revolutionary pressures for a new political order on the one hand and the ultimately successful attempts to preserve and restore capitalist economic structures and bourgeois society on the other. On the surface, these two developments seem quite distinct from one another. But are the two really so different as might appear at first sight? Writing about the mass working-class movements which played so important a role in German politics at this time, Gerald Feldman has noted that 'the very conditions that promoted the development of a mass movement in Germany between 1917 and 1920 were very often the same ones that limited, constrained and even destroyed its revolutionary potential and that fed the forces of counterrevolution'.[20] One suggestion in this chapter is that among those conditions was a widespread hostility towards the German state and state interference, which could be found in the camps of both revolutionary transformation and bourgeois restoration.

Throughout the upheavals of 1918 to 1920, antipathy towards the German state and its intrusion into people's everyday lives appears to have been the common denominator. The revolutionary impulses of 1918 and thereafter were in large measure an expression of antipathy towards the state and its demands. But at the same time many of the impulses which made possible a successful bourgeois restoration also were an expression of antipathy towards state intervention: the desire to see controls lifted as soon as possible, to retreat from the public sphere and return to the private sphere. It is, therefore, perhaps an error to see the revolution and restoration as clearly distinct phenomena. Perhaps the failure of the SPD Reich Economics Minister Rudolf Wissel and his *Unterstaatssekretär* Wichard von Moellendorf to put in place a new, state-run economic

20. Gerald D. Feldman, 'Socio–Economic Structures in the Industrial Sector and Revolutionary Potentialities, 1917–1922', in Charles L. Bertrand (ed.), *Revolutionary Situations in Europe, 1917–1922: Germany, Italy and Austria-Hungary*, Montreal, 1977, p. 160. See also Gerald D. Feldman, Eberhard Kolb and Reinhard Rürup, 'Die Massenbewegungen der Arbeiterschaft in Deutschland am Ende des Ersten Weltkrieges (1917–1920)', *Politische Vierteljahresschrift*, vol. 13, 1972, pp. 84–105.

order after 1918 was due in part to the same kinds of sentiment which had made possible the creation of government in which Wissell could have become a minister in the first place. Perhaps working-class radicalism, peasant conservatism and middle-class reaction after the First World War all found nourishment from the same source: distaste for state interference in everyday life.

The Ambiguities of State-Managed Demobilisation

The dilemmas facing the German state in the aftermath of the First World War can be seen in the activities of the Reich Demobilisation Office set up in November 1918 under Joseph Koeth. As Gerald Feldman stressed in his important article on economic demobilisation after the First World War, Koeth's work 'long outlasted the brief tenure of the Demobilisation Office' as it 'predetermined so many of the basic patterns of economic and social life in the Weimar Republic'.[21] Koeth regarded the demobilisation over which he had been put in charge as a two-stage process: first, overcoming the emergency created by the sudden return of the soldiers following the Armistice, and then attempting to sort out the fundamental structural problems involved in the transition from war to peace – including the coal shortage, the threats to agricultural production and the need to channel labour towards those sectors of the economy where it was most needed. With regard to the first, Koeth's efforts – characterised by a readiness to go to almost any lengths to ensure that the soldiers had jobs upon their return home – seemed to meet with startling success. With regard to the second, however, he was less effective.[22] The contrast is revealing. Koeth's apparent success with regard to the first phase of the demobilisation may have had less to do with his organisational skill or the competence of the Demobilisation Office which he headed than with the fact that, essentially, he was swimming with the tide. At a time when the vast majority of German soldiers wanted nothing more than to go back home and pick up the threads of their civilian lives once again, Koeth had the good sense not to try to stand in their way. Instead he was willing to try just about anything, and spend just about any

21. Gerald D. Feldman, 'Economic and Social Problems of the German Demobilization, 1918–19', *Journal of Modern History*, vol. 47, 1975, p. 7.
22. Ibid., pp. 17–18.

sum of money necessary to allow the soldiers' wishes to be granted. In other words, Koeth was successful where he sought to enable people to do what they wanted to do anyway. He was less successful with regard to the second task he had set himself, for this did involve state interference: attempts to direct labour, to control the distribution of raw materials.

These observations go some way towards explaining the responses to a key element of demobilisation policy: the guarantee to veterans of their old jobs back once they returned from military service, as stipulated in the decree of 4 January 1919 on the 'hiring, dismissal and payment of industrial workers during the period of the economic demobilisation'.[23] According to its provisions, firms with more than twenty workers had to re-employ war veterans who had been with them before the outbreak of war, as far as possible in their old positions. Certainly employers were justified in regarding this decree as a 'deep incursion into the rights of the entrepreneur';[24] the state was intervening in hiring practices to an extent which would have been difficult to imagine before 1914. Yet employers made great efforts to comply with the provisions of the decree.[25] Indeed, many re-hired their former employees as these returned from military service before there was legal compulsion to do so.[26] Three reasons for this behaviour can be put forward: first, it was assumed by almost everyone concerned with the planning of the economic demobilisation, including the employers, that the soldiers would return to their old jobs.[27] What is more, employers generally had viewed it as their patriotic duty to re-hire the soldiers

---

23. *Reichsgesetzblatt*, 1919, pp. 8–13.

24. Quoted in Jürgen Reulecke, *Die wirtschaftliche Entwicklung der Stadt Barmen von 1910 bis 1925*, Neustadt von der Aisch, 1973, p. 118.

25. See, for example, ZStAP, RMwD, Nr. 18/1, ff. 200–3: Wirtschaftsstelle Frankfurt a.M. für die Bezirke Hessen & Wiesbaden to the Reichsamt für die wirtschaftliche Demobilmachung, Frankfurt a.M., 18 January 1919; ibid., f. 168: The Regierungspräsident, Demobilmachungskommissar, to the Reichswirtschaftsamt (sic) für wirtschaftliche Demobilmachung, Stettin, 26 January 1919.

26. See, for example, Westfälisches Wirtschaftsarchiv Dortmund (WWA), K1, Nr. 171: letters from firms to the Dortmund Handelskammer during December 1918; ZStAP, RMwD, Nr. 18/1, ff. 2–3: Kriegsamtstelle Danzig to the Reichsamt für wirtschaftliche Demobilmachung, Danzig, December 1918; Staatsarchiv Potsdam (StAP), Rep. 2A, Regierung Potsdam I SW, Nr. 796, f. 150: Hirsch-, Kupfer- und Messingwerke Aktiengesellschaft to the Regierungspräsident als Demobilmachungskommissar, Messingwerk, 15 February 1919.

27. See, for example, WWA, K1, Nr. 172: letters of firms to the Handelskammer Dortmund during 1917 and 1918.

(an argument which, during the War, had been deployed to forestall regulations of the kind decreed in January 1919).[28] Secondly, employers already had agreed to take this step in the Stinnes-Legien Agreement (Point 4) of 15 November 1918.[29] And thirdly, despite misgivings about the consequences of such hiring practices for the profitability of their firms, compliance with what appeared to be an inevitable measure seemed better than provoking further state intervention by non-compliance. That is to say, the success of this state intervention came about, on the one hand, because the government was pushing against a (temporarily) open door, and, on the other, because compliance may have been due to a widespread desire to forestall further government interference.

Further clues in this direction are offered by a glimpse at the operations of the demobilisation machinery itself. As we have seen, in performing certain tasks, the demobilisation apparatus – set up at short notice under the direction of Koeth – was quite successful. The German economy did survive the economic crisis which sudden military demobilisation created, and the ways in which the Reich Demobilisation Office steered the German economy through troubled waters immediately after the Armistice were of great importance in shaping the economic and social constitution upon which the Weimar Republic was based. However, recognition of that success should not lead one to associate the history of post-war Germany with a picture of a massive demobilisation machinery feverishly working away at all levels within the state bureaucracy. Certainly feverish activity was the name of the game at the top. But what of the demobilisation machinery lower down the administrative structure, and what of how the decrees issued in Berlin actually were put into practice?

The demobilisation machinery hastily put into place in November 1918 was essentially three-tiered: the central authorities under Koeth's direction in Berlin, the 'Demobilisation Commissars' (in the case of Prussia, these were the *Regierungspräsidenten*) at regional level, and the local 'Demobilisation Committees' (*Demobilmachungsausschüsse*) at district (*Kreis*) level (composed of local

28. See Reulecke, *Die wirtschaftliche Entwicklung der Stadt Barmen*, p. 118.
29. See the text of the Agreement in Gerald D. Feldman and Irmgard Steinisch, 'The Origins of the Stinnes–Legien Agreement', *Internationale wissenschaftliche Korrespondenz zur Geschichte der deutschen Arbeiterbewegung*, vol. 19, 1973, pp. 84f.

representatives of business and labour and chaired by the local mayor or *Landrat*). The main tasks of the demobilisation machinery involved the regulation of the labour market – as the *Regierungspräsident* (and Demobilisation Commissar) in Merseburg put it, 'to keep the economy going, to place workers, insofar as they no longer can be employed in the armaments factories, as well as discharged soldiers, back in work and in their old regions'.[30] The great mass of the work involved in this – ensuring that the decrees emanating from Berlin were put into practice and sorting out conflicts which arose over carrying out the demobilisation measures – fell to the local Demobilisation Committees.[31]

But how much did these Demobilisation Committees actually do? Although some took their duties extremely seriously, in many cases the answer appears to have been not all that much. Particularly in more rural regions, the Committees rarely met, their unpaid members – the representatives of the local business communities and of labour organisations – had little to do with the working of the Committees, and it tended to be the Chairmen (the mayors or *Landräte*) who effectively carried out the tasks which fell to the local demobilisation organisations.[32] Similar observations may be made about the enforcement of that central piece of demobilisation legislation, the 'Decree on the Releasing of Jobs during the Period of the Economic Demobilisation', which allowed the authorities to

30. Staatsarchiv Magdeburg, Rep. C 50 Querfurt A/B, Nr. 2808, ff. 8–9: The Regierungs-Präsident to the Landräte and Ersten Bürgermeister der Kreisfreien Städte des Bezirks, Merseburg, 15 November 1918. See also Martin Sogemeier, *Die Entwicklung und Regelung des Arbeitsmarktes im rheinisch-westfälischen Industriegebiet im Kriege und in der Nachkriegszeit*, Jena, 1922, pp. 88f.; Jürgen Tampke, *The Ruhr and Revolution. The Revolutionary Movement in the Rhenish-Westphalian Industrial Region 1912–1919*, London, 1979, p. 76.

31. Staatsarchiv Weimar, Thüringisches Wirtschaftsministerium, Nr. 130, ff. 3–4: The Staatskommissar für die Demobilmachung in den Thüringischen Staaten to the Demobilmachungsausschüsse der Thüringischen Staaten, Weimar, 20 November 1918.

32. In March 1921, when the Demobilisation Committees were scheduled to be dissolved by the government ('Reichsverordnung über die Beendigung der wirtschaftlichen Demobilmachung vom 18. Februar 1921', *Reichsgesetzblatt*, 1921, p. 189), the Regierungspräsident in Stralsund wrote to the Chairmen of all the Demobilisation Committees in his region to ask what the Committees had been doing and what administrative arrangements would be needed in their place. In response he was informed that in most cases the Committees had met only once or twice over the previous two years, and that their tasks had been carried out by the normal state bureaucracy (the Landratsämter etc.). See the responses to the Regierungspräsident in Staatsarchiv Greifswald (StAG), Rep. 65c, Nr. 2903.

intervene to ensure that certain categories of workers (such as those judged not to depend on their jobs for their livelihoods) were dismissed.[33] Many local authorities simply had little or no cause to invoke this legislation, 'as even without the decree the local employers, as far as conditions permitted, employed their old people without any urging being necessary'.[34] What is more, the demobilisation machinery did not displace municipal employment offices and chambers of commerce and industry, which continued to concern themselves with the regulation of the labour market.[35] In other words, at the level where it directly affected individuals, this much-vaunted and extremely influential demobilisation machinery often was conspicuous largely by its absence.

This is not to argue that the whole demobilisation machinery at the regional and local level counted for nothing, or that there were no conflicts over the application of decrees affecting hiring practices. The demobilisation authorities could, and in many cases (particularly in the industrial cities of the Ruhr) did get involved deeply in the management of local job markets;[36] and their activities often provoked complaints from employers, particularly after the initial post-war crises had passed.[37] But in the main this involvement was exercised by the existing bureaucracy and owed its success not to compulsion enforced by a vast new state machinery but by general compliance with measures being monitored through the conventional bureaucratic framework. It succeeded in large measure because it was regarded as temporary, as a necessary step towards inevitable decontrol, and because in practical terms it did not really signify a massive new expansion of the state.

Not surprisingly, this limited demobilisation apparatus found itself virtually powerless to accomplish tasks when the German

33. *Reichsgesetzblatt*, 1919, pp. 355–9.

34. See reports to the Regierungspräsident in Schneidemühl in early 1920, in Archiwum Panstwowe w Poznaniu (APP), Rejencja w Pile, Nr. 1484. The quote is from a report of the Vorsitzender des Kreisausschusses to the Regierungspräsident, Schönlanke, 5 February 1920.

35. See Tampke, *Ruhr*, p. 76.

36. One example of an active Demobilisation Committee may be found in Bochum. See Stadtarchiv Bochum, B 265 and 266.

37. See, for example, Zentrales Staatsarchiv, Dienststelle Merseburg, Rep. 120, BB VII 1, Nr. 3o, Bd. 8, ff. 15–16: Vereinigung Erfurter Arbeitgeberverbände to the Minister des Innern, Erfurt, 5 January 1921; StAG, Rep 65c, Nr. 2903, f. 72: Arbeitgeber-Hauptverband für Industrie, Handel und Gewerbe Vorpommerns to the Demobilmachungskommissar, Stralsund, 17 December 1920.

population would not co-operate. Despite the desperate concern of the Reich Office for Economic Demobilisation that workers be channelled into farm labour and that regional demobilisation authorities make a major effort to bring this about,[38] and despite the unemployment in many German cities in early 1919, government ministers soon had to admit defeat: just a few months after the Armistice, and despite concern about the national composition of the population in eastern German border districts, they felt compelled to take the unwelcome step of encouraging the employment of foreign, Polish labour on the land.[39] Germans were unwilling to take up agricultural work in sufficient numbers.[40] The *Freikorps* may have had the strength to suppress left-wing revolts in German cities, but compelling hundreds of thousands of people to stick with work on the land was quite another matter. In the absence of a level of coercion which their government was not in a position to apply in the aftermath of the War and revolution, Germans were unprepared to be pushed by the state in directions they did not want to go. And yet, when it came to assigning blame for the failure to develop a successful agricultural policy, Germans naturally focused on the state. Probably no democratic state can accomplish such tasks when the population will not co-operate; the difficulty here was that the Weimar state was trapped between the impossibility of accomplishing such tasks and responsibility for the consequences of failing to accomplish them.

State Practice and Popular Expectations: The Interventionist State

The paradoxical nature of the relations between state and society in Germany after the First World War had another, deeper dimension:

38. See Hauptstaatsarchiv Düsseldorf, Reg. Aachen, Präsidialbüro, Nr. 1621: Reichsamt für wirtschaftliche Demobilmachung to the Demobilmachungskommissare usw., Berlin, December 1918; Niedersächsisches Hauptstaatsarchiv Hannover (NHStAH), Hann. 122a/XXXIV, Nr. 368, f. 397: Reichsamt für die wirtschaftliche Demobilmachung, 'Aufruf an die Landbevölkerung!' (January 1919).
39. APW, Rejencja Opolska I, Nr. 12410, ff. 764–5: Reichsministerium des Innern to the Regierungen der deutschen Freistaaten, Berlin, 19 March 1919.
40. See the reports on the labour market sent by various Kriegsamtstellen and Arbeitsnachweise to the Reichsamt für wirtschaftliche Demobilmachung in late 1918 and early 1919, in ZStAP, RMwD, Nr. 18/1.

the experience of the War and its aftermath had aroused expectations of the state which could not be met. Faced with enormous economic problems – including the sudden shift from war production, the return of millions of soldiers almost overnight, and desperate food shortages – the state was compelled to intervene extensively in the everyday lives of its citizens, but could not do so effectively. This produced both expectations of what the state *should* do and animosity towards the state for failing to do it. The problem was exacerbated by the revolutionary transformation of 1918 and 1919, and the heightened expectations it aroused. The new Weimar system thus inherited high popular expectations as to what the state could and should deliver; but it also inherited a widespread desire to see decontrol and deregulation, which undercut its ability to order a chaotic economy, and had insufficient means – both military and economic – either to meet the high expectations or to diffuse the popular hostility. This fundamental gap between expectations and the means to satisfy them burdened the Weimar Republic from start to finish. As such, it formed a damaging legacy of the First World War and subsequent demobilisation for the political viability of Weimar democracy.

It is common to note that the First World War, and the tremendous and indeed unprecedented demands it placed upon the belligerent countries, led to a vast expansion of state involvement in economic and social affairs. Government control was extended to a greater or lesser extent over the distribution of raw materials, prices, and the direction of labour. Not surprisingly, this extension of state activity led to growing animosity, particularly among businessmen (large and small) and farm producers who felt their freedom in the market-place restricted. Businessmen, who before the War had held attitudes which have been described as 'uncritical solidarity with the state', became increasingly critical of 'state socialism'.[41] In their anti-state polemics they stressed that the main item on the demobilisation agenda should be the casting off of state economic controls, the 'liberation from all the shackles brought about by the War'.[42] Yet German businessmen proved most willing to accept lucrative state contracts and to profit from the ramshackle system of controls

41. See Kocka, *Klassengesellschaft*, pp. 116–18. The quote is taken by Kocka from H. Jaeger, *Unternehmer in der deutschen Politik (1890–1918)*, Bonn, 1967, p. 260.
42. Quoted in Kocka, *Klassengesellschaft im Krieg*, p. 117.

where they could.[43] They may have loudly criticised state interference in the abstract, but they were not slow to urge that government contracts keep flowing in their direction, for example in order to tide them over the demobilisation period.[44]

Probably the most notorious example of this was the *Zwangswirtschaft*, the economic controls extended over agricultural production and distribution during the War in response to the critical problems of food supply and popular pressure for a fair system of distribution. Controls over the prices and deliveries of most key agricultural products continued in force until 1920–1 and were not lifted completely until the summer of 1923. But this massive state incursion into the everyday workings of the economy did not lead to a satisfactory regulation of food distribution. Instead, the result was chaotic marketing conditions, continued black-marketeering and anger on the part of both producers and consumers of food.[45] As Robert Moeller has put it, the continuing food crisis in which demand far exceeded supply and the consequent extension of wartime controls meant that 'tensions between producers and consumers of agricultural products, a central dimension of social conflict during the war and an inevitable consequence of chronic food shortages, survived undiminished in the transition from war to peace'.[46] State interference – even when it was continued in order to ensure that Germans had enough to eat and when a large proportion of the German population expected government action – inevitably brought a harvest of hostility. Thus by trying to hold the ring in the midst of intense social and economic conflict, the state could only lose.

Just how sharp the post-war antagonisms could be was illustrated by the fact that on occasion military expeditions were necessary to secure delivery of agricultural produce. Already during the winter

43. This is described masterfully by Gerald Feldman in *Army Industry and Labor*, and *Iron and Steel in the German Inflation 1916–1923*, Princeton, 1977.

44. See, for example, NHStAH, Hann 80, Hann. II, Nr. 1981: Handelskammer zu Hannover to the Regierungspräsident, Hannover, 19 December 1918; NHStAH, Hann 80, Hann. II, Nr. 1991: H. Wohlenberg Drehfabrik und Eisengiesserei to the Demobilmachungskommissar, Hannover, 20 December 1918.

45. See Robert Moeller, 'Winners as Losers in the German Inflation: Peasant Protest over the Controlled Economy, 1920–1923', in Gerald D. Feldman, Carl-Ludwig Holtfrerich, Gerhard A. Ritter and Peter-Christian Witt (eds.), *Die deutsche Inflation. Eine Zwischenbilanz*, Berlin and New York, 1982, pp. 255–88.

46. Ibid., p. 266.

of 1917/18 military squads had been sent to farms to enforce requisitioning orders,[47] and after the Armistice, with state authority weakened, the conflicts grew even worse. Farmers resisted giving their animals up for slaughter, sometimes violently, and rural gendarmes sometimes found themselves unable to enforce compulsory deliveries without the help of the army.[48] In March 1919 the Army Command in Upper Silesia decided that popular resistance to the compulsory purchase of cattle had grown so intense that it was necessary to create special twenty-man units in each garrison to help local officials collect livestock; and in the case of Klein Steinisch (a village of fewer than 1,000 inhabitants in *Kreis* Groß Strehlitz) a commando group of two officers and forty-five men were sent out in motor vehicles 'in order to carry through the collection of livestock and if necessary to break the resistance of the population'.[49] The effects of such expeditions upon the attitudes of the rural population are not difficult to imagine. Officials whose task it was to check agricultural production and deliveries also met extreme hostility. For example, in the district of Minden, in Westphalia, government inspection teams sent to ascertain farm production were greeted by peasants armed with clubs and pitchforks threatening to kill the intruders.[50] The *Zwangswirtschaft* may not have succeeded in controlling the marketing of agricultural products – indeed, Moeller argues convincingly that in many key areas it virtually had collapsed in practice before the controls were dismantled formally[51] – but it did succeed in fuelling antagonism between town and country and between the German state and the German people. In conditions of shortage, the German state hardly could refrain from involving itself in food distribution, but at the same time it could not but fail to satisfy popular expectations.

Similar observations may be made with regard to housing. During the First World War housing construction came to a virtual standstill, while rent controls prevented housing costs from keeping

47. Kocka, *Klassengesellschaft*, p. 99; Robert Moeller, 'Dimensions of Social Conflict in the Great War: The View from the German Countryside', *Central European History*, vol. 14, no. 2, 1981, p. 156.

48. See, for example, APW, Rejencja Opolska Pr.B., Nr. 326, ff. 283–4: The Landrat to the Regierungspräsident, Rybnik, 28 January 1919.

49. Ibid., pp. 329–31: The Landrat to the Regierungspräsident, Groß Strehlitz, 11 March 1919.

50. Moeller, *German Peasants*, pp. 73–4.

51. Moeller, 'Winners as Losers', pp. 266–7.

pace with the general rise in prices.[52] After the War, the predictable upsurge in marriages led to the creation of hundreds of thousands of new households and, therefore, tremendous additional pressure on an already tight housing market. Not surprisingly, the state was compelled to intervene, and in the demobilisation period the German housing market was shaped to a large extent by the state. Not only had the state intervened to regulate rent increases; it also circumscribed the rights of landlord and tenant, particularly with regard to the ways in which a landlord could dispose of his property.[53] The first moves had been made at the outbreak of the War, when the Law for the Protection of Servicemen of 4 August 1914 granted dependents of soldiers protection against eviction, and legislation enacted on 14 January 1915 prevented landlords from obtaining court eviction orders against fighting men.[54] During the closing stages of the War the certain prospect of massive housing shortages during the demobilisation led to the enactment on 23 September 1918 of measures to 'protect tenants' and work 'against the housing shortage'.[55] This spelled far-reaching state intervention in a sphere which before the War essentially had been a matter of private contract between landlord and tenant. No longer could flats be disposed of simply as the landlord (or tenant) saw fit. Now the state could, under certain circumstances, order that additional people be housed in a dwelling, and a landlord no longer had the final say about who would be his tenant. Local authorities were empowered to prevent dwellings from being torn down or used for commercial or industrial purposes, and to compel the owners of empty properties to advertise their availability. In larger communities 'rent settlement offices' (*Mieteinigungsämter*) were set up and had the power to prevent a landlord from evicting a tenant, extend a rental contract for a year, and decide whether a landlord

52. See Carl-Ludwig Holtfrerich, *Die deutsche Inflation 1914–1923. Ursachen und Folgen in internationaler Perspektive*, Berlin and New York, 1980, pp. 249–51.

53. For a concise discussion of this, see L. Pohle, 'Die Wohnungsfrage – Mieterschutz', in *Handbuch der Politik. Band IV. Der wirtschaftliche Wiederaufbau*, 3rd edn, Berlin and Leipzig, 1921, pp. 233–4.

54. See the discussion of this legislation, and of the fears aroused over what awaited men when they left military service and lost this protection, in GStA, Rep. 84a, Nr. 1764, ff. 165–6: (The Preußischer Justizminister) to the Staatssekretär des Reichsjustizamts, Berlin, 4 December 1918.

55. *Reichsgesetzblatt*, 1918, pp. 1140–3: 'Bekanntmachung zum Schutze der Mieter vom 23. September 1918'; ibid., pp. 1143–6: 'Bekanntmachung über Maßnahmen gegen Wohnungsmangel vom 23. September 1918'.

was justified in demanding a rent increase. In Prussia legislation came into force in December 1919 which obligated local authorities to fix rents and percentage rent increases as determined by the Prussian government.[56] Designed to prevent property owners from taking advantage of the tremendous shortages of housing, these regulations served to make the state, rather than the market, the final arbiter in landlord–tenant relations.

The state also intervened to restrict mobility, in particular to try to prevent large numbers of people congregating in the cities looking for work (and stirring up political unrest). The most serious problem was that faced by Berlin. Great efforts were made to ensure that the soldiers returned to their home communities – a goal often voiced by demobilisation authorities worried about the consequences of large numbers of unemployed ex-soldiers gathering in Germany's urban centres. And in some cases city councils banned immigration into their communities during the demobilisation period.[57]

However, these measures did not work. The state could neither control internal migration nor build enough housing in the short term to ease the desperate shortage. Indeed, by keeping the price of rented accommodation artificially low the state may have exacerbated the post-war housing shortage.[58] After the War housing became scarce almost everywhere in Germany. For example, in Ludwigshafen the municipal Statistical Office calculated on the basis of the census taken on 8 October 1919 that – even before the expected return of the prisoners of war – there were 1,379 fewer dwellings in the city than there were households.[59] Reports from the municipal Housing Office in neighbouring Heidelberg were no more heartening, noting in March 1919 that the number of flats available bore 'no relation' to the 'current extraordinary demand',[60] and two months later the position was worse still.[61] In the Ruhr the lack of housing limited the numbers of people who might be

56. See Pohle, 'Die Wohnungsfrage', p. 234.
57. This happened, for example, in Nuremberg in March 1919. See Eric G. Reiche, *The Development of the SA in Nürnberg 1922–1934*, Cambridge, 1986, p. 11.
58. See Pohle, 'Die Wohnungsfrage', p. 234.
59. Stadtarchiv Ludwigshafen, Nr. 1510: Statistisches Amt der Stadt Ludwigshafen am Rhein to the Bürgermeisteramt, Ludwigshafen am Rhein, 3 November 1919.
60. Stadtarchiv Heidelberg, Nr. 278,8: Städtisches Wohnungsamt, Heidelberg, 12 March 1919.
61. Ibid., Städtisches Wohnungsamt to the Stadtrat, Heidelberg, 2 May 1919.

brought in to supply desperately needed labour in the mines.[62] Even in small cities such as Neubrandenburg and Wismar the shortages of housing were desperate.[63] Many communities looked to the building of municipal or co-operative housing estates. Town administrations worked together with state governments and building co-operatives to provide capital for housing projects.[64] But these were essentially longer-term measures. The time required before such projects would bear fruit, the difficulties created by the inflation particularly for housing co-operatives struggling to finance projects,[65] and the huge scale of the housing shortages meant that it was difficult for such initiatives to have a significant impact during the demobilisation period.[66]

These problems took place against a general background of depressed housing construction and changes in population structures which put yet more pressure on the housing market. Smaller household and family sizes during the Weimar period meant that demand for separate dwellings outstripped population increase. For example, in Mannheim the total population in 1919 was 10.3 per

62. See Stadtarchiv Bochum, KrA 707: Amt Harpen, Landkreis Bochum, to the Demobilmachungsausschuß für den Landkreis Bochum, Gerthe, 24 December 1918; Tampke, *Ruhr*, p. 146.

63. Staatsarchiv Schwerin (StAS), Mecklenburg Strelitzer Ministerium, Abteilung des Innern, Nr. 5071, f. 48: Magistrat to the Meckl-Strelitzer Landesregierung, Abtlg. des Innern, Neubrandenburg, 25 October 1919; StAS, Mecklenburg-Schweriner Landeswohnungsamt, Nr. 21, f. 149: Stadtbauamt der Seestadt Wismar i.M. to the Landeswohnungsamt, Wismar, 16 December 1919.

64. For Berlin, see Frauke Bey-Heard, *Hauptstadt und Staatsumwälzung. Berlin 1919. Problematik und Scheitern der Rätebewegung in der Berliner Kommunalverwaltung*, Berlin, 1969, pp. 121–2.

65. For an example of the problems involved in raising the money to meet escalating building costs, see the correspondence relating to the 'Gemeinnützige Baugenossenschaft für Volks- und Kriegerheimstätten, Heidelberg', in Stadtarchiv Heidelberg, 281/53,1. This co-operative was founded in mid-1918, and was able to complete 174 flats by the end of 1920 (with another 42 flats underway), but only due to loans periodically made available by the Heidelberg city administration. See ibid., ff. 261–3: Badischer Verband gemeinnütziger Bauvereinigungen to the Gemeinnützige Baugenossenschaft für Volks- und Kriegerheimstätten Heidelberg G.m.b.H., 'Revisionsbericht', copy sent to the Stadtrat in Heidelberg, Heidelberg, 11 May 1921.

66. For example, the local administration of Langendreer, to the east of Bochum, reported in December 1921 that the 70 dwellings built there by the Miners' Housing Association and the 16 flats built by the town had done little to improve matters. During 1921 there had been 380 marriages in the town and during 1921 to December there had been 362. See Stadtarchiv Bochum, KrA 581: Amt Langendreer, Langendreer, 12 December 1921. At that time Langendreer had 29,000 inhabitants, a figure which – according to the town government – was a considerable increase over the number recorded in October 1919.

cent greater than it had been in 1910, but the number of households was 20.9 per cent greater; average household size in the city had fallen during this period from 4.58 to 4.18 people.[67] Yet during the post-war years the net increase in new dwellings in Germany remained quite low: it was a mere 56,714 in 1919 and 103,092 in 1920, and did not top 200,000 until 1926 (at which time rents were rising rapidly).[68] The result was continuing housing shortages during the 1920s, and increased state involvement in house construction; indeed, of the dwellings built in Germany between 1919 and 1932 more than four-fifths were financed to some extent by the state.[69] Thus the Weimar state got itself deeply involved in yet another thankless task involving the welfare of millions of Germans. Because of the problems created by war, demobilisation and inflation, the Weimar governments could not ignore the housing problem; but because of its scale and the limited resources available to deal with it, Weimar governments could not solve the problem either.

State Practice and Popular Expectations: Compensating the Victims of War

Perhaps the most revealing, but frequently overlooked, area of the Weimar state's involvement in the everyday lives of its citizens concerned war-related pensions and welfare benefits. As a result of the War, Weimar Germany contained a huge army of people dependent upon state benefits: men disabled as a consequence of combat injuries, war widows and other dependents of fallen servicemen. To be sure, the psychology of war victims is difficult to untangle.[70] However, it seems improbable that bringing millions of

67. Statistisches Amt der Stadt Mannheim (ed.), *Verwaltungs-Bericht der badischen Hauptstadt Mannheim für 1919/20*, Mannheim, n.d., p. 3.

68. For the figures on net increase in new dwellings, see *Statistisches Jahrbuch für das Deutsche Reich 1924/25*, Berlin, 1925, pp. 101–2; *Statistisches Jahrbuch für das Deutsche Reich 1926*, Berlin, 1926, p. 89; *Statistisches Jahrbuch für das Deutsche Reich 1934*, Berlin, 1934, p. 155. For evidence of the rapidly rising rent levels in the mid-1920s, see *Statistisches Jahrbuch für das Deutsche Reich 1927*, Berlin, 1927, p. 297; *Statistisches Jahrbuch für das Deutsche Reich 1929*, Berlin, 1929, p. 235.

69. Eberhard Kolb, *Die Weimarer Republik*, Munich, 1984, p. 100.

70. For a perceptive and at times brilliant discussion of Germany's war victims, see Robert Weldon Whalen, *Bitter Wounds. German Victims of the Great War, 1914–1939*, Ithaca and London, 1984.

Germans into contact with state bureaucrats to sort out entitlements to pensions and benefits won many enthusiasts for enhanced state involvement in everyday life. These pensions and benefits generally were regarded by their recipients (or potential recipients) as a right, while within the state administration there was a natural concern to keep expenditure on such benefits within bounds. The state bureaucracy became regarded as an obstacle in the way of people getting what was rightly theirs – a repayment for the sacrifices which the state had demanded of them during the War. Already in September 1915 the Prussian Interior Minister had expressed concern about a 'pension psychosis' developing among war invalids, who failed to display the necessary enthusiasm for job retraining that might remove them from dependence upon state welfare.[71] The sort of conflict which naturally arose as a consequence was neatly encapsulated by the Chairman of the 'Welfare Committee for War Invalids' for the Province of Posen in March 1918, when he looked with dismay at leaflets being distributed by a new organisation of war victims, the Association of Economic Organisations of Wounded Veterans:

> The leaflet represents in almost all respects an incursion into the domain of War Invalid Welfare proper. At the same time it stands in the sharpest contrast to the efforts of the Welfare Committee. The Welfare Committee is concerned to assist every war invalid to the point where he no longer needs outside help but rather is able care for himself and his family through his own work capability. The leaflet, however, emphasises the war invalid's claims to pension.[72]

According to the 'Sub-Committee for War Invalids' in Gnesen a few months later, the war disabled 'regard themselves as state pensioners'.[73] Here was an ideal recipe for hostility towards the state, a hostility fuelled by high expectations coupled with extreme

71. APS, Oberpräsidium von Pommern, Nr. 3932: The Minister des Innern to sämtliche Oberpräsidenten and the Regierungspräsident in Sigmaringen, 8 September 1915.

72. APP, Landeshauptverwaltung der Provinz Posen, Nr. 748, f. 104: Fürsorgeausschuß für Kriegsbeschädigte in der Provinz Posen to the Verband wirtschaftlicher Vereinigungen Kriegsbeschädigter, Ortsgruppe Posen, Posen, 9 March 1918.

73. APP, Landeshauptverwaltung der Provinz Posen, Nr. 749, f. 37: The Magistrat zu Gnesen, Unterausschuß für Kriegsbeschädigte, to the Fürsorgeausschuß für Kriegsbeschädigte in der Provinz Posen, Gnesen, 29 June 1918.

dependence upon state welfare provision.

During the Weimar years the German state faced huge financial and social obligations as a consequence of the War. It has been estimated that roughly 2.7 million German soldiers returned from the First World War with some sort of permanent disability, and in 1923 the Reich Labour Ministry estimated the number of war widows in Germany at 533,000 and of war orphans at 1,192,00.[74] The sheer scale of the problems created by the War overwhelmed the state welfare services. Already during the War it had been demonstrated that voluntary organisations, despite their good will and enthusiasm, could not cope; the government – horrified at the financial implications of attempts to supply the war victims with adequate pensions – tried to duck the issue; by the time of the Armistice, according to Robert Whalen, 'war victims were in open rebellion'.[75] And when the Reich government, in 1920, established a framework for aiding the war victims with the National Pension Law, this was done during an inflation which guaranteed constant conflict over the level of benefits. Even at the best of times it probably would have been impossible to shape a war-related pensions law which, without simultaneously destroying the state budget, could have satisfied the roughly five million people whose lives would be governed by its provisions.[76] And the prospects for success were not enhanced by the fact that the pensions had to be applied for, that their levels were dependent upon the extent to which the victims' earning capacity was judged (by doctors) to have been reduced, as well as upon eligibility for a range of special allowances ('location allowances' for those living in expensive parts of the country, 'care allowances' for those needing special medical care,

---

74. See Whalen, *Bitter Wounds*, p. 95. Other estimates put the number of war widows in Weimar Germany at roughly 600,000. See Karin Hausen, 'The German Nation's Obligation to the Heroes' Widows of World War I', in Margaret Randolph Higonnet, Jane Jenson, Sonya Michel and Margaret Collins Weitz (eds.), *Behind the Lines. Gender and the Two World Wars*, New Haven and London, 1987. Even though about 200,000 war widows remarried in the immediate postwar years, this still left 364,950 war widows and their 594,843 children receiving war-related state benefits in 1924. See Whalen, *Bitter Wounds*, pp. 109–10; Hausen, 'The German Nation's Obligation'.

75. Whalen, *Bitter Wounds*, p. 105.

76. See ibid., pp. 131–53. For a comparative discussion of welfare provision for the victims of the First World War, see Michael Geyer, 'Die Kriegsopferversorgung in Frankreich, Deutschland und Großbritannien nach dem Ersten Weltkrieg', *Geschichte und Gesellschaft*, vol. 9, 1983, esp. pp. 245–51.

etc.) What is more, the state bureaucracy was ill-equipped to handle the millions of applications generated by the new laws. During the 1920s hundreds of thousands of pension applications had to be handled every month; the high point was reached in March 1922, when over 200,000 applications were processed, but even in 1927 and 1928 more than 1.6 million cases had to be processed annually.[77] Inevitable delays caused anger and protests, the courts were overwhelmed with complaints about the decisions of pensions officials, and costs spun out of control while millions of people either received pensions they regarded as inadequate or failed to get their applications processed at all.[78] And this took place against a background of rapidly rising prices which made settlements inadequate within weeks or, in 1922 and 1923, within days after they had been made.

The problem did not end with the inflation, but plagued relations between the German state and its subjects throughout the Weimar period. As Robert Whalen has described so colourfully, the pension system remained 'trapped in a maze of red tape', creating enormous difficulties for overworked bureaucrats and enormous anger among the war victims whose cases sometimes took years to resolve.[79] The laws and bureaucratic procedures relating to the claims of war victims became ever more complicated; the costs of war-related pensions continued to rise, swallowing nearly one-third of the funds available to the Reich government; appeals to the National Pension Court against decisions made by the pensions bureaucracy trebled between 1924 and 1927 and the backlog of such cases doubled.[80] The results satisfied no one: organisations of war victims claimed that they were being short-changed; government officials claimed that the pensions system had to be pruned, and when the German economy went into a tailspin after 1929, things inevitably became even worse. Spending on war victims' pensions was cut (and payments were no longer calculated from the date of the application but rather from the date when the application was approved – in effect making the victim pay for bureaucratic delays!).[81] War victims responded with howls of protest, as hundreds of thousands demonstrated

77. Whalen, *Bitter Wounds*, p. 157.
78. Ibid., pp. 142–3.
79. See ibid., pp. 155–65.
80. Ibid., p. 156.
81. See ibid., pp. 168–70.

Richard Bessel

against the cuts. The predicament which the democratic Weimar state had created for itself was framed neatly in a protest to the Prussian Welfare Minister by a disabled war veteran from Stettin in October 1931, after the local welfare office (itself in poor financial straits) had turned down his request for additional help. 'Where are homesteads [*Eigenheime*] which were promised to us?' he cried, 'Where is work, bread, brotherhood?', 'Where is there justice left?' After borrowing phrases word-for-word from a recent resolution of the Social Democratic National Federation of War Wounded, Veterans and War Widows, he concluded that, having pursued his case unsuccessfully from one government office to the next, if he were refused yet again he would turn to Joseph Goebbels and Wilhelm Kube to raise the matter before the Reichstag.[82]

The unhappy history of Germany's administration of war-related pensions highlights the complicated and contradictory relationship between the state and its subjects during the Weimar period. The German state's new role as dispenser of benefits to millions of people did not necessarily imply a negative relationship with them, but in the specific context of Weimar Germany that is how it tended to develop. As a result of the tremendous financial obligations which the German state, for unavoidable political reasons, was compelled to accept, millions of Germans became directly and often desperately dependent upon state aid. While the German state had involved itself in people's everyday lives significantly before the War – through taxation, conscription, schooling, policing, and the judicial process – this often desperate dependence upon the state by millions of people for their livelihoods was something new. And it was not welcomed with gratitude; rather it was regarded as the paying back of a debt – the fulfilment of all those promises so unthinkingly made during the War that 'you can be sure of the thanks of the Fatherland'. Ideally, a debtor should pay the money owed without ado and then leave the creditor alone! That was what the war victims wanted. What they did not want was having to

82. APS, Oberpräsidium von Pommern, Nr. 3938: Bitte des Kriegsbeschädigten Walter Kosinsky um Zahnersatz und Nachzahlung von Militärgebührnissen to the Preußischer Minister für Volkswohlfahrt, Stettin, 18 October 1931; ibid.: The Landeswohlfahrtsamt to the Oberpräsident, 11 January 1932. The text of the resolution of the Reichsbund from a protest demonstration in Stettin on 26 April 1931 may be found in ibid.: Reichsbund der Kriegsbeschädigten, Kriegsteilnehmer und Kriegshinterbliebenen, Gau Pommern, to the Oberpräsident, Stettin, 27 April 1931.

battle with a government bureaucracy concerned to keep state expenditure under control. Popular expectations of what the state should provide its subjects had altered profoundly, as Weimar governments extended the social net and were compelled to face up to the social and economic consequences of the War. Huge new groups had arisen which regarded themselves as 'state pensioners' by right. Yet at the same time popular antipathy towards state interference had increased and the state could no longer effectively impose order. The post-war German state thus was caught in a trap of being a weak state, in terms of the coercive and economic resources at its disposal, with the responsibilities of a strong state, in terms of its functions.

Conclusions

This account of popular attitudes towards the German state offers stark contrasts with the clichéd picture of the law-abiding German standing in awe of the state. If any people were supposed to have had respect for the state and its representatives, it was the Germans. But popular attitudes towards the state had always existed on two levels, the abstract and the concrete. In the abstract, the state may have been regarded as a good thing, the final guarantor of the social order. In the concrete, however, it consisted of the unsympathetic bureaucrat, the rejected application for a pension, the unfair prices fixed for agricultural produce. Inevitably reactions to the latter were more critical than attitudes towards the former. One of the more important differences between the Wilhelmine and Weimar states was that after 1918 'the state' in the abstract was overshadowed as never before in peacetime by its concrete manifestations – as millions of Germans were given a desperate interest in the day-to-day decisions of the state (in the form of bureaucrats deciding upon levels of individual pensions). This was an ideal recipe for widespread popular antipathy towards the state.

In examining popular attitudes towards the German state during the immediate post-war period, one must remember that the nature of that state had changed significantly. In the place of a system in which political decision-making had remained largely insulated from popular influence or control there now was a constitutional structure in which – in principle at least – the German people were sovereign. But although the ways in which governments were formed and policies formulated had altered greatly, could the same be said for the behaviour of the state employees with whom the public came into contact? The transformation of 1918 did not serve to lessen antipathy towards state interference; if anything it complicated matters and exacerbated conflict. Antagonisms and fears among different groups and economic interests intensified. Democratic politics during a period of upheaval and economic crisis aroused, on the one hand, fears that desperately important economic policy decisions had become a function of popular pressures, and, on the other, inevitable cries of betrayal when political groupings claiming to represent particular sections of society felt compelled to implement unpopular policies. An example of the former were the fears of agricultural producers that urban interests would dictate the state's policies towards food production and distribution; an example of the latter was the hostility aroused among workers by an SPD-led government which came to rely on Freikorps units to suppress opposition. Thus the introduction of democratic government and politics, like the extension of the state's social functions, did not reduce popular antipathy towards the state, but instead often lent it a desperate character.

But, of course, the German state did not go away. Ultimately the name of the political game was not how to clip the state's wings but how to control them. During the immediate post-war period, firm control probably was impossible. The state was too weak; conditions were too chaotic. After war, defeat, revolution and economic problems of staggering proportions, the state was extremely limited in its ability to impose its will. The expansion of the role of the German state in the lives of its citizens during the War, the tremendous problems presented by the demobilisation, the heightened expectations of what government could do arising from the revolution, the collapse of a properly functioning market mechanism with the inflation – all these factors led Germans to expect much more of the Weimar state than they had of its predecessor. But in a country whose economic resources had been reduced significantly by war and in which structures of authority had been shaken severely by political upheaval, the ability of the state to meet such expectations had been reduced. The result was a crisis of the modern industrial state – a 'motivation crisis', as described by Jürgen Habermas, in which demands were generated which the state could not meet.[83] This was the essential dilemma of the German state in the demobilisation period. And it was not really until the economic and political 'stabilisation' of 1923 to 1924, that this problem was solved – if only temporarily and at a considerable cost.

83. Habermas's definition of a 'motivation crisis' – 'when the socio-cultural system changes in such a way that its output becomes dysfunctional for the state and for the system of social labour' – seems an apposite description of the dilemma of the Weimar state. See Jürgen Habermas, *Legitimation Crisis*, London, 1976, p. 75.

8
Municipal Finance in the Weimar Republic

Harold James

Introduction

Municipal politics during the Weimar Republic generated political clashes, the implications of which went far beyond a simply local arena. City government played a major economic role – in municipal utilities; as an employer; as the most important source of construction orders (60 per cent of house building in the later 1920s was publicly financed). Though enterprises such as water, gas and electricity works were as a rule run on business principles, many of the cities' economic activities were governed by a political rather than a commercial logic. Political clashes over how cities should run their activities took place in a framework of constitutional uncertainty, and critics of city government took up slogans about constitutional reform.

This chapter focuses on two related issues: first, the question of how far the failure to settle the financial relationship between Germany's different tiers of government produced economic destabilisation. The second question is concerned with the political response to the strains between central government and the municipalities. Municipal weakness was one of the chief arguments of those who wanted to carry out a fundamental constitutional reform in Germany. These arguments were canvassed throughout the 1920s, but they were articulated especially loudly during the depression in the final years of the Republic. There may even be a connection between the demand for constitutional change and the collapse of democracy. The fiscal erosion suffered by the Länder and municipalities in the later years of Weimar generated a willingness among higher civil servants (the *Ministerialbürokratie*) and among politicians of the centre and right to accept a radical constitutional revision. This wish played an important part in the carrying out of Papen's putsch against the Prussian government (July 1932);

and it also helps to explain the ease with which the Nazi Reich government in the spring of 1933 ended the autonomy of the Länder (*Gleichschaltung*).

The Nature of Municipal Politics

The most obvious form of government authority in Weimar was not the distant Reich or even the Land government, but rather the municipality and the commune. Communes were responsible for financing hospitals, school buildings, local roads, transport, amenities, water, gas and electricity supply, police, and for paying welfare support to those in need (determined by a means test) who were no longer eligible for support under the unemployment insurance scheme. They derived their income partly from a share of central taxes (sales tax and income and corporation taxes), partly from directly levied local taxes on real estate and business (*Grund-, Gebäude- und Gewerbesteuern*), and also from particular local taxes – on drinks, and on entertainment. A considerable income came from non-tax sources: fees and charges (for instance, for public utilities). Some of these revenues were sensitive to economic fluctuations: the commerce tax, or fees and charges; while others remained constant (property taxes), but represented a higher burden to taxpayers in times of depression. There was a double problem. Revenues that sank with the business cycle made communes fiscally vulnerable during economic crises; while revenues which did not seem to take into account the difficulties of local property owners made communes politically vulnerable.

Cities and communes had a great deal of independence in decisions on spending. A notion of self-administration (*Selbstverwaltung*) by local notables had originated in the Stein–Hardenberg period as a product of the need to reorganise Prussian local political life in the wake of the terrible defeats inflicted by the Napoleonic armies. Nineteenth-century local politics had been left to notables (*Honoratioren*); but before the First World War, the *Honoratioren* were giving way to a generation of spectacularly powerful professional *Oberbürgermeister*, elected by city parliaments but then virtually unsackable and not responsible to the city parliament.[1]

---

1. W. Hofmann, *Städtetag und Verfassungsordnung*, Stuttgart, 1966, pp. 26–56.

These men usually had a determination to modernise civic life at all costs. Often they had little but contempt for the old-fashioned notables and they liked to disregard the civic assemblies. Max Weber referred to 'plebiscitary city dictators'.[2] After 1918 these great mayors enlarged their powers and their position still further. To begin with, the areas they administered became much larger. A Prussian law of 1920 created Greater Berlin (Groß-Berlin): Berlin annexed seven formerly independent cities and increased its area by a factor of thirteen. The second largest city in the Reich was Hamburg, like Bremen and Lübeck not a city but a Hanseatic state immediate to the Reich: this constitutional peculiarity made it more difficult for Hamburg to swallow the adjacent conurbation of Altona, which belonged to Prussia as part of the province of Schleswig-Holstein. Altona was only handed over to Hamburg in 1938. But there were spectacular cases of city aggrandisement in the Rhineland. In 1922 Cologne swallowed Worringen. In July 1929 the whole Rhineland-Westphalian industrial area was reordered: Düsseldorf was enlarged to include Benrath and Kaiserswerth; Essen was extended to cover Werden, Steele, Karnap, Katernberg, Stoppenberg, Kary, and Kupferdreh. Duisburg was fused with Hamborn, Oberhausen with Sterkrade and Osterheld, Krefeld with Wertingen, Remscheid with Lennep and Lüttringhausen, Rheydt with Mönchen-Gladbach, and Barmen with Elberfeld (to form the new city of Wuppertal). In 1928 the area of the city of Frankfurt am Main was increased by 44 per cent as the city was extended to cover Griesheim, Sossenheim, Schwanheim, and Höchst. Stuttgart in 1922 expanded to include Obertürkheim, Hedelfingen, Botnang, and Kaltental; in 1929 Hofen; in 1931 Rotenberg and Münster; and in 1932 Zuffenhausen.[3]

City administrators had to deal directly with the social problems posed by the German revolution of 1918/19; and the solutions they produced were as characteristic of the nature of the Weimar compromise as the manipulations and intrigues of party leaders in Berlin. Konrad Adenauer, who had become *Oberbürgermeister* of

2. Quoted in H. Stehkämper (ed.), *Konrad Adenauer, Oberbürgermeister von Köln*, Cologne, 1970, p. 293.
3. Gesetz über die Bildung einer neuen Stadtgemeinde Berlin, 24 April 1920; Stehkämper (ed.), *Adenauer*, p. 582; D. Rebentisch, *Ludwig Landmann: Frankfurter Oberbürgermeister der Weimarer Republik*, Wiesbaden, 1975, p. 187; W. Kohlhaas, *Chronik der Stadt Stuttgart 1918–1933*, Stuttgart, n.d. [1964?], p. 130.

Cologne in 1917, was acutely aware of the problem faced by city administrators. He believed that it was the activity of the communal officials and the capacity of *Selbstverwaltung* to bring together all classes that had limited the extent of the damage done by the revolution. The cities in his eyes came closest to establishing a real corporatism based on social collaboration. His view of the revolution influenced Adenauer so profoundly that he later regarded with horror the deflationary policies pursued in the depression; if there were not immediate and large-scale work creation programmes, Adenauer claimed in the summer of 1930, there would be 'very great political difficulties'.[4] Ludwig Landmann, the *Oberbürgermeister* of Frankfurt am Main, was eloquent on the theme of how the cities were creating a new German culture and thus a new German stability: 'The justification from a socio-political standpoint of the cultural policy of the large cities in a time of crisis is to help ensure that the leaders rising out of the masses are filled with the spirit which flows from the spirit of art.'[5] Modern historians would describe the process Landmann was speaking of as the imposition of social control: for this task the communes were the most obviously suitable agents.

The cities resisted intervention from the outside with great determination. Adenauer, for instance, always attacked attempts of the Prussian and Reich regimes to 'stick their noses' into the affairs of the Rhenish cities, and he spoke of his fear that a centralised democracy of the type advocated by almost all the political parties except the Centre and the BVP would lead sooner or later to 'autocracy or dictatorship'. Gustav Böß in Berlin tried to run the capital of the Reich and Prussia without intervention from the Reich and Prussian governments.[6]

As the cities expanded and as they took on new tasks, their administrations grew larger. Cologne in 1913 employed 2,124 officials, while in 1924 there were 4,765 (the figure was later reduced, as part of a municipal economy drive, to 4,503 in 1928).[7] These officials were generally better paid than their opposite numbers in Reich and Land administrations, and the salaries of mayors were

4. Stehkämper (ed.), *Adenauer*, p. 451.
5. Rebentisch, *Landmann*, p. 217.
6. Stehkämper (ed.), *Adenauer*, p. 340; C. Engeli, *Gustav Böß: Oberbürgermeister von Berlin 1921 bis 1930*, Stuttgart, 1971, pp. 156ff.
7. Stehkämper (ed.), *Adenauer*, p. 252.

widely and critically discussed. The only way Böß could think of justifying his salary was to say that he was paid less than Adenauer, whose salary was generally believed to be 'somewhere between that of the Reich Chancellor and the Lord God, but nearer the latter's'. In 1929 Adenauer's salary was 33,000 RM but in addition he was paid 4,800 RM for expenses and 43,000 RM as 'living costs'.[8] (The Reich Chancellor was indeed only paid 45,000 RM.) During the depression, the Reich Savings Commissar's criticism of municipal life concentrated on the exorbitant incomes of the senior city employees.[9]

Wages and salaries for municipal employees at more humble levels also rose in the 1920s, though in general they moved closely in line with pay in the private sector. Between 1926 and 1928, an employee in Hamburg in category eight of the relevant pay scale had a rise of 21.9 per cent, while a foreman at Siemens on similar pay moved up by 22.5 per cent.[10] But even in this comparison, it should be noted that municipal employees had an advantage in that if – as was frequently the case – they had the status of civil servant (*Beamter*), they had a job security that could not be matched in the private sector: if they were laid off, they still had to be paid a substantial proportion of their previous salary in compensation (*Wartegeld*).

The cities of the 1920s embarked on tremendously expensive and ambitious projects, undertaken in accordance with the principle spelt out by Landmann and Adenauer of stabilising social conditions; even in the most extreme and difficult circumstances it was a foremost priority to keep up the ordinary circumstances of bourgeois life. Barmen was a relatively small city (population in 1925: 187,000), but it kept its city orchestra and opera until the worst days of the inflation in 1923, and started municipal culture up again in 1924 as soon as it could.[11] Other considerations guiding the city fathers were the necessity of keeping employment in the city, and a wish to compete with other cities. The favourite areas for

8. Stehkämper (ed.), *Adenauer*, p. 145; Engeli, *Böß*, p. 212.
9. Kohlhaas, *Chronik*, p. 106.
10. Figures from *Statistisches Jahrbuch für die Freie und Hansestadt Hamburg, Jahrgang 1930/31*, p. 222, and Siemens Archive SAA 11/Lf 100 (Köttgen).
11. J. Reulecke, 'Die Auswirkungen der Inflation auf die städtischen Finanzen', in G.D. Feldman (ed.), *Die Nachwirkungen der Inflation auf die deutsche Geschichte 1924–1933*, Munich, 1985, pp. 97–116.

municipal activity, and inter-city rivalry, were transport (trams, railways, underground systems in Berlin and Hamburg, and airfields), exhibition halls, sports stadiums, and swimming pools, as well as the more mundane business of municipal gas and electricity supply.

Berlin in the 1920s created a unified transport system. In 1926 the city bought the majority of shares in the *Hochbahngesellschaft* (underground railway) and in 1927 set up a 'community of interest' between the underground, tram and omnibus systems: this provided the basis for the creation in 1929 of a new company, the Berliner Verkehrs-Aktiengesellschaft (BVG). The BVG's personnel policy proved to be immensely expensive: in order to join different transport systems with different wage structures together into a unified operation, wage increases and reductions of hours of work were needed. In order to make the new company even more attractive for its employees, the BVG set up a subsidiary to construct houses for its workers (the Gemeinnützige Heimstättenbaugesellschaft der BVG GmbH). By the end of 1930 the BVG had put a total of 350m. RM into the construction of a new underground network, although *Oberbürgermeister* Böß had warned at the beginning of 1929 that in light of conditions on the capital market it would be wise to slow down the construction programme.[12]

In 1926 the city of Berlin took the initiative in constructing a new aerodrome on the site of the Kaiser's old parade ground at Tempelhof: this was supposed to guarantee Berlin's position as a centre of international aviation. Düsseldorf's municipal airport was opened in April 1926; Stuttgart in 1924 founded the Luftverkehr Württemberg AG in order to develop that city's aerodrome.

In 1924 Berlin created the Gemeinnützige Berliner Ausstellungs-, Messe- und Fremdenverkehrs GmbH to build exhibition halls; by 1926 there were three halls and by the end of the decade eight.[13] Exhibitions were just as fashionable in the west of Germany: Cologne was already in 1922 building exhibition halls during the inflation.[14] Neighbouring Düsseldorf in 1921 organised a confectionery exhibition; and after the stabilisation had to reply to Cologne

12. O. Büsch, *Geschichte der Berliner Kommunalwirtschaft in der Weimarer Epoche*, Berlin, 1960, pp. 91f., 94f.

13. Ibid., pp. 99–102.

14. Stehkämper (ed.), *Adenauer*, p. 570. F.W. Henning (ed.), *Düsseldorf und seine Wirtschaft: Zur Geschichte einer Region*, Düsseldorf, 1981, p. 623.

by staging a spectacular health, body culture, and physical exercise exhibition (May-October 1926) which according to the *Oberbürgermeister* Robert Lehr meant the 'Düsseldorf was no longer merely counted among the great cities of Germany: rather it was weighed and valued again.'[15] As permanent relics of this exhibition, Düsseldorf kept a municipal planetarium and a Reich Economic Museum. Cologne in 1928 hit on the idea of an International Press Conference. In 1929 the first big gardening exhibition in the world (the Gruga) was held in Essen. Stuttgart in 1926 organised an architectural exhibition to celebrate the new ethic: there were buildings by Le Corbusier, Walter Gropius, R. Behrens, and A.G. Schneck.[16] In Frankfurt am Main the cost of the exhibition halls, which required continual subsidies from the city, led to a political crisis in the municipality: Landmann had envisaged fairs as a part of the essential cultural mission of cities for discovering and developing new consumer tastes and demands. But Frankfurt's available fair and exhibition capacity was never used, and important fairs refused to come to Frankfurt: the automobile trade fair preferred to remain in Berlin. In 1928 the majority of the city council voted for the abolition of the Municipal Exhibition Company, the Messegesellschaft. Landmann simply ignored the resolution, and only one year later was prepared to make a compromise restricting Frankfurt to speciality fairs and ending the mass exhibition.[17]

Other aspects of city 'gigantomania' cost money too: Weimar mayors spent large sums lobbying companies to move their headquarters. They offered entertainment to company directors; more expensively, they promised tax concessions and expensive infrastructure. When Frankfurt incorporated Höchst, the centre of an important part of IG Farben's dyestuff business, it needed to make commitments about the future levels of commerce and land tax.[18] Cologne built an expensive new Rhine harbour in the hope of attracting new enterprise; it also tried to award contracts to local firms. The city chose for its new Rhine bridge linking Cologne and Mülheim not a box girder design of Krupp (Essen) but rather a much more costly suspension bridge which would lead to orders for

15. Stehkämper (ed.), *Adenauer*, pp. 570–1.
16. Kohlhaas, *Chronik*, p. 174.
17. Rebentisch, *Landmann*, pp. 237–42.
18. Ibid., pp. 184f.

steel cable produced by Felten & Guillaume, Mülheim. It justified the choice on aesthetic grounds.[19]

Finally, some parts of city spending had a purely aesthetic or environmental intention: Cologne's green belt offered a successful and attractive example of German city planning.[20]

Inevitably, when so much money was being spent, cases of corruption or near-corruption appeared. In light of the zeal with which opposition parties set about collecting examples of corruption, it is actually surprising that there were not more *causes célèbres*. Berlin attracted particular notoriety: it was much more difficult here than in other cities to control the city administration simply because of its enormous size. Some Berlin incidents were relatively harmless: firms were expected to give charitable donations to the city if they were awarded planning permission or if they sought public contracts. Thus when the department store Karstadt built a new branch on the Hermannplatz in 1928 it agreed to pay for the erection of a school retreat house in the country.[21] More sinister was the Sklarek scandal. The Sklarek brothers ran a wholesale textile and men's clothing business. In 1926 they had bought up low quality clothing stocks originally purchased by the city of Berlin for distribution to the needy during the war and inflation. In 1927 they extracted a substantial payment from the city on the grounds that, although there had been a warning that the clothing was of low quality, in fact it was even more shoddy than they had expected. At the same time the Sklareks won a monopoly contract on clothing supplies to the city. The reason was simple: the chairman of the municipal purchasing company, *Stadtrat* Gäbel, was bribed by the Sklareks. Other leading city officials too bought goods from the Sklareks at absurdly low prices, and the Sklareks also frequently delayed or even forgot to send bills to city employees. The case came into the open in late 1929, and eventually cost *Oberbürgermeister* Böß his job. Böß's wife had bought a fur coat from the Sklareks for 375 RM although Böß estimated that the real value was a thousand marks more: in order to make this up Böß had given 1,000 RM to charity (or rather he bought a painting from a poor artist for 800 RM and gave 200 RM to some poor relations of his

---

19. Stehkämper (ed.), *Adenauer*, pp. 164, 289.
20. Ibid., pp. 157f.
21. Engeli, *Böß*, pp. 142f.

wife's). Böß was clearly not bribed by the Sklareks in the way that Gäbel had been; but he had acted very incautiously and he had failed to supervise his administration effectively.[22]

In other cases there were accusations of corruption that were much less justified: these accusations belonged to the stock-in-trade of radical politicians. Cologne's Adenauer was frequently blamed for appointing in 1920 his brother-in-law Will Suth *Beigeordneter* (city director) with special responsibility for financial affairs. This was a key position in the municipal administration. Adenauer justified Suth's appointment on the grounds not only that Suth was extremely capable (he had been offered prestigious posts in many other German towns); but also that it was necessary for Adenauer to have someone he could trust completely in the light of the difficult financial situation created as a result of his spending plans.[23]

This story – and also that of the Sklarek brothers – illuminates one central difficulty facing municipal administration in the 1920s: the problem of the supervision of city affairs. Böß did not know what his subordinates were doing; and Adenauer needed to have a way of making sure that he did. Such were the problems of big government.

At the end of the 1920s, the Reich government and the Länder set out to exploit these difficulties in order to divert attention from their own very considerable problems. Communes, they believed, should take more of the share of political opprobrium. The Reich and the Länder faced falling revenues and rising social expenditure, and they reacted by imposing harshly restrictive budgets that generated political hostility. Why not shovel this hostility onto the communes by simply manipulating the division of revenue and expenditure in Germany? The Reich cut its transfers of tax to the Länder and in consequence forced them to impose new taxes; and the Länder complained that they were 'left with odious taxes and falling revenue'[24].

The Länder went on to carry out the same manoeuvre with respect to the communes. Transfers of shares of income and corporation taxes were cut back. In 1929/30 communes received 33.7 per cent of the total income and corporation tax paid in Germany. By

22. Ibid., pp. 230–47.
23. Stehkämper (ed.), *Adenauer*, pp. 259–61.
24. Bavarian State Archive (BStA) MA 103331, Oct. 1930 memorandum 'Wirtschafts- und Finanzprogramm der Reichsregierung'.

1931/2 the share had fallen to 27.8 per cent. The decline looks even more remarkable if expressed not as a proportion but in absolute terms: whereas in 1929/30 communes had received RM 1205.9 million from income and corporation tax, in 1930/1 they had 670.2 million and in 1931/2 only 404.6 million.[25]

Moreover, the Reich restricted the capacity of communes to raise revenue. In 1929 the tax reform packet proposed by the Great Coalition (SPD-Centre-Left and Right Liberal) government even included cuts of 10 and 20 per cent in communal taxes; and the essence of this proposal was incorporated into the second tax emergency decree of the Brüning government of December 1930, which forbade commerce and real estate tax increases for a ten-year period.

While communal spending reacted to strong local pressures to stimulate the local economy, communal revenues had become tightly controlled from the centre. The ideal of the Stein–Hardenberg period, autonomous local administration (*Selbstverwaltung*), had disappeared in the Weimar era because the communes were autonomous only when it came to spending, but not when it came to raising money.

This was the point of weakness exploited by the communes' enemies, including figures in the *Ministerialbürokratie* such as the powerful State Secretary in the Reich Ministry of Finance Johannes Popitz, as well as by heavy industry. Big business mounted a campaign against the extension of municipal economic activity, which it termed 'cold socialisation' (*kalte Sozialisierung*) – performing by stealth what the Socialisation Commissions of 1919 and 1920 had failed to achieve in open political discussion.[26] Industry scored some successes in this war against the municipalities and their enterprises.

The Ruhrgas AG, founded in 1927 by the Ruhr Coal Syndicate in order to extend the Syndicate's control over energy markets, dominated the gas market in the Rhineland, Hesse, and northern Germany, although southern Germany was still dominated by municipally controlled gas works.[27] By the end of the 1920s, the threats to

25. W. Heindl, *Die Haushalte von Reich, Ländern und Gemeinden in Deutschland von 1925 bis 1933*, Frankfurt, 1984, pp. 367 and 371.

26. C. Böhret, *Aktionen gegen die 'kalte Sozialisierung' 1926–1930: Ein Beitrag zum Wirken ökonomischer Einflußverbände in der Weimarer Republik*, Berlin, 1966.

27. D. Rebentisch, 'Städte und Monopol: Privatwirtschaftliches Ferngas oder

communes posed by large enterprises had abated, and there were
more and more cases of successful and profitable co-operation
between private and municipal enterprise. The Rheinisch-Westfälische Elektrizitätswerke AG, set up in 1893, provided a model for
such co-operation; and in 1930 municipalities were represented also
on the Supervisory Board of the Ruhrgas AG, despite its continued
domination by heavy industry.

Municipal Debt and Economic Collapse

At the end of the 1920s, the constitutional crisis of the communes
flared up as a credit crisis. Already long before the austerity decrees
imposed by the deflationary Brüning government, communes had
responded to the combination of pressures to spend more and
restrictions on their income by borrowing, often on the foreign
capital and credit markets (German industry of course also turned
in the later 1920s to foreign loans). Here there is a substantial
pre-history to the economic crisis at the end of Weimar.

At first much of the credit taken up by the communes was long
term. Cologne had borrowed abroad to pay for its new Rhine
harbour; Dresden to build a railway bridge across the Elbe; Munich
for electricity works and tram installations.[28] From the beginning,
the central bank (Reichsbank) and its President Dr Schacht tried to
restrict foreign borrowing.

In December 1924 an Advisory Office for Foreign Credit (Beratungsstelle für Auslandskredite) had been established through
agreements between the Reich and the Länder. In its original form,
the Beratungsstelle consisted of five permanent members (a representative of the Reichsbank, of the Reich Finance Ministry, and
the Reich Economics Ministry, and the Presidents of the Prussian
State Bank and the Bavarian State Bank); and in addition there was a
representative of the Land involved in the specific credit application. Thus there was numerical parity between the representatives
of the Reich and those of the Länder: the State Banks kept in close

---

kommunale Verbandswirtschaft in der Weimarer Republik', *Zeitschrift für Stadtgeschichte, Stadtsoziologie und Denkmalpflege*, vol. 3, 1976, pp. 38–80.
   28. See the meeting of the Beratungsstelle of 15 March 1928, Bundesarchiv
Koblenz (BAK) R2/2081; also R2/4126, 27 October 1930 meeting.

contact with the Prussian and Bavarian governments. On the other hand, there was no representative of the communes on the Advisory Board. In theory, the Board advised the Land government whether the communes should or should not be permitted to negotiate a foreign loan; in practice its verdict was authoritative. The Board also had the task of advising on the desirability of credit for the Länder.[29]

In its operations, the Beratungsstelle worked against the communes; after 1925 this discrimination was more and more pronounced. While by the end of 1925 the Beratungsstelle had approved 89 per cent of Länder loans and all the applications for Land-guaranteed agricultural and industrial loans, only 65 per cent of the communal applications had been agreed. In 1926 an even lower proportion of communal loans was allowed.[30] But despite the control of the Beratungsstelle, and despite a complete stop on public loans in 1927, German communes accounted for a sizeable part of the German foreign debt: 11.9 per cent of the long-term loans issued in the USA between 1924 and 1929 went to German municipalities.[31] The Beratungsstelle did, however, drive the communes to borrow on the domestic market, or to take short-term foreign loans which did not fall under Schacht's control: this may have helped to tighten an already narrow German capital market. In the later 1920s, communal borrowing represented the major part of total public borrowing in Germany. On the eve of the depression the increase in communal indebtedness represented an increasing share of total German investment, as shown in Table 8.1.

Schacht responded to what he believed was an evasion of the Reichsbank's control mechanism by demanding that the central bank should supervise domestic borrowing by public corporations as well. This principle was accepted, though only after Schacht had been succeeded as President of the Reichsbank by Hans Luther. In 1930 the Guide-lines on Credit of 1924 were revised: all Länder credit applications were to be submitted to the Beratungsstelle,

---

29. BStA MA 103859, 5 December 1924 Richtlinien; and 23 July and 12 November 1925 circulars of Reich Finance Ministry. In general see K. Hansmeyer (ed.), *Kommunale Finanzpolitik in der Weimarer Republik*, Stuttgart, 1973.
30. BStA MA 103859, 18 December 1925 and 1 April 1926 reports of Beratungsstelle meetings.
31. From Appendix in C. Lewis, *America's Stake in International Investments*, Washington, DC, 1938.

Table 8.1 Increase in German communal debt 1928/29–1930/31 (million RM)

	1928/29	1929/30	1930/31
As % of total increase in public debt	62.4	48.1	35.6
As % of net domestic investment in Germany	20.2	26.4	36.6
Increase in communal debt	2,221.4	1521.2	961.5

Sources: Wagemann, *Konjunkturstatistiches Handbuch 1936*, pp. 171–2; W.G. Hoffmann, *Das Wachstum der deutschen Wirtschaft seit der Mitte des 19. Jahrhunderts*, Berlin, 1966, p. 826.

while a new institution was created to deal with communal borrowing.[32]

There were other ways in which the operation of the Beratungsstelle had been unsatisfactory in the later 1920s: communes were encouraged to discount in advance the decision of the Beratungsstelle by applying for more funds than they needed. The existence of a central regulating body also helped to fan the inter-city rivalries that plagued German politics anyway: if Munich was allowed to borrow abroad in order to build new tramways, Nuremberg and Chemnitz wanted to be allowed to do the same.[33]

So the Reichsbank resorted to other means to brake communal credit demands. Schacht warned foreign investors directly: in 1925 he publicly attacked loans for Berlin and Cologne. He complained to American bankers about the wastefulness of the administration of Stettin. At the same time, the US State Department, prompted by warnings from Schacht and the Agent-General for Reparation Payments, Parker Gilbert, advised caution to the American public over loans to German Länder and municipalities because Article 248 of the Treaty of Versailles provided for a first claim on the Reich and the Länder by the Allies for reparation for wartime damage.[34] By the end of 1929 the communes were desperate for more funds from America as their expenditure rose uncontrollably. Gustav Böß went

32. Hansmeyer, *Finanzpolitik*, p. 188 ff.
33. BAK R2/4126, 27 October 1930 Beratungsstelle meeting.
34. Deutscher Städtetag Berlin Archive (DSTA) B2784, 2 October 1925 DST Giro Committee, and 24 October 1925 Stettin to DST. Also *Foreign Relations of the United States 1925 II*, pp. 177f.; Federal Reserve Bank of New York (FRBNY), Strong papers 1012.1, 18 October 1925 Gilbert to Winston.

with several Berlin officials on a trip to invite the New World to bail out the old. Mulert, the General Manager of the German Association of Cities, the Deutscher Städtetag (DST), told a Reichsrat Committee that 'the more money there is, the more the economic dangers can be avoided'.[35] But at the end of 1929 Schacht made a direct attack, similar to that of 1925, when he criticised the terms of a proposed one-year loan of RM 120 million by Dillon Read to the City of Berlin. Schacht justified his intervention by referring to the dangerously large volume of communal foreign short-term debt.[36] There were no exact figures as to how large this debt actually was in 1929: whereas the Deutscher Städtetag claimed that it amounted to RM 1,050–1,100 million, the Reich Finance Ministry and industry thought that the amount was nearer to RM 2,000 million, and the Reichsbank produced a figure of RM 3,000 million.[37]

At the end of 1929 Schacht believed that the only way of reducing this alarmingly large short-term foreign debt was by the drastic means of selective default, which would scare off new creditors. Berlin would be a spectacular case. Schacht suggested that if Berlin wished to save itself, it should privatise the municipal electricity works (the BEWAG) rather than continue to borrow.[38] The case of Berlin raised general issues about the position and future of the communes. The Deutscher Städtetag saw Schacht's action as an attack on all German cities, and Adenauer made the same point when he told the Reich Finance Minister, 'We must not let Berlin collapse because of the Reichsbank.' Schacht simply retorted by saying that the cities should face the consequences of the actions of 'tricksters and bankrupts'.[39]

That there was now a crisis was recognised by all. Adenauer was even prepared to admit that there had been severe mistakes in the communes' expansionary policies. In spring 1930, he said: 'I must make two critical comments: we [German *Oberbürgermeister*] have not in the past regarded sufficiently the limits of the financially

---

35. Engeli, *Böß*, pp. 227f.
36. Institut für Zeitgeschichte Munich (IfZ) ED93/7, 4 and 12 December 1929 Schäffer diary entries.
37. DStA B4159, 15 November 1929 Bracht to Benecke. Bank of England CBP 1.1., 30 November 1929 and 1 December 1929 Addis reports on Reichsbank Generalrat meetings; BStA MA 103861, 13 October 1929 von Wolf report.
38. BStA MA 103861, 13 December 1929 von Wolf report.
39. IfZ ED93/7, 4 and 12 December 1929 diary entries.

possible when we made spending decisions (particularly regarding extraordinary expenditures); and secondly, we should have used our rights vis-à-vis the communal parliaments more thoroughly.' Adenauer now recognised how thin his defence of the 1925 Cologne $15 million loan had been: then he said that 'the financial and economic circumstances of the City of Cologne are, according to my really detailed knowledge of the situation, as healthy and as favourable as those in Berlin'.[40] By 1929 Berlin was in great trouble; and Cologne's situation was precarious too.

The communes' position at the end of the 1920s was made much worse by the rise in unemployment in Germany: for under terms of legislation providing for the relief of the unemployed, substantial financial burdens were imposed on the communes. Under the regulations of February 1924, they were obliged to support the unemployed for thirty-nine weeks. As a result of the 1927 reforms, the communes bore some of the cost of 'crisis relief' after the end of eligibility for unemployment insurance benefit; and after fifty-eight weeks the unemployed were completely dependent on communal welfare relief. In June 1931 the burden on the communes was increased yet further as the eligibility period for insurance relief was cut for some classes of workers to twenty weeks. During the depression, the number of long-term unemployed, and hence the number dependent on communal support, rose.

In August 1930 453,000 workers in Germany depended on welfare support (15.7 per cent of the total registered as unemployed); one year later there were 1,131,000 (26.8 per cent) and in August 1932 2,030,000 (38.9 per cent).[41] Yet it was only in June 1932 that this problem was tackled by setting an upper ceiling for communal liability for welfare relief.

In addition to welfare payments, communes had on the eve of the depression been forced to take over new financial commitments: they complained how they had been forced by the Länder to pay for the building of new police stations, and for new pedagogical and commercial high schools. In Prussia communes after March 1930 were obliged to bid at compulsory auctions of over-indebted properties. In fact, an estimated four-fifths of communal expenditure was

---

40. Stehkämper (ed.), *Adenauer*, pp. 344 and 130f.
41. E. Wagemann, *Konjunkturstatistiches Handbuch 1936*, Berlin, 1935, pp. 16–17.

Table 8.2 Proportion of unemployed on welfare support in cities over 100,000 population[a]

	(%)
30. 6.1927	15.5
31.12.1928	18.0
30. 6.1929	20.4
31.12.1929	22.3
31. 3.1930	23.8

[a] Not including Munich, Karlsruhe, or Lübeck.
Source: BAK R2/20132 June 1930 Memorandum of Dr Köbner, 'Wohlfahrtserwerbslose und Gemeinden'.

Table 8.3 Tax revenue of communes 1928/29–1932/33 (million RM)

	Reich tax transfers	Communal taxes and Land transfers	Total
1928/1929	1,649.7 (100)[a]	2,747.0 (100)	4,396.7 (100)
1929/1930	1,595.8 (96.7)	2,794.0 (101.7)	4,390.0 (99.8)
1930/1931	1,427.1 (86.5)	2,877.5 (104.8)	4,333.1 (98.6)*
1931/1932	1,009.3 (61.2)	2,649.0 (96.4)	3,676.5 (83.6)*
1932/1933	785.0 (47.6)	2,065.0 (75.2)	2,957.5 (67.3)*

[a] Figures in brackets as a % of 1928/9 revenue.
* Totals from 1930/1 to 1932/3 include communal revenue from the poll tax.
Source: *Statistisches Jahrbuch*, 1930–5 issues.

laid down by law and thus could not be cut at will as part of an economy campaign.[42]

Meanwhile communal tax revenue was falling: particularly sharply in the case of the Prussian communes. Often communal parliaments obstructed attempts to impose new city taxes.[43]

Thus the communes were obliged to borrow more. Most of the new debt was funded domestically (though indirectly the money might still come from those foreign bankers who lent to such banks as the Dresdener and the Danat which specialised in communal business); and, although the total volume of debt was still rather

42. DSTA B3328, 13 October 1930 Elsass (DST) to Dorn (Reich Finance Ministry).
43. Kohlhaas, *Chronik*, p. 105.

Table 8.4 Debts of communes over 10,000 population 1928–1930 (million RM)[a]

	Cities over 10,000			Cities over 100,000		
	31.3.28	20.9.29	30.6.30	31.3.28	30.9.29	30.6.30
Foreign debt	524	718	708	413	593	578
	(100)	(137)	(135)	(100)	(144)	(140)
Internal debt	3,188	5,317	6,147	1,330	2,654	3,219
	(100)	(167)	(193)	(100)	(200)	(242)
(of which	1,267	2,338	2,621	576	1,286	1,585
short- and	(100)	(185)	(207)	(100)	(223)	(275)
medium-term)						

[a] (1928 = 100)
Source: DST B 3465, 11.12.1930 Memorandum on 'Level of Debt 1930'.

smaller than the pre-war communal debt had been, it was predominantly short-term.

Any attempts on the part of the cities to raise taxes in order to cover their deficits were strenuously resisted by pressure both from business and from the Reich. The Deutscher Städtetag noted that '1930 will be first and foremost a year of tax increases',[44] but Brüning did not want the new revenue to go to the communes. Instead the cities had to cut their capital expenditure radically: they drew up their own savings programmes (Düsseldorf 1930, Munich 1931), or called in the Reich Savings Commissar to advise on cuts (Halle, Mannheim, Stuttgart), or appointed commissions of economy experts (Frankfurt am Main, Ludwigshafen).[45] Though these cuts obviously increased local unemployment, particularly in the building trade, there seemed little alternative, and the communes could only hope that the depression would be short-lived. Most cities waited as long as possible before implementing their retrenchment programmes.[46] Böß had wanted to stop work on the Berlin underground in 1929, but the city council insisted that the project be carried on. Instead Böß tried to raise new funds in America.

44. DSTA B2731, 2 January 1930 meeting of Mulert (DST) with Mindir. Hag (Prussian Finance Ministry).
45. D. Rebentisch, 'Kommunalpolitik, Konjunktur und Arbeitsmarkt', in R. Morsey (ed.), *Verwaltungsgeschichte*, Berlin, 1977, p. 133; and DSTA B3328, 25 March 1931 Mulert memorandum.
46. DSTA B4159, 26 March 1930 meeting in Reich Labour Ministry.

Landmann in December 1929 asked the Reich Finance Ministry for help in getting foreign funds for building and construction programmes. Adenauer cancelled all building projects only in August 1931, after the banking collapse.[47] Stuttgart continued to build during the depression. The following projects were actually *started* during these dismal years: the construction of a hospital for skin diseases in Bad Cannstadt; the conversion and extension of a midwifery school in Berg; and preparations for the grand 1933 German gymnastic festival.[48]

One apparently easy option for the communes was to use the municipally owned savings banks (*Sparkassen*) as a source of funds. The DST repeatedly pressed for a 'consolidation action' to reduce the volume of short-term debt, and the Reich agreed to allow an alteration of the Prussian Savings Ordinance (which also served as a guide-line for other Länder). From December 1929 up to 50 per cent of deposits in savings banks could be used to consolidate communal debt. This step implied a great risk, for the savings of nervous small investors were locked into very long-term funding. More ambitious and wide-ranging plans to consolidate the communal short-term debt ran aground once more on the rocks of Reichsbank policy. The Reichsbank refused to offer Lombard facilities (loans against securities) on communal debt: 'Hoarding of gold and currency in recent months has increased – perhaps because of the discussions about the Young Plan. It is to be feared that an admission of communal loans to Lombard traffic would intensify the hoarding and would be interpreted as a beginning of new inflation methods.'[49]

The savings banks deposits locked into municipal loans in fact caused enough problems on their own: in some parts of Germany, where the mayors had been particularly pressing and powerful, the savings banks had put considerably more than 50 per cent of their deposits into communal business. Savings banks were supposed to hold highly liquid deposits with secondary banks (*Girozentralen* and *Länderbanken*) but these institutions had not always pursued conservative investment policies. In eastern Germany, the *Länderbanken*

---

47. O. Büsch, *Geschichte*, p. 186; DSTA B4159, 4 December meeting of Landmann and Hilferding; Stehkämper, *Adenauer*, p. 147.
48. Kohlhaas, *Chronik*, p. 96.
49. Negotiations reported in DSTA B4159; also BAK R2/13446, 6 February 1930 Reichsbank to Reich Finance Minister.

lent mostly to private firms, and the Landeskreditkasse in Kassel and the Nassauische Landesbank were engaged mostly in mortgages; but in Hanover, Rhineland-Westphalia and Schleswig-Holstein there was a heavy involvement in communal credit.[50] The most notorious case was that of the Rheinische Landesbank. At the end of July 1931, when the banking crisis blew the whistle on its activities, it had RM 250 million on deposit from the savings banks, and had loaned a total of RM 642 million, of which RM 522 million were credits to the communes. By far the largest of the Landesbank's debtors was the city of Cologne with RM 94 million. Cologne now reaped the harvest of the ambitious expansion of the 1920s.[51]

The 1930 consolidation through the savings banks could work only if the communes did not allow their short-term debt to increase further. Otherwise the effect of the action would be to reduce public confidence in the savings banks and thus undermine the stability of German credit. After September 1930, deposits in savings banks began to be withdrawn, and after May 1931 withdrawals exceeded new deposits.[52] The flow of new funds which might have been available to help the communes had become a trickle. A memorandum of late 1930 recorded that: 'These institutes [savings banks, *Länderbanken*, and *Girozentralen*] see the certain and inevitable moment approaching when the liquidity of our organisations will be seriously endangered if the credit demands of the communes resulting from unforeseen expenditure on unemployment relief continue.'[53] An increase in communal debt, the memorandum continued, would lead to a 'danger of financial collapse' of the savings banks. Yet this situation was bound to arise as the communes' optimism about future developments made almost any additional expenditure an unforeseen catastrophe.

The difficulties of the communes were increased too by the Reich's extension of the Beratungsstelle's control in order to elimin-

---

50. BAK R2/13634, 23 October 1931 memorandum of Landeshauptleute in East Prussia and Hesse-Nassau.
51. BAK R431/651, esp. 14 April 1932 report of Deutsche Revisions- und Treuhandgesellschaft.
52. J. Blatz, *Die Bankenliquidität im Run 1931: Statistische Liquiditätsanalyse der deutschen Kreditinstitutsgruppen in der Weltwirtschaftskrise 1929–1933*, Cologne, 1971, p. 212.
53. BAK R2/4057, 15 November 1930 memorandum of Deutscher Sparkassen- und Giroverband.

ate competition for scarce funds: 'The purpose of this extension of the Beratungsstelle's powers is the prevention of disturbances on the capital market as a result of the competition of the various borrowing groups. The internal market and the foreign market are to a great extent interdependent.'[54] A new set of guidelines laid down the principle that new communal loans should only be taken for productive purposes, and in cases of extraordinary need. The communes should ask permission of the Reich to take foreign loans, and in the case of domestic loans the Land government was to call a meeting of the Beratungsstelle augmented by the addition of a representative from the communes. Even this new system of control did not stop communes making approaches to foreign banks, though the loan contract could not be signed without the approval of the Beratungsstelle. In January 1931, in order to curb the embarrassment caused by such municipal appeals to American banks, the State Secretary in the Reich Finance Ministry sent a circular to the Länder governments asking that in view of the nervous state of the markets German cities should refrain from begging for credit.[55]

Finance Minister Dietrich was fundamentally sceptical about the purpose of much local government expenditure; both he and Luther had been career mayors who had discovered in their own experience that local government required vast sums to grease the wheels of its political machinery. Luther was very frank in expressing his views on communal finance, and his desire for a reform born out of catastrophe:

> He did not believe it right always to start from the premise that cities should not be allowed to go bankrupt. The communes had for years had the wrong idea of the world. In his eyes it would be most beneficial for the cities if some of them should go to the wall. From the point of view of self-administration, it was dangerous if communes always had the feeling that they would be helped.[56]

Deprived of loans and of central government support, the German cities started to sell off municipal enterprise. Bremen in January 1931 tried to sell its water and electricity works to a consortium

54. Hansmeyer, *Finanzpolitik*, p. 218; BAK R2/20151, 9 July meeting in Reich Finance Ministry.
55. BStA MA 103862, 20 January 1932 Reich Finance Ministry circular.
56. BAK R2/4057, 15 December 1930 meeting in Reich Finance Ministry.

headed by the Société Financière de Belgique (Sofina), but Brüning blocked the sale as it would place an important part of German industry under foreign control. The French aluminium and electrical industrialist Louis Marlio declared an interest in buying German municipal water and electricity works, and the Reich Finance Ministry's expert Norden warned that French financial imperialism was looking to the Rhenish cities.[57] Berlin had in June 1930 again been prevented from taking a $10 million credit by the Reichsbank's intervention, and had borrowed instead from the Danat bank: but it was clear that the Danat was not able to agree a renewal of this RM 150 million loan due on 31 July 1931. So in March the Berlin electricity works were sold to a foreign consortium in which the Sofina played a major role.[58] (The city overcame the political objections to a sale abroad by creating a holding company in which Berlin still held shares with especially privileged voting rights.)

The crisis for the German cities came with the general banking crisis: by 4 July 1931 there were signs of an imminent collapse of the credit of the big Rhenish cities. RM 75 million of the short-term deposits of the Rheinische Landesbank were withdrawn, as panic spread concerning the solvency of the cities. Düsseldorf needed to borrow RM 50 million to make payments due at the end of June, and Münster took RM 10 million. In June the temporary embarrassment of the Landesbank had been solved by a loan from the Prussian State Bank (Seehandlung), but the funds were exhausted by the middle of July. Luther was then called on to save the Landesbank, but was horrified at the amount of money involved, and in addition still believed that it was his mission to punish past municipal extravagance.[59]

But even the affair of the Landesbank and the similar difficulties of the Hanseatic banks did not deter the high spenders: Breslau was still suggesting at the end of July that a massive foreign loan could be raised on the security of communal enterprise.[60] The lenders however had learned the lessons of the summer of 1931, that over-enthusiastic borrowing caused spectacular collapse. Cities

---

57. BAK R2/4057, 17 March 1930 report of von Hoesch.
58. National Archives Washington StDep. 862.51, 19 February 1931 memorandum W.E. Beitz, 'Berlin's Financial Problems'; Büsch, *Geschichte*, p. 163ff.
59. IfZ ED93/11, 6 July 1931 diary entry; Prussian State Archive Dahlem, 109/6016 (Landesbank der Rheinprovinz); BAK R431/651.
60. BAK R2/4057, 27 July 1931 Stadtrat Przbilla to Reich Chancellor.

were no longer able to find sources of loan money, even when conditions on the credit market gradually improved in 1932 and 1933. Too many black marks had been made against municipal activity. In addition, the Reich Government stepped in, and the Dietramszell decree of October 1931 forbade the savings banks to lend to municipalities and provided for the banks to have greater political independence.

The financial erosion of the position of the cities continued in 1932; a combination of the alteration of tax rates by decree and a reduction in income from transfers of income and corporation tax cost the communes a total of RM 815 million. By the beginning of 1932 many cities were either in arrears on debt service, or had stopped payments altogether: Cologne, Dortmund, Gelsenkirchen, and Altona were in this situation. Luther, still following the course of using the crisis to push the Prussian state and the Prussian communes into accepting administrative reform, refused to help the communes by taking their bills for discount in the Reichsbank.[61]

A similarly dilatory and unhelpful approach was taken by the Reich authorities to a suggestion to solve the communal finance problem by consolidating the short-term debt. Such proposals involved the use of the communal house tax (*Hauszinssteuer*) as a pledge for a conversion loan: but this scheme produced fierce resistance from house owners who feared that they would for ever be burdened with the house tax as a result of the new plans. Most communes also preferred voluntary agreements with banks to convert short into long credits rather than compulsory rescheduling which would limit their future freedom of action.[62] In general the banks were co-operative in maintaining communal loans, despite the bitter experience of 1931. They actually preferred to keep their loans on a short-term basis because this meant that they could show the loans at par in their accounts, whereas they would have had to set a long-term consolidation loan at its market value. Moreover, they did not want to commit themselves to writing off parts of the communal loans as they believed that the position of the communes might improve quickly if the various government recovery programmes showed signs of being successful.[63] Thus the hope of an

---

61. BAK R2/20133, 21 March 1932 Mulert to Reich Finance Minister, and 16 January 1932 Deutsche Centralbodenkredit AG to Prussian Minister for Welfare.
62. BStA MA 103862, 4 November 1931 memorandum of Bayerischer Städtebund.

economic upswing in this case helped to obstruct consolidation measures which might well have increased the chances of such an upswing.

There were much more fundamental and political objections to a stabilising or rescheduling of the communal debt: the high debt levels had been a lever used by central governments in their efforts to control the political course of the communes. After the Nazi seizure of power in January 1933, dramatic changes took place in local politics. Nazi *Unterführer* demanded the resignation of mayors, and new communal elections in Prussia (12 March) in many cases produced Nazi majorities. In other Länder the pace of change was slower, but in the end the results were similar. By the end of the year, there had been an almost complete change in the administration of German communes. In towns with a population over 200,000 only 14 per cent of the *Oberbürgermeister* in office in January 1933 were still there twelve months later. There were also large-scale dismissals of communal officials: in Leipzig 1,600 were sacked and replaced by 1,150 loyal old party members. Such changes were often justified by the need to implement 'savings' in municipal administration and by reference to the old Nazi polemics against wasteful local government.[64]

The victors were not usually, however, the enthusiastic local Nazis who now saw an opportunity to build up their own style of municipal corruption or *Vetternwirtschaft*. In Prussia, the guiding hand behind the change of communal administration was not Minister-President Hermann Göring but the Prussian Finance Minister, Johannes Popitz, the centralising State Secretary of the late 1920s. In October 1930 Popitz had proposed to the Tax Committee of the RDI that communes should be subject to much tighter control from the centre: they should have uniform budget plans, tax schedules and auditing systems, and should require central permission to take up credit or to start public work programmes.[65] In 1931 Popitz set out a plan to reduce the communal *Realsteuern* (land and commerce taxes) by two-fifths. In 1933 he welcomed Hitler's Chancellorship

63. *Der deutsche Volkswirt*, 20 January 1933; BStA MA 103862, 3 September 1932 von Hammer report.
64. H. Matzerath, *Nationalsozialismus und kommunale Selbstverwaltung*, Stuttgart, 1970, pp. 79, 86.
65. J. Popitz, *Der Finanzausgleich und seine Bedeutung für die Finanzlage des Reichs, der Länder und Gemeinden*, Berlin, 1930, pp. 10f.

as a step towards the 'overcoming of pluralistic forces tied to material interest'.[66]

A new Prussian Communal Law (15 December 1933) provided for a very close state supervision of communal administration. It was opposed in vain by a large number of influential Nazis including the Director of the Kommunalpolitisches Amt of the NSDAP and new mayor of Munich, Karl Fiehler, and *Gauleiter* Florian of Düsseldorf, as well as by non-Nazi mayors such as Carl Goerdeler of Leipzig, who protested that the 'idea of self-regulation has been completely ended by the Prussian regulation'.[67]

The new constitutional settlement, which ended local elections, at first resembled much more closely the ideas of the Weimar centralisers than it did those of the new power-hungry local Nazi enthusiasts. Later the Nazis made up ground; by 1935 they had secured the appointment of a NSDAP party representative as first *Beigeordneter*, i.e. deputy mayor.

After the political uncertainty of 1931–3 had been ended by the Nazi local elections and the Nazi revolution in the communes, the question of debt rescheduling, so thorny in the past, became a trivial issue which was easily solved. Under the provisions of the Law of 21 September 1933, interest rates on the new conversion loan were set at 4 per cent, and all payments on non-converted short-term debt were blocked for five years.[68] In consequence, virtually all the RM 2.8 billion short-term communal debt was converted. At the same time regulations for unemployment relief were amended so as to lift the burden from the communes altogether.

These were not important decisions: for from the end of May 1933 communes had ceased to play an important role in German politics. Of the numerous opponents of communal administration of the 1920s, it was not the big industrialists nor even the refractory local parliamentary bodies, the city councils, that had won a victory: it was the central state. In order, however, for the plans of a Popitz to be implemented, the fomentation of discontent that produced the upheavals of the first half of 1933 was required. Communal administration had been the most obvious and the most controversial form of government intervention in the 1920s: it

66. H. Dieckmann, *Johannes Popitz: Entwicklung und Wirksamkeit in der Zeit der Weimarer Republik*, Berlin, 1960, pp. 113f., 139f.

67. Matzerath, *Nationalsozialismus*, p. 126.

68. *Reichsgesetzblatt*, 1933/I, p. 647.

disappeared as a result of the tensions produced by the economic crisis.

Conclusion

The municipalities represent a particular case of a more general fiscal problem in Germany. In the depression they had almost no room for manoeuvre: their revenues were restricted and now they had little control over their expenditure. Like the Länder and like the central state they were dependent on the behaviour of the German and especially the international capital market – a behaviour which they had only very limited opportunities to influence. The communes' weakness strengthened their enemies, and pushed the process of centralisation far further than the founding fathers of the Weimar constitution had envisaged.

The central state had, it may be thought, more latitude for action. But even here it might be argued that one of the reasons that in the constitutional issue it took such a harsh line against municipal independence lay in considerations imposed by the international financial and economic order. A vital part of any recovery programme was the securing of international co-operation, and perhaps also of new foreign loans. Yet Germany's creditors objected at least as vigorously as Brüning, Reichsbank President Luther or Reich Finance Minister Dietrich to what they regarded as Germany's Tammany Hall. As a memorandum prepared by the Federal Reserve Bank of New York put it, the Germans 'put coal in the German Mrs Murphy's cellar by furnishing social aid out of the budget and in addition providing jobs in the government for Mrs Murphy's boys'.[69]

One of the most intriguing questions raised in this chapter is how the public and private sectors behaved differently during the depression. The great banking collapse of the summer of 1931 which contributed significantly to the depth of Germany's slump was in part a consequence of mis-investment in the private sector – most notoriously the Danat Bank's overcommitment to the textile firm of Nordwolle. But it was also a result of a crisis in *public* finance: the Danat was vulnerable also as a result of its exposure to Berlin's

---

69. FRBNY German Government file, 9 June 1932 Galantiere memorandum.

municipal debt. The other major collapse of July 1931 – that of the Landesbank der Rheinprovinz – is directly attributable to the fiscal problems of the major cities in the Rhineland.

Public debt is volatile for two reasons: in the first place it is contracted as a result of decisions originating in a political process (how can a mayor such as Adenauer strengthen his political position?) that does not necessarily take into account problems of repayment or amortisement. This does not necessarily mean that private loans were more sensibly used in Germany in the 1920s: there was notoriously a great amount of mis-investment in private industry (most famously in the creation of overcapacities in the steel sector), Germany's public investments – the Berlin and Frankfurt housing estates, the Cologne Green Belt, even the Essen Gruga – represent long-term goods. But at the time not everyone thought so, and the financial markets were especially sceptical. And this was vital. The vulnerability occurred because of a second consideration: public finance is more immediately exposed to changes in sentiment ('market opinion') that are remarkably difficult to control through simple political decisions. This is why in the depression the existence of a relatively high level of relatively volatile debt led to a narrowing of choices. Their incomes had been cut and they could no longer borrow.

It would be foolish to argue that communes had a great deal of choice about what they did in the depression. On the other hand, the depression resulted partly from an instability stemming from earlier decisions by municipalities, when they had had more freedom of manoeuvre and had chosen a path of social stabilisation, high expenditure, and fiscal destabilisation. Luther's and Brüning's perception of the way in which the fiscal crisis had originated made them advocates of a kind of political control that laid the basis for the later dictatorship.

9
The *Gemeinden* as Agents of Fiscal and Social Policy in the Twentieth Century: Local Government and State-form Crises in Germany

Jeremy Leaman

Local Government in Materialist Theory

The consideration of this subject derives initially from observations on the failure of Keynesian politics in the late 1960s and early 1970s, in particular with regard to the key role of local authorities (LAs) in anti-cyclical strategies, and secondly from an interest in the changing relationship between state and economy in twentieth-century Germany, in which at second glance at least, the lower levels of the state apparatus seem to have played a significant role. The observer's task of surveying the role of local government in Germany this century has been made much easier and more rewarding by (recent) refinements in materialist state theory. First, the differentiation of the structural functionality of the state in modern capitalist society has allowed the identification of separate functions which the state is obliged to fulfil in order to sustain an increasingly critical reproduction of capital.[1] Secondly, each function is seen to operate according to a separate rationality and a separate dynamics which in

---

1. Elmar Altvater, 'Zu einigen Problemen des Staatsinterventionismus', in *Probleme des Klassenkampfes*, No. 3, 1972; Joachim Hirsch, 'Kapitalreproduktion, Klassenauseinandersetzungen und Widersprüche im Staatsapparat', in Volkhard Brandes *et al* (eds.), *Handbuch 5 Staat*, Frankfurt am Main, 1977, pp. 161ff; Heidrun Abromeit, 'Zum Verhältnis von Staat und Wirtschaft im gegenwärtigen Kapitalismus', *Politische Vierteljahresschrift*, vol. 17, 1976, pp. 2ff.; Dieter Läpple, 'Kapitalistische Vergesellschaftungstendenzen und Staatsinterventionismus', in Brandes *et al* (eds.) *Handbuch 5*, pp. 215ff.

part demand separate administrative institutions, thus creating the potential for conflict between 'particularised' elements of the state. Thirdly, the emergence of 'partial apparatuses'[2] is seen to reflect an increasing weakness of the capitalist state as it attempts to perform more and more fire-brigade duties, a view which confounds the assumptions by many bourgeois theorists, social democrats and orthodox communists of an increasingly powerful state monolith, of a leviathan moving inexorably towards socialism.[3] Refined materialist theories still contain predictions of an unavoidable fiscal crisis of *the* capitalist state, but this is qualified by reference to the tenacious strategies of defence which that state (in its variety of forms) has developed; local government, according to some observers, is not just affected passively by these strategies – in a variety of negative ways – but has been deliberately made a central element of that strategy.[4]

Materialist theory identifies some five fundamental functions of the modern capitalist state: (a) the maintenance of a basic framework of law relating to property and contractual rights; (b) the creation and maintenance of general conditions of material production (infrastructure) which includes increasingly certain external costs of production (research, development, training); (c) the maintenance of stable economic growth; (d) the regulation of social conflict, notably between capital and labour; and (e) the maintenance of mass loyalty.[5] While the primary function of guaranteeing the rights of disposition is rooted in the constitutional responsibilities of the central state and its subordinate judiciary,[6] the four

2. Thus Joachim Hirsch, *Staatsapparat und Reproduktion des Kapitals*, Frankfurt am Main, 1974, pp. 375f.

3. This linear conception of the expansion of 'the state' is shared by German Social Democrats with their strong Lassallean statist tradition (see below), by bourgeois critics of the deliberately expanded 'state quota' as a means of creeping towards socialism: Carl Böhret, *Aktionen gegen die "kalte Sozialisierung" 1926–1930*, Berlin, 1966; and more recently Kurt Biedenkopf and Meinhard Miegel, *Die programmierte Krise*, Bonn, 1979, pp. 35ff., and most significantly by Marxist-Leninist 'Stamokap' theories: see Autorenkollektiv, *Der Imperialismus der BRD*, Berlin, 1971, as just one example. These contrast with Abromeit's more differentiated view of a state whose growth reflects weakness, 'Zum Verhältnis', p. 15.

4. Thus Adalbert Evers, 'Staatlicher Zentralismus und Dezentralisation. Zur historischen Entwicklung einer politischen Problemstellung', in Brandes *et al* (eds.), *Handbuch 5*, p. 243.

5. Abromeit, 'Zum Verhältnis', p. 16.

6. Berhard Blanke and others have demonstrated the vital significance of the standardisation of law by an independent state apparatus as a precondition for the

other functions are performed to a varying degree by all levels of the state, including the LAs.

From the first stages of the process of industrialisation in Germany the LAs created and maintained the essential elements of the local economic infrastructure (local transport, water, gas, electricity and sewage services etc.) and contributed to the control of social conflict as major agents of welfare provision, public housing and primary education. As early as the 1920s the importance of local authority investment expenditure was recognised (albeit sporadically) as a potential instrument of counter-cyclical economic policy and state job-creation. In addition, the structurally vital role of the LAs in the maintenance of mass loyalty and hence the legitimacy of the politico-economic order has been strongly underlined recently.[7] Within a theoretical scheme which postulates an inevitable crisis of either the capitalist state form or the capitalist state as such, the LAs, as subordinate but vital institutions, must logically become exposed at an early stage in the crisis to a combination of severe pressures, where competing state functions collide and where in addition the central and regional effects of such collisions are pushed off onto this lowest level. Accordingly studies of the political economy of local government must represent an important focus for historians, political scientists and others.

It is important from the outset to dispose of the concept of 'self-government' (*Selbstverwaltung*) as a category of any validity for this analysis. This conception of a social institution distinct from the state is at best a heuristic fiction to describe the urban administrations after the vom Stein reforms up the end of the First World War; at worst it is an illusion fostered to create the impression of democratic participation, while the democratic substance of such participation is being consistently eroded.[8] On the other hand the

---

development of capitalism replacing localised systems of measurement and exchange: Berhard Blanke, Ulrich Jürgens, and Hans Kastandiek, *Kritik der politischen Wissenschaft*, Frankfurt am Main, 1975.

7. Claus Offe talks of the LAs as a 'buffer and filter zone' ideally suited for the concealment of central government responsibilities, 'Zur Frage der "Identität der kommunalen Ebene"', in *Lokale Politikforschung*, vol. 2, Frankfurt, 1975, p. 307; see also Evers, 'Zentralismus', pp. 243ff.

8. Heinz Zielinski, 'Die Erosion kommunaler Selbstverwaltung', in *Frankfurter Hefte*, vol. 35, part 4, 1980, pp. 29–36; Walter Buckmann, 'Planung, Kreditbeschränkung und kommunale Selbstverwaltung', *Archiv für Kommunalwissenschaften* (*AfK*), vol. 13, 1974, pp. 63–78; Horst Matzerath, 'Konjunkturrat und Finanzpla-

resilience of the 'ideology of self-government' is understandable for a number of reasons. First, the *Gemeinde* represents objectively – as well as through a variety of semantic associations ('community', 'parish', 'local authority') – the place in which social production and reproduction take place, where social needs are articulated most directly and where social conflict largely manifests itself;[9] 'nowhere else do the class structure of a society and the degree of social integration and disintegration ... become so clear as in the *"Gemeinden"*'.[10] In addition, the immediacy of the local environment as the policy-object of local government and as evidence of its success/failure subordinates policy formulation more to general social needs (in housing, welfare, education, recreation, infrastructure) than at higher (more distant) levels of the state; conversely it services directly the infrastructural needs of individual capitals in contrast to the central state which can be seen to service the general need of a putative 'national capital' often at the expense of individual (small) capitals. Moreover, the nature of LA economic activity requires both specific forms of organisation and a specific rationality which are often perceived by both proponents and critics of communal economics as contrasting with the prevalent private economy (collective economics, 'municipal socialism', 'creeping socialisation'). And the significance of local politics appears to be confirmed when the conquest of local positions of power by working-class (anti-capitalist) parties in 'red Vienna', Hamburg, Bremen and more recently in Greater London and Liverpool is considered by many to be fundamentally subversive of the general economic order.

The perceived 'ambivalence'[11] of LAs within and/or towards the state apparatus is however a natural reflection of both the contra-

---

nungsrat. Zum Wandel der kommunalen Position im modernen Bundesstaat', *AfK*, vol. 11, 1972, pp. 243–87; Adrienne Windhoff-Heritier, 'Politik der Abhängigkeit. Kommunale Sozialpolitik in der fiskalischen Krise', *AfK*, vol. 24, 1985, pp. 177–92; Rüdiger Voigt, 'Restriktionen kommunaler Sozialverwaltung', *aus politik und zeitgeschichte*, no. 3, 1977, pp. 3–30.

9. Already in 1905 Heinrich Herkner had stated that 'the nature of things forces the local authority to social-political action, whether it likes it or not. Social deprivation confronts the LA far more directly than the state authorities': *Die Arbeiterfrage*, Berlin, 1905, p. 576. The false differentiation between LA and state does not detract from the correctness of the basic perception.

10. Thus Wilhelm Ribhegge, 'Die Systemfunktion der Gemeinden. Zur deutschen Kommunalgeschichte seit 1918', *aus politik und zeitgeschichte*, no. 47, 1973, p. 4.

11. Ibid., p. 3.

dictory process of capital reproduction and the mirror contradictions of state functions within that process – the dynamics of unequal development within capitalism produce sectoral, local, regional and national disparities in the distribution of economic resources, as well as disparities between small, medium and large enterprises, which historically have produced corresponding disparities in the resources, perceptions and policies of differing state authorities at central, regional, local and ministerial/departmental level, and hence corresponding collisions of interest within the state apparatus. Along with all the other state institutions, the LAs are subject to the regular fluctuations of the economic cycle and to less regular structural economic crises (e.g. dying industries with specific local commitments), as well as to the exponential slide of general capital productivity/rate of profit which increases the state's obligations in respect of the infrastructure and external costs of production. More recently, they have also been subject to severe demographic fluctuations resulting from the effects of two world wars, economic crises and birth control. The combination of these factors produces the well-known general fluctuating pattern of increased state responsibilities and reduced state resources. In addition, however, the LAs have traditionally been subject to both structural political constraints on resources (limited access to tax revenue and other levies, ceilings on borrowing, etc.) and particular politico-economic developments, such as growing urbanisation and its implications for expenditure. Historically these two factors have tended to compound the contradiction between increased responsibilities and reduced resources within local government. The particular sensitivity of LAs to social *and* fiscal crises does not, however, remove them from consideration as state bodies; nor do communal forms of economic control represent 'phenomena which are alien to the [economic] system'.[12] Rather the 'dilemma of communal politics' is the dilemma of capitalist state politics in a clearer, distilled form. While the central (and regional) state bodies can often conceal the polarities of state functions by delegating responsibilities to lower levels of the state apparatus and retaining fiscal control, the local authorities regularly manifest the schizophrenia of conflicting obligations; equally social ownership of infrastructural facilities can clearly be seen to *complement* the

12. Ibid.

dominant private forms of control as an instrument of economic rationalisation and cost reduction.

The Wilhelmine Period

Up to 1918 local government in Germany reflected both the general rise in state responsibilities in a period of rapid industrialisation, and the specific economic and political conditions which obtained in Germany at the time. Thus apart from the general correspondence of local government to localised forms of commodity production and capital accumulation in the nineteenth century, the urban and semi-urban centres were a particular focus of bourgeois economic and political interests for three reasons; first, the political dominance of the aristocracy at the central and regional state level; secondly, the rapidity of industrial and hence urban development and the related need to establish (rapidly) comprehensive infrastructural services, and thirdly, the need to neutralise some of the misery of the urban poor. The political preconditions for the expansion of bourgeois-dominated local government were the relative fiscal autonomy afforded by reforms such as those of vom Stein in Prussia in 1808 and the persistence until 1918 of class-based franchise systems. This guaranteed a certain degree of self-determination by the bourgeoisie within a state which primarily protected the economic interests of the landowning aristocracy.

The particular importance of local government expenditure for industrial development in the second half of the nineteenth century is demonstrated by the 36-fold increase in LA expenditure in Prussia in this period compared to a mere 6-fold increase for the regional governments and even less for the central authorities.[13] This reflected the decentralised (localised) responsibilities for increasingly necessary social welfare (which after 1883 included the administration of local sickness insurance funds) and the creation or socialisation of infrastructural services. Whereas only half of Germany's larger towns possessed modern (communal) water and sewage systems in 1876, none of the 150 largest towns were without them in 1900. Similarly the number of gas-works rose from some 50

13. H. Göttrup, *Die kommunale Leistungsverwaltung*, Stuttgart, 1973, pp. 7ff., cited in Evers, 'Zentralismus', p. 255.

in all Germany in the mid-1850s to over 1,700 in 1914, most of which were under communal ownership. The number of power stations rose even more rapidly from a mere 16 in 1888 to over 2,500 in 1911.[14] The significance of the LAs as employers increased accordingly. In 1907, if one sets aside the vast labour force of the public railways of over 700,000, the LAs with a workforce of over 190,000 employed more people than all the other state enterprises combined.[15]

A particular feature of German local government up to 1918 was the creation and expansion of local and district savings banks, which functioned both as an instrument of self-help for the propertyless poor and also increasingly as an important source of credit for local small businessmen.[16] The unique strength of the communal savings banks, which rapidly developed into universal banks, reflects the particular character of German finance capital and the tenacious realisation of bourgeois self-interest through the institutions of 'municipal socialism'.

The Weimar Republic

Of the three severe state-form crises in the history of twentieth-century Germany the two which mark the beginning and end of the Weimar Republic are of particular interest for a consideration of the history of local government. The year 1918 marked the end of the period of relatively successful bourgeois manipulation of communal politics within an aristocratic state, but it did not mark the beginning of a corresponding manipulation of local government by working-class parties within a bourgeois state under the new conditions of universal franchise – there was no *real* municipal socialism to follow the bogus municipal socialism of the Kaiserreich. The period of revolutionary transition from 1918 to 1920 buried even this modest expectation of some sections of the labour movement.[17]

---

14. Figures from Gerold Ambrosius, *Der Staat als Unternehmer*, Göttingen, 1984, p. 40ff.

15. Ibid., p. 39.

16. The total balances of all German savings banks rose from RM 2 billion in 1876 to 19.7 billion in 1913, whereas the eight largest Joint Stock Banks could muster total balances of only 5.15 billion in 1913: Ambrosius, *Staat*, p. 49.

17. Georg Fülberth, *Die Beziehungen zwischen SPD und KPD in der Kommunalpolitik der Weimarer Periode 1918/19 bis 1933*, Cologne, 1985, pp. 18ff.

The speed with which the predominantly local-based revolutionary council system was swept aside and replaced by an orthodox system of bourgeois-democratic local administration was evidence not just of the primacy of national and international politics and the requirements of demobilisation, but also of specific and conflicting perceptions of structural-political priorities within the labour movement. However, these perceptions are not really covered by the polarity of reformist centralism and revolutionary syndicalism. The demands for a unitary centralised democratic state were not solely voiced by Lassallean 'statists' within German Social Democracy but also by Marxists within the party, in terms of both the preconditions for a proletarian class dictatorship and, more importantly, the absence of a bourgeois struggle for national political democracy. Consequently the left wing of the party did not really develop a significant line on local politics; rather it was the reformist right wing of the SPD – represented by Lindemann, Südekum and Bernstein – which produced a communal-political 'self-government line'.[18]

Nevertheless the pre-emptive parliamentarisation of national government in October 1918 and the requirements of demobilisation and social normality, combined with the centralist prejudices of the majority of leading Social Democrats to dilute and finally to neutralise the otherwise spontaneous manifestations of Soviet democracy. Despite this, the brief revolutionary episode – which at its height presented two parallel hierarchies of political power – reflected the persistent contradiction between the conflicting state functions within capitalism, of maintaining the basic order (*qua* 'national interest') and mass loyalty. The fact that the *disloyalty* of the masses was expressed temporarily through the Councils as predominantly communal institutions, which with some success administered essential services and secured essential supplies, underscored the susceptibility of the capitalist state to local functional crises and the need to deploy the instruments of the state in general to guarantee mass loyalty. The Stinnes–Legien agreement, by which the organised employers accepted the trade unions as

18. Ibid., pp. 380ff. Fülberth also locates Paul Hirsch 'in a more limited sense' on the right wing of the party. It is interesting that in 1898 already Paul Singer, a member of the left wing, had specifically warned Social Democratic councillors in Brandenburg of frittering away socialist principles for 'momentary advantages' in the LAs: ibid., p. 26.

legitimate negotiating partners, and the introduction of a liberal-democratic constitution were clearly intended to fulfil this function, but they also fuelled the resentment of capital towards the increasing irritation of democracy and thus pre-ordained the later state-form crisis of 1930–3 and the transition to fascism.

The constitutional reforms of 1919 and 1920 affected the local authorities significantly. The universal franchise brought many Social Democrats and later Communists into local government with labour or democratic republican majorities in many of the councils; even so bourgeois parties still held sway within the elected bodies and the national representative body for the German municipalities, the Deutscher Städtetag (DST), and the failure to reform the structure and personnel of the local bureaucracies made the representation of labour interests extremely difficult. The 'democratisation' of local government went hand in hand with increased responsibilities in both infrastructural and social affairs. On the other hand, the Erzberger fiscal reforms of 1920 brought a significant limitation of local authority finances with its general centralisation of taxation control and the specific suspension of LA quotas of both income and corporation tax, leaving only commercial and property rates and a number of bagatelle taxes at the exclusive disposal of the communes.

These changes placed the LAs in the Weimar Republic in a position of structural dependence on higher state authorities in terms of equalisation arrangements and also supervision, while they were given no representation in the national legislative process. Confronted with the objective demands of increasing urbanisation,[19] and increasing complexities of urban economies, the mostly bourgeois leaders of Germany's towns were forced into a critical and defensive stance against the constraints of the constitution and of real politics, not just in the periods of economic instability but also in the period of relative stabilisation. The resulting conflicts of perception over the social and fiscal priorities of the Weimar state contributed in large measure to the political paralysis of progressive forces at the end of the period and the demands for strong centralised government of the kind offered by fascism.

---

19. Between 1870 and 1910 the population of towns with more than 2,000 inhabitants had risen from 14.8 million to 39 million (or from 36% to 60% of the total population); by 1910 there were some 48 towns with a population of over 100,000.

The conflict within the state apparatus (overlaid as it was with the constraints of military defeat and post-war upheaval) was a logical reflection of conflicting rationalities within the capitalist state's functional role. On the one hand the financial centralisation of the Erzberger reforms represented a logical (if overdue) response to the centralised forms of capital reproduction, monopolisation, increased national economic susceptibilities and the corresponding need for remedial fire-brigade duties by the central state. On the other hand the insistence by the mayors and their administrations on an equitable and adequate funding of local government corresponded logically to increasing demands on local resources. Not only did economies of scale demand communal forms of control over many infrastructural services, but the costs of infrastructural operations rose considerably with the increasing size of conurbations.[20] The failure of the 1920 fiscal reforms both to mobilise sufficient tax revenue for state use and to distribute tax burdens more equitably compounded the tension between the central state and the *Gemeinden*; the tension would have been evident in any case, particularly in the period of recession and deflation 1929–32, because of differing budgetary priorities and the revenue dependence of the LAs. In 1925, a year of relative normality, the net revenue supplement of LAs of RM 1.4 billion from higher levels of the state (almost exclusively the Reich) represented some 28.5 per cent of LA's own revenues of RM 5.06 billions. This was despite the fact that in the same year the LAs controlled a larger share of total public expenditure (38 per cent) than either the Reich (35 per cent) or the Länder (26 per cent).[21]

LA expenditure was dominated by the four rubrics of housing construction (13 per cent of total *Gemeinde* expenditure in 1925), transport services (13.7 per cent), education (20.2 per cent) and social welfare (29.4 per cent). The increased expenditure on social

20. Within the area of local government the scale of infrastructural services varied dramatically between, say, medium-sized country authorities and Berlin with a population of over four million in the 1920s.
21. Figures from Willi Albers, 'Der Finanzausgleich' (III), in *Handwörterbuch der Sozialwissenschaften*, Göttingen, 1952f. The increased Reich share of total expenditure in 1928 was a deviation from the trend of expenditure ratios, being caused by sudden increases (over 1927) in both internal and external war-related expenditure (up RM 1.2 billion) and in social expenditure (up by RM 280 million), cf. K.H. Dederke, *Reich und Republik ' Deutschland 1917–1933*, Stuttgart, 1973, pp. 276f.

welfare (over 1913, for example, when it accounted for only 18.3 per cent of total expenditure by the *Gemeinden*) reflected a number of factors, including more extensive and in part more generous legislative guidelines of the central authorities.[22] Similarly the housing budgets of the LAs were affected by a variety of central government directives[23], as well as by the immensity of the post-inflation building back-log.[24] Characteristic of both these areas of LA responsibility was the discrepancy between centrally determined obligations on the one hand, and central government's indifference to the resource implications of these obligations on the other. As a result the larger authorities were forced to borrow large amounts of money in the stabilisation period (over RM 500 million) and, in the absence of domestic credit supplies, in the form of foreign loans.

The objective justification of LA borrowing (based as it was in both their constitutional obligations and their perceptions of basic local needs) was ignored in the bitter campaign waged subsequently by right-wing politicians, the right-wing press and the Reichsverband der deutschen Industrie (RDI) against the 'creeping socialisation' ostensibly taking place under the name of local government.[25] With a kind of primitive 'crowding-out' theory successive Reichsbank presidents, along with the RDI and the right-wing Hugenberg press empire, railed against the extravagance of LA expenditure, the pressure on interest rates caused by competition for credits and the subsequent deleterious effects of LA economic activity on private investment and private viability.[26] Dieter Rebentisch, on the other

22. Dieter Rebentisch, 'Kommunalpolitik, Konjunktur und Arbeitsmarkt in der Endphase der Weimarer Republik', in Rudolf Morsey (ed.), *Verwaltungsgeschichte*, Berlin, 1977, p. 108.

23. D. Silverman, 'A Pledge Unredeemed: The Housing Crisis in Weimar Germany', *Central European History*, vol. 3, 1970, pp. 112ff: see also J. Leaman, 'Handlungsspielräume der Gemeinden in der Zwischenkriegszeit', in C. Kopetzki, V. Lüken – Isberner *et al* (eds.) *Stadterneuerung in der Weimarer Republik und im Nationalsozialismus*, Kassel, 1987, pp. 132–62.

24. In 1920 the federal statistical office calculated a housing shortage of 1.4 million units, and there was general agreement on the need to build at least 250,000 units per year to reduce the shortage (Silverman, 'Pledge Unredeemed', p. 110). These figures were never achieved before 1927.

25. Böhret, *Aktionen*.

26. The campaign against the LA foreign debts was encouraged by the strong criticism expressed by Gilbert Parker, the American reparations commissioner, see Rebentisch, 'Kommunalpolitik', p. 110. This view is oddly echoed by Harold James in his recent book *The German Slump*, Oxford, 1986, where he makes much of the 'tremendously expensive and ambitious projects' of the big cities, of their 'gigantomania', determined by 'inter-city rivalry', by aesthetic considerations and by a

hand, stresses the emptiness of such criticism when he points out the modest borrowing quota of the LAs, which with 25 per cent of the total foreign debt of the public authorities in 1928 stood way below the Reich's own foreign debt quota;[27] the low debt quota of the LAs also compared favourably with its share of public expenditure (1928: 37.8 per cent).[28] Similarly Gerold Ambrosius defends the investment policies of the municipalities in the Weimar Republic in terms of the rationality of state infrastructural services,[29] where predominantly bourgeois local administrations proceeded not from the view of the polarity between public and private capital, but from the (correct) view of the subordinate complementarity of local state economic activity. The right-wing attack, (which was resisted vigorously by individual local politicians like Jarres [Duisburg], Landmann [Frankfurt], Küfner [Munich] and Mulert, the active head of the Deutscher Städtetag) was in some measure encouraged by the delusions of reformist elements within the labour movement, notably the trade-union leadership, which regarded the municipal enterprises as fortresses of communal economics, which could be used as instruments of further collectivisation.[30] However both right-wing critics and reformist supporters of communal economic policy misinterpreted the superficial evidence of an antagonism between private and public economics as something which was essentially subversive. It was like accusing the fire-brigade of arson. The apparently objectionable elements of local economic policy were rather the result of contradictory fiscal constraints. Thus the need to supplement local revenues by the surpluses of communal enterprises[31] was determined by pressing expenditure obligations;

---

general social and cultural 'mission' (pp. 88ff.) without examining the vital economic (and social) function of municipal expenditure, the multiplier effects of local state investment, and the proportion of expenditure on 'prestige' projects to total capital expenditure by the LAs.

27. Rebentisch, 'Kommunalpolitik', p. 110.

28. Willi Albers, 'Finanzausgleich', p. 556. James, *German Slump*, p. 95, tries to demonstrate that 'communal borrowing represented the major part of total public borrowing in Germany' in the late 1920s, but only produces figures for new debts, ignoring the significance of overall debt quotas, and for the ratio of the LAs' borrowing requirement to net domestic investment which, in view of the slump, was unsurprisingly increasing in 1930/1 despite the dramatic *fall* in absolute borrowing levels!

29. Ambrosius, *Staat*, pp. 68ff.

30. Böhret, *Aktionen*, pp. 30f., and Fülberth, *Beziehungen*, p. 59.

31. Communal enterprises provided some 10.6% of the revenue supplement of all

Table 9.1 State expenditure in Germany between the wars

	1925	1928	1932	1936
Reich in mill. RM	5,071	8,098	4,722	13,238
% of total state expenditure (TSE)	35	39	32.6	59.3
Länder in mill. RM	3,889	4,843	3,663	3,139
% of TSE	26.8	23.2	25.2	14
Local authorities in mill. RM	5,524	7,849	6,107	5,956
% of TSE	38.2	37.8	42.2	26.7
Total mill. RM	14,484	20,790	14,492	22,333

Source: W. Albers, 'Der Finanzausgleich', in *Handwörterbuch der Sozialwissenschaften*.

accordingly the pricing and accounting policies of many LA enterprises were 'consciously manipulated'[32] in order to cover deficits, such that rather than penalising capital interests in particular, the 'politically administered prices' functioned as a generalised 'tax on consumption', reducing the redistributive potential of local fiscal policy[33] and thus *protecting* capital interests.

It must be stressed that the fiscal dilemma of German LAs already existed in the period of relative stabilisation. As a result the economic and political crisis of 1929–33 pushed most LAs to the brink of ungovernability. It is well known that the cyclical character of capitalism produces a corresponding cyclical development of state finances and state responsibilities; in severe crises there is a normal discrepancy between reduced revenue and increased fire-brigade duties, to which the orthodox response was the balancing act of reducing budgetary deficits while redistributing expenditure to cover perceived priorities. This natural propensity of the state to act pro-cylically was characteristic of German fiscal policy since 1871, with the extreme exception of the unlimited discounting of the war and post-war reconstruction, and was significantly maintained in the 1929–33 crisis with severe reductions in overall state expenditure (see Table 9.1) and a restrictive monetary policy (higher interest rates etc.). The deflationary stance adopted by Chancellor Brüning

---

LAs in the year 1925/6 from their operating surpluses: Ambrosius, *Staat*, p. 92.
32. Ibid., p. 93.
33. Ibid.

in 1930, which predictably compounded the effects of the trade recession, proceeded not simply from a flawed doctrine of good husbandry and a deafness to progressive fiscalists like Wagemann and Friedländer-Prechtl, but also, as Rebentisch implies, from a kind of inverted *Katastrophenpolitik*, whereby the preparedness to fulfil reparations obligations 'even at the cost of increased mass suffering [would] demonstrate to the outside world [Germany's] inability to pay and hence the need to cancel reparations demands once and for all'.[34]

The 'success' of this policy, in the shape of the Hoover Moratorium, would have been little comfort to the LAs, which, from 1930 to 1932, were subject to a large array of restrictive pressures, both political and cyclical-economic: Brüning's emergency decree of 26 July 1930 imposed a 'citizens' tax' on the local authorities to compensate for withheld Reich taxation. This was resisted by the DST and individual authorities and stamped as an unfair poll-tax; nevertheless, despite its increasing importance as a source of revenue for many towns,[35] the revenue from communal taxes fell from RM 2.7 billion in 1929/30 to 2.2 billion in 1932/3. The Reich revenue supplement was reduced by over a half from RM 1.49 billion in 1929/30 to RM 649 million in 1932/3, reducing overall tax revenue by over 30 per cent from RM 4.2 billion to 2.8 billion. The emergency decree of 5 August 1931 forbade communal access to (communal) savings bank credits. The 'Dietramszell' emergency decree of 24 August 1931 empowered the Länder governments to 'prescribe all measures which are necessary for balancing the budgets of Länder and local authorities by means of a decree'.[36] The Reichsbank imposed effective ceilings on LA borrowing with new higher reserve levels. And the emergency decree of 6 October 1931 introduced mandatory examination of communal finances by Reich and Länder commissioners.[37]

This fiscal squeeze on the LAs coincided with increased demands on local services. As Rebentisch demonstrates, Reich social welfare legislation ultimately placed the greatest pressure on LA resources.[38]

34. Rebentisch, 'Kommunalpolitik', p. 123.
35. Ibid., p. 132.
36. Cited in: Werner Conze, 'Die Reichsverfassungsreform als Ziel der Politik Brünings', *Der Staat*, vol. 11, part 2, 1972, p. 213.
37. See Gerold Ambrosius, 'Aspekte kommunaler Unternehmenspolitik in der Weimarer Republik', *AfK*, vol. 19, part 2, 1980, p. 248.
38. Rebentisch, 'Kommunalpolitik', pp. 112ff.

Despite the introduction of unemployment insurance in 1927, by the end of 1930 already more of the unemployed population were excluded from insurance cover than were included in it and were eligible only for 'crisis support' (funded 20 per cent by the LAs) or for simple 'welfare support' which was funded exclusively by the LAs; by July 1932 most of the unemployed fell into the latter bracket, i.e. outside the responsibility of the Reich.[39] These direct social and fiscal consequences of the depression were reinforced by increased demand for local health services, child welfare, food, clothing and fuel. The unavoidability of basic social expenditure and the 'senseless' restrictions on LA borrowing (thus Mulert) forced many authorities to divert resources from investment budgets (housing and infrastructure, including autonomous and semi-autonomous communal enterprises) to manipulate accounting procedures and prices for services[40] in order to maximise income, and in certain instances even to withhold tax due to the Reich.[41] The ingenuity of *Gemeinde* treasurers – as well as the force of circumstance – is reflected in the maintenance of relatively high LA expenditure in the course of the recession compared to the expenditure of other state authorities (see Table 9.1). The good sense of the budget reform proposals by the DST[42] contrasts well with the blindness of Brüning and others to the value of remedial action at the lowest level of the state apparatus.

The polarity of central state and local state institutions in the last years of the Weimar Republic was a major element of the state-form crisis which was 'resolved' by the establishment of fascism. It was a collision not just between rival perceptions of differing bourgeois factions, but of fundamental state functions. The increasingly authoritarian modes of resolving social conflict collided with the requirements of the (democratic) maintenance of mass loyalty at a local level, while the state as a whole failed to produce stable economic growth. What the Weimar state-form crisis does demonstrate, however, is the central role the LAs perform in the maintenance of mass loyalty, as well as the urban infrastructure, particularly

39. Ibid., p. 114.
40. Ambrosius, 'Aspekte', pp. 250f.; in certain cases one-fifth of municipal budget deficits was covered by the surpluses of municipal enterprises during the recession.
41. Ribhegge, 'Systemfunktion', p. 14; this invariably only succeeded in bringing in the Reich Savings Commissioners.
42. Rebentisch, 'Kommunalpolitik', p. 128.

within a democratic constitution. The guarantee of minimum levels of subsistence, human comfort and social order is in large measure the responsibility of local government and with it the task of sustaining state legitimacy. The absence of these minimum conditions (through the neglect of central authorities, among other things) clearly fuelled the development of fascism with its strong ideological thread of anti-urbanism (strengthened by the perceived failures of urban existence) and its alternative modes of state legitimation. On the other hand it is a significant indictment of Weimar politics that the Nazis were able (successfully) to present themselves as defenders of 'self-government'.[43] The wolf as champion of the sheep-pen reflects worst on the previous shepherds.

National Socialism

In one sense the installation of a fascist dictatorship clearly destroyed the constitutional guarantees of *Selbstverwaltung*. The subordination of all lower authorities in the 1933 emergency legislation and later in the 1935 *Gemeindeordnung*, combined with the drastic purges of mayoral offices, local councils and local administrations rendered autonomous LA activity virtually impossible and ended the critical but open relationship between the highest and lowest levels of the state. In another sense the fascist state finished off the process begun in the First World War, continued after 1919 and accelerated under Brüning and his successors, Papen and Schleicher, of adapting the structure of the state to the economic order, i.e. in its marriage of cartelised (re-feudalised) relations of exchange with centralised authoritarian state powers.[44] The destruction of competition, the subordination of small capitals, the cartelisation and monopolisation of big capital produced problems which made a 'strong' state necessary and the messiness of democratic procedures both irritating and inefficient and thus unnecessary to bourgeois interests.

43. Volker Wünderich, *Arbeiterbewegung und Selbstverwaltung. KPD und Kommunalpolitik in der Weimarer Republik. Mit dem Beispiel Solingen*, Wuppertal, 1980, p. 268.
44. Joachim Perels postulates the logical confluence of authoritarian state and a constitutional reality of monopolised exchange relations: *Kapitalismus und politische Demokratie. Privatrechtsystem und Gesellschaftsstruktur in der Weimarer Republik*, Frankfurt am Main, 1973, pp. 73ff.

What is interesting about the development of local government under fascism (until 1943 at least) is the apparent ease with which the communes were manipulated, particularly as instruments of ideological control. Quite contrary to their anti-urban ideology the Nazis concentrated much material and propagandistic effort on the development of urban centres as symbols of renewal and political strength. Smaller authorities were merged and the most lavish of the urban planning schemes concentrated on the larger towns, such that the rural village style of housing development was 'recreated' along with monumental neo-classical buildings in or around the large towns.[45] The histories of small communities under fascism (by Tenfelde, Zofka, Zimmermann, Allen, Wagener and Willke and others) show how local party organisations insinuated themselves into most areas of social activity as elements of a new political culture as well as instruments of a war-economy. The reports of the Gestapo, local Nazi leaders and the Deutsche Arbeitsfront[46] also reflected a sensibility not just to the potential for resistance, but also to the potential for indifference, and thus a realisation of the need to maintain minimum levels of social existence and social morale which were ignored by many Weimar politicians.

Although fascism was an ultimately catastrophic 'solution' of the state-form crisis of the early 1930s, proving even more dysfunctional in terms of maintaining the framework for capital reproduction, it exploited perceptions of the value of local politics which were notably absent within central political circles in the Weimar Republic. This is reflected in part in the development of LA revenue and expenditure. In revenue terms the LAs were little worse off in 1936 than in 1925 (RM 4.9 billion against 5.05 billion), whereas the Länder lost almost half their revenue from RM 3.6 billion in 1925 to 1.9 billion in 1936. LA expenditure was also higher in 1936 than in 1925, compared to a fall in Länder expenditure of about one-fifth. The huge rise in Reich expenditure throughout the 1930s distorted

45. Horst Matzerath, *Nationalsozialismus und kommunale Selbstverwaltung*, Stuttgart, 1970, p. 335, etc.; also Joachim Petsch, *Baukunst und Stadtplanung im Dritten Reich*, Munich and Vienna, 1976, and by the same author, 'Architektur und Städtebau im Dritten Reich – Anspruch und Wirklichkeit', in D. Peukert and J. Reulecke (eds.), *Die Reihen fast geschlossen. Beiträge zur Geschichte des Alltags unterm Nationalsozialismus*, Wuppertal, 1981, pp. 175ff.

46. Timothy Mason, *Arbeiterklasse und Volksgemeinschaft*, Opladen, 1977 and M. Broszat *et al* (eds.) *Bayern in der NS-Zeit. Soziale Lage und politisches Verhalten der Bevölkerung im Spiegel vertraulicher Berichte*, Munich and Vienna, 1977.

the expenditure quotas (see Table 9.1) to the apparent detriment of the LAs, but the maintenance of relatively high LA expenditure underscores both the acknowledged importance of the *Gemeinden* as agents of state involvement and the relative constancy of their general social and economic obligations within the state apparatus, even in periods of strong growth – in contrast to other levels of the state, notably the regions.

West Germany since 1945

The state-form crisis which befell Germany after the capitulation of the fascist state coincided with a national crisis for the German people, both of which were 'resolved' by the respective occupying powers. The customary 'organic' relationship between state and economy was suspended, the specific interests of German capital or German labour set aside completely or marginalised by the 'interests' of the Allies. These interests were largely contradictory – a mixture of revenge, moral good intentions, indifference, prejudice, short- and long-term greed and a variety of perceptions of national security. There was also a shifting of priorities on the Western side before the particular solution of partition and a federal West German state was imposed on a slightly bewildered West German (and East German) population. The position of the new West German LAs in the constitutional reality of the Federal Republic (after some promising signs in the period 1945–9)[47] was certainly no improvement on the Weimar Republic. The demand of Weimar local government leaders for 'direct access' to the central state was studiously ignored by the architects of the Basic Law (otherwise noted for its awareness of the weaknesses of Weimar democracy), in that local government was subordinated to regional control and to regionally based fiscal arrangements. Bonn was seen to have 'betrayed' the LAs and missed a 'golden opportunity' to create a thorough-going democratic state structure with real power for local communities.[48]

The regionalisation of fiscal power (albeit subject to central

47. Wolfgang Rudzio, *Die Neuordnung des Kommunalwesens in der Britischen Zone*, Stuttgart, 1968.
48. Thus Ernst Böhme (SPD), Mayor of Brunswick, quoted in *Die Welt*, 5 August 1949.

Jeremy Leaman

Table 9.2 Share of individual state authorities in public revenue and
expenditure 1913–1958

	1913 Inc. exp.	1925 Inc. exp.	1936 Inc. exp.	1953 Inc. exp.	1958 Inc. exp.
Reich/Bund					
% of Total	29.7 32.0	37.6 35.0	66.1 59.3	55.6 48.0	51.5 44.3
Länder %	29.5 28.1	26.0 26.8	9.5 14.0	27.8 30.3	30.3 31.8
Local authorities					
%	40.8 39.9	36.4 38.2	24.4 26.7	16.6 21.7	18.2 24.0

Source: W. Albers, 'Der Finanzausgleich', in Handwörterbuch der Sozialwissenschaften.

legislative controls and equalisation procedures) contradicted the
trend in Germany towards greater centralisation which had followed the logic of centralised but critical capital reproduction. On
the other hand the reduction of direct LA access to revenue before
equalisation demonstrated the persistence of a general state (bourgeois) concern for the LAs as a potential drain on resources, rather
than as a primary agent of expenditure. (The reforms of 1957 and
1969 were perceived as marginal by most LA leaders.)[49]

The revenue weakness of the LAs has been compounded by the
reduction in the significance of the surpluses of communal enterprises. Energy production has been increasingly centralised and
removed from LA control; local gas production has been marginalised by the national network of natural gas; and in particular public
transport has declined in volume terms and in terms of profitability.
(Today with the huge increase in private transport, the tram, bus
and underground services perform as much social as economic
functions.)[50]

The fiscal weakness of the LAs was most noticeable in the
development of the state debt, which shows an increasing borrowing requirement as a proportion of expenditure in the 1950s, a
consistently higher debt quota for the LAs in the 1960s and early
1970s and a correspondingly high ratio of debt servicing to total
expenditure; from 1956 through to 1977 the burden of LA interest
payments was considerably higher than for the other authorities

49. Ribhegge, 'Systemfunktion', p. 26n.
50. Ambrosius, Staat, pp. 119ff.

272

Table 9.3 Interest burden of public authorities, 1950–1980

Year	Total in million DM	Bund	Länder	LAs	Total as % of expenditure	Bund	Länder	LAs
1950	624	151	421	52	2.2	1.2	3.9	0.7
1960	1,919	699	582	496	3.0	2.2	2.3	3.0
1961	2,615	710	716	702	2.8	1.6	1.9	2.9
1962	3,045	909	662	785	2.9	1.8	1.5	2.8
1963	2,834	988	644	901	2.4	1.8	1.4	2.9
1964	3,136	1,118	636	1,066	2.5	1.9	1.3	3.0
1965	3,584	1,166	768	1,299	2.6	1.8	1.4	3.3
1966	4,466	1,527	964	1,592	3.1	2.3	1.7	3.9
1967	5,482	2,009	1,250	1,807	3.6	2.7	2.1	4.4
1968	5,761	1,917	1,479	1,920	3.6	2.5	2.3	4.4
1969	6,355	2,191	1,607	2,075	3.6	2.7	2.4	4.3
1970	6,862	2,460	1,675	2,404	3.5	2.8	2.2	4.3
1971	7,720	2,597	2,000	2,810	3.4	2.6	2.2	4.2
1972	8,817	2,798	2,319	3,394	3.5	2.5	2.3	4.5
1973	10,556	3,330	2,704	4,205	3.8	2.7	2.3	5.0
1974	12,403	4,234	3,149	4,852	3.9	3.2	2.3	5.1
1975	14,462	5,211	3,881	5,246	4.0	3.3	2.7	5.2
1976	17,726	6,880	5,224	5,535	4.7	4.2	3.4	5.3
1977	20,725	8,534	6,383	5,828	5.2	5.0	3.9	5.4
1978	21,827	9,562	6,878	5,414	5.0	5.0	3.9	4.5
1979	24,481	11,259	7,813	5,500	5.2	5.5	4.1	4.3
1980	27,829	13,661	8,492	5,911	5.6	6.4	4.1	4.3

Source: Federal Ministry of Finance.

(see Table 9.3). The obvious conclusion from this is that within the fiscal arrangements of the Federal Republic the expenditure commitments of the LAs have exceeded their overall revenue to a higher degree than those of either central government or the Länder with their constitutionally better access to revenue. It would therefore seem to be correct to link the increasing revenue weaknesses of the LAs to a significant shift in their spending. The importance of LA infrastructural activity to capital reproduction has, as was indicated above, fallen with the increasing centralisation of control over certain areas (electricity, gas, water) and the greater importance of national transport with its emphasis on private haulage on trunk roads and central subsidies for the grossly indebted national railways (*Bundesbahn*). This leaves the focus of LA budgets on areas of expenditure with an exclusive or predominant social profile: public housing, education, cultural facilities, local transport, the bulk of social welfare outside the social insurance schemes and increasingly, health recreation and environment. The fact that these areas relate to the 'needs' of the general population rather than to specific economic interests means that (with notable exceptions) the limitations imposed by the supreme fiscal (and monetary) authorities are understandable reflections of the contradiction between specific state functions represented by separate state institutions – namely between the central authorities with their stress on optimal conditions for the reproduction of capital, and local government with its responsibilities for the maintenance of social order, prevention of social conflict and the sustaining of mass loyalty.

This contradiction remained latent during the 1950s and early 1960s because of the constant real increases in state revenue at all levels which made borrowing less problematic. However, significant economic and demographic shifts took place during this period which predetermined the later crises of town-hall and state expenditure. First, the absorption of expellees and refugees placed considerable burdens on the social infrastructure of West German LAs, which were compounded by the effects of the displacement of agricultural labour and the later importation of migrant labour. Secondly, the temporary rise in capital productivity in the 1950s came to an end in 1959/60 and was followed by a consistent decline throughout the subsequent period; this had implications for the fiscal stance of the state in general and for particular LAs which relied on the 'loyalty' and stability of particular capitals within their area. Thirdly, the latitude for flexible state responses to various forms of economic disequilibrium was reduced by the independence of the central bank, by remilitarisation, by the increasing export quota (rendering an increasing percentage of total demand independent of domestic demand management), by the increasing unprofitability of public transport (specifically the Bundesbahn), the increasing internationalisation and mobility of capital and other structural economic factors. Fourthly, the overdue reform and expansion of the education system was succesfully postponed by the governments of the Adenauer era with its 'planning-phobia'[51],

---

51. Ibid., p. 108; Marianne Welteke, *Theorie und Praxis der sozialen Marktwirtschaft*, Frankfurt am Main, 1976, p. 88.

creating an investment backlog which would, at some time in the future, have to be made good. Finally, the growth of productivity in the economic sectors controlled by the state was much lower than that of the private sectors which indicated increasing relative costs of state economic activity and reduced scope for cost rationalisation.[52]

The honeymoon years of constant growth in GNP and state revenues ended abruptly in 1966/7 and produced, as is well known, a Keynesian response under Schiller in the shape of two major state investment programmes, the latter of which involved the LAs as the main agents of investment. The sudden 'instrumentalisation' of the LAs made virtue out of necessity, inasmuch as the LAs normally presided over two-thirds of manoeuvrable investment,[53] and local building investment was at the time objectively more needed by the mass of the population. The experience of the Weimar recession, of the ignored demands for fiscal expansion by Friedländer-Prechtl and Ernst Wagemann and by municipal leaders like Landmann, Scharnagl, Jarres, Luppe and others, informed the new enthusiasm for technocratic state solutions. However, West Germany's surrender of Keynesianism in 1972 was as abrupt as its espousal and reflected, among other things, a simplistic assessment of both the nature of investment and the specific role of LAs as the main agents of state investment demand (simplistic in part because of the non-employment of demand management proper in the 1930s).

Briefly, the assumed multiplier effects of state demand stimuli are not necessarily identical to the real effects: private investment will not necessarily increase because of temporary increases in state demand or demand inducements; rather it is more likely to correspond to longer-term expectations of sales, profits and capacity utilisation. Any induced private investment may simply represent an acceleration of future plans, may serve not to extend capacity but to rationalise or replace existing capacity and may thus have neutral or negative effects on growth and employment. Moreover, the formulation of state investment plans in the depth of the recession may produce a pro-cyclical surge if the implementation of the plans is much delayed. And direct state investment projects have varying growth effects and varying costs effects – the long-term yearly cost effects of many local projects represent a high proportion of the

---

52. Evers, 'Zentralismus', p. 242.
53. Ibid., p. 241.

initial investment cost (a fact often ignored by central policy-makers).

In the event Schiller's Keynesian experiment achieved short-term anti-cyclical success for the national economy,[54] but because of predictable planning delays, long term post-investment costs and a combination of other factors the LAs were confronted with a pro-cyclical surge of expenditure, building price inflation (profiteering) and borrowing. The manoeuvrability of LA investment proved to be a supreme delusion of West German Keynesianism. Even if the Central Bank had not imposed monetarism on the Federal Republic in the summer of 1972, the local authorities are unlikely to have committed themselves to further involvement in anti-cyclical strategies, given that neither central nor regional governments have shown any willingness to share the long-term burden of such strategies. Rather the LAs have returned as far as possible to a pro-cyclical pattern of expenditure, reducing their borrowing requirement (particularly in the 1981/2 recession) and investment commitments to a minimum. This clearly runs against their instincts, given that the Deutscher Städtetag has calculated local investment needs of some DM 47 billion per annum (in 1984 prices) from 1976 to 1990, which contrasts with the actual level achieved of DM 38.3 billion up to 1984 with a rapidly declining trend.[55]

This financial retrenchment of the LAs has been a dominant feature of state economic activity in the last few years and both capital and labour interests have acknowledged the serious effects it has had on building and other investment.[56] It has been made even more critical by both the revenue shortfall caused by the recent reform of commercial rates and the expenditure pressures exerted on town-hall budgets by chronic unemployment and social deprivation. The development over the last decade in fact bears some similarity to the experience of the later years of the Weimar Republic. Despite the existence of a system of ostensibly comprehensive social insurance, an increasing number of people have become

---

54. The multiplier effects of wage restraint as a stimulus to private investment was probably more significant than any direct fiscal measures: Jeremy Leaman, *The Political Economy of West Germany*, London, 1988, p. 252, fn 22.

55. Quoted in *Der Spiegel*, 30 September 1984, p. 132.

56. Günter Samtlebe, 'Städtische Finanzen unter dem Druck von Bund und Ländern', *Gewerkschaftliche Monatshefte*, vol. 35, 1984, pp. 373ff.

eligible for social assistance (*Sozialhilfe*) since the institution of the Federal Social Assistance Law of 1962.[57] Designed as the 'last social safety net', it is becoming an increasingly important supplement to centrally administered funds; whereas in 1970 1.49 million people received some DM 3.3 billion in Social Assistance, in 1980 there were already 2.14 million receiving DM 13.3 billion and the indications are that this trend accelerated in the first half of the 1980s.[58] Given that the LAs are responsible for over 60 per cent of these expenditures, the burden of social security outside the insurance system can be seen to be falling increasingly on them. Within this inequitable distribution of responsibilities between different levels of the state (which even the Bundesbank acknowledges),[59] there is, as in Weimar, an urban–rural divide between the relatively prosperous authorities of the south and the less prosperous northern cities. This implies particular financial problems for particular poor authorities in poorer regions. In fact despite a system of horizontal equalisation between LAs the poverty of many town halls is clearly evident in the different levels of debt in individual authorities. Hanover, for example, was carrying a debt of almost DM 4,000 per head of population in 1981 compared to Heilbronn with an average debt per head of population of less than DM 400 and Munich of less than DM 1,000.

Overall the failure to reform West Germany's fiscal-political structures has weakened the power of many LAs to fulfil all their constitutional obligations and their (allied) politico-economic functions. The consolidation of town-hall debts and the maintenance of social expenditure has thus only been achieved recently at the expense of investment programmes, as in the recession of 1929–32. The apparent return of the latest Christian Democratic (CDU) government to the 'planning phobia' of the 1950s, the march towards deregulation and privatisation and the hamfisted (international) application of monetarist politics suggest that the present

57. In 1970 there were some 25 social assistance recipients to 1,000 people in the Federal Republic, in 1980 it was already 35: Bundesbank *Monatsberichte*, April, 1983.
58. The Bundesbank only gives figures to 1980. A 1986 report by the German Institute for Economic Research (DIW) in Berlin shows a dramatic increase of Social Assistance expenditure as a result of restricted access to unemployment benefit, an indirect result of a reduction of central government support for the Social Insurance Funds: *Frankfurter Rundschau*, 30 May 1986.
59. Bundesbank *Monatsberichte*, November, 1983.

generation of national politicians has learned little from the experience of the past. Local authorities are still caught in the structural trap of increased demand on resources which can be limited by higher fiscal authorities. Their structural weaknesses are compounded by the tendency of individual capitals to choose locations for investment with the best infrastructural facilities, which results in a (predictable) frenzied rivalry by regional and local state authorities to attract that investment with a variety of expensive inducements (as in the case of the recent Daimler-Benz test-track saga). But again this situation, which is evident in the Federal Republic, does not reflect the strength of 'national capital', but rather of individual oligopolies; their strength betokens a general weakness of capital overall to maintain stable conditions for its own reproduction, a weakness epitomised by the marked decline in the ratio of productive investment to GNP and the dominant role of vagabond capital in the world's financial markets. And it is predominantly the state that is forced to issue fixed (high) interest bonds in order to channel that vagabond capital into perceived priority areas of social expenditure, such as productive investment. The high interest rates of the 'golden twenties' and the period of crisis management since 1967 were in part determined by the unavoidable need of local authorities in particular to invest in the social and economic infrastructure and the corresponding need to attract capital. In both periods they were competing with other state authorities (at home and abroad) for the same funds. In both periods they were subject to accusations of 'crowding out' and uncontrolled extravagance. They were also largely excluded from decision-making within the state administration about fiscal priorities and to a considerable degree ignored as victims of central measures of fiscal reform.

Despite the high investment profile of LAs, as well as a growing burden of social expenditure, their budgets have been the subject of considerable criticism from other state authorities and private capital. More recently the appalling condescension of higher state authorities towards the concerns of town-hall budgets has been reflected in the discussions on taxation reform. The Liberal (FDP) spokesman on finance policy, Solms, was quoted as saying that 'taxation reform cannot be conducted from the perspective of provincial princes and town-hall treasurers'.[60] This widespread

---

60. Hermann Otto Solms, quoted in the *Frankfurter Rundschau*, 11 June 1987.

attitude towards the lower levels of the capitalist state is symptomatic of the present obsession of supply-side orthodoxy with reducing state budgets and the state's share of GNP, and betokens not just an ignorance of the effects of drastic reductions in state demand, but also an ignorance of the vital stabilising function that the LAs in particular have had to fulfil within the state apparatus as a whole. This ignorance of fundamental relations in Germany's political economy is strongly reminiscent of the later Weimar years. It is also reflected in the effective abandonment of full employment[61] as one of four components of the 'Magic Square' (stability of growth, prices, balance of payments and full employment) and in the central state's recent attempts to reduce state social provision in line with the demands of private capital.[62]

In summary, the fulfilment of the major functions of the state can be seen to be increasingly critical today as in the 1920s. In the absence of structural-political, let alone structural-economic reforms,

61. Even before the slide into the mass unemployment of the 1980s Kurt Biedenkopf (CDU) had called for the renunciation of the guarantee of full employment as a means of consolidating the state debt. See Biedenkopf and Miegel, *Die programmierte Krise*, p. 114.

62. The recent attacks on the 'social state' echo the sentiments of the Reichsverband der deutschen Industrie, the Reichslandbund, the Central Federation of Banks and others in the 1920s and share the fundamental desire to minimise state and mass consumption and maximise the cost advantages/profitability of capital. The RDI in 1929 blamed the social security system for putting 'too high a financial burden on the productive economy' (quoted in D. Abraham, *The Collapse of the Weimar Republic*, Princeton, 1981, p. 237) while in 1975 the BDA (Employers' Federation) talked of the social state pushing the economy and the public finances towards 'breaking point': 'Too much collective security can paralyse individual initiative': BDA, *Soziale Sicherung unter veränderten wirtschaftlichen Bedingungen*, Cologne, 1975. In the Bundestag right-wing politicians have likened the 'social safety net' to a 'hammock' or a 'sedan chair' which bears the recipient 'from molotov cocktail party to molotov cocktail party and then finally to Majorca for a holiday to recuperate' (thus Dr Riedl of the CSU in June 1981, quoted in W. Adamy and J. Steffen, 'Konservative Sanierungsstrategie in der Sozialpolitik', *Gewerkschaftliche Monatshefte*, vol. 33, 1982, p. 692). Since 1973 there has been a chorus of calls for the 'weeding out' of excessive social expenditure from leading representatives of the BDA, the BDI, the Chambers of Commerce and others, including a series of advertisements by the Federation of German Banks, one of which showed the picture of a cuckoo next to a text on the dangers of the social state (in *Die Zeit*, April 1983). Collectively capital shows a united front in support of budget cutbacks, but representatives of individual sectors, notably the construction industry, have expressed concern over the drastic reductions in state (i.e. local authority) investments. Even the BDA stresses the primacy of infrastructural investments in its submissions for general budget reductions. See BDA, *Mit Wachstum gegen Arbeitslosigkeit*, Cologne, 1977, p. 13.

the LAs will continue to be a particular focus of the general crisis of capitalism; the physical and social decay of particular (urban) areas will be an important factor in stretching the legitimacy of the system towards another state-form crisis. With the unresolved rivalry of the three levels of fiscal authority in protecting their hard-pressed budgets, the particular 'ungovernability of the towns'[63] will, as in the Weimar Republic, foreshadow that crisis.

63. Hans-Ulrich Klose, 'Die Unregierbarkeit der Städte', *aus politik und zeitgeschichte*, no. 41, 1975.

Select Bibliography

The following list of titles represents some of the more important books and articles which deal explicitly with the major themes of the present volume. The list is not exhaustive, but is designed to provide a brief overview of relevant recent research.

Heidrun Abromeit, 'Zum Verhältnis von Staat und Wirtschaft im gegenwärtigen Kapitalismus', *Politische Vierteljahresschrift*, vol. 17, 1976, pp. 2–22

Gerold Ambrosius, *Der Staat als Unternehmer*, Göttingen, 1984

K.J. Bade, 'Arbeitsmarkt, Ausländerbeschäftigung und Interessenkonflikt: der Kampf um die Kontrolle über Auslandsrekrutierung und Inlandsvermittlung ausländischer Arbeitskräfte in Preußen vor dem Ersten Weltkrieg', in L. Elsner (ed.), *Fremdarbeiterpolitik des Imperialismus*, no. 10, Rostock, 1981, pp. 27–47

——, 'Arbeiterstatistik zur Ausländerkontrolle: die "Nachweisungen" der preußischen Landräte über den "Zugang, Abgang und Bestand der ausländischen Arbeiter im preußischen Staate" 1906–1914', *Archiv für Sozialgeschichte*, vol. 24, 1984, pp. 163–283

D. Baudis and H. Nussbaum, *Wirtschaft und Staat in Deutschland vom Ende des 19. Jahrhunderts bis 1918/19*, Berlin, 1978

D. Blackbourn and G. Eley, *The Peculiarities of German History*, London, 1985

M. Boeger, *Die Haltung der industriellen Unternehmer zur staatlichen Sozialpolitik in den Jahren 1878–1891*, Frankfurt am Main, 1982

Jane Caplan, 'The Politics of Administration: the Reich Interior Ministry and the German Civil Service, 1933–1943', *The Historical Journal*, vol. 20, 1977, pp. 707–36.

——, '"The imaginary universality of particular interests": The "tradition" of the Civil Service in German History', *Social History*, vol. 4, 1979, pp. 299–317

D.F. Crew, 'German Socialism, the State and Family Policy 1918–1933', *Continuity and Change*, vol. 1, 1986, pp. 235–63

P. Cullity, 'The Growth of Governmental Employment in Germany 1882–1950', *Zeitschrift für die gesamte Staatswissenschaft*, vol. 123, 1967, pp. 201–17

R.N. Dorwart, *The Prussian Welfare State before 1740*, Cambridge, Mass., 1971

Select Bibliography

K. Dyson, *The State Tradition in Western Europe*, Oxford, 1980

G. Eley, *Reshaping the German Right*, New Haven, Conn., 1980

——, *From Unification to Nazism. Reinterpreting the German Past*, London, 1986

L. Elsner, 'Zur Politik der herrschenden Klassen Deutschlands gegenüber den eingewanderten polnischen Arbeitern in den Jahren 1900 bis 1918', in idem (ed.), *Fremdarbeiter*, no. 2, 1977, pp. 5–45

R.J. Evans (ed.), *Society and Politics in Wilhelmine Germany*, London, 1978

A. Faust, 'Arbeitsmarktpolitik in Deutschland: Die Entstehung der öffentlichen Arbeitsvermittlung 1890–1927', in T. Pierenkemper and R.H. Tilly (eds.), *Historische Arbeitsmarktforschung*, Göttingen, 1982, pp. 253–73

J. Flemming, *Landwirtschaftliche Interessen und Demokratie. Ländliche Gesellschaft, Agrarverbände und Staat 1890–1925*, Bonn, 1978

S. Graessner, 'Gesundheitspolitik unterm Hakenkreuz', in G. Baader and U. Schultz (eds.), *Medizin und Nationalsozialismus. Tabuisierte Vergangenheit – ungebrochene Tradition?*, Berlin, 1980, pp. 145–51

Claudia Hahn, 'Der öffentliche Dienst und die Frauen-Beamtinnen in der Weimarer Republik', in Frauengruppe Faschismusforschung, *Mutterkreuz und Arbeitsbuch*, Frankfurt am Main, 1981, pp. 49–77

E. Hansen, M. Heisig, S. Leibfried and F. Tennstedt (eds.), *Seit über einem Jahrhundert . . .: Verschüttete Alternativen in der Sozialpolitik*, Cologne, 1981

H. Henning, *Die deutsche Beamtenschaft im 19. Jahrhundert*, Stuttgart, 1984

V. Hentschel, *Geschichte der deutschen Sozialpolitik (1880–1980). Soziale Sicherung und kollektives Arbeitsrecht*, Frankfurt am Main, 1983

G. Hirschfeld and L. Kettenacker (eds.), *The 'Führer State': Myth and Reality*, Stuttgart, 1981

H.G. Hockerts, *Sozialpolitische Entscheidungen im Nachkriegsdeutschland. Alliierte und deutsche Sozialversicherungspolitik 1945–1957*, Stuttgart, 1980

N. Johnson, *State and Government in the Federal Republic of Germany. The Executive at Work*, 2nd edn, London, 1983

F.X. Kaufmann *et al*, *Guidance, Control and Evaluation in the Public Sector*, Berlin/New York, 1986

I. Kershaw, *The Nazi Dictatorship*, London, 1985

J. Kocka, 'Capitalism and Bureaucracy in German Industrialization before 1914', *Economic History Review*, vol. 33, 1981, pp. 453–68

A. Kunz, *Civil Servants and the Politics of Inflation in Germany 1914–1924*, Berlin, 1986

A. Labisch and F. Tennstedt, *Der Weg zum Gesetz zur Vereinheitlichung des Gesundheitswesens*, Düsseldorf, 1985

J. Leaman, *The Political Economy of West Germany*, London, 1988

A. Lüdtke, *"Gemeinwohl", Polizei und "Festungspraxis", Staatliche Gewaltsamkeit und innere Verwaltung in Preußen 1815–1850*, Göttingen, 1982

H. Matzerath, *Nationalsozialismus und kommunale Selbstverwaltung*, Stuttgart, 1970

H. Mommsen, *Beamtentum im Dritten Reich*, Stuttgart, 1966

——, 'Die Stellung der Beamtenschaft in Reich, Ländern und Gemeinden in der Ära Brüning', *Vierteljahrshefte für Zeitgeschichte*, vol. 21, 1973, pp. 151–65

W.J. Mommsen and W. Mock (eds.), *Die Entstehung des Wohlfahrsstaates in Großbritannien und Deutschland 1850–1950*, Stuttgart, 1982

R. Müller and D. Milles (eds.), *Beiträge zur Geschichte der Arbeiterkrankheiten und der Arbeitsmedizin in Deutschland*, Bremerhaven, 1984

K. Naujeck, *Die Anfänge des sozialen Netzes 1945–1952*, Cologne, 1984

J. Noakes (ed.), *Government, Party and People in Nazi Germany*, Exeter, 1980

M. Nussbaum, *Wirtschaft und Staat in Deutschland während der Weimarer Republik*, Berlin, 1978

H.-J. Puhle, 'Historische Konzepte des entwickelten Industriekapitalismus. "Organisierter Kapitalismus" und "Korporatismus"', *Geschichte und Gesellschaft*, vol. 10, 1984, pp. 165–84

D. Rebentisch, 'Städte und Monopol: Privatwirtschaftliches Ferngas oder kommunale Verbandswirtschaft in der Weimarer Republik', *Zeitschrift für Stadtgeschichte, Stadtsoziologie und Denkmalpflege*, vol. 3, 1976, pp. 38–80

——, 'Kommunalpolitik, Konjunktur und Arbeitsmarkt in der Endphase der Weimarer Republik', in R. Morsey (ed.), *Verwaltungsgeschichte*, Berlin, 1977, pp. 104–35

G.A. Ritter, *Social Welfare in Germany and Britain: Origins and Development*, Leamington Spa/New York, 1986

K.H. Roth (ed.), *Erfassung und Vernichtung. Von der Sozialhygiene zum 'Gesetz über Sterbehilfe'*, Berlin, 1984

C. Sachße, *Betriebliche Sozialpolitik als Familienpolitik in der Weimarer Republik und im Nationalsozialismus*, Hamburg, 1987

—— and F. Tennstedt, *Geschichte der Armenfürsorge in Deutschland. Vom Spätmittelalter bis zum 1. Weltkrieg*, Stuttgart/Berlin/Cologne/Mainz, 1980

D. Stegmann *et al* (eds.), *Industrielle Gesellschaft und politisches System*, Bonn, 1978

W. Struve, *Elites against Democracy. Leadership Ideals in Bourgeois Political Thought in Germany 1890–1933*, Princeton, 1973

F. Tennstedt, 'Sozialgeschichte der Sozialversicherung', in M. Blohmke et al (eds.), *Handbuch der Sozialmedizin*, 3 vols., Stuttgart, 1976, pp. 385–492

——, *Vom Proleten zum Industriearbeiter. Arbeiterbewegung und Sozialpolitik in Deutschland 1800–1914*, Cologne, 1983

P. Weindling, *Health, Race and German Politics between National Unification and Nazism*, Cambridge, 1989

E. Wickenhagen, *Geschichte der gewerblichen Unfallversicherung*, 2 vols., Munich, 1980

H.A. Winkler (ed.), *Organisierter Kapitalismus. Voraussetzungen und Anfänge*, Göttingen, 1974

G. Zang (ed.), *Provinzialisierung einer Region*, Frankfurt am Main, 1978

Notes on the Contributors

Richard Bessel is Lecturer in History at the Open University. His publications include (ed. with E.J. Feuchtwanger) *Social Change and Political Development in Weimar Germany* (London, 1981), *Political Violence and the Rise of Nazism* (New Haven, Conn. and London, 1984) and (ed.), *Life in the Third Reich* (Oxford, 1987).

Helen Boak is Principal Lecturer in Languages at the Polytechnic of East London. Her major research interest is the position of women in German society in the early twentieth century.

Martin Forberg studies at the University of Bielefeld. He is currently completing his PhD on the attitude of free trade unions towards foreign workers, with special reference to the period between 1890 and 1914.

Harold James is Professor of History at Princetown University, USA. He has published extensively on the economic and financial history of twentieth-century Germany. His major books include *The Reichsbank and Public Finance in Germany 1924–1933: A Study of the Politics of Economics during the Great Depression* (Frankfurt am Main, 1985) and *The German Slump: Politics and Economics 1924–1931* (Oxford, 1986).

Andreas Kunz is currently undertaking research at the Zentralinstitut für Sozialgeschictliche Forschung, Arbeitsbereich Wirtschafts- und Sozialgeschichte Forschung, at the Free University of Berlin. He is the author of a major monograph, *Civil Servants and the Politics of Inflation in Germany, 1914–1924* (Berlin and New York, 1986) and numerous articles on German economic, social and political history.

Jeremy Leaman is Senior Lecturer in European Studies at the Loughborough University of Technology. He is the author of *The*

Political Economy of West Germany (London, 1988) and of chapters and articles on German economic, social and political history.

W.R. Lee is the Chaddock Professor of Economic and Social History at the University of Liverpool. He has published widely on the demographic, economic and social history of Germany.

Dietrich Milles is Director of the Archive and Library of the recently established Zentrum für Sozialpolitik at the University of Bremen. He has become one of the leading experts on the social history of medicine in West Germany, publishing (with R. Müller) *Beiträge zur Geschichte der Arbeiterkrankenheiten und der Arbeitsmedizin in Deutschland* (Dortmund, 1984) and (as co-editor) *Sozialpolitik und Sozialstaat* (3 vols., Bremen, 1985).

Eve Rosenhaft is Senior Lecturer in the Department of German at the University of Liverpool. She is the author of *Beating the Fascists? The German Communists and Political Violence 1929–1933* (Cambridge, 1983) and is currently working on a social and political history of the German Communist Party from 1917 to 1936.

Paul Weindling is Interim Director of the Wellcome Unit for the History of Medicine, Oxford. He has edited *The Social History of Occupational Health* (London, 1985), co-edited *Information Sources for the History of Science and Medicine* and is the author of *Health, Race and German Politics between Unification and Nazism* (Cambridge, 1989).

Index

Index

Index

Index

Index